Through its collection of essays from Europe, the United States, and non-Western countries, *Police–Citizen Relations Across the World* both expands the horizons of the police trust and legitimacy literature, and challenges the generalizability of procedural justice assumptions. By providing a comparative and global perspective, it substantially enriches scholarly understanding of the causes of police legitimacy and effectiveness. It is an essential reading for scholars and policy makers interested in procedural justice, police legitimacy, or police effectiveness.

Professor Sanja Kutnjak Ivković, *School of Criminal Justice, Michigan State University, USA*

Issues of trust in the police and of police legitimacy are among the most pressing matters facing politicians and academics. Bringing together the best scholars and the most up-to-date data, *Police–Citizen Relations Across the World* offers a comprehensive, global perspective on the subject. No one interested in the subject can afford to be without it.

Professor Tim Newburn, *Department of Social Policy, LSE, UK*

This volume offers police scholars what is sorely needed – a truly cross-national, comparative perspective on the fundamental challenges of police legitimacy and public trust. The thirteen chapters present rigorous empirical inquiry by leading police researchers, who illuminate the complexities of forging strong police-community relations in a variety of settings – the U.S., Europe, and non-Western nations. They explore similarities and differences across and within national borders. They raise serious questions about the impact of procedural justice in different national settings. *Police-Citizen Relations Across the World* will broaden your perspective on a timeless issue for democracies around the world and shows the path for a rich new global trajectory for police research.

Stephen Mastrofski, *University Professor, Department of Criminology, Law and Society, George Mason University, USA*

Police–Citizen Relations Across the World

Police–citizen relations are in the public spotlight following outbursts of anger and violence. Such clashes often happen as a response to fatal police shootings, racial or ethnic discrimination, or the mishandling of mass protests. But even in such cases, citizens' assessment of the police differs considerably across social groups. This raises the question of the sources and impediments of citizens' trust and support for police. Why are police–citizen relations much better in some countries than in others? Are police–minority relations doomed to be strained? And which police practices and policing policies generate trust and legitimacy?

Research on police legitimacy has been centred on US experiences, and relied on procedural justice as the main theoretical approach. This book questions whether this approach is suitable and sufficient to understand public attitudes towards the police across different countries and regions of the world. This volume shows that the impact of macro-level conditions, of societal cleavages, and of state and political institutions on police–citizen relations has too often been neglected in contemporary research.

Building on empirical studies from around the world as well as cross-national comparisons, this volume considerably expands current perspectives on the sources of police legitimacy and citizens' trust in the police. Combining the analysis of micro-level interactions with a perspective on the contextual framework and varying national conditions, the contributions to this book illustrate the strength of a broadened perspective and lead us to ask how specific national frameworks shape the experiences of policing.

Dietrich Oberwittler is a Senior Researcher at the Max Planck Institute for International and Foreign Criminal Law (Department of Criminology) in Freiburg, Germany, and extracurricular professor of sociology at the University of Freiburg.

Sebastian Roché is a Research Professor at the National Center for Scientific Research (CNRS) at Sciences Po, University of Grenoble-Alpes, France. First secretary general of the European Society of Criminology after its foundation, he is today the regional editor (Europe) of *Policing and Society.*

Routledge Frontiers of Criminal Justice

Police–Citizen Relations Across the World

Comparing Sources and Contexts of Trust and Legitimacy

Edited by Dietrich Oberwittler and Sebastian Roché

Routledge
Taylor & Francis Group

LONDON AND NEW YORK

First published 2018 by Routledge

2 Park Square, Milton Park, Abingdon, Oxfordshire OX14 4RN
52 Vanderbilt Avenue, New York, NY 10017

Routledge is an imprint of the Taylor & Francis Group, an informa business

First issued in paperback 2019

British Library Cataloguing in Publication Data
A catalogue record for this book is available from the British Library

Library of Congress Cataloging in Publication Data
Names: Oberwittler, Dietrich, editor. | Roche, Sebastian, editor.
Title: Police-citizen relations across the world : comparing sources and contexts of trust and legitimacy / edited by Dietrich Oberwittler and Sebastian Roche.
Description: 1 Edition. | New York : Routledge, 2018. | Series: Routledge frontiers of criminal justice ; 54 | Includes bibliographical references and index.
Identifiers: LCCN 2017025610| ISBN 9781138222861 (hardback) | ISBN 9781315406664 (ebook)
Subjects: LCSH: Police-community relations–Case studies. | Police–Complaints against–Case studies.
Classification: LCC HV7936.P8 P565 2018 | DDC 363.2–dc23
LC record available at https://lccn.loc.gov/2017025610

ISBN: 978-1-138-22286-1 (hbk)
ISBN: 978-0-367-22769-2 (pbk)

Typeset in Times New Roman
by Wearset Ltd, Boldon, Tyne and Wear

Contents

Figures

Tables

Contributors

Oluwagbenga Michael Akinlabi is currently a Lecturer in Criminology at the University of New England, Australia. He has a PhD in Criminology and Criminal Justice from Griffith University in Australia. He was previously educated in his home country, Nigeria, as well as at Cambridge University in the United Kingdom. He undertook the research in this chapter while he was still studying as a PhD student at Griffith University's School of Criminology & Criminal Justice.

Ömer Bilen is Research Assistant at Statistics Department of Yıldız Technical University. He received his PhD degree on the statistical modeling of factors that influence crime at Yıldız Technical University. He has an MSc degree in statistics. He has worked at various national and international projects, as a statistician including crime, policing, police–citizen relations, and police job satisfaction, urban-related studies, etc. He specialises in research methodology, data preparation and quality, statistical methods, multivariate statistics, GIS and data mining applications.

Ben Bradford (PhD, LSE) is Departmental Lecturer in Criminology at the Centre for Criminology, University of Oxford. His areas of research include public trust, police legitimacy, procedural justice theory and police–public interactions, particularly in relation to stop and search and associated powers. He has published in journals including *British Journal of Criminology*, *British Journal of Sociology*, *European Journal of Criminology*, *Journal of Empirical Legal Studies*, *Journal of Experimental Criminology*, *Law and Society Review*, *Regulation and Governance*, *Psychology*, *Public Policy and Law* and *Policing and Society*. His book, *Stop and Search and Police Legitimacy*, was published by Routledge in 2016; he is also co-editor of the *SAGE Handbook of Global Policing* (2016) and co-author of *Just Authority? Trust in the Police in England and Wales* (Routledge 2013). He is on the editorial boards of the *British Journal of Criminology* and *Policing and Society*.

Adrian Cherney is Associate Professor of Criminology at the School of Social Science at The University of Queensland, Brisbane, Australia. He holds a PhD in Criminology from the University of Melbourne. One major focus of his work is on institutional legitimacy and cooperation with authorities (e.g. police and government). He is currently undertaking research on community cooperation in counter-terrorism and examining grass root efforts to counter violent extremism. He has secured both national and international competitive grants from the Australian Research Council, US Air Force and the Australian Institute of Criminology. He has published in leading journals such as *Policing and Society*, *British Journal of Criminology*, *The Australian and New Zealand Journal of Criminology* and the *European Journal of Criminology*, and he is a co-author of *Procedural Justice and Legitimacy in Policing* (Springer 2014) and *Crime Prevention: Principles, Perspectives and Practices* (Cambridge University Press 2013).

Mike Hough (MA, University of Oxford) is Visiting Professor at Birkbeck, University of London. He was previously University of London Professor of Criminal Policy and Director of the Institute for Criminal Policy Research, which he set up. For the first 20 years of his career, he was a criminological researcher at the British Home Office, where he was one of the small team that started the British Crime Survey. He has around 250 publications, some of which can be found in the *British Journal of Criminology*, *Criminology and Criminal Justice*, *The European Journal of Criminology* and *Policing and Society*. His current research interests include procedural justice theory and young people's experience of crime as victims and offenders.

Jonathan Jackson (PhD, LSE) is a Professor of Research Methodology at the LSE. He has held visiting appointments in criminology at Oxford, Sydney, Griffith and Cambridge; in psychology at New York University and John Jay College of Criminal Justice; in law at Yale; and in public policy at Harvard (Kennedy School). He is an editor of the *British Journal of Criminology*. His areas of research include legitimacy, trust, police–citizen relations, fear of crime and public attitudes towards punishment. His work has been published in *Journal of Social Policy*, *Journal of Empirical Legal Studies*, *Journal of the Royal Statistical Society: Series C (Applied Statistics)*, *Risk Analysis*, *Psychology, Public Policy & Law*, *British Journal of Criminology*, *Journal of Research in Crime & Delinquency*, *British Journal of Sociology* and *European Journal of Criminology*. He is a co-editor of *Routledge Handbook of Criminal Justice* (Routledge 2016) and co-author of *Just Authority? Trust in the Police in England and Wales* (Routledge 2013) and *Social Order and the Fear of Crime in Contemporary Times* (Oxford University Press 2009).

Juha Kääriäinen (Doctor of social sciences, University of Tampere, Finland) is a Postdoctoral Researcher at the Institute of Criminology and Legal Policy, University of Helsinki (Finland). His areas of research include social capital, policing, violence research and penal attitudes research. His work has been published in *European Societies*, *European Journal of Criminology*, *Journal of Scandinavian Studies in Criminology and Crime Prevention*, *Violence and*

Victims, Homicide Studies, Journal of Ethnicity in Criminal Justice, European Journal of Crime, Criminal Law and Criminal Justice and *Journal of Gambling Issues.*

Tammy Rinehart Kochel (PhD, George Mason University, USA) is Associate Professor and the Graduate Program Director for Criminology and Criminal Justice at Southern Illinois University (USA). She conducts research on policing and communities, examining public perceptions of police and how policing strategies and behaviours may influence those views. Her focus addresses the factors that promote and the consequences of police legitimacy and procedural justice. She also examines the effectiveness of policing strategies on crime, with an emphasis on targeted approaches such as problem solving, hot spots policing and focused deterrence. She has published in *Criminology, Journal of Experimental Criminology, Justice Quarterly* and elsewhere.

Jacques de Maillard is Professor of Political Science at the University of Versailles-Saint-Quentin, deputy-director of the Cesdip (a research centre affiliated to the CNRS, the University of Versailles, the University of Cergy and the ministry of Justice). His interests lie in the questions of local governance of security, plural policing, police reforms and the comparative study of policing in Western countries. He has recently published 'Plural policing in Paris. Variations and pitfalls of cooperation between national and municipal police forces' (with M. Zagrodzki), *Policing & Society* 2017, 'Les logiques professionnelles et politiques du contrôle: Des styles de police différents en France et en Allemagne'(with D. Hunold, S. Roché, D. Oberwittler, M. Zagrodzki), *Revue française de science politique*, 2016, and 'Studying policing comparatively: obstacles, preliminary results and promises' (with S. Roché), *Policing & Society*, 2016. He has also co-authored *Sociologie de la police* (with F. Jobard, Armand Colin 2015).

Kristina Murphy (PhD, ANU) is Professor of Criminology in the Griffith Criminology Institute at Griffith University, Brisbane, Australia. Her research draws on social psychological theory to understand how citizens respond to authorities and their laws. Her major research interest focuses on the concept of procedural justice; the idea that dealing with citizens in a procedurally fair and respectful manner, and providing citizens voice in decision-making, will promote trust in authorities, will reduce marginalisation, will enhance social cohesion and identity with society, and will encourage cooperative behaviour and voluntary compliance with authorities and rules. She has examined this in the policing, taxation, prison, social security and environmental contexts. She has been awarded numerous competitive grants by the Australian Research Council to undertake research on this topic. She has widely published in leading journals such as *Policing and Society, British Journal of Criminology, The Australian and New Zealand Journal of Criminology* and the *European Journal of Criminology*, and she is a co-author of *Procedural Justice and Legitimacy in Policing* (Springer 2014).

Dietrich Oberwittler (Dr. phil, University of Trier, Germany) is Senior Researcher at the Max Planck Institute for Foreign and International Criminal Law, Dept. of Criminology, in Freiburg (Germany), and extracurricular Professor of Sociology at the University of Freiburg. From 2004 to 2006, he was a Marie Curie Fellow at the Institute of Criminology, University of Cambridge (UK). His areas of research include communities and crime, policing, adolescent delinquency and violence research. His work has been published in *the European Journal of Criminology, European Sociological Review* and *Policing and Society*. He is co-author (together with Per-Olof Wikström, Kyle Treiber and Beth Hardie) of *Breaking Rules. The Social and Situational Dynamics of Young People's Urban Crime* (Oxford University Press 2012) and editor (together with Susanne Karstedt) of *Soziologie der Kriminalität* (VS Verlag für Sozialwissenschaften 2004).

Mine Özaşçılar is a member of faculty in the Sociology Department at Bahcesehir University, Istanbul. Her current research focuses on criminology and victimology. Under her major area of study in criminology, she is particularly working on risky behaviours among young adults, and police perception among adolescents. In addition to these fields, she also focuses on victimology by researching on fear of crime in Turkey and Sweden.

Stephan Parmentier (Dr, KU Leuven, Belgium) studied law, political science and sociology at the universities of Ghent and Leuven (Belgium) and sociology and conflict resolution at the Humphrey Institute for Public Affairs, University of Minnesota-Twin Cities (USA). He currently teaches sociology of crime, law and human rights at the Faculty of Law of the University of Leuven and previously served as the Head of the Department of Criminal Law and Criminology (2005–2009). He was elected Secretary-General of the International Society for Criminology in 2010 and re-elected in 2014. Furthermore, he is on the Advisory Board of the Oxford Centre of Criminology and the International Centre for Transitional Justice (New York). Parmentier is the founder and co-general editor of the international book *Series on Transitional Justice* (Intersentia Publishers), and editor of the *Restorative Justice International Journal* (Routledge).

Mina Rauschenbach (Dr, University of Lausanne, Switzerland) is a lecturer at the Institute of Social Sciences of the University of Lausanne and a Research Affiliate at the Leuven Institute of Criminology (LINC). Her main areas of interest concern the role of interpretations of the past, as well as identity concerns, in relation to transitional justice processes and their significance in shaping justice perceptions and needs for justice stakeholders, such as victims, perpetrators or diaspora communities. Some recent publications include 'Accused for involvement in collective violence: The discursive reconstruction of agency and identity by perpetrators of international crimes' (*Political Psychology*, 2015), and 'The perfect data-marriage: Transitional justice research and oral history life stories' (*Transitional Justice Review*, 2016).

Sebastian Roché is Research Professor at the National Center for Scientific Research (CNRS), PACTE research unit at Sciences-Po (Institute of Political Science), University of Grenoble-Alpes, France. He specialises in crime (self-reported delinquency, juvenile justice), and on criminal justice policies. He has published more than ten books (including *The Governance and Oversight of the Internal Security Sector in Turkey and 7 EU Countries*) as well as articles in political science and criminology journals (*Crime and Justice, European Journal of Criminology, Canadian Journal of Criminology, Revue Française de Science Politique*). Presently, he works on a) the causes of pre-radicalisation among adolescents and the comparative measurement of crime and of the causes of juvenile crime (ISRD project), and b) on police legitimacy and citizen-police relations in comparative perspective.

Mai Sato received her PhD from King's College London in 2011. She worked for the Centre for Criminology (University of Oxford) and the Institute for Criminal Policy Research (Birkbeck, University of London) before joining the School of Law as Lecturer in September 2015.

Anina Schwarzenbach is a PhD candidate at the International Max Planck Research School on Retaliation, Mediation and Punishment (IMPRS REMEP) of the Max Planck Institute for Foreign and International Criminal Law, Freiburg (Germany). For her PhD thesis she has investigated the relationship between young people and the police in Germany and France's multi-ethnic cities. Currently she studies prevention policies to counter radicalisation in the European context. Her main areas of interest are policing, juvenile delinquency, migration and crime and radicalisation of ethnic minorities.

Wesley G. Skogan is Professor of Political Science and a Faculty Fellow of the Institute for Policy Research, Northwestern University. His research includes studies of fear of crime, the impact of crime on communities, public participation in community crime prevention, victimisation, victim responses to crime and policing. Beginning in 1993, he directed a large-scale evaluation of Chicago's community policing initiative. His newest projects include an evaluation of the Chicago Police Department's procedural justice and legitimacy initiatives and a redesign of the National Crime Victimization Survey. His books are *Police and Community in Chicago* (Oxford University Press, 2006), *On the Beat: Police and Community Problem Solving* (Westview Press, 1999) and *Community Policing, Chicago Style* (Oxford University Press, 1999). In 2003, he edited *Community Policing: Can It Work?* (Wadsworth/Thomson Learning, 2004), a collection of original essays on innovation in policing. His 1990 book, *Disorder and Decline: Crime and the Spiral of Decay in American Cities* (University of California Press, 1990), won the Distinguished Scholar Award of a section of the American Sociological Association. In 2000, he organised the Committee on Police Policies and Practices for the National Academy of Sciences and served as its chairman. He is the co-author (with Kathleen Frydl) of the committee report that appeared as a book: *Fairness and Effectiveness in Policing: The Evidence*. He is a fellow of the American Society of Criminology. In 2015, he received the Distinguished Achievement Award in Evidence-Based Crime Policy from the Center for Evidence-Based Crime Policy.

Michael Tonry is McKnight Presidential Professor of Criminal Law and Policy, University of Minnesota, and formerly was Professor of Law and Public Policy and Director of the Institute of Criminology, University of Cambridge, UK. He edits the journal *Crime and Justice* and has written and edited a number of books.

Maarten Van Craen is Postdoctoral Researcher at the Leuven Institute of Criminology (University of Leuven, Belgium). His research is supported by the Research Foundation – Flanders (FWO). His research interests include police–citizen relationships and work relationships within police organisations. He has published articles on internal and external procedural justice, trust relationships and ethnic minorities. His work has appeared in journals such as *Justice Quarterly*, *Journal of Experimental Criminology*, *Criminal Justice and Behavior* and *European Journal of Criminology*.

Ronald Weitzer is Professor of Sociology at George Washington University. He has conducted research on police–minority relations in Israel, Northern Ireland, South Africa and the United States and is the author of *Policing under Fire: Ethnic Conflict and Police–Community Relations in Northern Ireland* (State University of New York Press 1995) and co-author of *Race and Policing in America* (Cambridge University Press 2006).

Foreword

Michael Tonry

Police–Citizen Relations Across the World is a milestone. It demonstrates the maturation of European research on procedural justice and legitimacy in policing. It provides richer understanding than heretofore of when and why people trust the police, and why that is, and sometimes is not, important. Probably most significantly, it offers the first genuinely comparative and cross-national examination of its subject, covering but also reaching far beyond Europe and the wealthy English-speaking countries.

The ideas underlying procedural justice theory are simple. Public officials who treat people fairly and respectfully are more likely themselves to be trusted and respected. Citizens attribute greater legitimacy to officials and institutions when they are trusted than when they are not. Officials who treat people unfairly or disrespectfully are unlikely to be trusted. These processes operate both personally and vicariously. Bystanders who observe unfair and disrespectful treatment of others, especially others with whom they identify, also become less trusting.

Those assertions seem self-evident. It should be in the nature of things that public officials in democratic societies treat people fairly and with respect. That is implicit in the limited powers a rational citizenry would grant to the state. The term 'police state' by contrast conjures up images of authoritarianism, disrespect and abuse of power. No rational person in a democratic state, where the state's authority rests on the consent of the governed, would want to live in a police state or would want public officials to treat people unfairly or disrespectfully.

If police functioned as in principle they should, there would be no need for theorising or research on procedural justice and legitimacy. Unfortunately, police do not always act as they should. Failures sometimes are aberrational and situational, but sometimes they are structural and systemic. Those latter general failures raise a series of interrelated questions.

The first is whether police do treat people fairly and respectfully. The answer varies widely from country to country and place to place, ranging from nearly always to only sometimes. That 'sometimes' often means that members of some groups are usually treated fairly and respectfully, and members of other groups, especially ethnic, racial and religious minorities, often are not. This common pattern raises issues of distributive justice.

A second question is whether public perceptions of police legitimacy decline when police treat people unfairly and disrespectfully. The answer is usually yes but sometimes, when police legitimacy is chronically low, the answer is no.

A third question is whether police legitimacy matters. The answer here is complicated. If procedural justice theory is right, people whom the police treat well should react more positively than do people whom police treat badly. They should be more likely to report crimes, cooperate during investigations and testify against others.

The preceding paragraphs offer a conventional and, I believe, uncontentious overview of procedural justice theory and its underlying logic. Research in English-speaking countries and elsewhere has validated some of its main claims. Unfair and disrespectful police behaviour reduces affected peoples' trust and cooperation. So does aggressive street-level law enforcement, variously called zero-tolerance, order maintenance, stop-question-frisk and misdemeanor polic-ing, that is much more often directed at racial and ethnic minority groups than at majority populations. Opinion and attitude surveys regularly show that affected minority communities are more alienated from the police than are whites, and less willing to cooperate with them.

Research, including some discussed in this book, has confirmed these propo-sitions, both positively and negatively. The positive confirmation is reassuring. In democratic societies based on liberal values, it is axiomatic that representa-tives of the state, including the police, should always treat citizens fairly and respectfully. That doing so is sometimes instrumentally useful, because it makes state actors more effective or more efficient, is a happy by-product.

The negative confirmation, that disrespectful and unfair treatment reduces peoples' trust in the police, and in the state, is devastating. Interactions with the police become tenser, more hostile, and more likely to result in violence. Cooperation with the police then and later becomes less likely. Fundamental bonds of citizenship weaken. None of that is good.

Systematic research on procedural justice and the causes and consequences of police legitimacy dates back only three decades. It emerged from psychological research in the United States on why people obey the law and cooperate with officials. The earliest studies focused mostly on courts.

The literature's origination and flowering in the United States was no acci-dent. One mundane reason was the emergence in the 1970s, earlier than in other countries, of systematic empirical research on the criminal justice system. This was partly a by-product of the proliferation of new university departments in criminology, also beginning in the 1970s, which provided cadres of researchers looking for subjects on which to prove themselves, at a time when substantial federal and foundation funding for research was available.

The politicised, assembly line character of American criminal justice and a long-term history of bad relations between the police and African Americans are substantive reasons why procedural justice research emerged. Most state judges and chief prosecutors are chosen in partisan local elections. This is different from other developed countries, sometimes results in improper influence on the handling of cases, and often means that offices are small and poorly managed. Prosecutors dispose of most cases by means of plea negotiations with defendants' lawyers. There are no dossiers. Judges are involved only perfunctorily except in the 1 to 5 per cent of cases resolved by trials. Put more vividly, the vast majority of criminal cases in the 1970s were and today are resolved behind closed doors, with no or little judicial oversight.

The combination of partisan politics and assembly line processes inevitably produces injustices and high risks of unfair and disrespectful treatment. That by itself provided an understandable reason why American researchers wanted to understand how things work and with what effects. The centuries-long history of unjust treatment of black people by the criminal justice system, especially by police, provided a compelling reason. The widespread adoption of aggressive street-level police tactics targeting young minority men in disadvantaged neighbourhoods exacerbated racial tensions.

By the beginning of the twenty-first century, the primary focus in the United States had shifted from courts to police, and related work began to blossom in Europe. The Russell Sage Foundation sponsored a small conference in Paris in 2005 that brought together American and European researchers. The book that resulted, *Legitimacy and Criminal Justice: International Perspectives* (2007), edited by Tom R. Tyler, showed that European research on procedural justice and legitimacy was beginning to emerge.

This book, and papers prepared for the 2015 Paris conference from which it derives, show that research in Europe has surpassed American efforts. The chapters covering policing in diverse countries within Europe, and even more those on policing in Japan, Nigeria and Turkey, show that many other issues deserve attention in addition to procedural justice, legitimacy and effectiveness. Support for the police, for example, may turn more on perceptions of their effectiveness than of their legitimacy. Support for the police may turn, for another example, not on peoples' interactions with police but on their trust in the state generally. The effects of citizens' interactions with the police, even positive ones, may be swamped by negative attitudes in countries with endemic police corruption or recent colonial histories. Membership in particular ethnic or religious groups, or support for particular political parties, may have more influence on peoples' views of the police than do personal experiences.

Global dispersion of research has enormously enriched understanding of the significance and causes of police legitimacy and effectiveness. Here are some examples drawn from chapters in *Police–Citizen Relations Across the World*. Starkly different minority group perceptions of the police in Germany and France show that alienation is not inevitable, even among disadvantaged groups. That Turkish and German young people in Germany view the police in comparably positive ways is heartening. That North African young people in France, aboriginal people in Australia, and African Americans in the United States view the police much more negatively than do majority populations is disheartening. Policing can be done in better and worse ways. And if greater police legitimacy improves police effectiveness, everyone gains.

   That police legitimacy is sometimes high throughout a society is cause for optimism. The more common pattern is that legitimacy varies enormously between racial, ethnic, religious and political groups. That is cause for pessimism, especially when historical patterns of corruption, conflict between groups, and levels of confidence in the state generally appear to explain why people do and do not trust the police. There are no easy or quick ways to offset longstanding historical and cultural influences. The United States, France, Nigeria, Japan or Turkey are unlikely soon to become exemplars of Scandinavian- or German-style social or political culture.

   Police–Citizen Relations Across the World constitutes a giant step forward. Police legitimacy is more complicated than earlier conceptions of procedural justice acknowledged. Improved understanding of those complexities is necessary if policing is better to serve the purposes for which, in principle, in civil societies, it exists. Countries need effective crime control and prevention, but they also need social cohesion and public confidence in the state including the police. All of those goals are important. *Police–Citizen Relations Across the World* shows that they can be achieved, illustrates the problems to be overcome, and offers insights into how that can be done. Those are no small accomplishments.

Acknowledgements

Most of the chapters in this volume have been presented at the International Conference 'Police–Citizen Relations' in Paris, 19–21 April 2015. The conference was generously supported by the Fritz Thyssen Foundation, Pacte research unit at Sciences Po/University of Grenoble-Alpes, and the Max Planck Institute for Foreign and International Criminal Law, to which we are grateful.

The editors thank all participants for their contributions to the Paris conference, and especially Hans-Jörg Albrecht, Jacques de Maillard, Jeffrey Fagan, Michael Tonry and Tom R. Tyler in their role as discussants, and all those involved in the review process.

Financial support for the language editing and assistance during the editing process was again generously provided by the Fritz Thyssen Foundation. The formal editing was meticulously assisted by Tanja Strukelj, and Jenna Milani and Dominic Aitken as well as Jenny Fleming skillfully improved the language of many chapters.

Dietrich Oberwittler, *Freiburg*
Sebastian Roché, *Grenoble*

Part I
Introduction

1 Towards a broader view of police–citizen relations

How societal cleavages and political contexts shape trust and distrust, legitimacy and illegitimacy

Sebastian Roché and Dietrich Oberwittler

Introduction

How to think of relations between the police and the public across countries and in different regions of the world? The intention of this book is to broaden and expand current perspectives on the sources of police legitimacy and citizens' trust in the police. While research on police–citizen relations has proliferated in the last two decades, much of it is still centred on the USA, the United Kingdom, and a few other, predominantly Western countries. In contrast to what was observed ten years ago, research outside the USA has left its 'nascent' phase (Tonry 2007: 3; foreword, this volume) behind and contributed considerably to the field, calling for an expanded focus on cross-national comparisons. Among the many advantages of comparative research is the greater attention paid to national contexts. The impact of macro-level conditions, of societal cleavages, and of state and political institutions on police–citizen relations has been neglected in most contemporary research. Procedural justice theory, the dominant approach, has provided a theoretical basis for the study of public attitudes towards the police. It has gained strong empirical support and has started to inform public policies (Tyler, Goff, and MacCoun 2015). Yet with its focus on micro-level social interactions and citizens' experiences of policing, it may neither help us to fully grasp the sources of trust in the police and police legitimacy, nor always be suitable for understanding police–citizen relations in different countries.

Police–citizen relations are embedded in the broad context of polities and states. Polities are 'systems of authority' or 'of domination', to use Max Weber's words (Weber 1947). Governments dispose of coercive powers. Police forces are a visible branch of state authority, legally entrusted to protect society and maintain order by force when deemed necessary. However, governments cannot rely solely on force. They need to claim and obtain support from their citizens, and to promote national integration and a sense of cohesion among diverse segments of population, or face the risk of discontent and possibly violent conflict. In many countries, the reality is that some social groups do not perceive the political or social order as fair, and do not feel protected by the police. Some individuals or groups may perceive the police as a partisan instrument or the ally of one group in a conflict situation. Thus, to understand police–citizen relations in general and police legitimacy in particular, we must take into account nation-states, the cultural pillars of the political order (e.g. its core values), government and major societal cleavages.

Legitimacy has been studied for longer than the police for a simple reason: The police as a government agency, distinct from the judiciary and the army, did not exist when political philosophers, following in the tradition of social contract theories, started to address the issue of public consent to state authority. When the most revered attempt to conceptualize legitimacy was carried out by Max Weber at the beginning of the twentieth century, policing was not his concern, to say the least (Smith 1970; Terpstra 2011). For very long, it was possible to write about morality, trust, and use of force, notions key to the legitimacy of the state, without touching the issue of policing. It was only in the post-World Word II era that the police became an object of theoretical and empirical examination. During the last 20 years, studies of police legitimacy have blossomed in many different countries. This book does not try to present a comprehensive overview but rather to stimulate the study of policing in a global perspective by including state- and society-level dimensions into the analysis. It brings together case studies from Europe and the USA as well as non-Western countries, in order to promote comparative perspectives on the conditions of police–citizen relations, and to question the generalizability of assumptions and models shaped by research in Western democracies.

From community policing to trustworthiness and legitimacy of the police

During the last 20 years, police legitimacy has emerged as an important academic theme and a political issue, but empirical studies of police–citizen relations have existed in the USA as early as 1930 (Bellman 1935; Parrat 1936). A major catalyst of early research was police use of force and other experiences of unfairness as well as recurrent race riots (often triggered by such incidents) since the 1960s in the USA and the 1980s in the UK (Bowling and Phillips 2008). However, anti-police riots did not prompt a comparable governmental or academic interest in other countries. The largest of such episodes of unrest in Europe took place in France in 2005 without a noticeable impact on research.

For many years, interest in police–citizen relations started from the 'police end' of the relationship and took the path of policing strategies. Many studies were concerned with various forms of community policing as a strategy to bridge the gap with segments of the population (see definition by Skogan 1998), leading to an interest in countries like Japan and their *koban* system (see Bayley 1976; cf. for reviews of research in Australia and Europe Coquilhat 2008; Mackenzie and Henry 2009). Only later did research shift its focus to the other end of the relationship: the citizen. Tom Tyler, in the introduction to his book *Why People Obey the Law*, gathered quotations illustrating that 'the nature and underpinnings of legitimacy are among the most neglected aspects of the dynamics of society', noticing 'the virtual absence of empirical examination of legitimacy' (Tyler 1990: 27).

More than 25 years later, the situation is very different in criminology, political science, and policing studies, with an unabated growth in the number of publications. Together with trust, the return of legitimacy to the forefront of research interests indicates a paradigm shift, 'a turn toward soft variables' (Sztompka 1999: 1) as opposed to 'hard' institutional structures and class stratification. There is an ongoing debate about the notions of trust and legitimacy. While some say that that the two notions are theoretically distinct and assert that it is possible to view an institution as a legitimate authority while simultaneously having little trust in it (Kaina 2008: 511), others present evidence that it is not the case empirically that 'constructs are distinguishable at a conceptual level' and that 'they are not empirically separable' (Maguire and Johnson 2010; Johnson *et al.* 2014). In this introduction, we will not draw a definitive distinction between the notions.

The critical element of legitimacy theory is its subjective nature, the subjective interpretations of reality, in line with Max Weber's 'interpretative sociology': 'The basis of every system of authority, and correspondingly of every kind of willingness to obey, is a belief, a belief by virtue of which persons exercising authority are lent prestige', Weber (1947: 382) writes. Such a reading of societies as made of individuals places a particular emphasis on the consciousness of actors as they interpret their actions and those of others. Individuals use their subjectively derived interpretations of the behaviour of others to predict the outcome of certain behaviours and, for example, whether to trust an organization, its principles, and its agents. In this line of thinking, interactions (as well as expectations about interactions) and related attitudes about fair interactions are key, and in empirical research survey questions about the feelings of the duty to obey and perceived fairness and trustworthiness are central. Many survey studies following procedural justice theory have stressed that people grant the police legitimacy if they feel they are being treated with fairness and dignity, irrespective of the outcome of the treatment (Donner *et al.* 2015; Jackson *et al.* 2013; Tyler 2011).

The contribution of this micro-level, socio-psychological approach to the field is undeniable. In its early stages, research on attitudes towards the police was driven by various poorly connected assumptions, for example on racial, class, and neighbourhood effects or a combination of these. No 'grand hypothesis' on the key dependent variables and the roots of obedience guided analyses (Webb and Marshall 1995: 49). It was only later with the interest in procedural justice in interactions that researchers have explored the complex structure of attitudes towards the police. The development of a multidimensional construct of citizen's perceptions (Shafer *et al.* 2003) led to the establishment of four core components of 'just procedure', formal and informal decision making and quality of treatment (Blader and Tyler 2003; Mazerolle *et al.* 2013b). The implementation of these concepts into opinion polls has resulted in a better and more nuanced understanding of attitudes regarding procedural fairness and to their standardized measurement that is applied across many countries. This allows researchers to test comparable hypotheses in various cultural and political contexts.

The study of trust and legitimacy: the micro and the macro perspective

However, a theoretical alignment always comes at a price. An interactional orientation deflects the attention away from the impact of social and political structures (like the state, culture, and the economy) on individual attitudes and behaviours, and it tends to ignore political cleavages, policy alternatives (Miller 1974; Miller and Listhaug 1998), political power, social inequalities, and class relations (Farganis 2008: 322). The concept of emergence of larger social processes and structures from individual-level actions and social interactions is important. However, macro structures are critical as 'frameworks' which shape the situations in which individuals act and supply to actors a certain set of symbols that allow them to act. This is of particular relevance for the study of the police forces since they are state-controlled organizations, placed under the direction of elected officials operating in a political system. Thus, theoretically speaking, trust in the police and police legitimacy relate to trust in the political system and its legitimacy. In fact, empirically, we have indications that overall support for the political system has a very large influence on trust in the police and that attitudes vis-à-vis the police are influenced by national contexts regarding the quality of police organizations, societal homogeneity, and cohesion and crime levels (see below; cf. Kutnjak Ivkovic 2008; Morris 2001; Weitzer and Tuch 2006). These macro-level foundations of attitudes towards the police become visible in cross-national comparisons and need to be accounted for.

Scholars of political trust have highlighted the role of performance and satisfaction (for example in service delivery or respecting human rights), the importance of *institutional* procedures (equality before the law and free elections being the master legitimation processes) and participation in decision making mechanisms (Norris 2017). Weber insisted on respect for legal procedures (*versus* substance, see discussion and critique by Coicaud 2002). Psychologists have also studied procedures, however, at the *interactional* level, in micro-settings, as John Thibaut and Laurens Walker (1975) did in their seminal experimental work entitled *Procedural Justice, A Psychological Analysis*, and later in numerous opinion surveys about the feeling of fairness and its impact on attitudes towards the police and police legitimacy (Donner *et al.* 2015; Mazerolle *et al.* 2014). The name of procedural justice is used on the micro-level of interactions or attitudes towards such interactions as well as on the macro-or institutional level. The two traditions both of political scientists of input, 'throughput' (internal processes), and output processes as well as of psychologists of fair interactions with legal officials (again versus its substance or outcomes) highlight the importance of procedures in modern democracies. Similarities also exist in terms of the importance of utilitarian versus normative types of explanation among systems analysts and interactions analysts. Among political scientists, David Easton (1965) made a still accepted distinction between diffuse and specific support, suggesting the role of the former for the stability of the political system: Diffuse support is not of a utilitarian nature while specific support may more often be of that sort. Fairness in interactions was also differentiated by psychologists from distributive justice (the output of the interaction) in courts and later in front of police officers.

Here, we contend that those two research streams need to be combined into a mixed approach as it was proposed almost two decades ago for the study of political support in order to fully grasp the nature and sources of trust in the police and police legitimacy (Booth and Seligson 2009; Mishler and Rose 2001). This avenue has started to be explored regarding the relation between trust and penal policies (Lappi-Seppälä 2008) and regarding attitudes towards the welfare state and their correspondence with welfare state regimes (Larsen 2016). On the one hand, there is evidence of the benefit of a micro-level approach to asking citizens about their subjective perceptions, their levels of trust or legitimacy, and about their experiences of interactions with the police. On the other hand, we defend the idea that variables relating to the national context, indicators of ideological, religious, and racial-ethnic cleavages, and the state's response to these as well as indicators of social integration at city and neighbourhood levels have a more important role to play (Taylor and Lawton 2012; Wu *et al.* 2009). Comparing studies from different countries and pursuing genuinely comparative studies provide opportunities for combining the analysis of micro-level interactions with a perspective on the contextual framework and varying national conditions. The contributions to this book can illustrate the strength of such a perspective and lead us to ask how specific national frameworks shape the structure of institutions and the experiences of policing. The findings indicate that generalizations of current theories about the sources of police trust and legitimacy across different types of societies are problematic.

State, culture, and history: the need for incorporating a broader societal context

The importance of institutions and political contexts

Procedural justice theory posits that perceptions of fair procedures have a strong causal influence on whether the public ascribe legitimacy to legal authorities. Legitimacy, in turn, will influence people's voluntary compliance with the directives of authorities and encourage cooperation (Jackson *et al.* 2013; Tyler 2011). It has often been confirmed in survey studies in Western nations that perceived police fairness rather than perceived effectiveness predicts police legitimacy (see Murphy and Cherney, Chapter 7 in this volume; cf. Bradford *et al.* 2014; Murphy *et al.* 2013; Sunshine and Tyler 2003; Tyler 2006). However, Weitzer (Chapter 2, this volume) insists that 'procedural justice is a micro-level variable but we know that police–citizen relations are influenced by factors at the meso and macro levels as well', providing a review of studies of neighbourhood and racial effects. What seems to be undervalued in these findings is the impact of trust ('specific support' and 'diffuse support') in state institutions on police legitimacy.

In order to be certain both of the importance of 'specific support', most notably to the ruling political party or its policies, and of 'diffuse support' to the political system which can be measured through general trust in state institutions (Easton 1965), those concepts need to be more systematically taken into consideration and empirically measured. Political scientists have stressed the importance of people's overall perception of the institutions: They foster generalized trust in society as well as trust in the police. Several studies, mainly cross-national, have looked at the correlates of trust in state institutions, generalized social trust, and trust in the police. You (2012) found that generalized social trust was primarily linked to the existence of *institutional* procedural rules (democracy), an administration free from corruption, and distributive justice in terms of income distribution. Concerning police trust, studies found positive influences by trust in institutions in general and overall satisfaction with democratic functioning (Christensen and Lægreid 2005; Jang *et al.* 2010), i.e. stable and 'high level democracy' (Kutnjak Ivkovic 2008; Morris 2015). In comparative surveys, corruption is regularly a decisive variable when accounting for trust in the police at national level (Morris 2015; Rothstein and Uslaner 2005). Other research has found that trust in the political system is the strongest or among the strongest predictors of support for the police, at the world level, in Europe, and also in Latin America (Cao and Zhao 2005; cf. Thomassen 2013; Thomassen and Kääriäinen 2016). In fact, police systems are embedded in larger polities and the former are influenced by the latter, as can be observed in Nordic countries where police are 'heavily influenced by the Scandinavian welfare model' (Høigård 2011). While it seems safe to conclude from these studies that citizens' assessment of the trustworthiness of the police is embedded in a more generalized assessment of state institutions, a mono-causal interpretation remains difficult, and direct and indirect experiences of police fairness may well contribute to citizens' positive attitudes towards state institutions generally. This may especially be the case if individuals accumulate such experiences over time or 'when there are a *series* of incidents in a compressed time period that gain massive traction in the media and popular discourse' turning such personal and collective experiences in a longer-term impact. We do not see those micro and macro explanations as being mutually exclusive, on the contrary, and their possible linkage would require further exploration.

Testing procedural justice theory beyond Western societies

Two in-depth studies in this volume from Nigeria and Japan test the key assumption of procedural justice theory about the link between fairness perceptions and legitimacy. The study of Nigeria by Oluwagbenga Michael Akinlabi (Chapter 6, this volume) portrays a complex reality: The perception of police fairness does not explain the legitimacy granted to the police and the willingness to cooperate – both of which are relatively low compared to developed democracies. At least three findings are notable from his study. First, anticipated cooperation with the police is not accounted for by perceptions of fairness, corruption or 'predatory policing' (a tendency to use police power for personal gains). Second, and contrary to findings from developed countries, citizens' assessment of police legitimacy is instead driven by perceptions of their efficiency. And, third, those who recognise the police as originating from the British colonial legacy are less likely to perceive the police as legitimate, reflecting the rather bleak historical roots of policing in Nigeria. The major purpose of colonial policing in Africa was to safeguard economic exploitation and to protect colonial interests against the resistance of the African people. Nigerian police officers until today have been guilty of arbitrary arrests, unlawful treatment of suspects, and extrajudicial killings. In sum, police forces were 'alien organizations established by foreigners' while the 'post-independence governments are guilty of malevolent indifference in their continuous neglect of police reform' that 'rendered the police largely unaccountable' (Akinlabi, Chapter 6, this volume). If we study the Afrobarometer (2010–2012), we learn that Nigerians very rarely disagree about the notion that 'people must obey the law' (7 per cent do so), far less than its neighbours (in Ivory Coast and Burkina Faso 15 per cent, in Benin 14 per cent), or that they should pay taxes (5 per cent compared to 24 per cent in Ivory Coast and Burkina Faso and 21 per cent in Benin), and Nigerians also show a higher degree of satisfaction with democracy. The rejection of the police might therefore not be based on the rejection of the idea of a national state (that would incorporate all ethnic groups) but on the failure of the state to regulate the police and prevent abuses. What seem to be at stake are the basic police functions in a modern state. Interactional fairness, in such a context, is probably perceived as a luxury that is not of major relevance in citizens' daily expectations. A second lesson learned is that obedience to the police and the law, often conflated when police officers are described as law enforcement agents, are not identical in nature: In contexts where police officers are not strictly bound by and frequently violate the law, citizens do not perceive them as representing the law.

In fact, these are not isolated findings in the African context. The perception of risks and the level of crime directly contribute to the attitudes of citizens towards the police in South Africa (Bradford *et al.* 2014) and Ghana, where Tankebe (2009) also showed that police legitimacy and public cooperation with the police were most strongly predicted by instrumental concerns, i.e. the perception of police effectiveness against crime. Even in Western nations such as Australia, Sargeant *et al.* (2014) found that perceived fairness was not at the core of trust and anticipated willingness to cooperate. In fact, a large set of studies shows that risk perceptions and crime experience matter (Hind and Murphy 2007; Ho and McKean 2004; Jang *et al.* 2010; Kääriäinen and Niemi 2014; Thomas and Hyman 1977; and the longitudinal analysis of Sindall *et al.* 2012).

In Japan, Tsushima and Hamai (2015) demonstrated that the procedural justice model was not applicable. Japan is well known for community policing in the academic domain since the work of Bayley (1976). The system of *koban*, dating back to 1971, consists of 'small neighbourhood police units [that] patrol the streets, make home visits to establish links, receive feedback on community safety, and respond to crime reports' (Sato, Chapter 5 in this volume). Mai Sato further investigates the main result of Tsushima and Hamai's study: 'The procedural justice model failed: While the first link (between trust in police fairness and legitimacy) worked, the second link (from legitimacy to cooperation) did not. Cooperation was also not explained directly by trust in police fairness'. And, contrary to Ghana or Nigeria, neither is willingness to cooperate with the police in Japan explained by perceived police effectiveness. Although untested in that survey, one possible explanation in the case of Japan may be that the *institutional* unfairness of a police system marked by high levels of corruption and illegal police actions for achieving high conviction outweighs the *interactional* fairness of the *koban* system (Johnson 2003; Miyazawa 1992). Mai Sato lets us feel how desperate Tsushima and Hamai were to try to find some good reasons why the model did not work, breaking the population into males and females or arguing that the police do not use stop and search enough, implying that it should have. But should it? What if the exception were the rule at a global level?

When comparing surveys from different national settings, two conclusions stand out. First, the interrelations of attitudes vis-à-vis the police prove inconsistent (in some countries, perceived fairness is related to willingness to cooperate/obey, in some others not). Second, the expectations about police performance and perceived levels of security are important and in some countries, they are the largest determinants of trust in the police and police legitimacy while perceived police fairness is less relevant. There are good reasons for these differences. In fact, we learn from comparative studies that perceptions of fairness, trust, and legitimacy of the police are dependent on macro-level conditions, in particular diffuse support of the state institutions of which the police are a part (or their rejection when they are perceived as colonial police) and of the levels of corruption (see above) as well as violent crime in the country (Jang *et al.* 2010; Stack *et al.* 2007). An important implication is that procedural justice theory cannot claim universal applicability across different criminal, cultural, and political contexts. Another implication is that one theory is not enough to determine the level of anticipated obedience and cooperation with the police, and in particular the importance of the outcomes of an encounter with the police need to be addressed (on *distributive justice* importance, see Weitzer, Chapter 2 in this volume).

Beyond attitudes: voluntary and involuntary interactions with police as state officials

Studies of the complex structure of attitudes towards the police in Anglo-Saxon countries tend to display stable findings. In Chapter 7 in this volume, Kristina

Murphy and Adrian Cherney, drawing on survey data of residents in ethnically diverse neighbourhoods in Brisbane and Melbourne (Australia), find that attitudes towards procedural justice policing enhances both feelings of belonging to the local community and trust in the police. The authors confirm a number of previous studies in which trust and perceived fairness were correlated, underscoring the importance of the latter on the production of what is frequently described as an essential lubricant of social life, trust. They also suggest that it would be particularly effective in building trust if it were possible to increase the number of marginalized people who assess the police as fair. This is an important issue since those are the segments of the population with the lowest levels of trust.

What remains to be understood is the relationship between attitudes and *actual* behaviour, a crucial issue in many research fields in the social and behavioural sciences. In survey research (as opposed to experimental research), one has to rely on declarations of intended behaviours or at best on self-reports of past behaviours which are more specific than intentions.

In a study of Nordic countries, Juha Kääriäinen (Chapter 13 in this volume) tests the notion that 'public trust in the police and the willingness of citizens to report offences or anti-social behaviour should go hand in hand'. Procedural justice theorists have maintained that victims who believe that the police are helpful and treat them well will be more inclined to turn to the police for assistance (Jackson *et al.* 2013; Tyler and Huo 2002). However, Juha Kääriäinen argues, few studies on actual reporting behaviour have been conducted, and they 'do not seem to confirm the hypothesis that public trust in the police translates into increased readiness among citizens to report offences'. Based on the Finnish 'Police Barometer' survey asking about actual victimization and victims' reactions, he finds a weak correlation only for one of three types of victimization (cf. also Kääriäinen and Sirén 2011). It is well established that at the individual level 'only some reasons for not reporting an offence have anything to do with the police', including attitudes towards the police. At the macro level of European countries, trust in the police and crime reporting behaviour are uncorrelated (see Figure 13.1). Likewise, no or even negative correlations between trust in the police and reporting behaviour have been found in studies from the Netherlands (Goudriaan *et al.* 2006) and Germany (Guzy and Hirtenlehner 2015). In the US, according to Barbara Warner (2007), trust in the police was not found to affect attempts to mobilize public authorities, another form of cooperation.

Such findings raise essential questions about the validity of core assumptions of procedural justice theory, even if more systematic research in more countries is necessary before definitive conclusions can be drawn. And these results echo other studies of a longitudinal or experimental nature, which included the measurement of actual behaviour (although not as an outcome but as an independent variable).

Some experimental studies of traffic stops have found beneficial effects of procedural treatment on general orientations towards the police (Mazerolle *et al.* 2013a; Murphy *et al.* 2013), and the use of some components of procedurally fair policing in pre-existing studies (such as of community policing) have also displayed significant effects on some attitudes but not on legitimacy (Mazerolle *et al.* 2013b). However, and contrary to findings of cross-sectional surveys on attitudes, other recent research based on randomized control trials in the UK found that fairness-based interventions did not improve legitimacy in the police (MacQueen and Bradford 2015), and that procedurally just interventions did not affect drivers' views of police during random breathalyser tests (Lyndel *et al.* 2015). In some studies, if police behaviour was fairer, perceptions of police behaviour changed but without affecting more general attitudes towards police, at least in the case of the US (Lowrey *et al.* 2016) and Turkey (Shahin 2014). In a study of two US cities, Worden and McLean (2016) did not record positive changes in citizen attitudes after fair policing was introduced over several months, neither using police recorded behaviour or a direct observation based indicator. These findings leave us with two puzzles. Why do procedurally just interventions not affect people's perceptions of police legitimacy, and why do we observe an inconsistent effect of procedural fairness on general attitudes towards the police?

In conclusion, there is evidence that the procedural interactional model works at the attitudinal level in some Western countries: Perceptions of fair policing are correlated with the declared willingness to obey and cooperate with the police. Several attitudinal dimensions are intercorrelated, suggesting that those may in fact be part of one single consistent attitudinal complex. A robust debate on this issue has already taken place and will probably continue (Bottoms and Tankebe 2012; Gau 2011; Hough *et al.* 2013; Johnson *et al.* 2014; Tankebe *et al.* 2016). The cross-sectional nature of many surveys on which studies of the Procedural justice model rely casts some doubts on causal relationships. Respondents who trust the police more are also more likely to assess interactions with police officers positively, hinting at a reciprocal relationship between perceptions and attitudes (Hawdon 2008). Such an effect of pre-existing attitudes on the assessment of encounters with the police has been documented before (Brandl *et al.* 1994; Rosenbaum 2005). The notion that some variables are the causes or antecedents of the variations of others is still unclear and cannot be tested unless studies of behaviours are undertaken, preferably also using longitudinal designs with sufficient time duration. When asked about reporting crime to the police in cross-sectional surveys, citizens do not seem to act based on trust. When tested in real life experiments, the expected causal chain form perceived or observed fairness to positive attitudes is not always and, in fact, very rarely verified regarding changes in legitimacy (Lowrey *et al.* 2016; MacQueen and Bradford 2015; Shahin 2014; Worden and McLean 2016). A logical conclusion would be that other social processes may contribute to explaining citizen support for the police. Some relate to the structure of encounters, i.e. the suspect intoxication, disrespect, education of officer, social support of bystanders as theorized by Turk *et al.* (see Weidner and Terrill 2005) or Mastrofski *et al.* (2002), and others to the structure of society, which we discuss now.

Trust and legitimacy among ethnic minorities: social integration and policing policies make a difference

In many counties, there seems to be a strained relationship between the police and ethnic minorities (Rice and White 2010; Weitzer 2014). Minority adolescents have been prominently involved in almost all anti-police riots in the USA and across Western Europe, and police forces in these countries are suspected of widespread discriminatory treatment of minorities, most notoriously in the case of 'racial' or 'ethnic profiling' (Bradford and Loader 2016; Jobard and Lévy 2011; Newburn *et al.* 2016). Research conducted in Australia (Murphy and Cherney, Chapter 7 in this volume), Canada (Wortley and Owusu-Bempah 2009), Finland (Kääriäinen, Chapter 13 in this volume), France (Oberwittler and Roché, Chapter 4 in this volume), Turkey (Roché *et al.* Chapter 10 in this volume) and the USA (Weitzer, Chapter 2 in this volume) has found that attitudes towards the police are clearly more negative among ethnic or racial minority groups than among the majority population. In the developed democracies of Europe and North America, the ethnic dividing lines are mainly between 'White' and some sort of visibly 'Non-White' groups, while in other countries different kinds of ethnic cleavages may matter. In most societies, an ethnic minority status is associated with lower or marginal socio-economic status and a lower position in political and religious hierarchies. Social marginalization combined with the fact that in many countries police officers are recruited mostly from one ethnic group are seen as the main reasons for the strained relationship with the police (Davis and Henderson 2003; Weitzer 2010).

Several chapters in this volume aim to understand the roots of minorities' perceptions of the police in the USA, in European countries and in Turkey, focusing on societal, institutional, and policy factors. For example, perceptions of the police and other social institutions in the US correspond to a White-Latino-African American hierarchy, which 'is deeply rooted in racialized structural inequalities' (Weitzer, Chapter 2 in this volume). It remains an essential task to better understand how attitudes are connected with national structural and cultural contexts, since it can help us understand what makes fairness, trust, and cooperation thrive.

National variations in police–minority relations

Ben Bradford, Jonathan Jackson and Mike Hough (Chapter 3 in this volume) use data from the European Social Survey to assess whether accounting for 'modes of incorporation' (or societal integration) reduce the statistical effect of a dichotomous majority versus minority indicator on police legitimacy ('felt obligation to obey' and 'normative alignment with police' measured by support for the way police behave). Modes of incorporation consist of the felt discrimination, the age of respondents at the time of immigration (as a measure of voluntariness to adopt a place), citizenship status, decisions not to participate in elections, and economic precariousness. The authors find 'no consistent association between ethnic minority status and police legitimacy'. In 11 countries, the felt obligation to obey is higher for minority members; in 14 others, it is lower. They find that, in general, the less minority members are integrated economically and politically, the less they see the police as legitimate. An important exception is that natural-ized minority members are less inclined to obey the police than those still holding foreign citizenship as are those who are eligible to vote. In the multivari-ate model, immigrant status is no longer significant in explaining legitimacy.

These findings are remarkable in two respects. First, the assumption that ethnic minorities hold more negative views of the police is rejected in many European countries and, thus, not universally valid. Second, ignoring the unex-pectedly negative effect of citizenship, the results indicate that the salience of ethnicity is found in social and economic integration into a host society. In the same vein, in Chapter 4, Dietrich Oberwittler and Sebastian Roché reveal that residence in socially and ethnically segregated French 'banlieues' proves a signi-ficant predictor of distrust in the police, thus, suggesting the formation of an anti-police culture in line with previous US studies (e.g. Berg *et al.* 2016; Weitzer 1999; Wu *et al.* 2009), a situation not seen in Germany. Again, the context seems to influence minority integration and relations with the police in nationally specific ways. These findings invite us to scrutinize the characteristics of state institutions and policies supporting minority cultural and economic integration.

Another avenue that has been explored is the contrast between minorities' experiences of institutions in their host countries and expectations formed in their countries of origin, a phenomenon that has been referred to as 'dual frames of reference' (Suarez-Orozco 1987). If the difference is positive, high confidence of first-generation immigrants in Europe may be explained by such contrasts as has been observed in the USA and Canada (Correia 2010; Wortley and Owusu-Bempah 2009). Röder and Mülhau (2012; cf. Nannestad *et al.* 2014) report similar findings about immigrants' attitudes towards criminal justice institutions in EU countries. The role of institutions rather than culture in shaping immig-rants' attitudes need to be given proper attention.

Taken together, comparative analyses of the sources of police trust and legiti-macy indicate that they are not only about policing. Minority groups' attitudes are also driven by their relation to the host societies and their political institu-tions, and in comparison to their countries of origin.

Policing policies and policing styles

Another aspect of political systems refers to how the state and elected officials implement policies. Police structures and policing policies are very divergent across cities and nations. In terms of citizens' involuntary contacts with police, for example, Mai Sato (Chapter 5 in this volume) presents the contrast within the EU between states like Finland and Sweden with many contacts and states like Portugal and Bulgaria with few contacts (see Table 5.2). Three chapters, two about two continental European countries and one on the USA, study the impact of policing strategies, and another proposes avenues for improving the management of officers. They all find that aggressive policing has a deleterious effect on trust.

Wesley Skogan (Chapter 11 in this volume) studies the consequences on trust in police of 'stop-and-frisk' as a law enforcement strategy, which he explains has become the crime deterrence strategy of choice in Chicago since 2013 and, more largely, in American policing. No less than 29 per cent of people (and 40 per cent of those under 35) were checked in Chicago in 2015, compared to 20 per cent a decade before. He explores the risks of this for police efficiency on the one hand, since 'the ability of the police to accurately select suitably at risk people from among [residents of high crime places] is very limited, further reducing the 'hit rate' for seizing contraband and making arrests'; and for police–citizen relations on the other hand, since 'even in crime hot spots, most people, most of the time, are just going about their daily lives', and from their point of view these stops may be unjustified and ethnically unfairly distributed. Sixty-eight per cent of young African American men were stopped and 56 per cent searched and questioned, five times more than average. Use of physical force or threat with a gun was distributed unevenly to the detriment of minority groups.

Dietrich Oberwittler and Sebastian Roché (Chapter 4 in this volume) present findings from the POLIS study, a comparative research project, which compares adolescents in two cities in France and two cities Germany and support the notion that police strategies affect adolescents' trust in the police. While almost no difference in the prevalence of proactive stops is found in Germany between the majority and all minority groups (e.g. 29 per cent for native and 28 per cent for Turkish boys), in France, the largest minority group of Algerian origin is far more exposed to proactive stops (42 per cent for boys) than the majority group (20 per cent for boys), and this difference remains after accounting for a large number of relevant control variables.

Similar consequences are found on both sides of the Atlantic. Aggressive and discriminatory policing practices send a message that is contrary to the idea that the police are doing their best for the people. In line with other US studies, Wesley Skogan (Chapter 11 in this volume) finds that the level of trust in the police is lowest for Blacks and lower for Hispanics compared to White Chicagoans. In addition, those caught up in stop-and-frisk are less trusting of the police. In the POLIS study, trust in the police is considerably lower for minority compared to majority adolescents only in France, in line with the ethnic disproportionality of stops by French police, whereas in Germany very small ethnic differences in trust and no indications of ethnic profiling are found.

Maarten Van Craen, Stephan Parmentier and Mina Rauschenbach (Chapter 12 in this volume) indicate with their study in Belgium that disrespectful treatment of officers by their management equally encourages lack of fairness vis-à-vis citizens. Ron Weitzer (Chapter 2 in this volume) suggests that the American public want reform, that police chiefs are learning from ongoing events, and that its content should focus on how police departments are ethnically populated and police accountability.

These results from various countries show that there is no general law that demands a greater distance between minorities and the police. Learning that a specific ethnic group will not have the same relation to the police in different national settings casts doubt on the nature of the 'ethnic effect'. Moreover, this distance varies across time as much as across nations. Police may serve the minority against the majority (as in South Africa during the apartheid regime) since they are not meant to represent the people but to respond to the orders of the political authority that may be ethnically defined. Police may also be service oriented and not ethnically biased, most likely in political systems with a culture of equality and in which policies are oriented towards that aim. The case studies in this volume illustrate the existence of divergent relations between minority groups and the police. Lower levels of trust and legitimacy granted by minorities are in some cases accounted for by levels of integration into host societies, and strong evidence is found for the impact of policing strategies which are a source of tensions between minorities and police, underlining the relevance of fairness in policing. The convergence of US and European studies is striking in regard to the negative effects of stop-and-search strategies.

Ethnic, religious, and political identities and cleavages

While ethnic divisions have received substantial attention in studies on police–citizen relations, religious and political divisions have not. Such partitions do not necessarily make themselves felt constantly: They depend on identities that can be activated by conflicts, a series of events and processes through which they become expressed in the public arena and politicized. Examples are police killings of Black citizens in the USA and the subsequent ethnic mobilization (as in Black Lives Matter) or political discourses during elections campaigns, e.g. about secularism in France or national identity in Turkey. Studies that are able to capture the dynamics of cleavages and their consequences for police legitimacy in such instances are important but very rare. This volume brings together analyses of the Ferguson shooting in the USA, ethnic-religious tensions in France and political divides in Turkey, and all these examples highlight the interplay between societal tensions and social identities.

Unlike in Europe, the USA has frequent incidents of lethal police violence, with 991 citizens killed by police in 2015 and 963 in 2016 according to the *Washington Post* (Fatal Force 2017), and more than 1,000 each year according to the *Guardian* (The Counted 2016). After White Police Officer Darren Wilson shot and killed African American Michael Brown on 9 August 2014 in Ferguson, there three weeks of large protests, rioting, and looting. 'Police responded with fortified vehicles, riot gear, skirmish lines, beanbag bullets, and tear gas. The heaviest period of civil unrest lasted from 9 August and into September', Tammy Rinehart Kochel (Chapter 9 in this volume) writes. She assesses how such a high-profile incident affected citizens' attitudes towards the police, using a local panel survey with measurements before and after the incident. In the short term, a gulf along ethnic lines widened: Trust and perceived fairness diminished significantly for Blacks (−26 per cent) but increased for Whites (+1.5 per cent), suggesting that the latter group did not judge the killing as relevant for themselves. In line with Easton's theoretical framework and empirical findings from Kaminski and Jefferis (1998), Tammy Rinehart Kochel observes that citizens who hold lower levels of diffuse support for police appear to have been more negatively affected by use of force. Important conclusions are that in the assessment of police use of lethal force, the impact of racial divisions and polarization are reinforced by a critical event and the way it is managed by authorities.

A Turkish case study (Roché *et al.* Chapter 10 in this volume) analyses public support for the use of violent and non-violent illegal means by the police, i.e. granting a moral right to use coercive powers which constitutes another aspect of state legitimacy. In order to explain who does agrees to deviant policing and who does not, Sebastian Roché, Mine Özaşçılar and Ömer Bilen take into account various societal divides, and it appears that political party orientation is the main predictor with supporters of the incumbent political party, the Justice and Development Party (AKP), most inclined to condone unlawful police actions. The AKP is a nationalistic, religiously conservative and free market-oriented party, and political cleavages in Turkey seem to be an amalgam of religious identity (Sunni Muslim versus other), ethnicity (Turkish versus Kurdish) and socioeconomic preferences. Respondents' own experiences of police-initiated stops reinforce a critical assessment of illegal police actions only for supporters of the two oppositional parties, the CHP (a secular party) and HDP (a Kurdish-based party), which display the largest political distance vis-à-vis AKP. The authors suggest that political ideology organizes the subjective understanding both of policing policies and personal experiences with police. It is important to consider that central police forces in Turkey are organizations that take their orders from the executive branch of government. Hence, it is no surprise that legitimacy to act illegally is granted to the police primarily by supporters of the ruling party. For them, it seems that the end justifies the means. Political preferences are very strong determinants of the public evaluation of the morality of the government and its police (cf. Anderson and Tverdova 2003 on corruption). The role of political ideologies has been hinted at in recent research on attitudes towards the police: Political ideology predicts support for excessive use of force (Gerber and Jackson 2017), while conservative and authoritarian worldviews, which often include punitiveness, are ideological bases for seeing the police in a more positive light, as an agency defending social order against deviance (Dugan 2015; Hough *et al.* 2013: 46; Jackson *et al.* 2011; Messner *et al.* 2006; Silver and Pickett 2015).

The history of state building in some countries is marked by foreign domination, with long-lasting effects on how the police is perceived, such as in Nigeria (Akinlabi, Chapter 6 in this volume) or Ghana (Tankebe 2008). Others are deeply divided by religion or ethnicity to the point where different people live largely separately, as in Israel with corresponding distrust of the Israeli state and its police by the Arab minority (Hasisi 2008). Less extreme divides exist in European countries and adherence to the political community always manifests itself as 'diffuse support' with significant effects on attitudes towards the police. In Chapter 8, Sebastian Roché, Anina Schwarzenbach, Dietrich Oberwittler and Jacques de Maillard analyse the role of religious beliefs and ethnic identities in minority adolescents' attitudes towards the police in France and Germany. Supporting the group engagement model (Bradford *et al.* 2014; Tyler and Blader 2003), they find that trust in the police is dependent on the identification of minority adolescents with the host society in both France and Germany, whereas adolescents who strongly identify with their group of origin are less trusting. And, importantly, they find that religiosity among Muslim minority adolescents (of Maghrebian origin in France and of Turkish origin in Germany) has diverging effects in both countries: Stronger religiosity *increases* trust the police in Germany but *decreases* trust in France. Depending on national contexts and the institutionalization of state-religion relationships (a means of building a political community), religion can turn into a political cleavage that may weaken the legitimacy of state institutions. We relate this divergence in the effect of social identification to the possible existence of a conflict (Sambanis and Shayo 2013), a tension about the legitimacy of institutional arrangements. When the state has legitimacy problems or a trust deficit with a large minority, it will in turn affect the group's relationship with the police (Brewer 1991). The conditional effect of religious identification underscores the importance of national political institutions. On a more general level, we propose that ethnicity, race, religion, or region play a role for trust only if they are 'expressed' (in an analogy to 'gene expression' in biology). While in Germany religious identity is not expressed, in France it is, and since the police are part of a larger political system, this process negatively impacts adolescents' trust in police.

Towards a renewed research agenda

The chief intention of this volume is to learn from the comparison of different experiences of police–citizen relations across various countries where the relationship between the governors and the governed, of which trust and legitimacy are a part, may vary. We have classically addressed legitimacy as the moral right to rule vested in government and police, i.e. voluntary compliance and cooperation, on the one hand, and the right to use coercive powers, on the other hand. Summing up the major points of our introductory discussion based on the case studies presented in this volume and on the relevant literature, we have identified four core issues for future research on police–citizen relations.

First, a major question is 'what are the main theories that may be needed in order to explain trust in the police and police legitimacy?' We believe that several theories are needed and we categorize them in four blocks: (a) adherence to the political and social order (and related institutions); (b) group position, integration into society and corresponding societal cleavages of various kinds (socio-economic, religious, ethnic); (c) policing policies (and in particular stop and search strategies) and performance of the police (the quality of service and efficacy against crime); and (d) those that deal with the interactions, i.e. the structure of interaction, the procedural justice during interaction, and the out-comes of interactions or distributive justice.

A second issue is under which circumstances does the procedural justice model work at the attitudinal level? It appears that its core tenets apply mainly to Western liberal democracies but not necessarily beyond. Which countries should we then judge as the rule and which as an anomaly? There is some weight to the argument that political liberalism and the rule of law have combined to con-tribute to higher standards of living (although unevenly distributed), and have laid the groundwork for people's appreciation of fair procedures and rules. In other regions of the world, people may cooperate with the police for different reasons, but we need more systematic analyses to substantiate this hypothesis, starting with definitional issues. Cross-country comparisons have revealed that the concept of two components of legitimacy (duty to obey to and value align-ment with police) do not match countries as Ghana, Nigeria, Japan or Israel, for example.

A third important problem is the disconnect between subjective and objective measures of fairness and legitimacy and the lack of studies which are able to combine survey data with observational or experimental data. Subjective assess-ments of interactions as recorded in surveys may well be coloured by ideology, strong identity, and other non-interactional factors. We echo other scholars' calls for assessments of specific examples of police conduct to be incorporated into surveys (Waddington *et al.* 2015). This is important if we want to ascertain the effects of interactional procedures on trust and legitimacy. In addition, we do not yet have at our disposal a shared and agreed upon measurement rod for observed interactional fairness. This situation may help explain why several programmes focusing on improving police interactions (recorded and coded by an observer) do not alter public perceptions.

A fourth issue is about the role for cross-national studies that can help to clarify the effects of macro-level variables (e.g. state institutions, culture, level of crime, cleavages). National contexts may impact all four blocks of theories mentioned in the first major issue. We advocate cross-national comparative surveys supplemented by measures of state institutions, criminal context, and socio-political cleavages. The chapters in this volume have been examples of research underscoring the impact of these dimensions on police–citizen relations.

A series of hypotheses relating to the role of institutions might be worth testing in future research. First, states have distinct regimes and quality of gov-ernment. An effect of those two major aspects of states on generalized trust and attitudes towards the welfare state have started to be observed with various methodologies (Larsen 2016; Rothstein and Eek 2009). Extant research already has found effects on trust and other attitudes towards the police of police respon-siveness and competence, impartiality and fairness, transparency and account-ability, all being classic notions useful for measuring the quality of service rendered to citizens by police, before, during, and after interactions take place. Regimes and quality of government may influence the quality of policing and, as a consequence, attitudes vis-à-vis police in different ways. The quality of policing may matter for producing support to the political system, a sense of belonging to a superordinate group, and a sense of citizenship. That makes it a candidate explanation for diffuse system support (Rodgers and Taylor 1971). And we know that such trust has lot to do with the legitimacy of the police. Second, police forces across the world are hardly comparable in their organization, their control by the political authority, and the behaviour of their units and members. Trust and legitimacy might depend on those factors directly or indirectly and in combination with other factors. For example, centralization of forces with strong government oversight may promote more homogeneous policing and may, in combination with a policy of equal treatment of all citizens, explain the privileged situation of Nordic European countries. Conversely, a poorly supervised and decentralized set of forces might lead to open police distrust. Third, political ideologies are likely to influence judgements about the police and policing in a diversity of states (Stack and Cao 1998). It is also well established that supporters of the incumbent party are more positive about the policies and it is likely that they are in the same mood regarding policing, i.e. ready to endorse the actions of the police for reasons of ideological proximity with the government (Anderson *et al.* 2005). A cross-national analysis of the correspondence between citizens' political leaning, ideological distance to incumbent office holder, and trust or legitimacy of police might help to unveil the importance of ideology. Fourth, levels of violence and crime may vary greatly across states, affecting support for the police. Their systematic incorporation to research protocol would help to include contextual data that are correlated to state performance. Fifth, societies are more or less divided along fault lines, and the police are often placed in the middle of opposing groups in the case of tensions (Waddington 2003). Group cleavages are related to the politicization of group identities, and governments contribute to feeding or defusing such cleavages by their identity policies and their use of police forces (Brewer 1991). Attitudes vis-à-vis the police may vary according to support to the government's policies in handling such cleavages. A measurement of the degree of division of the country combined with a measurement of the related government policies might enlighten support given to police deviance as well as fair policing.

Bibliography

Afrobarometer Round 5 (2010–2012). 'Afrobarometer online data analysis', online. Available www.afrobarometer-online-analysis.com/aj/AJBrowserAB.jsp (accessed 27 April 2017).

Anderson, C., Blais, A., Bowler, S., Donovan, T., and Listhaug, O. (2005). *Losers' Consent: Elections and Democratic Legitimacy*, Oxford: Oxford University Press.

Anderson, C. J. and Tverdova, Y. V. (2003). 'Corruption, political allegiance, and attitudes toward government in contemporary democracy', *American Journal of Political Science* 47, 91–109.

Bayley, D. (1976). *Forces of Order: Policing Modern Japan*, Berkeley, CA: University of California Press.

Bellman, A. (1935). 'A police service rating scale', *Journal of Criminal Law and Criminology*, 26: 74–114.

Berg, M., Stewart, E., Intravia, J., Warren, P., and Simons, R. (2016). 'Cynical streets: neighborhood social processes and perceptions of criminal injustice', *Criminology*, 54: 520–47.

Blader, S. L. and Tyler, R. T. (2003). 'A four-component model of procedural justice: defining the meaning of a "fair" process"', *Personality and Social Psychology Bulletin*, 29: 747–58.

Booth J. A. and Seligson M. A. (2009). *The Legitimacy Puzzle in Latin America: Political Support and Democracy in Eight Nations*, Stanford, CA: Stanford University Press.

Bottoms, A. and Tankebe, J. (2012). 'Beyond procedural justice: a dialogic approach to legitimacy in criminal justice', *Journal of Criminal Law and Criminology*, 102: 119–70.

Bowling, B. and Phillips, C. (2008). 'Policing ethnic minority communities', in Newburn, T. (ed.), *Handbook of Policing*, Cullompton: Willan, 611–41.

Bradford, B. and Loader, I. (2016). 'Police, crime and order: the case of stop and search', in B. Bradford, B. Jauregui, I. Loader, and J. Steinberg (eds) *The SAGE Handbook of Global Policing*, London: Sage, 241–60.

Bradford, B., Murphy, K., and Jackson, J. (2014). 'Officers as mirrors: policing, procedural justice and the (re)production of social identity', *British Journal of Criminology*, 54: 527–50.

Brandl, S., Frank, J., Worden, R., and Bynum, T. (1994). 'Global and specific attitudes toward the police: disentangling the relationship', *Justice Quarterly*, 11: 119–34.

Brewer, J. (1991). 'Policing in divided societies: theorizing a type of policing', *Policing and Society*, 1: 179–91.

Cao, L. and Zhao, J. (2005). 'Confidence in the police in Latin America', *Journal of Criminal Justice*, 33: 403–12.

Christensen, T. and Lægreid, P. (2005). 'Trust in government: the relative importance of service satisfaction, political factors, and demographics', *Public performance and Management Review*, 28: 487–511.

Coicaud, J.-M. (2002). *Legitimacy and Politics. A Contribution to the Study of Political Right and Political Responsibility*, Cambridge: Cambridge University Press.

Coquilhat, J. (2008). *Community Policing: An International Literature Review*, Wellington: New Zealand Government.

Correia, M. (2010). 'Determinants of attitudes toward police of Latino immigrants and non-immigrants', *Journal of Criminal Justice*, 38: 99–107.

Davis, R. and Henderson, N. (2003). 'Willingness to report crimes: the role of ethnic group membership and community efficacy', *Crime and Delinquency*, 49: 564–80.

Donner, C., Makaly, J., Fridell, L., and Jennings, W. (2015). 'Policing and procedural justice: a state-of-the-art review', *Policing: An International Journal of Police Strategies and Management*, 38: 153–72.

Dugan, A. (2015), 'Trust differs most by ideology for church, police, presidency', online. Available www.gallup.com/poll/183875/trust-differs-ideology-church-police-presidency. aspx?version=print (accessed 27 April 2017).

Easton, D. (1965). *A Framework for Political Analysis*, Englewood Cliffs, NJ: Prentice-Hall.

Farganis, J. (2008). *Readings in Social Theory*. Columbus, OH: McGraw Hill.

Fatal Force (2017). 'Fatal force', *Washington Post*, online. Available www.washington post.com/graphics/national/police-shootings-2016 (accessed 5 May 2017).

Gau, J. (2011). 'The convergent and discriminant validity of procedural justice and police legitimacy: an empirical test of core theoretical propositions', *Journal of Criminal Justice*, 39: 489–98.

Gerber, M. and Jackson, J. (2017). 'Justifying violence: legitimacy, ideology and public support for police use of force', *Psychology, Crime and Law*, 23: 79–95.

Goudriaan, H., Wittebrood, K., and Nieuwbeerta, P. (2006). 'Neighbourhood characteristics and reporting crime effects of social cohesion, confidence in police effectiveness and socio-economic disadvantage', *British Journal of Criminology*, 46: 719–42.

Guzy, N. and Hirtenlehner, H. (2015). 'Trust in the German police: determinants and consequences for reporting behavior', in: Mesko, G. and Tankebe, J. (eds), *Trust and Legitimacy in Criminal Justice. European Perspectives*, Cham: Springer International Publishing, 203–29.

Hasisi, B. (2008). 'Police, politics, and culture in deeply divided societies', *The Journal of Criminal Law and Criminology*, 98: 1119–45.

Hawdon, J. (2008). 'Legitimacy, trust, social capital, and policing styles: a theoretical statement', *Police Quarterly*, 11: 182–201.

Hinds, L. and Murphy, K. (2007). 'Public satisfaction with police: using procedural justice to improve police legitimacy', *Australian and New Zealand Journal of Criminology*, 40: 27–42.

Ho, T. and McKean, J. (2004). 'Confidence in the police and perceptions of risk', *Western Criminology Review*, 5: 108–18.

Høigård, C. (2011). 'Policing the North', in M. Tonry and T. Lappi-Seppälä (eds) *Crime and Justice in Scandinavia (Crime and Justice, vol. 40)*, Chicago, IL: The University of Chicago Press, 265–348.

Hough, M., Jackson, J., and Bradford, B. (2013). 'Legitimacy, trust and compliance: an empirical test of procedural justice theory using the European Social Survey', in J. Tankebe and A. Liebling (eds), *Legitimacy and Criminal Justice: An International Exploration*, Oxford: Oxford University Press, 326–52.

Jackson, J., Bradford, B., Hough, M., Kuha, J., Stares, S. R., Widdop, S., Fitzgerald, R., Yordanova, M., and Galev, T. (2011). 'Developing European indicators of trust in justice', *European Journal of Criminology*, 8: 267–85.

Jackson, J., Bradford, B., Stanko, E., and Hohl, K. (2013). *Just Authority? Trust in the Police in England and Wales*, London: Routledge.

Jang, H., Joo, H.-J., and Zhao, J. (2010). 'Determinants of public confidence in police: an international perspective', *Journal of Criminal Justice*, 38: 57–68.

Jobard, F. and Lévy, R. (2011). 'Racial profiling: the Parisian police experience', *Canadian Journal of Criminology and Criminal Justice*, 53: 87–93.

Johnson, D. (2003). 'Above the law? Police integrity in Japan', *Social Science Japan Journal*, 6: 19–37.

Johnson, D., Maguire, E., and Kuhn, J. (2014). 'Public perceptions of the legitimacy of the law and legal authorities: evidence from the Caribbean', *Law and Society Review*, 48: 947–78.

Kääriäinen, J. and Niemi, J. (2014). 'Distrust of the police in a Nordic welfare state: victimization, discrimination, and trust in the police by Russian and Somali minorities in Helsinki', *Journal of Ethnicity in Criminal Justice*, 12: 4–24.

Kääriäinen, J. and Sirén, R. (2011). 'Trust in the police, generalized trust and reporting crime', *European Journal of Criminology*, 8: 65–81.

Kaina, V. (2008). 'Legitimacy, trust and procedural fairness: remarks on Marcia Grimes's study', *European Journal of Political Research*, 47: 510–21.

Kaminski, R. and Jefferis, E. (1998). 'The effect of a violent televised arrest on public perceptions of the police: a partial test of Easton's theoretical framework', *Policing: An International Journal of Police Strategies and Management*, 21: 683–706.

Kutnjak Ivkovic, S. (2008). 'A comparative study of public support for the police', *International Criminal Justice Review*, 18: 406–34.

Lappi-Seppälä, T. (2008). 'Trust, welfare, and political culture: explaining differences in national penal policies', *Crime and Justice*, 37: 313–87.

Larsen, C. (2016). *The Institutional Logic of Welfare Attitudes: How Welfare Regimes Influence*, London: Routledge.

Lowrey, B., Maguire, E. R., and Bennett, R. R. (2016). 'Testing the effects of procedural justice and overaccommodation in traffic stops: a randomized experiment', *Criminal Justice and Behavior*, Advance online publication, doi: 10.1177/0093854816639330.

Lyndel, J. B., Antrobus, E., Bennett, S., and Martin, P. (2015) 'Comparing police and public perceptions of a routine traffic encounter', *Police Quarterly*, 18: 442–68.

Mackenzie, S. and Henry, A. (2009). *Community Policing: A Review of the Evidence*, Edinburgh: Scottish Government Social Research.

MacQueen, S. and Bradford, B. (2015). 'Enhancing public trust and police legitimacy during road traffic encounters: results from a randomised controlled trial in Scotland', *Journal of Experimental Criminology* 11: 419–43.

Maguire, E. and Johnson, D. (2010). 'Measuring public perceptions of the police', *Policing: An International Journal of Police Strategies and Management*, 33: 703–30.

Mastrofski, S. D., Reisig, M. D., and McCluskey, J. D. (2002). 'Police disrespect toward the public: an encounter-based analysis', *Criminology*, 40: 519–52.

Mazerolle, L., Antrobus, E., Bennet, S., and Tyler, T. (2013a). 'Shaping citizen perceptions of police legitimacy: a randomized field trial of procedural justice', *Criminology*, 51: 33–63.

Mazerolle, L., Bennett, S., Davis, J., Sargeant, E., and Manning, M. (2013b). 'Legitimacy in policing: a Systematic Review', *Campbell Systematic Reviews*, 9.

Mazerolle, L., Sargeant, E., Cherney, A., Bennett, S., Murphy, K., Antrobus, E., and Martin, P. (2014). *Procedural Justice and Legitimacy in Policing*, New York: Springer.

Messner, S. F., Baumer, E. P., and Rosenfeld, R. (2006). 'Distrust of government, the vigilante tradition, and support for capital punishment', *Law and Society Review*, 40: 559–90.

Miller, A. (1974). 'Political issues and trust in government: 1964–1970', *American Political Science Review*, 68: 951–72.

Miller, A. and Listhaug, O. (1998). 'Policy preferences and political trust: a comparison of Norway, Sweden and the United States', *Scandinavian Political Studies*, 21: 161–87.

Mishler, W. and Rose, R. (2001). 'What are the origins of political trust? Testing institutional and cultural theories in post-communist societies', *Comparative Political Studies*, 34: 30–62.

Miyazawa, S. (1992). *Policing in Japan: A Study on Making Crime*. New York: University of New York Press.

Morris, C. S. (2011). *A cross-national study on public confidence in the police*. PhD thesis, Northeastern University, online. Available https://repository.library.northeastern.edu/files/neu:1022/fulltext.pdf (accessed 27 April 2017).

Morris, C. (2015). 'An international study on public confidence in police', *Police Practice and Research. An International Journal*, 16: 416–30.

Murphy, K., Mazerolle, L., and Bennett, S. (2013). 'Promoting trust in police: findings from a randomised experimental field trial of procedural justice policing', *Policing and Society*, 24: 405–24.

Nannestad, P., Svendsen, G., Dinesen, P., and Sønderskov, K. (2014). 'Do institutions or culture determine the level of social trust? The natural experiment of migration from non-Western to Western Countries', *Journal of Ethnic and Migration Studies*, 40: 544–65.

Newburn, T., Diski, R., Cooper, K., Deacon, R., Burch, A., and Grant, M. (2016). '"The biggest gang"? Police and people in the 2011 England riots', *Policing and Society*, online. Available www.tandfonline.com/doi/abs/10.1080/10439463.2016.1165220 (accessed 11 May 2017).

Norris, P. (2017). 'The conceptual framework of political support', in S. Zmerli and T. van der Meer (eds) *Handbook on Political Trust*, Cheltenham: Elgar Publishing, 19–32.

Parratt, S. D. (1936), 'A critique of the Bellman police service rating scale', *Journal of the American Institute of Criminal Law and Criminology*, 27: 895–905.

Rice, S. and White, M. (2010), *Race, ethnicity and policing*, New York: New York University Press.

Röder, A. and Mühlau, P. (2012). 'What determines the trust of immigrants in criminal justice systems in Europe?', *European Journal of Criminology*, 9: 370–87.

Rodgers, H. and Taylor G. (1971). 'The policeman as an agent of regime legitimation', *Midwest Journal of Political Science*, 15: 72–86.

Rosenbaum, D. (2005). 'Attitudes toward the police', *Police Quarterly*, 8: 343–65.

Rothstein, B. and Eek, D. (2009). 'Political corruption and social trust: an experimental approach', *Rationality and Society*, 21: 81–112.

Rothstein, B. and Uslaner, E. (2005). 'All for all: equality, corruption, and social trust', *World Politics*, 58: 41–72.

Sahin, N. M. (2014). *Legitimacy, procedural justice and police–citizen encounters: A randomized controlled trial of the impact of procedural justice on citizen. Perceptions of the police during traffic stops in Turkey*, Phd thesis, State University of New Jersey, online. Available https://rucore.libraries.rutgers.edu/rutgers-lib/43841/PDF/1/ (accessed 27 April 2017).

Sambanis, N. and Shayo, M. (2013). 'Social identification and ethnic conflict', *The American Political Science Review*, 107: 294–325.

Sargeant, E., Murphy, K., and Cherney, A. (2014). 'Ethnicity, trust and cooperation with the police: testing the dominance of the process-based model', *European Journal of Criminology*, 11: 500–24.

Schafer, J. A., Huebner, B. M., and Bynum, T. S. (2003). 'Citizen perceptions of police services: race, neighborhood context, and community policing', *Police Quarterly*, 6, 440–68.

Silver, J. R. and Pickett, J. T. (2015). 'Understanding politicized policing attitudes: conflicted conservatism and support for police use of force', *Criminology*, 53: 650–76.

Sindall, K., Sturgis, P., and Jennings, W. (2012). 'Public confidence in the police', *British Journal of Criminology*, 52: 744–64.

Skogan, W. (1998). 'Community policing in Chicago', in Alpert, G. and Piquero, A. (eds), *Community Policing: Contemporary Readings*, Prospect Heights, NY: Waveland Press, 159–74.

Smith, R. (1970). 'The concept of legitimacy', *Theoria: A Journal of Social and Political Theory*, 35: 17–29.

Stack S. and Cao L. (1998). 'Political conservatism and trust in the police: a comparative analysis', *Journal of Crime and Justice*, 21: 71–76.

Stack, S., Cao, L., and Adamzyck, A. (2007). 'Crime volume and law and order culture', *Justice Quarterly*, 24: 291–308.

Suarez-Orozco, M. (1987). 'Becoming somebody: Central American immigrants in U.S. inner-city schools', *Anthropology and Education Quarterly*, 18: 287–99.

Sunshine, J. and Tyler, T. (2003). 'The role of procedural justice and legitimacy in shaping public support for policing', *Law and Society Review*, 37: 513–48.

Sztompka, P. (1999). *Trust: A Sociological Theory*. Cambridge: Cambridge University Press.

Tankebe, J. (2008). 'Colonialism, legitimation, and policing in Ghana', *International Journal of Law, Crime and Justice*, 36: 67–84.

Tankebe, J. (2009). 'Self-help, policing, and procedural justice: Ghanaian vigilantism and the rule of law', *Law and Society Review*, 43: 245–69.

Tankebe, J., Reisig, M., and Wang, X. (2016). 'A multidimensional model of police legitimacy: a cross-cultural assessment', *Law and Human Behavior*, 40: 11–22.

Taylor, R. and Lawton, B. (2012). 'An integrated contextual model of confidence in local police', *Police Quarterly*, 15: 414–45.

Terpstra, J. (2011). 'Two theories on the police. The relevance of Max Weber and Emile Durkheim to the study of the police', *International Journal of Law, Crime and Justice* 39: 1–11.

The Counted (2016). 'The Counted. People killed by police in the US', *Guardian*, online. Available www.theguardian.com/us-news/ng-interactive/2015/jun/01/the-counted-police-killings-us-database (accessed 5 May 2017).

Thibaut J. J. and Walker, W. (1975), *Procedural Justice. A Psychological Analysis*, Hillsdale, NJ: Lawrence Erlbaum Associates.

Thomas, C. and Hyman, J. (1977). 'Perceptions of crime, fear of victimization, and public perceptions of police performance', *Journal of Police Science and Public Administration*, 5: 305–16.

Thomassen, G. (2013). 'Corruption and trust in the police: a cross-country study', *European Journal of Policing Studies*, 1: 152–68.

Thomassen, G. and Kääriäinen, J. (2016). 'System satisfaction, contact satisfaction, and trust in the police: a study of Norway', *European Journal of Policing Studies*, 3: 437–48.

Tonry, M. (2007). 'Preface', in T. Tyler (ed.), *Legitimacy and Criminal Justice*, New York: Russell Sage Foundation, 3–8.

Tsushima, M. and Hamai, K. (2015). 'Public cooperation with the police in Japan: testing the legitimacy model', *Journal of Contemporary Criminal Justice*, 31: 212–28.

Tyler, T. (1990). *Why People Obey the Law*, New Haven, CT: Yale University Press.

Tyler, T. (2006). 'Psychological perspectives on legitimacy and legitimation', *Annual Review of Psychology*, 57: 375–400.

Tyler, T. (2011). *Why People Cooperate: The Role of Social Motivations*, Princeton, NJ: Princeton University Press.

Tyler, T. and Blader, S. (2003). 'The group engagement model: procedural justice, social identity, and cooperative behavior', *Personality and Social Psychology Review*, 7: 349–61.

Tyler, T. and Huo, Y. (2002). *Trust in the Law: Encouraging Public Cooperation with the Police and Courts*, New York: Russell-Sage Foundation.

Tyler, T., Goff, P., and MacCoun, R. (2015). 'The impact of psychological science on policing in the United States: procedural justice, legitimacy, and effective law enforcement', *Psychological Science in the Public Interest*, 16: 75–109.

Waddington, P. A. J. (2003). Policing public order and political contention, in Newburn, T. (ed.), *Handbook of Policing*, Cullumpton: Willan, 394–421.

Waddington, P. A. J., Williams, K., Wright, M., and Newburn, T. (2015). 'Dissension in public evaluations of the police', *Policing and Society*, 25: 212–35.

Warner, B. (2007). 'Directly intervene or call the authorities? A study of forms of neighborhood social control within a social disorganization framework', *Criminology*, 45: 99–129.

Webb, V. J. and Marshall, C. E. (1995). 'The relative importance of race and ethnicity on citizen attitudes toward the police', *American Journal of Police*, 14: 45–66.

Weber, M. (1947). *The Theory of Social and Economic Organization*, New York: The Free Press.

Weidner, R. R. and Terrill, W. (2005). 'A test of Turk's theory of norm resistance using observational data on police–suspect encounters', *Journal of Research in Crime and Delinquency*, 42: 84–109.

Weitzer, R. (1999). 'Citizens' perceptions of police misconduct: race and neighborhood context', *Justice Quarterly*, 16: 819–46.

Weitzer, R. (2010). 'Race and policing in different ecological contexts', in Rice, S. and White, M. (eds), *Race, Ethnicity and Policing*, New York: New York University Press, 118–39.

Weitzer, R. (2014). 'The puzzling neglect of Hispanic Americans in research on police–citizen relations', *Ethnic & Racial Studies*, 37: 1995–2013.

Weitzer, R. and Tuch, S. (2006). *Race and Policing in America: Conflict and Reform*, Cambridge: Cambridge University Press.

Worden, R. and McLean, S. (2016). 'Measuring, managing, and enhancing procedural justice in policing: promise and pitfalls', *Criminal Justice Policy Review*, advance online publication, doi: 10.1177/0887403416662505.

Wortley, S. and Owusu-Bempah, A. (2009). 'Unequal before the law: immigrant and racial minority perceptions of the Canadian criminal justice system', *Journal of International Migration and Integration*, 10: 447–73.

Wu, Y., Sun, I., and Triplett, R. (2009). 'Race, class or neighborhood context: which matters more in measuring satisfaction with police?', *Justice Quarterly*, 26: 125–56.

You, J.-S. (2012). 'Social trust: fairness matters more than homogeneity', *Political Psychology*, 33: 701–21.

Part II

Police–citizen relations

Multilevel and comparative approaches: neighbourhoods and states

2 Recent trends in police–citizen relations and police reform in the United States

Ronald Weitzer

Introduction

Policing in America has become highly controversial in the past three years. Several well-publicized violent incidents, in a short time span, have rattled public confidence in the police and sparked fresh debate on reforms. This is a fairly unique moment in American history, surpassing the level of popular alarm that followed some high-profile policing incidents in the twentieth century (Lawrence 2000).

Research shows that public confidence in the police typically erodes after a controversial event is heavily publicized in the news media. But, over time, public opinion typically rebounds to its pre-incident level (Weitzer 2002). Recent events, however, may have a longer-term impact—especially when there are a series of incidents in a compressed time period that gain massive traction in the media and popular discourse. This contamination-by-association is occurring in America today, in a cumulative manner—with each incident pollinating subsequent ones—in part because activists and the media are drawing connections between them. And this perfect storm gained added momentum with the creation in December 2014 of the President's Task Force on 21st Century Policing, which signaled to the public that police killings are not isolated incidents. Also important is the growing role of video recordings of police actions, featured in both mainstream and social media. Videos can provide a counter-narrative to the police account, and contribute to policing's "new visibility": "Whereas, by comparison, there was once the occasional, localized performance of police impropriety achieving notoriety, we now can expect more frequent, globalized spectacles of such impropriety" (Goldsmith 2010: 931). Patrol officers today are aware that their actions may be recorded and widely distributed. And some recent studies suggest that this new visibility may be having some constraining effect on officer behavior (Ariel et al. 2014; Brown 2016; Goold 2003; Jennings et al. 2015).

Many of the recent police-involved killings of civilians have been politicized by activists, politicians, media pundits, and law enforcement officials. Time and again, we have seen protestors on the streets and commentators in the media (1) operating with a presumption of guilt toward the officer or officers involved, (2) asserting that misconduct is widespread and systemic, or (3) imputing racial animus as a motive. For example, when it was announced that charges would not be brought against the officer who killed Tony Robinson in Madison, Wisconsin, a protestor filmed on the street shouted, "This is *not* what democracy is about," which clearly presumes that the officer should have been prosecuted. For their part, senior police officials are typically slow to provide the public with information about an incident, and the police union (if not the chief of police) typically jumps to the defense of the accused officer (Baker 2015). And the media have sometimes provided biased coverage or have generalized beyond the specific incident—blaming an entire police department or "the police" in general. Reporting on a police killing of a Black man in Chicago, for example, *New York Times* reporters wrote that the incident "exposed a deeper culture of secrecy and impunity in Chicago that implicated the entire police force and much of the city's government" (Davey and Smith 2016). The *Washington Post*'s editorial board claimed that the Chicago police department "suffers not from a few bad apples but from a rotten culture of racist policing and official impunity" (*Washington Post* 2016, April 16). And generalizing about policing nationwide, the *New York Times* editorial board stated, "[t]he shootings seem part of some gruesome loop of episodes of law enforcement gone amok" (*New York Times* 2016, July 8).

Most research shows that Americans' perceptions and reported personal experiences with the police are racially stratified. Older studies often lumped racial minorities into a "Nonwhite" category that was compared to Whites, but we now know that this masks important differences between Blacks, Latinos, and Asians. In fact, numerous polls show a *White-Latino-African American hierarchy* (see Weitzer and Tuch 2006). The attitudes of Asian Americans either parallel those of Whites or fit between the modal opinions of Whites and Latinos. For example, when asked to assess the seriousness of the killings of African Americans by the police, a representative sample of individuals aged 18 to 30 fits the hierarchical pattern: the "extremely serious" option was selected by 24 percent of Whites, 35 percent of Asians, 45 percent of Latinos, and 73 percent of African Americans (GenForward/Associated Press/NORC 2016).

The racial hierarchy pattern is evident in citizen perceptions of other criminal justice agencies and other social institutions in the United States, and is deeply rooted in structural inequalities:

> Among racial minority groups, the level of alienation [from major social institutions] would vary based on differences in the persistence, pervasiveness across domains of life, and extremity of inequality of life chances. This argument implies that members of more recent and voluntarily incorporated minority groups will feel less alienation than members of long-term and involuntarily incorporated minority groups.
>
> (Bobo 1999: 461)

Just as African Americans have a deeper and more crystallized experience of political, social, and economic subordination than is true for Hispanics and Asians, they also have a longer and more fractious history with the police in

America. This is a central reason why Blacks' opinions of the police are significantly more negative than those of Hispanics and Asians. And their collective history and contemporary racial-group affinity help to explain why they tend to view Black victims of police misconduct vicariously as an attack against the racial group as a whole. As the dominant racial group in the United States, Whites tend to individualize police abuse of White individuals, rather than seeing these incidents as a threat to Whites more generally. This has been described as the "group position" explanation for racial groups' perceptions of authority figures (Weitzer and Tuch 2006). Membership in a particular racial group shapes individuals' relations with the police, over and above their individual experiences.

The chapter examines several key factors that condition perceptions of the police at both the individual and group level and then discusses a set of reforms that have been proposed in the United States.

Underlying factors

Citizens' attitudes toward the police are shaped by several factors, including the dynamics of their interactions with officers, exposure to media reporting, and various structural factors. At the interactional level, it is now well established that procedural justice during encounters can make a big difference in citizens' willingness to cooperate with officers, their evaluation of the contact, and their overall opinion of the police (Tyler and Huo 2002; Wiley and Hudik 1974). *Procedural justice* takes place when officers give citizens a reason for a stop, treat them courteously, allow them to explain their actions, and demonstrate that police procedures are fair. When a person is deprived of due process, verbally demeaned, given no reason for being stopped, told to "shut up," detained in public for a long time, or subjected to excessive force, it is almost guaranteed that he or she will define this treatment as unjust and that these experiences will color the individual's general opinion of the police.

But procedural justice at the micro level is only part of the equation. An exclusive focus on procedural justice downplays the importance of *distributive justice*: the outcomes of an encounter with the police. Such outcomes have been shown to influence people's views of the police, over and above the perceived fairness of the procedures followed (Peffley and Hurwitz 2010). As one study noted, "[s]ome police stops are recognized to be fundamentally unjust no matter how 'polite' or 'nice' the officer. [...] The problem is not simply the 'manner' in which these stops are carried out; the problem is investigatory stops themselves"—i.e. stops and questioning not directly related to any observable offense (Epp et al. 2014: 5, 133). Second, many citizens have had either limited or no contact with a police officer during their lifetime, thus rendering encounter-based procedural justice irrelevant. Third, having a *neutral* or even *good* interaction with an officer does not necessarily enhance one's general opinion of the police. Some individuals hold highly negative views of the police that are not improved by a positive contact with an officer (Jacob 1971; Miller 2004; Skogan 2006). Their attitudes are shaped by other factors.

In addition to direct personal experiences, a person's "vicarious experiences" can influence their opinions of the police. *Vicarious experiences* are formed by observations of another person's treatment by an officer or the narratives of friends, family members, neighbors, or remote others (as portrayed in the media) that are then internalized by an individual. One study found that both personal and vicarious experiences lowered opinions of the police but since negative vicarious experiences were more plentiful than negative personal experiences, their net impact was greater. Interestingly, people who reported positive vicarious experiences tended to view the police similarly to people who had no contact with police (Miller 2004). Hispanics and African Americans are much more likely than Whites to hear about instances of officer mistreatment from people in their social networks and to internalize these experiences (Weitzer and Tuch 2006). In a recent poll, 44 percent of Blacks aged 18–30 stated that someone they knew had experienced "harassment or violence" by a police officer, whereas 22 percent said this had happened to them (GenForward/Associated Press/NORC 2016). Among African Americans, policing is a much more frequent topic of conversation than among White Americans, which increases the chances of a multiplier effect, i.e., personal experiences morphing into others' vicarious experiences. And these conversations often have a proactive motive: There is a long tradition among African Americans of elders attempting to transmit "proper" conduct norms to young people in the hope of preventing them from having altercations with police officers (Brunson and Weitzer 2011). These norms include keeping hands in full view, speaking softly and respectfully, avoiding furtive movements, and complying with officer commands. There is no evidence that White parents routinely caution their children in this way.

Another problem with an exclusive focus on encounter-based procedural justice as an explanation for police–citizen relations is demonstrated by research showing the obverse pattern: individuals' general opinions of the police influence how they view their interactions with officers (Brandl et al. 1994; Rosenbaum 2005). While direct experiences may indeed influence general appraisals of the police, the latter may influence or overdetermine how people interpret their face-to-face experiences with officers.

Procedural justice is a micro-level variable but we know that police–citizen relations are influenced by factors at the meso and macro levels as well. A substantial research literature documents the importance of contextual factors, such as the type of residential neighborhood a person lives in (Weitzer 2010). In middle-class and affluent communities, for example, a police presence is typically episodic and, on the rare occasions when officers are called to the neighborhood, they are likely to treat residents with a measure of respect (Fassin 2013; Mastrofski et al. 2002; Sykes and Clark 1975; Weitzer 1999). Officers are aware of neighborhood social capital and the degree of access and influence residents have vis-à-vis local authorities, and officers may be cognizant of these status characteristics in their interactions with residents (Reck 2015: 214–18; Weitzer 1999). Regardless of their racial composition, police are less likely to show respect toward residents of economically disadvantaged communities (Mastrofski et al.

2002). It is well known that some residents of these neighborhoods engage in unconventional survival practices (e.g., theft, panhandling, drug dealing), and police often assume that individuals are involved in criminal behavior in these communities. Under U.S. law, officers may stop individuals if they have "probable cause" or "reasonable suspicion" that the person may be involved in wrongdoing, and are allowed to search (under the probable cause requirement) and frisk or pat down the person (under reasonable suspicion). But there is evidence that many frisks are conducted without reasonable suspicion and instead as a more general practice in certain neighborhoods (Epp et al. 2014; Fagan et al. 2010; Lerman and Weaver 2014; on France, see Fassin 2013). A minor infraction—such as littering, jaywalking, or loitering—can serve as a pretext for an interrogation whose real purpose is to discover other types of wrongdoing (drug or gun possession, an arrest warrant, etc.). Young residents of these neighborhoods are not only uniquely vulnerable to being stopped and questioned by the police[1] but are also much more likely than their White counterparts to be stopped *repeatedly* (American Civil Liberties Union of Illinois 2015; Department of Justice 2016; Epp et al. 2014; Weitzer and Tuch 2006).

There is thus a dynamic interaction between (1) high neighborhood-level disadvantage (poverty, unemployment), (2) residents' involvement in illicit survival strategies (property crime, victimless crime), and (3) intrusive and aggressive police practices. This syndrome contributes to residents' alienation from and avoidance of the police. And the syndrome is marked by reciprocal effects: Hyperpolicing does not just *reflect* neighborhood-level disadvantage but also *reinforces* existing inequalities by routinely entangling residents with the criminal justice system, often for minor infractions that are ignored in middle-class and affluent neighborhoods—infractions such as loitering, consuming alcohol in public, and riding bikes on sidewalks.

Research indicates that socio-economic disadvantage is a key determinant of police–community relations but neighborhood racial composition is also important. Moving from the neighborhood context to racial factors more generally, it is clear that at least some police officers hold overtly racist views toward ethnic minorities in the United States and other multi-ethnic countries (e.g., Fassin 2013; Moskos 2008; Weitzer 1995). And racial bias may be widespread in at least some police squads or departments. For example, the U.S. Justice Department's investigation of the Ferguson, Missouri police department concluded, "[w]e have found substantial evidence of racial bias among police and court staff in Ferguson" (Department of Justice 2015: 5). And even where racial animus is not widespread, officers' latent racial stereotypes may be quite consequential. In one study, researchers showed a sample of 182 police officers color photos of the faces of White and Black men, told them that some of the faces might be those of criminals, and instructed the officers to indicate whether each face "looked criminal" (Eberhardt et al. 2004). Officers were significantly more likely to identify Blacks as criminals (Eberhardt et al. 2004).

Racial disparities have been documented in arrest rates and police killings of civilians. Regarding arrest rates, a recent meta-analysis of 27 datasets found that, controlling for a wide variety of factors that might influence arrest rates, the citizen's race made a difference: Individuals from minority groups had a higher likelihood of arrest, net of other factors (Kochel et al. 2011). Racial disparities are also evident in both public perceptions and the actual incidence of police-involved shootings. A majority of Blacks (64 percent) but only 31 percent of Whites believe that there has been an increase in the past year in the number of unarmed Black people killed by the police (*New York Times*/CBS News 2015, July 23). Similarly, nearly six out of ten Whites but less than one-fifth of Blacks, believe that "race does not affect police use of deadly force" (*New York Times*/CBS News 2015, July 23).[2] Data on killings suggest that a citizens' race may indeed be a factor. Of the 965 police killings of civilians in the United States in 2015, Black males (6 percent of the U.S. population) accounted for 40 percent of the unarmed men killed by police that year (Kindy et al. 2015). Analysis of 771 incidents recorded in the *U.S. Police Shootings Database* from 2011–2014 show that armed and unarmed Black and Hispanic individuals were shot by police at much higher rates, in most U.S. counties, than their armed and unarmed White counterparts; in some counties, *unarmed* Blacks were shot at significantly higher rates than *armed* White civilians (Ross 2015; cf. Kindy 2015). The *Guardian* newspaper maintains its own database on police-involved killings, which shows that such killings vary from one to eight per day in the U.S. and that African American shooting victims are twice as likely as Whites to have been unarmed.[3] Unfortunately, neither database contains complete details for all killings, so caution is needed in drawing conclusions about the role of race in police shootings.[4] But if these statistics approximate reality, they would give external validity to experimental laboratory findings on how implicit racial bias affects individuals' decisions to interpret ambiguous behavior as aggressive, to mistake harmless objects for weapons, and to shoot a firearm quickly (Correll 2007; Eberhardt et al. 2004).

Reforms

During the past three years, significant reforms have been discussed in the media and by government and police officials. Sustained media coverage of policing problems rarely occurred in the past, as Regina Lawrence (2000) demonstrated in her study of news coverage of policing in the 1980s and 1990s. But today, the media and the wider public have been engaged in an ongoing debate regarding both the causes of police misconduct and a host of reforms. An editorial in the *Washington Post* in 2015 proclaimed, "[w]hat's beyond doubt is that the Ferguson imbroglio [in 2014] led directly to important policy changes. [...] Americans are more focused on these issues now than they have been in many years—and that's having positive, real-world effects" (*Washington Post* 2015, July 30). The accuracy of this conclusion can be debated, given how difficult it is to implement and sustain reforms in policing. Certain types of reform, however, have the potential to reduce police misconduct and enhance police professionalism. I discuss a few of these here.

The proposed changes include body cameras for police officers, better screening of recruits, sensitivity training, racial diversification, community policing, demilitarization, civilian review boards, abandoning zero-tolerance and stop-and-frisk policies, and prohibiting racial profiling.[5] These corrective measures are not new: Each of them has been advocated for *decades* by critics as well as official commissions of inquiry.[6] The President's Commission (1967), for example, advocated better screening of police recruits, creation of community policing units, and racial diversification of police departments. Even the newest of the remedies—police video cameras—has been proposed for years (Reaves 2010; Weitzer and Tuch 2006) but their adoption has been slow. Only 6 percent of all fatal police-involved shootings in 2015 were captured on police body cameras (Kindy et al. 2015). Yet randomized experiments in Rialto, California and Orlando, Florida found that equipping officers with cameras correlated with reductions in the use of force (i.e., coercive response-to-resistance incidents) and decreased complaints from the public (Ariel et al. 2014; Jennings et al. 2015). The Orlando study found that police officers were generally in favor of body cameras and would feel comfortable wearing them but Nonwhite officers were more likely than White officers to say that wearing a camera would reduce their own use of force (Jennings et al. 2014).

Racial diversification of police departments is frequently advocated. Data from 269 American police departments serving populations of 100,000 or more shows that Blacks, Hispanics, and Asians were underrepresented in 2013 by a combined 25 percent (Maciag 2015). During the past two years, the media and other commentators have almost universally assumed that racial diversification of police departments will reduce misconduct. The issue dates back to the President's Commission on Law Enforcement and the Administration of Justice (1967), which considered the lack of minority officers one of the central problems in policing at that time. Almost 50 years later, the report of President Obama's commission similarly recommended diversification:

> Many agencies have long appreciated the critical importance of hiring officers who reflect the communities they serve. [...] The federal government should create a Law Enforcement Diversity Initiative designed to help communities diversify law enforcement departments to reflect the demographics of the community.
>
> (President's Task Force 2015: 16–17)

The report also offered a rather impractical and dubious hiring strategy: "Since people are less likely to have biases against groups with which they have had positive experiences, police departments should seek candidates who have had positive interactions with people of various cultures and backgrounds" (President's Task Force 2015: 17).

The Task Force offered little justification for diversification, treating it as a self-evident benefit; the same faith in the diversity principle is common in Europe (Zauberman and Lévy 2003).

Behaviorally, the available evidence shows that the vast majority of police officers are "blue": their occupational training and on-the-job socialization by fellow officers trump racial background in their conduct toward civilians. It appears that the police subculture is relatively autonomous from incremental change in the direction of demographic inclusiveness.[7] A few studies have documented some differences among White and Black officers working in a particular city[8] but, for the most part, the literature points to overall *similarities* in police behavior irrespective of officers' racial background (National Research Council 2004).[9] The key variable is not officers' background characteristics but instead the nature of their contextually-specific working conditions, spatial deployment, and oversight by supervisors.

It is not well known that several big American police departments are majority-Black or majority-Hispanic in officer composition.[10] In some of these cities the racial/ethnic representation of Black or Latino police officers is even greater than that of the city population (Maciag 2015). And Black or Hispanic police chiefs and/or mayors are in office in many of these cities. There is very little research on whether a shift to a majority-Black or -Hispanic department leads to any appreciable change in the pre-existing police subculture or in department-wide behavior patterns. Longitudinal studies or multi-city comparisons (varying on racial complexion) are needed to determine whether a major transition in racial/ethnic demographics, from minority to majority, has an impact on the police subculture and behavior patterns (e.g., Howell et al. 2004; Weitzer et al. 2008).

Irrespective of how patrol officers of different races behave toward civilians, racial diversification of police departments in multi-racial cities can have *symbolic* benefits, enhancing the overall reputation of a department (Sklansky 2006). A department like Ferguson's, where 50 out of 53 officers are White in a city that is two-thirds African American, is a glaring mismatch and is almost guaranteed to lead at least some Black residents to racialize their encounters with officers. Diversity is not a sufficient condition for building public confidence but it can be considered a necessary condition—providing a foundation on which to build trust. A diverse police force not only symbolizes equal opportunity and racial integration but can also help decrease the sense that individuals are being stopped and questioned solely because of their race. This clearly applies when the officers and citizens are of the same race but even encounters between White officers and minority citizens may be perceived as less racialized when the department has a critical mass of minority officers. Unfortunately, the recent string of police-involved killings and subsequent street protests makes the job of recruiting minority officers even harder than it has been in the past.

Public support for reform

Americans overwhelming support police reform. In one poll, more than 70 percent of Whites, Blacks, and Hispanics believed that a city's police department should have a similar racial complexion to that of the city (Weitzer and Tuch 2006). Regarding civilian review boards—responsible for reviewing complaints against officers—63 percent of Whites, 72 percent of Hispanics, and 80 percent of African Americans believe that creation of such a board will improve policing in their city (Weitzer and Tuch 2006). Similar or even higher proportions of all three groups endorse equipping officers with body cameras, creating early-warning systems to flag and monitor rogue officers, appointment of outside prosecutors to investigate police-involved killings, retraining, demilitarization, and various types of community policing (Langer 2014; *New York Times*/CBS News 2014, August 21, 2016, May 6; Weitzer and Tuch 2006). What is especially noteworthy here is the *cross-racial consensus* on the value of these reforms. Equipping officers with cameras, for example, was endorsed by 93 percent of both Blacks and Whites in April 2015 (*New York Times*/CBS News 2015, May 4) and in August 2016 by 85 per cent of Blacks, 93 per cent of Hispanics, and 95 per cent of Whites (Morin and Stepler 2016). Such widespread support for reforms is consistent with Americans' opinions on other proposed reforms of the criminal justice system. When given the choice of favoring increasing punitiveness vs. fixing the social problems that appear to generate crime, for example, a majority of both Blacks and Whites support the latter (Peffley and Hurwitz 2010: 152–3).

Yet, Whites' support for reforms does not mean that they believe there are indeed problems to be corrected. Although a large majority supports the reforms mentioned above, 75 percent of Whites believe that the police do a good or excellent job of treating racial and ethnic groups equally, compared to 35 percent of Blacks (Morin and Stepler 2016). Perhaps because the number of highly publicized killings of Blacks has increased in the past two years, Whites are becoming less likely to view such killings as "isolated incidents" (60 percent in 2014, 44 percent in 2016) and more prepared to view them as "a sign of broader problems" (54 percent in 2016) (Morin and Stepler 2016). Still, Hispanics (66 percent) and Blacks (79 percent) are much more likely than Whites to subscribe to the "broader problem" view (Morin and Stepler 2016). Similar race gaps exist for other issues:

- Whites are much more likely than Blacks or Hispanics to be "confident" that American police officers are adequately trained to avoid using excessive force (Langer 2014).
- Sixty-five percent of Blacks think that their city's police department is doing only a fair or poor job in "holding officers accountable" for misconduct, compared to 30 percent of Whites and 35 percent of Hispanics (Morin and Stepler 2016).
- Seventy-one percent of Blacks believe that officers who injure or kill civilians are treated too leniently by the criminal justice system, compared to 33 percent of Whites. Whites are more likely (46 percent) than Blacks (20 per cent) to think that such officers are treated fairly (Associated Press 2015).

Clearly, there is a wide racial gap in public perceptions of police accountability. These perceptions are partly shaped by publicized instances of officers involved in a shooting of a civilian either not being prosecuted at all or prosecuted and acquitted by a court. Over the past decade, 65 officers have been prosecuted in the United States for fatal shootings of civilians, 11 of whom were convicted; to put this in perspective, in 2015 alone, American police officers shot and killed 965 individuals (Kindy et al. 2015). Civilian complaint review boards are another mechanism of accountability, existing in most large cities. These boards generally have low substantiation rates, due to evidentiary deficiencies.[11] And the rulings of some of these boards may be racially disparate. Analysis of civilian complaints lodged against police officers in Chicago from March 2011 to September 2015 found that the civilian's racial background made a difference: 62 percent of complaints were filed by Blacks, yet only 28 percent of them resulted in officer discipline; the respective figures for Whites were 20 percent and 57 percent (Davey and Williams 2015).

There is racial polarization on the issue of whether the police should engage in more robust or aggressive practices as well: Over one-third of Whites and Hispanics nationwide favor police "stopping and searching more people on the streets," compared to about one-fifth of Blacks (Weitzer and Tuch 2006), and in New York City, 50 percent of Whites but only 30 percent of Hispanics and 20 percent of Blacks want the city's intrusive stop-and-frisk practice to continue (*Wall Street Journal* 2013). Stop rates are racially disproportionate: While Blacks and Hispanics comprise 55 percent of New York City's population, they were the targets of 85 percent of stop-and-frisk actions between 2002 and 2015; roughly half were 14–24 years old; and 90 percent of those stopped were innocent (New York Civil Liberties Union 2015). Similar disparities were found in Chicago: Whereas Blacks and Hispanics comprise 61 percent of the city's population, they accounted for 89 percent of stops from May–August 2014, and the disparity for Blacks was particularly pronounced: 32 percent of the population and 72 percent of those stopped and frisked (American Civil Liberties Union 2015).

In sum: There is substantial cross-racial support for most of the reforms that have been proposed but also a reluctance among many Whites to believe that police misconduct is serious or widespread. Support for reform among Whites is rooted in *principle* (a reasonable innovation that is hard to reject) as opposed to *practice* (policing as problematic). Blacks and Latinos, by contrast, are more likely to perceive police misconduct as serious and widespread, and they support reforms not just in principle but also because they see the need for concrete corrective measures to address police misconduct.

Institutionalizing reform

Despite the impression that American policing is at a crossroads and that meaningful reforms may be on the horizon, there are reasons to be pessimistic that this is pivotal moment in policing. First, it is not known how many police chiefs are learning lessons from the cities where officers have recently been embroiled in controversy. How many are reviewing their own department's practices or considering new measures to curb misconduct and enhance accountability among their officers? How many of them have read the consent decrees and settlements that the Federal Justice Department has entered into with the departments it has investigated for systemic "pattern or practice" violations in the past 20 years? How many police departments have thoroughly institutionalized community policing as a philosophy and practice in their departments, rather than simply giving it lip service or marginalizing it in a "community relations" unit? A majority of departments mention community policing in their mission statements, give officers some training in community policing, and have a specialized community affairs unit (Reaves 2010, 2015). But these superficial indicators cannot be used to measure *departmental institutionalization* of community policing as a policy and practice, which remains the exception rather than the rule. We do know, however, that at least a few police departments have made substantial changes in the recent past in the direction of a more community-oriented model (e.g., Chanin 2015; Greene 1999; Lowery 2015; Stone et al. 2009; Zernike 2014).

Second, some reforms are expensive and require funding over a lengthy period of time. The fact that American policing is decentralized among 18,000 police departments means that most funding depends on local budgets, not the federal government, and many municipalities have limited resources to finance reform measures.

Third, even when reforms are initiated, social scientists know just how hard it is to make them "stick"—institutionalizing them in training, codes of conduct, performance evaluations, and rewards and punishments, or being embraced in the police subculture (Chanin 2015; Sherman 1978; Skogan 2008; Walker 2012). The record is mixed for departments that have introduced reforms under the guidance of the Justice Department (Chanin 2015; Kelly et al. 2015; Office of the District of Colombia Auditor 2016; Walker 2012). Some of the departments that have complied and instituted reforms have made clear progress (e.g., Washington, DC [ODCA 2016]), while others have had difficulty *sustaining* the reforms after the period of Justice Department oversight has ended. This is partly due to resistance to change from patrol officers, mid-level managers, and police unions (Baker 2015; Skogan 2008), but mostly because of the very nature of policing on the ground. It is axiomatic that patrol officers enjoy a substantial amount of discretionary authority, which can be curbed only to a limited extent by any reform. And most officers patrol alone, unfettered by the checks that a fellow officer or supervisor might provide. For these reasons, we should expect more officer misconduct in the future, including unjustified killings. And we should also expect a growing public *perception* that misconduct is *dramatically increasing*, even if this is simply an artifact of policing's "new visibility" via increasing media reporting of altercations, including footage from video recordings. The growing display of visual images gives the impression, as one woman at a protest in Baltimore exclaimed, that police brutality is a "skyrocketing epidemic." Scholars would challenge this claim by pointing out that misconduct was more hidden and more prevalent in the twentieth century. Overall, policing has become more professional in recent decades (National Research Council 2004), yet, as recent events illustrate, such progress has not been uniform across the country.

Conclusion

The current debate about policing in the United States has neglected a central fact: variation among police departments. Media representations and assertions by protestors and pundits give the impression that police brutality and racism are pervasive throughout the nation. Rarely do we get a more nuanced, poly-morphous picture—recognizing that there are 18,000 law enforcement agencies and 800,000 police officers in the United States, cautioning against sweeping generalizations. Unlike some other countries, policing is decentralized in America and police departments differ significantly in their size, resources, com-position, leadership, training, and accountability mechanisms. And, although dif-ficult to measure—given the invisibility of most police–citizen interactions—both cities and neighborhoods vary in rates of police misconduct (e.g., Fagan et al. 2010; Greene 1999; Kane 2002; Reck 2015; Terrill and Reisig 2003). In the public square today, these important contextual distinctions have too often been replaced with blanket indictments of "the police" nationwide – claims that may have a cumulative long-term effect in eroding public confidence in law enforce-ment agencies, even for people whose local department has a fairly clean record.

This points to the need to focus on the *performance of specific departments* in order to identify those most in need of reform. The creation in 2015 of a pres-idential commission on policing is a rare opportunity for federal engagement and promotion of "best practices" in police departments with serious patterns of mis-conduct. Responding to recent incidents, several state legislatures passed bills that seek to enhance police accountability (Wilson 2015) but other bills failed to pass (Kindy and Tate 2015). Major reform efforts are expensive and usually face steadfast resistance from police unions, if not police chiefs themselves. There-fore, it remains to be seen whether, or to what extent, top-down reforms will improve officer behavior on the ground and help to rebuild public trust in the police in the United States.

Notes

1 When asked, in a 1999 Gallup poll, whether they had ever been stopped by the police solely because of their race or ethnicity, Black males aged 18–34 were much more likely to answer affirmatively (73 percent) than older Black males (40 percent), same-age Black females (38 percent), and same-age White males (11 percent) (Weitzer and Tuch 2002). When asked generically about being stopped (rather than about racially-biased stops), one study found that Blacks were twice as likely as Whites to report being stopped in just the past year: 25 versus 12 percent, respectively (Epp et al. 2014: 52).
2 Three-quarters of Blacks and one-third of Whites believe that police are more likely to use deadly force against Blacks (*New York Times*/CBS News 2015, July 23).
3 This database is available at: www.theguardian.com/us-news/ng-interactive/2015/jun/01/the-counted-police-killings-us-database#. A majority of civilians killed were White; the vast majority of all civilians killed were brandishing a gun, firing a gun, or attacking an officer by other means (Brittain 2015).
4 A study of St. Louis, Missouri examined 230 police shootings, most of which involved White police officers and young Black male victims. The shootings were concentrated in a small number of neighborhoods, and were highest in areas with

large minority populations, high levels of economic disadvantage, and high rates of violent crime. The latter (particularly gun-related violence in an area) was the strongest predictor of police use of deadly force (Klinger et al. 2016).

5 At present, 30 states have laws banning racial profiling and 18 require officers to collect data for all stops and searches (Stolberg 2015). As a result of a court ruling (*Floyd* v. *City of New York*, 2013) that New York's stop-and-frisk practice violated citizens' rights, the number of such stops in the city declined dramatically, from 685,000 in 2011 to 24,000 in 2015 (Baker 2016).

6 See the reports of the 1967 President's Commission, 1972 Knapp Commission, 1981 Commission on Civil Rights, 1991 Christopher Commission, 1994 Mollen Commission, and others.

7 Although it has long been assumed that gender does not influence a police officer's behavior toward civilians, some data suggest otherwise. A study of seven American cities found that female officers were much less likely than their male counterparts to receive citizen complaints regarding excessive force, to have accusations sustained against them, and to be responsible for civil liability lawsuit payouts (National Center for Women and Policing 2002). One explanation is that female officers are more adept in using communication skills rather than coercion to resolve conflicts with civilians. If these results also apply more broadly to other cities, it suggests that measures should be taken to increase the percentage of women in policing, which is 12 percent in the United States.

8 Some studies find that minority officers treat citizens better than White officers, while other studies find the opposite (Sklansky 2006). An example of the latter is a study of eight precincts in San Diego, which found (surprisingly) that the higher the percentage of Black officers in a precinct, the greater the racial disparity in vehicle stops of civilians (a higher stop rate for Black drivers than White drivers) (Wilkins and Williams 2008). In a 2003 survey of drivers in Kansas City, officers' race had no effect on either their demeanor toward drivers or their "intrusions and sanctions" (Epp et al. 2014: 105).

9 Hispanic and Asian officers have not been included in the few studies that have examined this question (Weitzer 2014).

10 Atlanta, Birmingham, Detroit, El Paso, Hialeah, Jackson, Laredo, Las Cruces, McAllen, Memphis, Miami, New Orleans, San Antonio, Washington.

11 From 2011–2015 in Chicago, only 3 percent of the 28,500 citizen complaints against police officers resulted in any punishment; police-involved shootings were almost never ruled unjustified. In over 400 such shootings since 2007, only two were ruled unwarranted (Davey and Williams 2015).

Bibliography

American Civil Liberties Union (ACLU) of Illinois (2015). *Stop and Frisk in Chicago*, American Civil Liberties Union.

Ariel, B., Farrar, W., and Sutherland, A. (2014). 'The effect of police body-worn cameras on use of force and citizen complaints against the police', *Journal of Quantitative Criminology*, 31: 509–35.

Associated Press-NORC Center for Public Affairs Research (2015). 'Law enforcement and violence: the divide between Black and White Americans', online. Available www.apnorc.org/PDFs/Police%20Violence/Issue%20Brief_PoliceFinal.pdf (accessed 19 December 2016).

Baker, A. (2015, April 18). 'Police unions, facing public anger, rethink how to address shootings', *New York Times*, online. Available www.nytimes.com/2015/04/19/us/police-unions-facing-public-anger-rethink-how-to-address-shootings.html?_r=0 (accessed 19 December 2016).

Baker, A. (2016, February 17). 'City police still struggle to follow stop-and-frisk rules, report says', *New York Times*, online. Available www.nytimes.com/2016/02/17/ny region/new-york-police-struggle-to-follow-new-street-stop-policy-report-finds.html (accessed 30 March 2017).

Bobo, L. (1999). 'Prejudice as group position', *Journal of Social Issues*, 55: 445–72.

Brandl, S., Frank, J., Worden, R., and Bynum, T. (1994). 'Global and specific attitudes toward the police: disentangling the relationship', *Justice Quarterly*, 11: 119–34.

Brittain, A. (2015, October 24). 'On duty, under fire', *Washington Post*, online. Available www.washingtonpost.com/sf/investigative/2015/10/24/on-duty-under-fire/ (accessed 19 December 2016).

Brown, G. (2016). 'The blue line on thin ice: police use of force modifications in the era of camera phones and YouTube', *British Journal of Criminology*, 56: 293–312.

Brunson, R. and Weitzer, R. (2011). 'Negotiating unwelcome police encounters: the inter-generational transmission of conduct norms', *Journal of Contemporary Ethnography*, 40: 425–56.

Chanin, J. (2015). 'Examining the sustainability of pattern or practice police misconduct reform', *Police Quarterly*, 18: 163–92.

Correll, J. (2007). 'Across the thin blue line: police officers and racial bias in the decision to shoot', *Journal of Personality and Social Psychology*, 92: 1006–23.

Davey, M. and Williams, T. (2015, December 17). 'Chicago pays millions but punishes few in killings by police', *New York Times*, online. Available www.nytimes.com/2015/12/18/us/chicago-pays-millions-but-punishes-few-in-police-killings.html (accessed 19 December 2016).

Department of Justice (2015). *Investigation of the Ferguson Police Department*, Washington, DC: Civil Rights Division.

Department of Justice (2016). *Investigation of the Baltimore Police Department*, Washington, DC: Civil Rights Division.

Eberhardt, J., Goff, P. A., Purdie, V., and Davies, P. (2004). 'Seeing Black: race, crime, and visual processing', *Journal of Personality and Social Psychology*, 87: 876–93.

Epp, C., Maynard-Moody, S., and Haider-Markel, D. (2014). *Pulled Over: How Police Stops Define Race and Citizenship*, Chicago, IL: University of Chicago Press.

Fagan, J., Geller, A., Davies, G., and West, V. (2010). 'Street stops and broken windows revisited: the demography and logic of proactive policing in a safe and changing city', in S. Rice and M. White (eds.), *Race, Ethnicity, and Policing*, New York: NYU Press, 309–48.

Fassin, D. (2013). *Enforcing Order: An Ethnography of Urban Policing*, Cambridge: Polity Press.

Floyd et al. v. *City of New York* (2013).

GenForward/Associated Press/NORC (2016). *GenForward July 2016 Survey Report: A survey of the Black Youth Project with the AP-NORC center for Public Affairs Research*, online. Available http://genforwardsurvey.com/assets/uploads/2016/08/Gen Forward-July-2016-Report-_-Final-copy.pdf (accessed 19 December 2016).

Goldsmith, A. (2010). 'Policing's new visibility', *British Journal of Criminology*, 50: 914–34.

Goold, B. (2003). 'Public area surveillance and police work: the impact of CCTV on police behavior and autonomy', *Surveillance and Society*, 1: 191–203.

Greene, J. (1999). 'Zero tolerance: a case study of police policies and practices in New York City', *Crime and Delinquency*, 45: 171–87.

Howell, S., Perry, H., and Vile, M. (2004). 'Black cities, White cities: evaluating the police', *Political Behavior*, 26: 45–68.

Jacob, H. (1971). 'Black and White perceptions of justice in the city', *Law and Society Review*, 6: 69–90.

Jennings, W., Fridell, L., and Lynch, M. (2014). 'Cops and cameras: officer perceptions of the use of body-worn cameras in law enforcement', *Journal of Criminal Justice* 42: 549–56.

Jennings, W., Lynch, M., and Fridell, L. (2015). 'Evaluating the impact of police officer body-worn cameras on response-to-resistance and serious external complaints', *Journal of Criminal Justice*, 43: 480–6.

Kane, R. (2002). 'The social ecology of police misconduct', *Criminology*, 40: 867–96.

Kindy, K. (2015, May 30). 'Fatal police shootings in 2015 approaching 400 nationwide', *Washington Post*, online. Available www.washingtonpost.com/national/fatal-police-shootings-in-2015-approaching-400-nationwide/2015/05/30/d322256a-058e-11e5-a428-c984eb077d4e_story.html?utm_term=.ac8efcceec27 (accessed 19 December 2016).

Kindy, K. and Tate, J. (2015, October 8). 'Police withhold videos despite vows of transparency', *Washington Post*, online. Available www.washingtonpost.com/sf/national/2015/10/08/police-withhold-videos-despite-vows-of-transparency/ (accessed 19 December 2016).

Klinger, D., Rosenfeld, R., Isom, D., and Deckard, M. (2016). 'Race, crime, and the micro-ecology of deadly force', *Criminology and Public Policy*, 15: 193–222.

Kochel, T., Wilson, D., and Mastrofski, S. (2011). 'Effect of suspect race on officers' arrest decisions', *Criminology*, 49: 473–512.

Langer, G. (2014, December 27). 'In police/community controversies, vast majorities back special prosecutors, body cams', *ABC News/Washington Post*, online. Available www.langerresearch.com/wp-content/uploads/1165a6RaceandCriminalJustice.pdf (accessed 19 December 2016).

Lawrence, R. (2000). *The Politics of Force: Media and the Construction of Police Brutality*, Berkeley, CA: University of California Press.

Lerman, A. and Weaver, V. (2014). 'Staying out of sight? Concentrated policing and local political action', *The Annals*, 651: 202–19.

Lowery, W. (2015, May 8). 'A softer approach to policing gains believers in Calif. City', *Washington Post*, online. Available www.pressreader.com/usa/the-washington-post/20150508/textview (accessed 19 December 2016).

Maciag, M. (2015, August 28). 'Where police don't mirror communities and why it matters', *Governing Magazine*, online. Available www.governing.com/topics/public-justice-safety/gov-police-department-diversity.html (accessed 19 December 2016).

Mastrofski, S., Reisig, M., and McCluskey, J. (2002). 'Police disrespect toward the public: an encounter-based analysis', *Criminology*, 40: 519–51.

Miller, J. (2004). *Public Opinions of the Police*, New York: Vera Institute of Justice.

Morin, R. and Stepler, R. (2016). *The Racial Confidence Gap in Police Performance*, Pew Research Center.

Moskos, P. (2008). 'Two shades of blue: Black and White in the blue brotherhood', *Law Enforcement Executive Forum*, 8: 57–86.

National Center for Women and Policing (NCWP) (2002). *Men, Women, and Police Use of Excessive Force*, Los Angeles, CA: NCWP.

National Research Council (2004). *Fairness and Effectiveness in Policing: The Evidence*, Washington DC: National Academies Press.

New York Civil Liberties Union (NYCLU) (2015). *Stop and Frisk Data, 2002–2015*, New York: NYCLU, online. Available www.nyclu.org/content/stop-and-frisk-data (accessed 19 December 2016).

New York Times/CBS News (2014, August 21). Poll, August 19–20, online. Available www.nytimes.com/interactive/2014/08/21/us/poll-nyt-cbs.html (accessed 19 December 2016).

New York Times/CBS News (2015, May 4). Poll, April 30–May 3, online. Available www.nytimes.com/interactive/2015/05/05/us/05poll-doc.html (accessed 19 December 2016).

New York Times/CBS News (2015, July 23). Poll, July 14–19, online. Available www.nytimes.com/interactive/2015/07/23/us/document-new-york-timescbs-news-poll-on-race-relations-in-the-us.html?_r=0 (accessed 19 December 2016).

New York Times (2016, May 6). Poll of Chicago, April 21–May 3, online. Available www.nytimes.com/interactive/2016/05/06/us/document-Chicago-Trn-Final.html (accessed 19 December 2016).

New York Times (2016, July 8). 'When will the killing stop?' [Editorial], online. Available www.nytimes.com/2016/07/08/opinion/when-will-the-killing-stop.html (accessed 19 December 2016).

Office of the District of Columbia Auditor (ODCA) (2016). *The Durability of Police Reform: The Metropolitan Police Department and Use of Force, 2008–2015*, Washington, DC: ODCA.

Peffley, M. and Hurwitz, J. (2010). *Justice in America: The Separate Realities of Blacks and Whites*, New York: Cambridge University Press.

President's Commission on Law Enforcement and the Administration of Justice (1967). *The Challenge of Crime in a Free Society*, Washington, DC: United States Government Printing Office.

President's Task Force on 21st Century Policing (2015). *Final Report*, Washington, DC: Office of Community Oriented Policing Services.

Reaves, B. (2010). *Local Police Departments, 2007*, Washington, DC: Bureau of Justice Statistics.

Reaves, B. (2015). *Local Police Departments, 2013*, Washington, DC: Bureau of Justice Statistics.

Reck, P. (2015). 'Variations in patrol officers' concerns about racial profiling across communal contexts', *Journal of Qualitative Criminal Justice and Criminology*, 3: 195–230.

Rosenbaum, D. (2005). 'Attitudes toward the police', *Police Quarterly*, 8: 343–65.

Ross, C. (2015). 'A multi-level Bayesian analysis of racial bias in police shootings at the county level in the United States, 2011–2014', *PLOS One*, 10: e0141854.

Sherman, L. (1978). *Scandal and Reform: Controlling Police Corruption*, Berkeley, CA: University of California Press.

Sklansky, D. (2006). 'Not your father's police department: making sense of the new demographics of law enforcement', *Journal of Criminal Law and Criminology*, 96: 1209–43.

Skogan, W. (2006). 'Asymmetry in the impact of encounters with police', *Policing and Society*, 16: 99–126.

Skogan, W. (2008). 'Why reforms fail', *Policing and Society*, 18: 23–34.

Stolberg, C. (2015, August 26). 'Maryland restricts racial profiling in new guidelines for law enforcement', *New York Times*, online. Available www.nytimes.com/2016/02/17/nyregion/new-york-police-struggle-to-follow-new-street-stop-policy-report-finds.html (accessed 20 March 2017).

Stone, C., Foglesong, T., and Cole, C. (2009). *Policing Los Angeles Under a Consent Decree: The Dynamics of Change at the LAPD*, Cambridge: Harvard Kennedy School.

Sykes, R. and Clark, J. (1975). 'A theory of deference exchange in police-civilian encounters', *American Journal of Sociology*, 81: 584–600.

Terrill, W. and Reisig, M. (2003). 'Neighborhood context and police use of force', *Journal of Research in Crime and Delinquency*, 40: 291–321.

Tyler, T. and Huo, Y. (2002). *Trust in the Law: Encouraging Public Cooperation with the Police and Courts*, New York: Russell-Sage Foundation.

Walker, S. (2012). 'Institutionalizing police accountability reforms: the problem of making police reforms endure', *St. Louis University Public Law Review*, 32: 57–92.

Wall Street Journal/NBC News/Marist (2013). Poll, September 15–16.

Washington Post (2015, July 30). 'After the death of Samuel Dubose, an officer is indicted in Cincinnati' [Editorial], online. Available www.washingtonpost.com/opinions/an-officer-indicted-in-cincinnati/2015/07/30/c0169cf6-36fa-11e5-b673-1df005a0fb28_story.html?utm_term=.6360f6e29f15 (accessed 19 December 2016).

Washington Post (2016, April 16). 'Chicago's lawless police culture' [Editorial], online. Available www.washingtonpost.com/opinions/chicagos-racist-policing-culture-must-be-fixed/2016/04/16/89474bf4-033b-11e6-9d36-33d198ea26c5_story.html?utm_term=.3b168770dea5 (accessed 19 December 2016).

Weitzer, R. (1995). *Policing Under Fire: Ethnic Conflict and Police–Community Relations in Northern Ireland*, Albany, NY: SUNY Press.

Weitzer, R. (1999). 'Citizens' perceptions of police misconduct: race and neighborhood context', *Justice Quarterly*, 16: 819–46.

Weitzer, R. (2002). 'Incidents of police misconduct and public opinion', *Journal of Criminal Justice*, 30: 397–408.

Weitzer, R. (2010). 'Race and policing in different ecological contexts', in S. Rice and M. White (eds.), *Race, Ethnicity, and Policing*, New York: NYU Press, 118–39.

Weitzer, R. (2014). 'The puzzling neglect of Hispanic Americans in research on police-citizen relations', *Ethnic and Racial Studies*, 37: 1995–2013.

Weitzer, R. and Tuch, S. (2002). 'Perceptions of racial profiling: race, class, and personal experience', *Criminology*, 40: 435–56.

Weitzer, R. and Tuch, S. (2006). *Race and Policing in America: Conflict and Reform*, New York: Cambridge University Press.

Weitzer, R., Tuch, S., and Skogan, W. (2008). 'Police–community relations in a majority-Black city', *Journal of Research in Crime and Delinquency*, 45: 398–428.

Wiley, M. and Hudik, T. (1974). 'Police–citizen encounters: a field test of exchange theory', *Social Problems*, 22: 119–27.

Wilkins, V. and Williams, B. (2008). 'Black or blue: racial profiling and representative bureaucracy', *Public Administration Review*, 68: 654–64.

Wilson, R. (2015, February 4). 'Police accountability measures flood state legislatures after violent events', *Washington Post*, online. Available www.washingtonpost.com/blogs/govbeat/wp/2015/02/04/police-accountability-measures-flood-state-legislatures-after-ferguson-staten-island/?utm_term=.bd31288c7ef7 (accessed 19 December 2016).

Zauberman, R. and Lévy, R. (2003). 'Police, minorities, and the French republican ideal', *Criminology*, 41: 1065–100.

Zernike, K. (2014, September 1). 'Camden turns around with new police force', *New York Times*, online. Available www.nytimes.com/2014/09/01/nyregion/camden-turns-around-with-new-police-force.html (accessed 19 December 2016).

3 Ethnicity, group position and police legitimacy

Early findings from the European Social Survey[1]

*Ben Bradford, Jonathan Jackson and
Mike Hough*

Introduction

Relations between police and ethnic minority groups have been of perennial interest to criminologists, serving as they do as indicators of key fault-lines in policing. Academic, policy, and media debates have circled constantly around the often fraught nature of this relationship – a level of interest entirely justified by a history that includes landmark events such as the Brixton riots in 1981, the beating of Rodney King in 1991, the 2005 riots in Paris, and the killing of Michael Brown in Ferguson, Missouri, in 2014 – and it is hard not to conclude that this history, which resonates across multiple national and local contexts, explains why it has been claimed that race/ethnicity is one of only three individual level variables consistently associated with attitudes towards the police (Brown and Benedict 2002). Across many different contexts, older people seem to have more favourable views of police than younger people; people who have had recent contact with the police seem to express less favourable views (the quality of the contact is also important, particularly when it comes to procedural justice); and people from ethnic and other minority groups seem to be less positive about police than those from the majority group.

It is, indeed, the case that research conducted in the United States has almost universally found that views of the police are significantly less positive among Black and other minority groups than among the white majority (Brown and Benedict 2002; Weitzer 2010). Similar findings have been reported in many other contexts, for example Australia (Murphy and Cherney 2012), Canada (Wortley and Owusu-Bempah 2011) and France (Roché 2008). The marginal position of ethnic minority groups and their location in implicit or explicit racial hierarchies in many national contexts are frequently cited as the reason for such findings – these are characteristics of groups and individuals likely to be associated with negative experiences of police and policing.

Yet, the negative association between minority status and negative assessments of police is not universal, and there can be significant variation between different ethnic minority groups. The best evidence of this latter phenomenon comes from the UK, with a London-based study showing, for instance, that net of a wide range of relevant controls, there is no consistent association between ethnicity and police legitimacy (Jackson *et al.* 2012). Among some minority groups, levels of legitimacy were lower than among the white British majority. But among others – most notably those of south Asian origin – they were higher (see also Bradford *et al.* 2015). In the UK, at least, it seems that it is not ethnic minority status per se that is important in explaining variation in beliefs about police legitimacy, but instead the membership of particular minority groups and the particular set of historical, cultural and personal experiences associated with such membership.

It might be argued that these results merely suggest the UK is an outlier in international terms. This could be true, but such findings do also caution against simply assuming that views of the police in general – and police legitimacy in particular – are always less favourable (on average) among minority group members. One relevant factor, as suggested by Weitzer (2010; Weitzer and Tuch 2006), may be the 'mode of incorporation' of different minority groups (see also Oliveira and Murphy 2015). Minority (and majority) groups are differentially stratified across different societies and within the same society over time, and the extent to which they are alienated from social institutions (and perhaps particularly the police) could well vary as a function of the specific histories of exclusion or repression (or inclusion and incorporation) they have experienced (Weitzer 2010).[2]

Supporting this idea, research has shown that contextual or class-based characteristics can confound the association between ethnicity and opinions of the police. For example, Weitzer (1999) found that residents of White and Black middle-class neighbourhoods were both less likely to perceive or experience police abuse than residents of a 'lower-class' Black neighbourhood. Bradford and Jackson (2016) found that there was very little ethnic variation in trust in the police among residents of seven particular London neighbourhoods (neighbourhood perceptions were far more important). Relatedly, Sampson and Bartusch (1998) found that objective neighbourhood characteristics (particularly concentrated disadvantage) entirely explained the association between race and satisfaction with police in their Chicago sample. On these accounts, people – from any ethnic group – who are socially or geographically marginalized will tend to have less favourable views of the police, and some or all of the apparent association between ethnicity and police legitimacy may therefore be explained by variation in the economic and social patterning of different groups within a particular national or local context.

There is also an increasingly rich vein of research that suggests people's views of the police are related to social identity. The legitimacy the police command as 'proto-typical' representatives of nation, state and/or community may be shaped in important ways by people's sense of identification with these categories (Sunshine and Tyler 2003). Oliveira and Murphy (2015), for example, demonstrate a strong association between identification with the 'nation' and police legitimacy in their Australian sample – a finding that is replicated in the UK (Bradford 2016) and the United States (Huo 2003). The judgements people make about their inclusion within a particular context ('Do I belong here?', 'Am I made to feel welcome?') may, by extension, be important in shaping the extent to which they grant police legitimacy.

In this chapter, we draw on these ideas to consider the association between ethnic minority status and police legitimacy across 27 European countries. Considering social, legal and economic aspects of incorporation, we explore how people's experiences and circumstances may relate to their relationships with the police. Pooling data from the 27 countries, we fit a series of joint models. Estimating the average statistical effects of individual-level variables that are themselves averaged across the 27 countries, we focus on some of the factors that predict legitimacy judgements of minority (and majority) group members across multiple jurisdictions (rather than those which may or may not be important within one particular culture or country – a task we leave for another study). We do not assess whether the 'modes of incorporation' of different minority groups helps to explain heterogeneity in legitimacy judgements across different minority groups. We instead assess the importance of 'modes of incorporation' in explaining variation in legitimacy and we test whether accounting for these factors reduces the statistical effect of a dichotomous majority versus minority indicator on legitimacy.

Modes of incorporation and group positions

Weitzer (2010) uses Alexander's (2001) notion of modes of incorporation to sketch out the idea that police–minority relationships may be influenced by the extent to which minority groups are incorporated into the wider society in which they live. Alexander (2001) identifies three such modes: *assimilation*, where minority group members are allowed to fully enter in public life as long as they hide or obscure their original identities; *hyphenation*, where minorities are allowed to be simultaneously (and contingently) 'in' and 'out' of the mainstream of society; and *multiculturalism*, where minority identities are not just 'allowed' but also 'accepted', and the majority culture itself changes as a result of the presence of minority groups. These are, therefore, also all modes of inclusion; the antithesis of each and all of them is *exclusion*, i.e. the denial of the right of minority groups to inhabit the social and perhaps even physical space of the majority.

Each mode has a different form and different likely set of consequences for police–minority relations (and the full acceptance suggested by Alexander's vision of multiculturalism seems likely to be linked with the highest levels of police legitimacy). However, there may be a shared set of factors driving the inclusion of minority groups across different social and political contexts. When these are low or absent, the outcome will be exclusion, and it seems *prima facie* possible that one result will be poor police–minority relations – not least because processes of social exclusion will trigger aggressive styles of policing that seek to control the tensions they create. Exclusion and marginality should predict views of the police – that is because these are social-structural locations linked to particular experiences of policing.

Weitzer (2010: 130) identifies five groups of variables that will define the extent and form of a minority group's incorporation within the wider social and political sphere: voluntariness of initial incorporation (which might be very different for a Chinese immigrant working in the City of London than for a Native American living in the southwestern United States), socio-economic status, ethno-cultural orientation, population size, and political power. Variation across these factors may well explain variation in direct experiences of policing. But the claim here is also that the socio-economic, cultural and political position of a particular minority group will, *net* of individual and situational factors, predict the views of police among its members.

In developing his theory of 'prejudice as group position', Bobo (1999: 448) argues that racial prejudice can best be seen in the light not only of 'orthodox prejudice models' but also of a sociologically informed understanding of group relations that brings insight into the 'historical development of group relations and [...] the collective or group interests that naturally flow from the institutionalization of racially or ethnically stratified social order' (Bobo 1999: 448). On this account, social groups have objective characteristics and positions within the social order, and group positions exert influence on how group members perceive members of *other* groups with *different* positions. Weitzer and Tuch (2006: 8–9) extend this idea to groups' relations with social institutions, arguing that groups feel an affinity with institutions that serve their interests, but are likely to taken an oppositional stance if the reverse is the case.

The integration and location of minority groups within the dominant social order may take two forms. Vertically, they may have varying positions in hierarchies of power, wealth and influence (and in many contexts, of course, ethnic minority groups can be found towards the lower end of such hierarchies). Horizontally, they may be more or less included within legal and/or affective social groups, most obviously in the current context those associated with the nation, state and/or community. In the European context, such categories tend to be ideologically inclusive – all those living in a particular polity can at least potentially belong, whatever their vertical positioning – yet are often exclusionary in practice, often being based, for example, on racialized visions of who can be a member and who cannot.

There are implications for police legitimacy across both these axes. Vertical integration may shape direct experiences of police activity, most pertinently via the well-established focus of police on those towards the bottom of the economic and political hierarchies, with consequences for legitimacy arising from such experiences (Bradford 2016). Equally, those towards the 'top of the pile' may cleave to police as protectors of a social order that seems to be serving them well. Horizontal integration may influence relations with police in a more symbolic or ideological sense. Members of groups that identify more strongly with dominant social categories seem likely, all else likely, to grant police more legitimacy for reasons essentially related to in-group favouritism.

There is a considerable amount of evidence in support of these ideas. Judgements concerning not only the condition of nation and state but also about relationships with and within society seem to have an important influence on peoples' views of police. Those who feel that they 'belong' to a society that includes them (and people like them), and those who feel that the state functions properly and serves and protects them, are more likely to have positive views of police (e.g. Bradford *et al.* 2014; Kääriäinen 2007; Thomassen and Kääriäinen 2016).

Group position and police legitimacy

While Weitzer and Tuch (and indeed Bobo) are concerned with the characteristics of groups *qua* groups, we confine our discussion here to the individual level and consider a subset of socio-economic and other factors that define 'group positions' and which might as a result shape the way people view police. Our aim is to explore whether: (a) any or all of these factors are associated with legitimacy judgements and (b) whether any or all explain differences in legitimacy between minority and majority groups. Each of the five factors outlined below captures a distinct form of inclusion/exclusion and may affect views of the police across one or other, or both, of the vertical and horizontal axes outlined above.

Discrimination

This is perhaps the most obvious variable to include in any analysis of police–minority relations. If an individual living in a particular context feels discriminated against on the basis of race, ethnicity or religion this may have a significant effect on their relationship with police, whether or not they feel the police are responsible for that discrimination. Such an experience may indicate to them that they are not welcomed, included or valued in the society within which they live, undermining their identification with dominant social categories and thus the extent to which they hold police legitimate. And, of course, for some the police may have been the vector of discrimination.

> H1: Those who believe they are discriminated against on the basis of race, ethnicity or religion will grant the police less legitimacy

Immigrant status

A significant body of research has shown links between immigration status and opinions of police. The direction of this association is, however, inconsistent. Some studies have found that immigrants have less trust or evaluate police more negatively (e.g. Piatkowska 2015); others have found that immigrants trust more or evaluate more positively (e.g. Nannestad *et al.* 2014); still others have concluded that there is little difference in views of the police between first-generation immigrants and the native-born population (e.g. Röder and Mühlau 2012). Recall, however, that Weitzer (2010) argues that voluntariness of initial incorporation should be an important factor. What this may mean at the individual level is that there will be a difference between those who chose to migrate to a new country and those who moved involuntarily. All else being equal, those who chose to submit themselves to a particular set of social and political arrangements – by migrating – may well take a different view of the authority structures governing those arrangements than those who did not make such a choice. This idea is supported by a recent UK-based study which found that net of relevant controls people who immigrated as adults tended to trust police more than those who arrived as children, whose views were essentially the same as the native-born population (Bradford *et al.* 2015).

> *H2: Immigrants who arrived in the destination country as adults will grant the police more legitimacy than those who arrived as children.*

Citizenship

Increasingly in the twenty-first century, a significant proportion of those subject to the authority of the police in a particular country are not citizens of that country. Citizenship may solidify a person's legal and subjective identity and strengthen their bonds with those around them (Heater 1990) – fellow citizens – and hence with the police as an important representative of the group to which all belong. Conversely, non-citizens may feel less of an affiliation with 'society' and thus the police. These processes might be particularly important for people from ethnic minority groups, at least some of whom may be inhibited or even prevented from gaining full citizenship in particular context. Here, a lack of citizenship becomes a marker of exclusion and, precisely, low or absent incorporation into the wider polity.

> *H3: Citizens will grant the police more legitimacy than non-citizens.*

Voting

Intimately linked to citizenship, participation in democratic processes can be an important marker of belonging and inclusion in society. Conversely, a lack of political engagement may mark subjective or objective exclusion – an inability to 'participate in the normal activities of citizens' (Burchardt *et al.* 1999: 229). While there may be many reasons why people may or may not choose to vote, in the present context not voting may indicate one of two things. An (adult) individual who *cannot* vote is in an important sense not a full citizen and may, therefore, be subject to some of the pressures on non-citizens outlined above.

However, an individual who can vote but chooses not to may be indicating through their behaviour a sense of distance from or weakness in relation to structures of social and political authority. In their review of the evidence concerning why people vote, Harder and Krosnick (2008) suggest a number of correlates of low turnout which suggest either social marginality (lack of education, low income, low participation in civic organizations) or an indication of status uncertainty and political weakness (a perceived lack of political efficacy and/or sense of civic duty, low group solidarity). A failure to vote may indicate, in Weitzer's terms, low political power and socio-economic status and thus less favourable views of the police. It may also indicate in a direct sense distancing from the dominant social order and, again, lower police legitimacy.

H4: Police legitimacy will be lower among those who are eligible to vote but choose not to.

Economic security

Bobo's (1999) theory of group position is premised on a stratified social order; people's interests, and the way they express them, are influenced by their economic status. Economic insecurity may indicate a subordinate position in vertical structures of social ordering, predicting a particular set of experiences of police and/or a sense that the system is failing. Yet, it could also indicate a marginal position within horizontal structures of social ordering, representing distancing or even exclusion from dominant social categories.

H5: People who are economically more precarious will grant the police less legitimacy.

It is important to stress that these five factors are not intended to constitute an exhaustive list. Rather, they reflect some pragmatic decisions shaped by what was available in the dataset used in the current chapter. However, they do represent a diverse set of measures of the vertical and horizontal integration of individuals – and indeed social groups – within a given national context, and together may go a some way to explaining variation in police legitimacy within ethnic minority populations and between majority and minority groups. Our final hypothesis is therefore:

H6: Once the variables outlined above are taken into account, any association between minority group status and police legitimacy should be attenuated.

Data and methods

The European Social Survey (ESS) is an academically-driven social survey that affords the charting and explanation of the interaction between Europe's changing institutions and the attitudes, beliefs, and behaviour patterns of its diverse populations. Running every two years, the ESS was established in 2001 and is funded by the European Commission. The survey is run by a central coordinating team survey, with each participating country covering the costs of employing its own country coordinator, translating the questionnaire, and commissioning fieldwork. Although not all countries achieve it fully, the aspiration is that countries should have probability samples of the adult (aged 15 plus) population with high response rates and face-to-face interviews using computer assisted personal interviewing (CAPI). The questionnaire comprises an invariant core of questions asked of all respondents in each round. Rotating modules are included with academics invited to bid for rotating module space on the questionnaire in each round. With other colleagues, we successfully bid for one of these modules, on trust in justice, in Round 5 of the survey (ESS 2010).

We draw here upon data from our trust in justice module and elsewhere in the Round 5 questionnaire.[3] The fieldwork for this was conducted in 28 countries in 2010/2011. We use a dataset comprising 27 countries (excluding Austria) and the overall sample contains 52,437 interviews.

Dependent variables

We are concerned with the empirical rather than normative legitimacy of the police (Tyler 2006a, 2006b) – i.e. on citizen perceptions of legitimacy rather than outside-expert judgements about the fitness of an institution to wield authority, judged against criteria such as legality, decency or democratic accountability (Hinsch 2008, 2010). Defining empirical legitimacy along two connected dimensions (Trinkner *et al.* 2016), we assume that the police are said to be legitimate when citizens in a given political community believe (a) that the police wield their power in normatively appropriate ways and (b) that they as citizens have a positive moral duty to obey police instructions (for a fuller discussion, see; Bradford *et al.* 2014; Hough *et al.* 2013; and Jackson *et al.* 2011).

First, three survey items tapped into respondent's sense of normative alignment with police. Normative alignment is the extent to which people believe that police act according to societal expectations regarding appropriate conduct. Reciprocity is central to the concept of normative alignment: a positive belief reflects normative justification of power in the eyes of citizens, and moreover, when people feel that police act appropriately, this activates a corresponding that they, as citizens, should respect societal norms regarding law-related behaviour (Jackson *et al.* 2012; Jackson 2015). The items included the agree/disagree statements: 'I support how the police usually act'; and 'The police stand up for values that are important to people like me.'

Three further items tapped into respondents' sense that they had a moral duty to obey the instructions of police officers (e.g. 'To what extent is it your duty to back the decisions made by police even when you disagree with them?'). This component of legitimacy relates to classic conceptions concerned with the ability of authorities to command willing obedience from subordinates. The assumption here is that people who view the police as having rightful authority also believe that they are entitled to be obeyed (for discussion, see Bottoms and Tankebe 2012; Jackson *et al.* 2016; Tankebe 2013; Tyler and Jackson 2013; Huq *et al.* 2016).

Before we outline the independent variables, it is important to say something about our approach to scaling the dependent variables. In the original documentation of the 'trust in justice' module, police legitimacy was defined in terms of reflective measurement. This approach means (a) that normative alignment and duty to obey are assumed to be unobservable psychological constructs that cannot by directly measured, but (b) that indirect measures can nevertheless be used and that variation in such indicators can be attributed to variation in the underlying psychological construct.

Whether one takes a reflective or formative approach is, of course, down to one's philosophical stance on the constructs and measures at hand, and one can reasonably approach scaling legitimacy in a formative way. This means combining in some more pragmatic manner answers people give to the various questions in some way to constitute (to form not reflect) the construct. Contrary to our starting point in 2010, we have in this analysis taken a formative approach. Taking the mean of the three indicators for each of normative alignment and duty to obey represents a practical and relatively straightforward way to address issues of (cross-national) measurement equivalence. In the current analysis we assume that police legitimacy within a particular country, and across the 27 countries included in the analysis, can be assessed by taking the mean of the three indicators available for each component, and that the resulting indicator has the same substantive meaning across the individuals and countries included in the dataset.[4]

Independent variables

Ethnicity is a tricky concept to measure on a cross-national basis. Ethnic categories and ethnic group membership are heavily context-dependent, and it would be almost impossible to come up with a list of ethnic categories applicable across the 27 countries included in the dataset used here. We therefore rely on a question that simply asked 'Do you belong to a minority ethnic group in (this country)?' (1 = yes; 0 = no). This at least has the advantage of allowing ESS respondents to self-identify themselves as members of minority group – and, overall, some 6 per cent did so. Note that the size of the ethnic minority sample varied significantly by country, from 22 per cent in Israel, 18 per cent in Bulgaria and 14 per cent in Russia to just 1 per cent in Poland and Finland, and 2 per cent in Portugal, Slovenia and the Czech Republic.

A range of survey items tapped into the five group position variables outlined above. To measure experience of *ethnic discrimination* answers to a range of questions were combined into a binary indicator which was coded 1 if a respondent indicated they were members of a group discriminated against on the grounds of colour or race, nationality, religion, language, or ethnic group (7 per cent said this was the case).

Immigrant status was included in the models as two dummy variables, the first coded 1 if a respondent was an immigrant who arrived in the country in which they were interviewed as an adult, and the second coded 1 if they were an immigrant who had arrived as a child (under the age of 16). The reference category was 'non-immigrant' (9 per cent of the overall sample were immigrants).

Voting behaviour was also captured by two dummy variables. The first was coded 1 if a respondent did not vote in the last national election because they were *ineligible* to vote (7 per cent of the sample fell into this category), while the second was coded 1 if the respondent was *eligible* to vote but did not do so; some 21 per cent of the sample fell into this category. The reference category was 'voted in the last national election'.

Economic security was measured by two different items. The first, *unemployment*, captures the objective experience of being outside paid employment (8 per cent of the sample were unemployed at the time of interview). The second, *coping on income*, captures a more subjective experience of economic insecurity. Respondents were asked 'Which of these descriptions […] comes closest to how you feel about your household's income nowadays?' with the possible responses: 'living comfortably on present income'; 'coping on present income'; 'finding it difficult on present income'; and 'finding it very difficult on present income'. Responses to this item were entered into our models as three dummy variables with the reference category set as 'living comfortably'. Overall, 23 per cent of respondents felt they were living comfortably, 43 per cent felt they were getting by, 23 per cent said they found it difficult to cope, and 11 per cent said they found it very difficult to cope.

An additional important measure was *contact with the police*, which may mediate associations between some or all of the above variables and legitimacy. Respondents were first asked if police in their country had approached, stopped or made contact with them for any reason in the last two years (32 per cent indicated this was the case); they were then asked how satisfied they were with the conduct of the police on the last occasion this occurred. Police contact was therefore entered into the models as three dummy variables, representing satisfactory contact, 'neutral' contact, and unsatisfactory contact (the reference category was therefore 'no contact').

Displaying results from the full ESS sample, Table 3.1 shows the distribution of the explanatory variables across majority and minority groups. Minority group members were consistently in a different and usually less favourable position than majority group members. They were more likely to have experienced discrimination, more likely to be immigrants, less likely to be citizens, less likely to have voted at the last election even when they were eligible to do so, more likely to be unemployed, and more likely to be finding it 'difficult to get by'.

Table 3.1   Measures of group position: by minority/majority status

	Majority group (in per cent)	Minority group (in per cent)
Experience of ethnic discrimination		
No	98	72
Yes	2	28
Immigrant?		
No	93	66
Yes – arrived as a child	3	9
Yes – arrived as an adult	5	26
Citizen?		
No	3	20
Yes	97	80
Vote at last election?		
Yes	72	57
No	22	26
Not eligible	6	17
Unemployed?		
No	93	85
Yes	8	15
Getting by economically?		
Living comfortably	24	13
Coping	43	35
Difficult	22	27
Very difficult	10	24

Analytical strategy

Analysis proceeds in three stages.[5] On a descriptive basis, we first show country-by-country variation in police legitimacy across majority and minority ethnic group members. Switching to the pooled dataset, we then estimate random effects models predicting police legitimacy among minority group members only. This allows us to explain variation in legitimacy judgements among such individuals with a particular focus on group position and police contact (although we also control for gender, age, years of full-time education, and victimization). Third, we essentially repeat these models but with the full sample and utilizing random coefficients models to allow the association between minority status and legitimacy to vary across countries. This allows us to test whether the inclusion of modes of incorporation and police contact (as well as the control variables) shrinks towards zero the statistical effect of minority group status on legitimacy.

Results

Variation in police legitimacy between minority and majority group members

Figures 3.1 and 3.2 plot the basic associations between ethnic majority/minority status and police legitimacy across the 27 countries included in this analysis. Specifically, the figures show the regression coefficients from a series of country-by-country linear regression models predicting each measure of legitimacy, where ethnicity was the sole explanatory variable. A dot to the left of the zero line indicates that police legitimacy was lower among the ethnic minority population in that country, while a dot to the right indicates that legitimacy was higher among the ethnic minority population. Bars show the 95 per cent confidence intervals – these are often very wide due to the small size of the ethnic minority sample in many countries.

Overall, there appeared to be no consistent association between ethnic minority status and police legitimacy. In 18 of the 27 countries, people from ethnic minority groups tended to feel less normatively aligned with police,

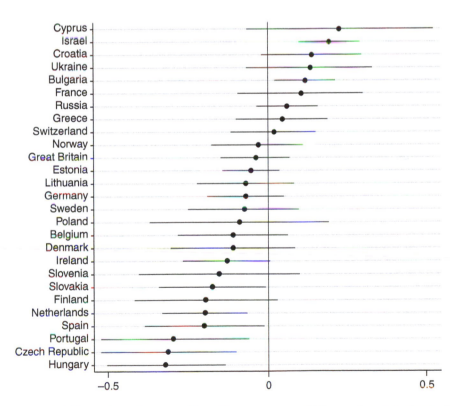

Figure 3.1 Normative alignment with police, by country. Difference between views of minority and majority group members.

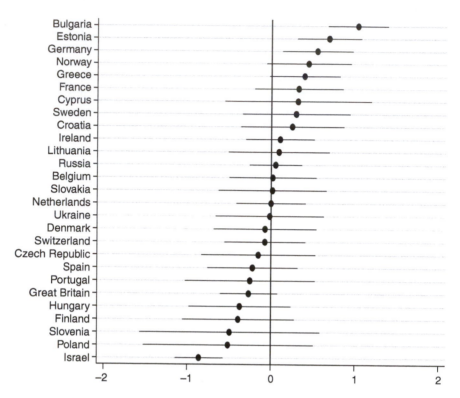

Figure 3.2 Felt obligation to obey police, by country. Difference between views of minority and majority group members.

although this association was statistically significant in only six. Felt duty to obey police was lower among minority group members in 11 countries but only in Israel was this statistical effect significant. Normative alignment with police was higher among ethnic minority group members in nine countries, although the distinction between majority and minority groups was significant in only two (Bulgaria and Israel). Similarly, felt obligation was higher among minority group members in 14 countries, yet the majority/minority group difference was significant in just three (Bulgaria, Estonia and Germany). Any idea that police legitimacy is always lower among ethnic minority groups appears to be called into question by this data, although there was significant variation across countries, and it is important of course to remember that the composition of the category 'ethnic minority' varies hugely over the 27 countries in this dataset.

The apparently anomalous position of Israel in this data is worthy of a little further comment. On a bivariate basis ethnic minority group members in Israel – most but not all of whom were Muslim – were more likely to feel normatively aligned with police but less likely to feel a duty to obey police. One reason for this may be ambivalent views of the police among the *majority* Israeli population. In general, police legitimacy in Israel seems to be quite low (Perry and Jonathan-Zamir 2014), and it has been suggested that one reason for this is that Jewish Israelis feel the amount of time and energy police spend on counter-terrorism activity comes at the expense of more traditional policing concerns. As Metcalfe *et al.* (2016: 1) put it, at least some people from the majority population have the impression that police 'protect our homeland but neglect our community'. This may weaken their sense of the normative appropriateness of the police, who they see as failing to live up to societal expectations concerning the proper function of police (e.g. dealing with local crime and disorder) – while their sense of duty towards police as 'protectors of the homeland' is less affected by such concerns. This divergence underlines that legitimacy is a complex and multi-faceted phenomenon, and demonstrates the utility of measuring it as a multi-dimensional construct.

Police legitimacy among ethnic minority group members

Moving on to consider whether group position-related variable predict police legitimacy, Table 3.2 shows the results of six multi-level regression models predicting normative alignment (Models 1–3) and duty to obey (Models 4–6) among minority group members only. Models 1 and 4 are empty variance components models; Models 2 and 5 contain the main explanatory variables plus controls; Models 3 and 6 add the police contact measures. This design allows us to test for any mediating statistical effect of police contact.

Across both measures of legitimacy, being an immigrant who arrived as an adult was associated with higher levels of legitimacy. Equally, across both measures not voting when eligible to do so was associated with lower levels of legitimacy. For the normative alignment component of legitimacy, the experience of discrimination and economic insecurity was also associated with lower legitimacy. Economic insecurity was also associated with lower perceived duty to obey, albeit somewhat less consistently. All these findings were as hypothesized. Some results, however, did not match our original hypotheses. First, there was no independent association between unemployment and either aspect of police legitimacy. Second, being a citizen of the country where the respondent lived was associated with *lower* legitimacy, although this statistical effect only achieved significance in relation to normative alignment. Third, the experience of discrimination had no association with perceived duty to obey police.

In Models 3 and 6 in Table 3.2, we find, as would be expected, that contact with the police was strongly associated with legitimacy judgements. Yet, little if any of the other statistical effects identified appear to be mediated by police contact: coefficients elsewhere in the models remain almost unchanged upon the addition of police contact. It seems that people in an economically precarious position, for example, do not grant the police less legitimacy because they have more contact with officers. We return to this point in the discussion below. Note also the size of the statistical effects associated with some of the key measures. For example, the standardized coefficients for discrimination ($\beta = -0.10$) and

Table 3.2 Random effects linear regression models predicting police legitimacy. Ethnic minority group members only

Standardized betas	Normative alignment			Duty to obey		
	Model 1	Model 2	Model 3	Model 4	Model 5	Model 6
Age		0.09***	0.06**		0.08***	0.07***
Gender (ref: male)						
Female		-0.02	-0.04*		-0.02	-0.03
Years in full time education		-0.07***	-0.08***		-0.03	-0.03
Victim of crime (ref: no)						
Victim		-0.04*	-0.02		-0.05**	-0.04*
Immigrant (ref: no)						
Arrived as a child		0	0.01		-0.01	-0.01
Arrived as an adult		0.08**	0.08***		0.08**	0.08**
Perception of discrimination? (ref: no)						
Yes		-0.12***	-0.10***		-0.03	-0.02
Citizen of country (ref: no)						
Citizen		-0.08**	-0.08**		-0.03	-0.03
Voted at last election (ref: yes)						
Eligible but did not vote		-0.08***	-0.08***		-0.08***	-0.08***
Not eligible		-0.03	-0.02		-0.02	-0.02

	A1	A2	A3	B1	B2	B3
Employment status (ref: others)						
Unemployed	−0.01	−0.01	−0.01	−0.01	−0.01	−0.01
Coping on income (ref: living comfortably)						
Coping		−0.08**	−0.07*		−0.01	0
Finding it difficult		−0.12***	−0.10***		−0.06*	−0.05+
Finding it very difficult		−0.16***	−0.14***		−0.03	−0.02
Contact with police (ref: none)						
Yes and bad			−0.19***			−0.10***
Yes and neutral			−0.07***			−0.04+
Yes and good			0.09***			0.04*
ICC	0.07	0.02	0.01	0.08	0.05	0.05
n	2,804	2,804	2,804	2,831	2,831	2,831

Notes
+ $p < 0.1$;
* $p < 0.05$;
** $p < 0.01$;
*** $p < 0.001$.

'finding it very difficult to cope' ($\beta=-0.12$) in the normative alignment models are close in size to those of the coefficients of the police contact measures. Some measures of group position had almost as large a statistical effect on their legitimacy judgements as did direct contact with the police, albeit that negative police contact trumped everything else.

Finally, note that the Intra-class Correlation (ICC) values fall significantly with the addition of the group position and other explanatory variables – from 0.07 to 0.02 in the normative alignment models and from 0.08 to 0.05 in the duty to obey models. This suggests that a large proportion of the across country variation in police legitimacy among minority group members is explained by characteristics of the minority populations in those countries.[6]

Police legitimacy across the European population

The final step is to compare the views of minority and majority group members in multivariate analysis. Table 3.3 shows results from a series of random coefficients linear regression models predicting the two legitimacy measures, estimated using the full ESS sample. These are specified in a similar way previously with the important exception that they contain the majority/minority indicator and that the association between minority status and legitimacy was allowed to vary across countries.[7]

Models 7 and 10 contain only ethnic minority status as a predictor. These show that there was a small but statistically significant negative association between minority status and normative alignment with police. Across Europe, people from ethnic minority groups tended on average to feel less normatively aligned with police. By contrast, there was no association between minority status and perceived duty to obey police.

Turning to the multivariate models, results appear similar to those shown in Table 3.2 above. Holding constant minority status and the other variables included in the models, immigrants who had arrived as adults felt, on average, more normatively aligned with police than the native born. Those who felt discriminated against, were finding it hard to get by – and, here, who were unemployed – and those who chose not to vote all granted less legitimacy across both measures. Citizens, again, tended to be more critical than non-citizens. Also as before, adding the police contact variables had little effect elsewhere in the models, confirming that the statistical effect of the measures of interest on legitimacy did not seem to be mediated by contact experiences to any great degree.

A few findings vary across the two sets of models, however. All else being equal, across the whole sample those who were ineligible to vote tended to feel a slightly greater obligation to obey police than those who had voted at the last election. There was, by contrast, no independent association between immigrant status and perceived duty to obey police. Most importantly, though, Model 9 shows that once the other predictors were taken into account, the association between ethnic minority status and normative alignment with police was broken, suggesting that the reason why this aspect of police legitimacy is on average lower among minority groups is indeed that they tend to have different 'group positions' (and demographic profiles).[8] Note also that the ICC values fall again with the addition of the explanatory variables, although this effect is not as marked as it was in the minority group only models described above. Considering the European population as a whole, at least some of the across-country variation in police legitimacy was explained by the variables included in models.

The use of random coefficients models means it is possible to estimate, from the pooled data, the association between ethnic minority status and police legitimacy in each of the 27 countries. The results of doing so are plotted in Figures 3.3 (normative alignment) and 3.4 (duty to obey). These display the strength and direction of the bivariate minority/legitimacy relationship generated, first, from Models 7 and 10 (the darker bars). This essentially replicates the analysis shown in Figures 3.1 and 3.2 above. There was a negative association between minority status and normative alignment in 22 countries. By contrast, although there was no significant association overall, the bivariate relationship between minority status and felt duty to obey police was positive in 17 countries.

Second, estimates derived from Models 9 and 12 are also plotted (the lighter bars). These show the association between minority status and legitimacy conditional on the other variables in the models. The change in the size and direction of the coefficients is striking. In Figure 3.3, all negative coefficients either shrink essentially to zero or reverse signs to become positive. That is, across all the countries shown any negative correlation between ethnic minority status and normative alignment was fully, or very nearly fully, accounted for by the other variables in the models. In those countries where the bivariate association between minority status and normative alignment was either very close to zero (Cyprus, Greece and France) or positive (Russia, Croatia, Bulgaria, Israel and Ukraine), the coefficients become more strongly positive upon the addition of the other measures. Conditional on the other predictors, minority group members in these countries were more likely to feel normatively aligned with police.

A similar pattern is observed in Figure 3.4. In those countries where the bivariate association was negative, the addition of the other predictors reduced the coefficient to near zero or switched it to positive. The one exception was Israel, where minority group members felt less of a duty to obey police even when conditioning on the other variables (c.f. Hasisi and Weitzer 2007). In those countries were the bivariate association was positive, the coefficient was strengthened by the addition of the other variables. In most of the countries included in this analysis a minority group member felt somewhat more of a duty to obey police than an otherwise similar (in terms of the variables included in the model) majority group member.

Table 3.3 Random coefficients linear regression models predicting police legitimacy. Full ESS sample

Standardized betas	Model 7	Model 8	Model 9	Model 10	Model 11	Model 12
Ethnic minority (ref: no)						
Yes	−0.02*	0.01	0.01	0	0.01	0.01
Age		0.11***	0.09***		0.06***	0.06***
Gender (ref: male)						
Female		0.02***	0.01*		0.01*	0.01
Years in full time education		−0.01**	−0.01**		−0.01*	−0.01*
Victim of crime (ref: no)						
Victim		−0.05***	−0.04***		−0.03***	−0.02***
Immigrant (ref: no)						
Arrived as a child		0	0		−0.01	0
Arrived as an adult		0.02**	0.02**		0.01	0.01
Perception of discrimination? (ref: no)						
Yes		−0.06***	−0.05***		−0.01**	−0.01*
Citizen of country (ref: no)						
Citizen		−0.02***	−0.02***		−0.01*	−0.01*
Voted at last election (ref: yes)						
Eligible but did not vote		−0.05***	−0.04***		−0.04***	−0.03***
Not eligible		0	0		0.01*	0.01*

Employment status (ref: others)						
Unemployed		−0.04***	−0.03***		−0.03***	−0.03***
Coping on income (ref: living comfortably)						
Coping		−0.05***	−0.04***		−0.03***	−0.03***
Finding it difficult		−0.07***	−0.06***		−0.04***	−0.04***
Finding it very difficult		−0.09***	−0.08***		−0.03***	−0.02***
Contact with police (ref: none)						
Yes and bad			−0.16***			−0.06***
Yes and neutral			−0.07***			−0.03***
Yes and good			0.06***			0.05***
Intra Class Correlation	0.13	0.12	0.11	0.13	0.12	0.12
n	46,077	46,077	46,077	46,883	46,883	46,883

Notes

Age and years in full time education were group-mean centred.

* $p < 0.05$;
** $p < 0.01$;
*** $p < 0.001$.

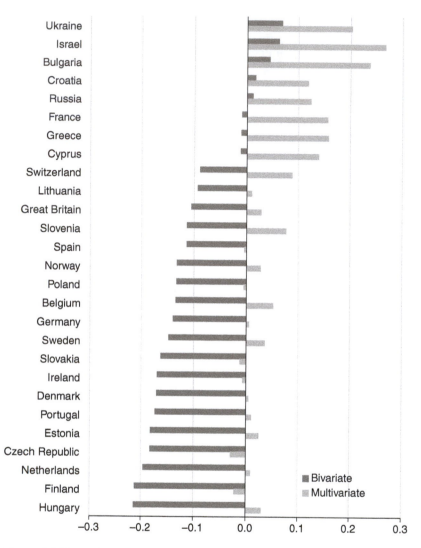

Figure 3.3 Normative alignment with police, by country. Difference in conditional means, majority vs. minority groups.

Discussion

Six hypotheses guided the analysis above. As predicted, we found that both among the ethnic minority population of Europe and across the population as a whole, those who felt discriminated against tended to grant police less legitimacy (H1); those who had immigrated as adults tended to grant more legitimacy (H2); those who chose not to vote granted less legitimacy (H4); and that economic insecurity tended to be associated with lower legitimacy (H5). One

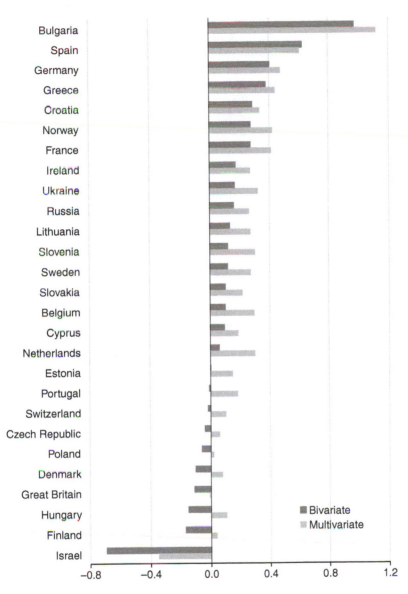

Figure 3.4 Felt obligation to obey police, by country. Difference in conditional means, majority vs. minority groups.

finding flatly contradicted our hypothesis: citizens tended to grant less, not more, legitimacy to police than non-citizens (H3). Strikingly, we also found that across almost all of the 27 countries included in the ESS sample, any negative bivariate association between ethnic minority status and police legitimacy disappeared once a range of theoretically interesting variables were taken into account.

Indeed, in many countries, people who identified as ethnic minority group members tended, all else equal, to grant police *more* legitimacy than their majority group counterparts. Negative associations between minority status and police legitimacy were often attenuated by the addition of the key variables of interest (H6). Yet, *positive* associations were often also strengthened.

This analysis has, of necessity, operated at a very high level of abstraction (being unable to take in account the social and cultural conditions of specific minority groups in particular countries). However, we believe our results will have implications for police–minority relations within specific national and indeed local contexts. There are significant associations between group position and police legitimacy: individual and in all likelihood collective locations within social, economic, and political structures seem to predict police legitimacy across both measures used. Importantly, these effects are not unidirectional. Recall that people from minority groups were more likely to feel discriminated against, less likely to vote even when eligible and more likely to be in an economically precarious position. These were all characteristics associated with lower levels of police legitimacy. However, minority group members were also less likely to be citizens, and more likely to be immigrants who had arrived as adults – these were characteristics associated with higher levels of police legitimacy.

The ways in which these different factors come together in particular contexts will therefore likely influence the extent to which people from a particular ethnic group – i.e. those with a particular position in that context – view the police. We might surmise, for example, that a minority group subject to high levels of discrimination and economic insecurity and with low levels of engagement in the democratic process but with many members born *in* the country concerned will confer significantly less legitimacy on the police than a group, similarly subject to discrimination and insecurity but which contains many members born *outside* that country and who are not yet citizens of it. This seems to describe well the situation in the UK, where police legitimacy is lowest among the most long-established ethnic minority group, the Black Caribbean, and significantly higher among other groups, such as the Bangladeshi and Black African groups, who have broadly similar experiences of social exclusion and discrimination but which contain a much higher proportion of first-generation immigrants (Jackson *et al.* 2012).

The net result of this complex interplay between group position, ethnic minority status and police legitimacy seems to be that across the 27 countries included in the analysis there is no consistent bivariate association between minority status and police legitimacy. Overall, the 'positive' and 'negative' implications of differential group positions seem to cancel each other out. It will be by drilling down into local contexts and, it seems, by taking into account group and individual location within the social order that the association between minority status and legitimacy can properly be explored.

Our results also throw up some puzzles. First, why is police legitimacy lower among citizens than among non-citizens? There are two possible reasons for this. It may be that citizens are allowed, and feel themselves able, to be more critical of the police. And in a related sense, there may be greater normative pressure on non-citizens, whose status and indeed very presence in a particular context remains uncertain, to legitimize police (or at least express opinions that suggest they hold police legitimate). Alexander (2013: 66) argues that the 'patterned normative order' that structures a particular society applies not only to its members but also to those who are excluded from membership. The latter are often 'expected' to adhere to dominant norms and values – and legitimacy has been positioned precisely as a social norm by many authors (e.g. Horne 2009). Indeed, this may help explain the positive conditional associations between ethnic minority status and legitimacy shown in Figures 3.3 and 3.4. It does not seem unreasonable to suggest that in many national contexts, and all else being equal – i.e. controlling for group position-related factors and contact with police – a minority group member might feel a greater pressure to express support for police than a majority group member.

Second, the lack of any significant mediating effect of police contact also raises questions. It seems that an individual's position in the social order and their contact with police officers had largely separate and distinct associations with legitimacy. It did not seem that economically insecure individuals tended to grant police less legitimacy because they had more contact with officers, for example, in contrast to what would be expected if social exclusion predicted more, and more problematic, personal experience of policing. Naturally, it is neither to claim that such contact is not important nor that it is not differentially patterned across social and geographic space. Both these things are likely to be true. Rather, it seems that 'group position' has an association with police legitimacy above and beyond differential experiences of police activity (at least as far as all this is captured by the ESS). It may indeed be that the association between group position and police legitimacy functions on a symbolic or ideological level as well as an experiential one.

Conclusion

We hope that this analysis of Round 5 of the ESS has made a contribution to the study of police legitimacy – even if it offers somewhat cautionary messages about the need to avoid over-generalization. The clearest and most important of these is that minority ethnic group status is not *in itself* a consistent predictor of negative attitudes towards the police. We have pointed to some key correlates of minority group status that explain why minority groups *sometimes* tend to confer less legitimacy on the police than majority groups – while also identifying correlates which predict more positive attitudes. Factors such as age and economic security appear in our analysis as consistent predictors of orientations towards the police but ethnic minority status does not. This said, one does not have to look hard to locate minority groups in a range of countries whose citizenship, economic, and social statuses seem corrosive of police legitimacy.

The second cautionary finding is that experience of police activity seems to shape legitimacy in important ways. Yet so too do factors unrelated – or only loosely related – to policing. Economic, social, and political marginalization all appear to be linked to lower police legitimacy. There are obvious but important policy implications to this, concerning both the need for policing to continue to focus on constructive strategies of legitimation and the need for broader political responses to social exclusion. These may address not only the underlying problems of marginalization but also the symptoms of these problems that manifest in some-times disastrously poor relations between minority groups and the police. Given the complexity of the factors that build police legitimacy, there is a need for realism in setting expectations about the scope for consolidating police legitimacy whether through improvements to policing itself or though broader inclusionary initiatives.

Clearly, there is plenty of scope for further work to flesh out the mechanisms of inclusion and exclusion though which some minority groups become fully incorporated into social and economic systems – including systems of social control – while others do not. Our analysis demonstrates, we hope, that large-scale comparative surveys have a role to play in doing this. Even if their essentially reductionist methodology makes them blunt tools, the scale of an enterprise such as the ESS enables it to detect relationships that may inform future research across multiple national and local contexts.

Notes

1 This work was supported by the Economic and Social Research Council [grant number ES/L011611/1].
2 Nor should it be forgotten that in some societies, political power is actually seized and retained by minority ethnic groups.
3 Other relevant topics included victim experience, citizenship, perceived societal discrimination against one's group and financial security, as well as demographics.
4 The resulting scales had the following characteristics: normative alignment (mean 2.46; SD 0.79; min. 1; max. 5); duty to obey (mean 5.65; SD 2.61; min. 0; max. 10).
5 All analyses used unweighted data.
6 Further analysis, not shown here, suggested that the group position variables explained more of the across country variation than those included as control measures (age, gender, education and victimization).
7 Continuous predictor variables were group-mean centered, i.e. centred on the mean value of that variable for the country in which the respondent lived.
8 Additional models – not shown here – demonstrated that addition of *either* the group position/police contact variables *or* the control variables was sufficient to break the link between minority status and normative alignment with police.

Bibliography

Alexander, J. (2001). 'Theorizing the modes of incorporation', *Sociological Theory*, 19: 237–49.
Alexander, J. (2013). *The Dark Side of Modernity*, Cambridge: Polity Press.
Bobo, L. (1999). 'Prejudice as group position: microfoundations of a sociological approach to racism and race relations', *Journal of Social Issues*, 55: 445–72.
Bottoms, A. and Tankebe, J. (2012). 'Beyond procedural justice: a dialogic approach to legitimacy in criminal justice', *Journal of Criminal Law and Criminology*, 102: 119–70.
Bradford, B. (2016). *Stop and Search and Police Legitimacy*, London: Routledge.

Bradford, B. and Jackson, J. (2016). 'Cooperating with the police as informal social control: trust and neighbourhood concerns as predictors of public assistance', *Nordisk politiforskning* [*Nordic Journal of Policing Studies*], 3: 109–29.

Bradford, B., Murphy, K. and Jackson, J. (2014). 'Officers as mirrors: policing, procedural justice and the (re)production of social identity', *British Journal of Criminology*, 54: 527–50.

Bradford, B., Sargeant, E., Murphy, T. and Jackson, J. (2017). 'A leap of faith? Trust in the police among migrants in England and Wales', *British Journal of Criminology*, 57(2): 381–401, doi: 10.1093/bjc/azv126.

Brown B. and Benedict W. (2002). 'Perceptions of the police: past findings, methodological issues, conceptual issues and policy implications', *Policing: An International Journal of Police Strategies and Management*, 25: 543–80.

Burchardt, T., Le Grand, J. and Piachaud, D. (1999). 'Social exclusion in Britain 1991–1995', *Social Policy and Administration*, 33: 227–44.

European Social Survey Round 5 Data (2010). NSD – Norwegian Centre for Research Data, Norway – Data Archive and distributor of ESS data for ESS ERIC.

Harder, J. and Krosnick, J. (2008). 'Why do people vote? A psychological analysis of the causes of voter turnout', *Journal of Social Issues*, 64: 525–49.

Hasisi, B. and Weitzer, R. (2007). 'Police relations with Arabs and Jews in Israel', *The British Journal of Criminology*, 47: 728–45.

Heater, D. (1990). *Citizenship*, London: Longman.

Hinsch, W. (2008). 'Legitimacy and justice', in J. Kühnelt (ed.), *Political Legitimization without Morality?*, New York: Springer, 39–52.

Hinsch, W. (2010). 'Justice, legitimacy, and constitutional rights', *Critical Review of International Social and Political Philosophy*, 13: 39–54.

Horne, C. (2009). 'A social norms approach to legitimacy', *American Behavioral Scientist*, 53: 400–15.

Hough, M., Jackson, J. and Bradford, B. (2013). 'Legitimacy, trust and compliance: an empirical test of procedural justice using the European Social Survey', in J. Tankebe and A. Liebling (eds.), *Legitimacy and Criminal Justice: An International Exploration*, Oxford: Oxford University Press, 326–52.

Huq, A., Jackson, J. and Trinkner, R. (2016). 'Legitimating practices: revisiting the predicates of police legitimacy', *British Journal of Criminology*, doi: 10.1093/bjc/azw037.

Huo, Y. (2003). 'Procedural justice and social regulation across group boundaries: does subgroup identity undermine relationship-based governance?', *Personality and Social Psychology Bulletin*, 29: 336–48.

Jackson, J. (2015). 'On the dual motivational force of legitimate authority', in B. Bornstein and A. Tomkins (eds.), *Cooperation and Compliance with Authority: The Role of Institutional Trust. Nebraska Symposium on Motivation*, New York: Springer, 145–66.

Jackson, J., Bradford, B., Hough, M., Kuha, J., Stares, S., Widdop, S., Fitzgerald, R., Yordanova, M. and Galev, T. (2011). 'Developing European indicators of trust in justice', *European Journal of Criminology*, 8: 267–85.

Jackson, J., Bradford, B., MacQueen, S. and Hough, M. (2016, September 3). 'Truly free consent? Clarifying the nature of police legitimacy', *SSNR*, online. Available https://papers.ssrn.com/sol3/papers.cfm?abstract_id=2620274 (accessed 03 September 2016).

Jackson, J., Bradford, B., Stanko, B. and Hohl, K. (2012). *Just Authority? Trust in the Police in England and Wales*, London: Routledge.

Kääriäinen, J. (2007). 'Trust in the police in 16 European countries: a multilevel analysis', *European Journal of Criminology*, 4: 409–25.

72   B. *Bradford* et al.

Metcalfe, C., Wolfe, S., Gertz, E. and Gertz. M. (2016). 'They protect our homeland but neglect our community: overemphasis, legitimacy and public cooperation in Israel', *Journal of Research in Crime and Delinquency*, 53: 814–39.

Murphy, K. and Cherney, A. (2012). 'Understanding cooperation with police in a diverse society', *British Journal of Criminology*, 52: 181–201.

Nannestad, P., Svendsen, G., Dinesen, P. and Sønderskov, K. (2014). 'Do institutions or culture determine the level of social trust? The natural experiment of migration from Non-western to Western countries', *Journal of Ethnic and Migration Studies*, 40: 544–65.

Oliveira, A. and Murphy, K. (2015). 'Explaining negative attitudes toward police: does race or social identity matter more?', *Race and Justice*, 5: 259–77.

Perry, S. and Jonathan-Zamir, T. (2014). 'Lessons from empirical research on policing in Israel: policing terrorism and police–community relationships', *Police Practice and Research*, 15: 173–87.

Piatkowska, S. (2015). 'Immigrants' confidence in police: do country-level characteristics matter?', *International Journal of Comparative and Applied Criminal Justice*, 39: 1–30.

Roché, S. (2008). 'Minorities, fairness, and the legitimacy of the criminal-justice system in France', in: T. Tyler (ed.), *Legitimacy and Criminal Justice: International Perspectives*, New York: Russell Sage, 333–80.

Röder, A. and Mühlau, P. (2012). 'What determines the trust of immigrants in criminal justice systems in Europe?', *European Journal of Criminology*, 9: 370–87.

Sampson, R. and Bartusch, D. (1998). 'Legal cynicism and (subcultural) tolerance of deviance: the neighbourhood context of racial differences', *Law and Society Review*, 32: 777–804.

Sunshine, J. and Tyler, T. (2003). 'Moral solidarity, identification with the community, and the importance of procedural justice: the police as prototypical representatives of a group's moral values', *Social Psychology Quarterly*, 66: 153–65.

Tankebe, J. (2013). 'Viewing things differently: the dimensions of public perceptions of police legitimacy', *Criminology*, 51:103–35.

Thomassen, G. and Kääriäinen, J. (2016). 'System satisfaction, contact satisfaction and trust in the police', *European Journal of Policing Studies*, 4: 437–48.

Trinkner, R., Jackson, J. and Tyler, T. (2016, October 2). 'Expanding "appropriate" police behavior beyond procedural justice: bounded authority & the legitimation of the law', *SSRN*, online. Available https://papers.ssrn.com/sol3/Papers.cfm?abstract_id=2846659 (accessed 10 February 2017).

Tyler, T. (2006a). *Why People Obey the Law*, Princeton, NJ: Princeton University Press.

Tyler, T. (2006b). 'Psychological perspectives on legitimacy and legitimation', *Annual Review of Psychology*, 57: 375–400.

Tyler, T. and Jackson, J. (2013). 'Future challenges in the study of legitimacy and criminal justice', in J. Tankebe and A. Liebling (eds.), *Legitimacy and Criminal Justice: An International Exploration*, Oxford: Oxford University Press, 83–104.

Weitzer, R. (1999). 'Citizens' perceptions of police misconduct: race and neighborhood context', *Justice Quarterly*, 16: 819–46.

Weitzer, R. (2010). 'Race and policing in different ecological contexts', in S. Rice and M. White (eds.), *Race, Ethnicity and Policing: New and Essential Readings*, New York: NYU Press, 118–39.

Weitzer, R. and Tuch, S. (2006). *Race and Policing in America*, Cambridge: Cambridge University Press.

Wortley, S. and Owusu-Bempah, A. (2011). 'The usual suspects: police stop and search in Canada', *Policing and Society*, 21: 395–407.

4 Ethnic disparities in police-initiated contacts of adolescents and attitudes towards the police in France and Germany

A tale of four cities

Dietrich Oberwittler and Sebastian Roché

Introduction

'Stop and search' – or the proactive police power to stop and check individuals in public spaces – is a standard law enforcement procedure for police forces around the world, and one of the most frequent ways by which individuals come into contact with police. As an involuntary form of police contact that is largely at the discretion of individual officers, stop and search has been widely seen as a contentious issue and a potential source of strain between police and citizen (Bradford and Loader 2016; Delsol and Shiner 2015; Weber and Bowling 2013). This is particularly true for urban, young, male, and minority populations, who are thought to be disproportionally affected by stop and search in many countries, especially in the context of alleged strategies of 'ethnic [or racial] profiling' (Engel and Cohen 2014; Fagan 2002). Discriminatory stop and search practices have been named as a major factor behind the recent outbursts of collective youth violence across several European cities (Newburn 2016; Roché 2010). Interviews with participants in the 2011 England Riots, for example, found that the 'most common complaints related to people's everyday experience of policing, with many expressing deep frustration at the way people in their communities were subjected to stop and search' (Lewis *et al.* 2011). Similarly, following the 2005 riots in France, adolescents living in deprived neighbourhood reported that 'tensions between youth and police' best accounted for the violence (57 per cent), even ahead of a general sense of discrimination (15 per cent) (Fourquet 2007). Indeed, after the Brixton Riots almost exactly 30 years earlier, the Scarman Report concluded that anger was largely fuelled by the 'heavy-handed use of stop and search [which] impacted disproportionately on black and minority ethnic communities' (quoted by Delsol and Shiner 2015: 4). The immediate trigger of the largest riot in France in 2005 was the lethal accident of two adolescents fleeing from an anticipated police control (Mucchielli 2009; Roché and de Maillard 2009). Similar events were also 'flashpoints' (Waddington 2010) for 2011 riots in England and 2013 riots in Stockholm.

Against this backdrop, France and Germany make interesting comparative case studies as they are neighbouring countries that share many socio-economic and political similarities, yet differ greatly in their respective police–citizen relations. Specifically, France has had several large anti-police riots in recent years whereas Germany has not had any. Germany has also scored higher in ratings of public trust in the police in cross-national surveys (Billiet and Pleysier 2012). A comparative micro-analysis of individuals' daily experiences of policing in these two countries therefore might better reveal the possible sources (and inhibitors) of positive police–citizen relations. This was the rationale behind the joint French–German research project POLIS, a mixed-methods study of police relationships with adolescents in multi-ethnic cities.[1] While findings of participant observations and in-depth interviews have been discussed elsewhere (de Maillard *et al.* 2016a, 2016b; Hunold 2015; Hunold *et al.* 2016), this chapter focuses on results from a standardized survey of a sample of nearly 21,000 adolescents of various ethnic origins on their experiences of police-initiated contact. While street-level policing has received more attention in France (Fassin 2013; Goris *et al.* 2009; Roché 2016) than in Germany (Hüttermann 2003; Schweer and Strasser 2003), large-scale and systematic research has been lacking in both countries, and French–German comparisons have been even rarer (Gauthier 2012). We use POLIS survey data to address questions about the frequency and distribution of stop and search among majority and minority adolescent communities, and the potential consequences it has had for attitudes towards the police.

Police-initiated contact and its impact on police–citizen relations

Police officers have a considerable degree of discretion in deciding whom they proactively stop, question, and search in public spaces, especially because in many cases, police contact is not prompted by an evident norm violation or call for service. As in many other countries, the legal framework in Germany and in France provides the police with broad powers of discretionary controls for the protection of 'public safety and order' (Police Law Baden-Württemberg 1992; Republique Francaise 2014). High-crime or disorderly neighbourhoods can be formally declared 'dangerous places' in both countries (by the public prosecutor in France, by the police in Germany), after which anybody may be stopped regardless of behaviour. In the absence of elaborated state strategies for the use of proactive contact, stop and search procedures are in many ways at the whim of local policing styles, public prosecutors' preferences, and most considerably, frontline officers' individual discretion in how, when, and upon whom they use these powers.

In particular, the wide discretionary latitude accorded to local criminal justice authorities has resulted in allegations of discriminatory practices against vulnerable groups of citizens, especially ethnic minorities (Bowling and Phillips 2008; Weitzer 2014). At the core of these allegations is the claim that an individual may be treated differently not on the basis of *what* he or she is doing, but because on the basis of *who* he or she is (i.e. physical appearance) (Jackson *et al.*

2013). The European Union Agency for Fundamental Rights (2010b: 15) has defined police controls as discriminatory if 'based only or mainly on that person's race, ethnicity or religion,' rather than suspicious behaviour, which results in 'treating an individual less favourably than others who are in a similar situation'. On a legal dimension, many experts agree that the discriminatory application of policing violates basic citizen rights, although only very few cases have been adjudicated in national or international courts, and policing practices seem to be largely oblivious to such concerns (Schicht 2013). On a socio-psychological dimension, there has been strong support for the hypothesis that discriminatory police controls violate people's fairness expectations (which strongly correspond with legal principles of equality). According to procedural justice theory, public trust and the willingness to obey the police depends on the perception that the police exercise their authority in a fair manner (Sunshine and Tyler 2003). What is considered 'fair' policing is often the amalgamation of state or federal directives, managerial practices (e.g. organizational targets), local police culture (as sociologists of police have pointed out since Wilson 1968), the perceived neutrality of an agent's decisions (e.g. why an individual is subjected to contact), as well as the quality of the encounter (e.g. whether an individual is treated with dignity and respect) (Tyler 2011; Tyler and Wakslak 2004). The Group Engagement Model adds to this list the salience of collective identity shared by members of ethnic minorities (Murphy *et al.* 2015; Tyler and Blader 2003). Encounters between the police and members of these groups often carry symbolic messages about the status of that group, the values of the society from which it is a part, and the government that represents that society.

Many studies from various countries have tested these hypotheses. Evidence for the disproportional use of police-initiated contact primarily comes from the few countries and places where official data of stop and search is collected, such as England and Wales (Borooah 2011; Chainey and MacDonald 2012; United Kingdom Ministry of Justice 2013), New York City (Gelman *et al.* 2007) and Toronto (Meng *et al.* 2015). In other places, survey data has filled the gap left by a lack of official records. Survey data has also better accounted for differences in the so-called 'availability' of certain population subgroups and the discrepant police attention affecting them (i.e. adolescent males are more likely to be in public spaces late at night than elderly women) (Bowling and Phillips 2007; Quinton 2015). Yet, some of these studies still found higher control rates of minority adolescents in England and Wales (Medina Ariza 2014) and Toronto (Hayle *et al.* 2016), though this was not true in Amsterdam (Svensson and Saharso 2015). There have been few national or local investigations of this kind in France, and none in Germany. A covert observation at Paris train and metro stations revealed a grossly disproportionate stopping of visible minorities by factor six to seven (Goris *et al.* 2009). The cross-national European Minorities and Discrimination Survey (European Union Agency for Fundamental Rights 2010a) reported higher control rates for Turkish minority respondents in Germany and even more for North African minority respondents in France compared to the respective majority populations.

Numerous qualitative, interview-based studies have documented perceptions of discriminatory treatment and its relationship with distrust and resentment towards the police among minority youths in Europe (Gesemann 2003; Parmar 2011; Pettersson 2013; Sharp and Atherton 2007), and the USA (Brunson 2007; Gau and Brunson 2010; Weitzer 1999). Dirikx et al. (2012) has added a nuance to these findings in the context of Belgium, arguing that adolescents' low trust in the police may be an expression of a general 'teenage aversion to authority' independent of negative experience with the police.

Standardized survey data may be better suited to link actual experiences to attitudes towards the police. Many scholars have found that contact with the police was correlated with lower trust (Berg et al. 2016; Hagan et al. 2005; Sindall et al. 2016; Tyler et al. 2014; Weitzer and Tuch 2004; cf. Mazerolle et al. 2013 for a systematic review). Though Skogan (2006) has argued that negative experiences of police encounters deteriorate trust while positive experiences do not help to improve trust, others have found some positive effects of fair and respectful police behaviour on respondents' attitudes (Bradford et al. 2009; Norman 2009). However, this research was predominantly based on cross-sectional survey data which precludes a causal interpretation. Some longitudinal studies were able to show that perceptions of fair procedures improve attitudes towards police over time (Bradford et al. 2014; Slocum et al. 2016; Tyler and Fagan 2008). The evidence of positive effects of 'procedurally justice policing' in the case of victims' experiences (Koster et al. 2016) and randomized traffic stops (Lowrey et al. 2016; MacQueen and Bradford 2015) has often been mixed or inconclusive.

We hope to contribute to this large body of existing research by analysing the practice of police-initiated contact towards adolescents using cross-sectional survey data from two large European countries, France and Germany. We address the issue of disproportionality in police contact for ethnic minorities and low-income neighbourhoods, investigate the quality of these interactions, and examine the possible impact of police behaviour on adolescents' attitudes towards the police.

Data

The data used in these analyses are from a binational school survey conducted in France and Germany as part of the research project POLIS. In addition to this standardized survey, the study also includes 800 hours of participant observations and 115 in-depth interviews with police officers (de Maillard et al. 2016a, 2016b; Hunold 2015). The study design was almost identical in both countries in an effort to make a cross-national comparison possible.

Two large and two medium sized metropolitan areas in each country were chosen as research sites for this project: Lyon (c.1.3 million inhabitants) and Grenoble (c.440,000 inhabitants) in France, and Cologne (c.1 million inhabitants) and Mannheim (c.300.000 inhabitants) in Germany. All four cities have ethnic minority populations well above the national averages, with almost 50 per cent among children and adolescents.[2] The minority populations in both German cities are primarily dominated by Turkish and South European labour migrants and their descendants as well as by Eastern Europeans and 'resettlers' of German origin who immigrated from countries of the former Soviet Union. In Lyon and Grenoble, minority communities are primarily comprised of North Africans (particularly Algerians), Sub-Saharan Africans, and Southern Europeans.

The survey was administered in all major types of secondary schools[3] as a paper-and-pencil interview conducted by trained survey staff during one or two school hours. In Germany and France, the sample of schools was based on a spatial selection reflecting the geographic and socio-demographic city structures. The school-level response rate was 69 per cent in Grenoble, 37 per cent in Lyon, 68 per cent in Cologne and 93 per cent in Mannheim. Within schools in France, 698 classes from eighth to eleventh grades were randomly selected, yielding a total sample of 13,679 respondents (response rate within selected classes 82.0 per cent). In Germany, 351 classes from eighth to tenth grades were randomly selected, yielding a total sample of 6,948 respondents (response rate within selected classes 78.0 per cent).

Dependent variables

Contact with the police was measured by asking adolescents about the frequency of seven different types (plus an open residual category) of contact with police officers during the last 12 months. Open frequency answers were summed up to a count variable, and outliers were trimmed to a maximum of 20 contacts for each item. We use two of these items ('I was approached or checked on the street/in a park/on a public square' and contact 'as a traffic participant, for example, on a bike') to measure *police-initiated contact*. Because police-initiated contact on the suspicion of an offence was captured by a different item, these two items are seen as an approximation of cases in which the police acted pro-actively and with discretion. For comparison, we use four items from this list to measure self-initiated, victim- or witness-related police contact (contact with police 'as witness of a crime', 'as victim of a crime', 'as a witness or victim of a traffic offence/accident', 'I have approached a police officer to ask a question or for help'). Overall, 18 per cent of French and 23 per cent of German respondents reported police-initiated contacts, and 31 per cent respectively 29 per cent reported self-initiated or victim-/witness-related contacts.[4]

For those who reported police contact, there were a series of follow-up questions about the actions and demeanour of police officers and the behaviour of adolescents during the most recent contact (in Germany, this module was randomly applied to half of the sample).

Attitudes towards the police were measured with seven items which tapped into the concepts of both trust in the police (e.g. '[o]verall the police can be trusted') as well as police legitimacy (e.g. 'one should follow the commands of a police officer in any case'). Scale analyses revealed a single latent dimension (Cronbach's alpha=0.79 in Germany, 0.81 in France, see Table 4.A1, appendix).

We computed factor scores using polychoric correlation matrices rescaled to values ranging from 1 (no trust at all) to 4 (complete trust). For simplicity, the resulting scale is called 'police trust'.

Independent variables

The descriptive statistics of all socio-demographic variables except ethnicity are found in Tables 4.A2 and 4.A3 (appendix). Respondents were between 12 and 18 years old, with 91 per cent of the German and 87 per cent of the French sample within the age bracket of 13 to 16 years. Both samples were roughly split half by sex.

Ethnicity or migrant background (which will be used interchangeably in this chapter) was established by asking respondents for their country of birth, as well as that of their parents and grandparents. Using a wide definition, respondents were labelled as having a 'migrant background' if they had at least one parent or more than two grandparents born abroad. Conversely, they were categorized as 'native' only if both parents or most of their grandparents were born in Germany or France. Following this classification, 49 per cent of respondents in Germany and 50 per cent of respondents in France were considered 'native'; 12 per cent of respondents in Germany and 18 per cent of respondents in France were classified as having 'mixed native-migrant parents'; and 39 per cent of respondents in Germany and 32 per cent of respondents in France were grouped as being from 'migrant families' (see Table 4.1). Because of its large sample sizes, the POLIS survey offers a unique opportunity to analyse the experiences and attitudes of a wide variety of adolescents from different ethnic minorities.

Table 4.1 gives an overview of the ethnic composition of the survey samples in both countries.[5] In the German sample, the largest ethnic minority was by far Turkish migrants (1,302 or 19 per cent of all respondents), with all other ethnic

Table 4.1 Respondents by migration background

France			Germany		
(n = 13.679)	abs.	%	(n = 6.948)	abs.	%
Native	6,799	50.6	Native	3,400	49.1
Mixed native/other	1,572	11.7	Turkey	1,302	18.8
Algeria	1,308	9.7	Mixed native/other	687	9.9
Mixed native/Maghreb	979	7.3	Rest of world	262	3.8
Europe	801	6.0	Maghreb/Mid-East	248	3.6
Rest of world	725	5.4	Ex-Soviet Union	221	3.2
Other Maghreb/Mid-East	577	4.3	Other East Europe	220	3.2
Sub-Saharan Africa	455	3.4	Poland	196	2.8
Turkey	229	1.7	West/South Europe	194	2.8
Unknown	*234*	–	Mixed native/Turkey	128	1.9
			Sub-Saharan Africa	70	1.0
			Unknown	*22*	–

groups much smaller. In France, the most significant migrant population was primarily from the Maghreb region (Algeria, Morocco, Tunisia, and Mauritania) with 1,885 respondents or 14 per cent of the total sample. Algeria alone accounted for 1,308 or 10 per cent of the respondents' backgrounds.

Three questions served as indicators of the families' *socio-economic status* that is difficult to measure in youth surveys: Family structure (complete vs. incomplete), parental educational status and parental unemployment or welfare dependency (see Table 4.A2, appendix).

In order to capture the routine activities and life styles of respondents, similar (though not identical) questions were asked in both the French and German versions of the questionnaire. 'Time spent on streets' was measured by asking how often respondents spent their free time 'on the streets, outside the houses' (France) and 'meeting and hanging around with friends on the streets/on a square' (Germany). Similarly, the frequency of meeting with friends on weekday evenings was measured in the French context by days per week, while in Germany it was measured with the hour they usually returned home at night. Finally, alcohol consumption was measured by asking how often respondents had been drunk (during the last 12 months in France, during lifetime in Germany).

Delinquent behaviour was measured using a self-reported delinquency scale consisting of 14 items related to criminal offences (criminal damage, property, violence, and drug offences) during the last 12 months, and open frequency answers were recoded into ordinal categories. Finally, *deviant attitudes* were measured by a scale using four items as 'sometimes it is OK to act illegally as long as one is not caught' (Cronbach's alpha=0.62 in Germany, 0.68 in France).

Neighbourhood-level data

The residential locations of respondents were geocoded by looking up the ID numbers of small administrative units in address directories, which in Germany was restricted to those living within the city limits of Cologne and Mannheim. This procedure yielded valid information about neighbourhood locations for 87 per cent of all respondents in Cologne, 83 per cent in Mannheim, and 92 per cent in both Lyon and Grenoble.[6] For multilevel regression analyses, we excluded neighbourhoods with less than ten respondents, which led to a loss of 16 per cent of respondents in Cologne and Lyon, 10 per cent in Grenoble, and 4 per cent in Mannheim.

We use official data from the French National Statistical Office (INSEE) and from the city statistical offices in Cologne and Mannheim to measure neighbourhood socio-economic conditions. 'Social disadvantage' is a factor score combining the rate of unemployment with the percentage of immigrants, computed separately for the two countries (see Table 4.A3, appendix).[7] We use the geometric distance to the city centre, the percentage of residents living at the same address for five years or longer, and (in France only) the percentage of social housing (HLM or Habitation à Loyer Modéré) as additional indicators of neighbourhood structure (see Table 4.A3, appendix).

Frequency and disproportionality of police controls

Police-initiated contact is a common experience for many urban, especially male adolescents. A quarter of boys in Lyon and Grenoble, and almost 30 per cent of boys in Cologne and Manheim reported a police-initiated contact in the year before the interview (see Tables 4.2a and 4.2b). Girls were much less likely to experience police controls (10 per cent in French and 17 per cent in German cities). The descriptive results also showed a pronounced difference in the

Table 4.2a Prevalence and incidence of discretionary police controls by migration background, French cities

Countries of origin	N =	Prevalence		By frequency of contacts (boys only)		
		Boys	*Girls*	*1–2 times*	*3–5 times*	*6+ times*
Native	6,799	20.0	8.6	11.8	3.6	4.7
Europe	801	26.6	8.3	13.7	5.0	7.8
Algeria	1,308	42.0	14.2	15.6	8.3	18.1
Other Maghreb/Mid-East	577	30.2	10.9	8.3	7.4	14.5
Mixed native-Maghreb	979	30.4	13.1	14.5	5.6	10.3
Turkey	229	29.1	9.3	7.7	10.3	11.1
Sub-Saharan Africa	455	28.8	9.1	18.0	3.4	7.3
Rest of world	725	25.9	12.2	11.6	3.8	10.5
Mixed native-other	1,572	25.6	12.2	12.5	5.0	8.1
Total	13,445	24.9	10.3	12.9	5.3	4.1

Notes
Lyon and Grenoble, *n*=13,445, missing cases 1,976 (7.9%).

Table 4.2b Prevalence and incidence of discretionary police controls by migration background, German cities

Countries of origin	N =	Prevalence		By frequency of contacts (boys only)		
		Boys	*Girls*	*1–2 times*	*3–5 times*	*6+ times*
Native	3,381	29.3	19.0	19.3	5.9	4.1
West/South Europe	194	28.7	10.0	17.0	8.5	3.2
Poland	195	20.8	16.9	11.3	3.8	5.7
Ex-Soviet Union	219	29.0	17.9	19.6	4.7	4.7
Other East Europe	216	20.6	16.0	7.2	9.3	4.1
Turkey	1,290	27.5	10.4	18.1	5.3	4.2
Mixed native-Turkey	126	32.7	11.7	14.3	4.1	14.3
Maghreb/Mid-East	247	28.4	16.0	14.7	6.9	6.9
Sub-Saharan Africa	68	35.7	10.0	21.4	14.3	–
Rest of world	254	29.1	16.5	15.0	7.1	7.1
Mixed native-other	681	33.9	20.9	22.8	7.3	3.8
Total	6,871	28.9	16.8	18.4	6.1	4.4

Notes
Cologne and Mannheim, *n*=6,928, 77 missing cases (1.1%).

prevalence rates between native and migrant adolescents in France: 20 per cent of native boys and 25 per cent to 42 per cent of migrant boys reported a police-initiated contact, with boys of Algerian descent clearly on the top. Boys of non-Algerian Maghrebian, Turkish, and Sub-Saharan African descents all had shares of around 30 per cent, and migrant boys of European origins reported more contacts than native French boys, too. In contrast, boys in Cologne and Mannheim from Turkish and Maghrebian/Mid-Eastern backgrounds (27.5 per cent and 28.4 per cent, respectively) did not report any more police contact than native boys (29.3 per cent). Only boys of Sub-Saharan African descent reported slightly more contact (35.7 per cent). For migrant girls, the likelihood of police contact was in fact considerably *lower* than for native girls. Thus, at first glance, the survey results suggest a targeting of minority adolescents by the police in French but not German cities.

To capture the experience of repeated police contact, we focused on adolescent boys, as they were much more likely to be stopped by police officers than girls (see Tables 4.2a and 4.2b). Participant observations conducted as part of the POLIS project showed that officers often knowingly perform identity checks on the same adolescents several times (Hunold *et al.* 2016; de Maillard *et al.* 2016a). Within the highest frequency category (five or more police encounters), native French boys reported the lowest rates of repeated contact (*c.*5 per cent) and boys of Algerian descent the highest (18 per cent), followed by boys of other Maghrebian and Mid-Eastern origins (*c.*15 per cent). By comparison, only 2.5 per cent of girls of Algerian or other Maghrebian origin reported five or more police-initiated contacts. Again, in Germany there were no pronounced differences in repeated police contact between native boys (4.1 per cent) and those of Turkish (4.2 per cent) and Maghrebian/Mid-Eastern (6.9 per cent) descent, except for a small group from mixed native-Turkish families (14.3 per cent) and an even smaller group of boys of Sub-Saharan African origin (14.3 per cent in the category '3–5 times').

Multivariate analyses

In order to isolate the relevance of ethnicity in the frequency of police-initated contact, we must rule out other possible influences that could explain the increased likelihood of police contact as the 'availability' in public spaces (Quinton 2015). It is possible that individual socio-economic status, routine activities, deviant behaviour, and neighbourhood context could all influence the likelihood of police contact, over and above any effect of minority status (Svensson and Saharso 2015). In order to test these effects, we ran a series of multilevel regression models to include individual- and neighbourhood-level predictors. Because the dependent variable was a highly skewed and over-dispersed count variable, we used a negative binomial regression analysis and report incidence rate ratios (IRR), which are the factor by which the predicted number of police contacts in- or decreases. While the full model results are documented in the appendix (see Tables 4.A4a and 4.A4b), we focus here on the most relevant effects supported by graphs of the predicted IRRs. A first series of models analysed the frequency of police-initiated contacts for boys separately by country. In the first models for France (see Figure 4.1 and Table 4.A4a, appendix, models 1) and Germany (see Figure 4.1 and Table 4.A4b, appendix, models 1), only ethnicity and a control variable for city were included as independent variables to look at ethnic differences *before* controlling for other relevant effects. The point estimates and 95 per cent confidence intervals for model 1 (see Figure 4.1) show that in France, all except one ethnic minority groups had IRRs significantly above 1 which means that the predicted number of police contact was higher than for the reference group, native French boys. Boys of Algerian descent lead the rank order with 4.7 times more police-initiated contacts than native French boys, followed by boys of other Maghrebian descent with 3.4 times more contacts. Contrary to expectations, only boys from Sub-Saharan African families did not report more police contact. Results for Germany are very different, with *no* ethnic minority group showing any significant difference in police-initiated contact than native Germans.

Model 2 includes more independent variables representing socio-demographic and behavioural risk factors that could increase adolescents' visibility for police officers. As the model results show (see Figure 4.1 and Tables 4.A4a and 4.A4b, appendix, models 2), few socio-demographic variables, but all of the behavioural predictors had significant and often extremely strong effects on the likelihood of

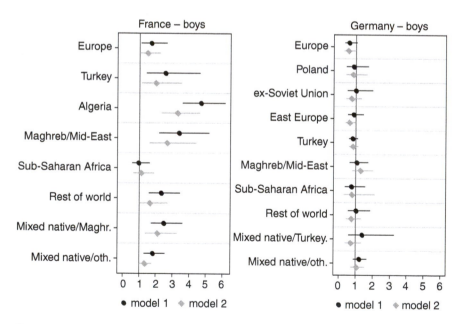

Figure 4.1 Proactive police contacts of boys by ethnicity (predicted IRRs compared to majority group).

Notes
IRR: Incidence rate ratios; predicted from models in tables 4.A4a and 4.A4b, appendix.

police contact – especially for those boys who reported meeting frequently with friends, spending a lot of time on the streets, getting drunk often, and committing delinquent acts. This was true for both French and German cities. From this, one might conclude that the police in both countries clearly target 'the right people,' i.e. male adolescents with delinquent inclinations and a high exposure to potentially risky situations in urban spaces at late hours. In this sense, police-initiated contact conforms to principles established by citizen rights agencies (European Union Fundamental Rights Agency 2010b).

Controlling for socio-demographic characteristics and risky behaviour in Model 2, however, hardly reduced the higher likelihoods of police-initiated contact for ethnic minority boys in France (see Figure 4.1 and Tables 4.A4a and 4.A4b, appendix, models 2). In fact, the inclusion of these predictors rendered ethnicity insignificant only for three categories (Europe, Rest of World, mixed native/other), whereas all other ethnic groups were still significantly more likely to be subjected to contact. Boys of Algerian descent were still 3.3 times more likely to experience police-initiated contact than native French boys, and boys from other Maghrebian backgrounds were 2.7 times more likely. Thus, empirical evidence supports the suspicion that French police in Lyon and Grenoble disproportionately stop ethnic minority male adolescents, in particular of Maghrebian descent, and of Algerian descent more than any other group.

Multilevel analyses also give insights into possible (residential) neighbourhood-level influence on the frequency of police-initiated contacts. The city variable revealed no differences in frequencies between the German cities of Cologne and Mannheim, but in France, there were 25 per cent more police-initiated contacts in Lyon than in Grenoble. Concentrated neighbourhood disadvantage increased the incidence of police contact in Lyon, but not in Grenoble, nor in the two German cities. Controlling for all individual factors represented in the regression model, residing in a neighbourhood with very high concentrations of unemployed and minority residents compared to a neighbourhood with very low levels of disadvantage additionally increased the incidence of contact roughly by factor two. Alternatively, the same effect size was found in Lyon but not in Grenoble for the percentage of social housing (Habitation à Loyer Modéré), which is highly correlated with concentrated disadvantage ($r=0.85$ in Lyon). We did not find any significant neighbourhood-level effects of geographic centrality or residential stability in any of the four cities.

Police behaviour during stops and the quality of interactions

In order to understand more about the actual experience of police-initiated stops and about the *quality* of these interactions, we asked follow-up questions about the most recent police encounter. Actual checks of identity were less frequent in France (around 60 per cent of native French, and close to 70 per cent of ethnic minorities; see Table 4.3a) than they were in Germany (*c*.80 per cent with no differences between ethnic origins; see Table 4.3b). But bag controls – ostensibly in search for illegal drugs – were more frequent in France (50 per cent of

Table 4.3a Details of police and adolescent behaviour during last discretionary police contact, French cities (% agreement)

Countries of origin	N =	Bag control	Identity check	'Police explained reasons'	'Police became violent'	'I (we) resisted the police'
Native	876	50.3	58.4	53.6	12.5	15.9
Europe	116	66.4	70.7	49.1	23.2	21.8
Algeria	301	67.1	66.8	43.8	36.2	33.8
Other Maghreb/Mid-East	95	67.7	69.9	44.3	40.0	28.1
Sub-Saharan Africa	69	65.2	62.3	56.1	21.7	21.2
Rest of world	121	66.4	66.4	41.0	27.8	31.9
Mixed native-Maghreb	181	60.0	58.9	44.6	23.9	29.9
Mixed native-other	267	56.2	58.5	48.1	20.2	22.1

Table 4.3b Details of police and adolescent behaviour during last discretionary police contact, German cities (% agreement)

Countries of origin	N =	Bag control	Identity check	'Police explained reasons'	'Police became violent'	'I (we) resisted the police'
Native	336	36.9	77.8	66.6	3.9	4.7
Europe	61	50.0	75.0	68.9	6.6	5.1
Turkey	92	48.7	78.4	57.5	5.6	4.4
Maghreb/Mid-East	19	53.3	80.0	47.4	5.3	5.6
Mixed native-other	71	50.0	87.0	49.3	7.3	11.6

native French, 66 per cent for most ethnic minorities) than in Germany (37 per cent of native Germans, 50 per cent of most ethnic minorities). Concerning checks and searches, police officers in both France and Germany tended to treat minority adolescents as more suspicious than native adolescents.

The officers' demeanour and the 'atmosphere' of the social interaction was captured by questions about positive and negative aspects of behaviour. Following procedural justice theory, explaining the reasons for actions and executing actions in a polite and respectful manner are key elements of building public trust and legitimacy (President's Task Force 2015). However, in France, only about half of native and other European adolescents, and only 44 per cent of Algerian and other Maghrebian and Middle East adolescents, reported a belief that police officers had 'honestly explained the reasons for their actions'. In Germany, the share of native and other European adolescents reporting this belief was higher, with c.66 per cent, but as in France, adolescents of Turkish and Maghrebian or Middle East descent judged the officers' transparency considerably less positive (58 per cent and 47 per cent, respectively).

Evidence pertaining to the escalation of conflict and the police use of force was captured by asking respondents whether police officers 'became violent' and whether they 'had resisted police'. Both indicators were very rare in Germany for all ethnic groups, with only about 4 to 6 per cent of both native German and minority adolescents claiming to have experienced this. In France, 12.5 per cent of native French adolescents reported that the police officers became violent, and 16 per cent reported that they had resisted the police. Among adolescents of Algerian and other Maghrebian or Middle Eastern descent, the figures were almost three times higher for police officers becoming violent, and nearly double for claiming to have resisted police. Thus, around a third of police stops of adolescents with Algerian and other Maghrebian backgrounds resulted in a violent confrontation, compared to only one in 20 such cases for Turkish adolescents in Germany. This contrast marks a striking degree of failure of the French police in establishing positive or at least neutral relations with many minority adolescents.

The impact of police-initiated contact on trust in police

Using a broad definition of police trust, we attempt to assess the effects of police-initiated contact on adolescents' attitudes towards the police. A great deal of scholarly research has been devoted to understanding experiences with police and their perceptions, starting with Bayley and Mendelsohn (1969). Direct experience of police-initiated contact has usually been found to be a major source of strain in individuals' attitudes towards the police (Bradford *et al.* 2009; Li *et al.* 2016). Testing this hypothesis with the POLIS survey data faced many conceptual and methodological difficulties. First, and importantly, cross-sectional data does not allow for a causal interpretation of effects and creates concern about possible endogeneity between police actions and adolescents' attitudes. Second, the negative consequences of police practices are not limited to the people subjected to a police contact, but extend vicariously to others around them, in particular to fellow group members who will identify more strongly with grievances against the police. Bearing in mind these caveats, we interpret the following results of our analyses with caution.

Police trust among ethnic minority adolescents

In the POLIS survey, police trust was generally higher among adolescents in the two German than in the two French cities. For example, the general statement '[o]verall, the police can be trusted' was supported by 74 per cent of respondents in Germany but only by 58 per cent of respondents in France. Whereas 57 per cent of French respondents and only 31 per cent of German respondents agreed with the statement, '[t]he police treat foreigners worse than French [resp. Germans]'. The scale 'police trust' consisting of these and five other items ranges from 1 (completely disagree to all items on police trust) to of 4 (completely agree to all items on police trust). The overall mean of police trust in France was 2.7 – only just above the 2.5 midpoint of the scale – and 0.4 scale-points lower than the mean score in Germany (3.1). Differentiated by sex and ethnicity and controlling for socio-demographic influences, Figure 4.2 shows that girls generally reported higher police trust than boys in both countries and

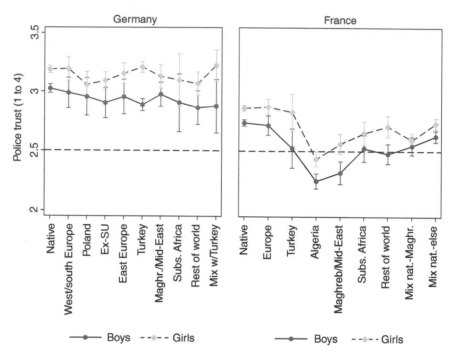

Figure 4.2 Police trust by ethnicity and sex.

Notes

Predicted values controlling for age, family composition, parental educational status, parental unemployment/welfare dependence, city, and neighborhood concentrated disadvantage.

across all ethnic groups. Many ethnic minority groups in France showed significantly lower police trust than the French majority, and particularly adolescents from Algerian and other Maghrebian or Middle East backgrounds reported much lower trust, even compared to adolescents from sub-Saharan African, Turkish or other non-European backgrounds. The trust gap between native French adolescents and those from Algerian backgrounds, controlling for other socio-demographic influences, was almost 0.5 points on the scale from 1 to 4. Boys from all ethnic minorities except other European countries or mixed-ethnicity families scored below 2.5 in France, indicating a pervasive negative attitude to the police.

Results from multilevel models also showed considerable neighbourhood effects on police trust in Lyon and Grenoble, with 8 per cent of the variation in police trust between neighbourhoods (see Table 4.A5a, appendix). More than half of this neighbourhood-level variation could be accounted for by the ethnic composition of respondents, but beyond the effects of individual minority status, neighbourhood concentrated disadvantage reduced police trust further. In Lyon, adolescents residing in disadvantaged neighbourhoods reported significantly lower police trust, even after controlling for all individual differences, including the experiences of police-initiated stops. The findings from the two French cities support previous studies from the USA (Schuck *et al.* 2008; Stewart *et al.* 2009; Weitzer 1999; Wu *et al.* 2009).

Not only was police trust generally higher among adolescents in Germany, but also the trust gap between native Germans and ethnic minorities was much smaller, with only about 0.1 scale-point difference for individuals from ex-Soviet Union countries and other non-European backgrounds. All ethnic minority groups were well above the scale midpoint, indicating a relatively positive attitude towards the police.

Boys from Turkish and mixed German-Turkish families scored only about 0.1 scale-points lower than native German boys, but girls from these backgrounds even reported slightly *higher* police trust than native German girls. Ethnicity explained only 1 per cent of the variation in police trust in Germany, in contrast to 9 per cent in France. Also compared to France, we did not find significant differences in police trust between neighbourhoods in Germany. The intraclass correlation coefficient of neighbourhood-level variance was less than 1 per cent, and concentrated disadvantage did not add significantly to the explanation of police trust (see Table 4.A5b, appendix).

The effects of police-initiated contacts on police trust

To what extent does the experience of police-initiated contact diminish police trust? In order to isolate this specific effect, we ran multilevel regression models with extensive control variables, including not only socio-demographic influences and neighbourhood concentrated disadvantage, but also behavioural predictors which proved significant in the previous models for police-initiated contact, as well as self-initiated and victim-/witness-related police contacts and deviant attitudes. Figures 4.3a shows the levels of trust among boys and Figure 4.3b among girls by number of contacts. We narrow our scope to include native adolescents and the largest and most relevant ethnic minority group in each respective country –Turkish descendants in Germany, Maghrebian (including Algerian) and Middle Eastern descendants in France. The full model results are documented in the appendix (see Tables 4.A5a and 4.A5b). The predictions plotted in Figures 4.3a and 4.3b differ from these models in an additional interaction effect between police controls and ethnicity.

The model results for France indicate that both boys and girls experience a decline in police trust as the frequency of police-initiated contact increases, amounting to about 0.4 scale-points. The decline was steeper for Maghrebian boys who had experienced between six and ten police stops; but for Maghrebian girls, there was a slight unexpected increase in trust for those with more than ten police contacts. However, due to the small sample size, this effect was not significant.

In Germany, there seemed to be a nonlinear decrease in police trust by boys only after the initial contact, and amounting to $c.0.3$ scale-points. As in France,

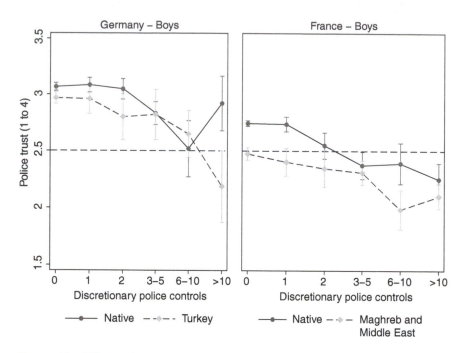

Figure 4.3a Effects of proactive police contacts on police trust of boys, French and German cities.

Notes
Estimates predicted from models in tables 4.A5a and 4.A5b, appendix.

these effects were highly significant. In Germany, the effects of police contact for girls' trust in police were less pronounced and barely significant, partly due to the scarcity of repeated police contacts for girls.

It is interesting to note that self-initiated and victim-/witness-related police contact were *not* associated with decreased police trust in either countries, indicating the divergent effect of different kinds of police contact. In fact, boys in France with multiple self-initiated contacts even showed significantly higher levels of police trust.

Conclusion

The survey findings from two French and two German cities contribute to a large body of research on the relationship between the police and adolescents, particularly from ethnic minorities, and advance our knowledge by contrasting strikingly diverging accounts from two neighbouring countries. Police-initiated contact is a common experience for many adolescents in France and Germany, yet while police in the two German cities appear to maintain equal treatment of ethnic groups, the practice of stop and search by French police is clearly biased

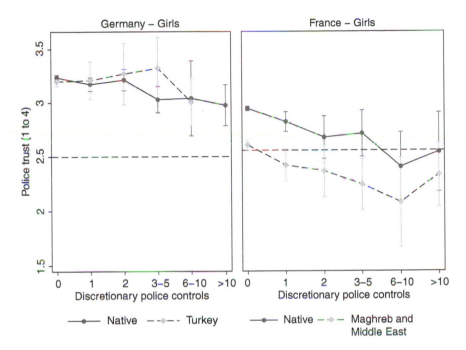

Figure 4.3b Effects of proactive police contacts on police trust of girls, French and German cities.

Notes
Estimates predicted from models in tables 4.A5a and 4.A5b, appendix.

against minority adolescents generally, and grossly disproportionate to the largest minority group – Maghrebians – in particular. This ethnic group faces double discrimination in Lyon where the police also stop adolescents residing in disadvantaged neighbourhoods more frequently. The frequency of police contact was not only captured by the number of adolescents stopped, but also by of the incidences of repeated contact for these individuals. France and Germany diverged drastically not only in the frequencies of police-initiated contact, but also in the quality of those interactions: In Germany, only about one in 20 adolescents of Turkish descent reported contact that escalated into confrontation, whereas in France, one in three Maghrebian adolescents reported such experiences. Additionally, adolescents from all ethnic groups reported much higher satisfaction with police in Germany.

This picture is supported by the results of participant observations undertaken as part of the POLIS project. These observations add detail and context to otherwise standardized data, and are independent of the respondents' subjective views. Police-initiated contacts in Lyon and Grenoble frequently happened in a tense or hostile atmosphere, whereas in Cologne and Mannheim, officers actively worked for an informal and relaxed atmosphere. Some French police officers viewed stop and search primarily as a crime fighting tool and consciously targeted minority adolescents for a better 'hit rate', assuming that they were more delinquent. German police officers, on the other hand, – especially those engaged in 'community policing' work – more frequently and successfully used proactive contacts as a longer-term strategy to establish positive communication with adolescents (Hunold *et al.* 2016; de Maillard *et al.* 2016b; cf. also Gauthier 2012, and for the Netherlands van Steden and Broekhuizen 2015). This may be in part the result of the professionalization of training for German police officers, which includes a curriculum focused on public and cross-cultural relations. In France, however, organizational and political issues resulting from the administrative centralization of police forces has resulted in a side-lining of citizens' expectations as other issues take priority. We only touch here on some of the differences accounting for the divergent beliefs about policing in these two countries and more should be addressed in future research.

The vast difference in police-adolescents relationships in these two countries correspond with the different levels of trust by adolescents in France and Germany. There is a much smaller trust gap between majority and minority groups in Germany and there are virtually no neighbourhood-level differences in trust. This seems to support procedural and distributive justice theories, or the idea that trust and legitimacy are granted by citizens as a reward for fair police behaviour. The low levels of trust in France raise questions about the consequences of aggressive policing styles and their consequences in urban areas of concentrated disadvantage.

The implications of our comparative findings offer practitioners and politicians a basis by which to improve police–citizen relations. Considerate and community-oriented policing appears to have a beneficial impact on police–public relations. Yet, we do not claim to have proven a causal relationship. The statistical association between police-initiated contact and attitudes towards the police was weaker than procedural and distributive justice theories alone would predict. Although multiple police contacts were linked to lower trust in the police in both countries, this predictor was far from being the only significant effect in multivariate models. Strong ethnic and neighbourhood differences in police trust still persisted in France to a much larger extent than in Germany. If aggressive stop and search tactics strains police–adolescents relations, these are likely to have an effect not only on the individual level but to extend collectively through peer and community networks. In addition, police–citizen interactions do not take place in a vacuum but are embedded in complex social and political cleavages in which group identities play a role (Bradford *et al.* 2014: chapter 20; see also Roché *et al.* in this volume). In this respect, the formation of 'banlieues' in French cities as places of concentrated disadvantage with a specific subculture adds to the forces which make police work more adversarial, and echoes the difficulty of achieving social cohesion and the integration of minorities.

Appendix

Table 4.A1 Descriptive statistics of scale 'police trust'

	France			Germany		
	Mean	Std. dev.	Item-total-corr.	Mean	Std. dev.	Item-total-corr.
The police protect adolescents.	2.44	0.89	0.61	2.75	0.82	0.56
The police disrespect adolescents. (r)	2.72	0.95	0.65	2.77	0.93	0.56
Overall the police can be trusted.	2.54	0.96	0.65	2.99	0.89	0.62
One should in any case follow the instructions of the police.	2.73	0.93	0.52	3.35	0.75	0.54
Even if having a serious problem, I would never contact the police. (r)	2.84	1.00	0.38	2.88	0.97	0.39
If adolescents protest violently and with riots against the police, I would join them. (r)	3.34	0.92	0.51	3.67	0.71	0.48
The police treat foreigners worse than French/Germans. (r)	2.41	0.99	0.50	2.91	0.99	0.47
Cronbach's Alpha			*0.81*			*0.79*

Note
(r) – reversed item.

Table 4.A2 Descriptive statistics of categorial independent variables

	France	Germany		France	Germany
	%	%		%	%
Sex			*Has been drunken*		
Male	51.0	48.1	Never	74.8	70.0
Female	49.0	51.9	1–2 times	7.7	11.6
Family setting			3–5 times	8.4	10.9
Complete	73.5	66.5	6+ times	9.0	7.5
Incomplete	26.5	33.5	*Delinquency last year*		
Parents' education			Never	59.1	69.4
Up to ISCED-3	53.1	76.3	1–2 times	16.6	13.9
Higher	46.9	23.7	3–5 times	7.1	6.3
			6+ times	17.2	10.5
Parents' unemployed/welfare					
No	72.3	74.4	*Discretionary police controls*		
Yes	17.7	18.3	Never	82.3	76.6
Unclear	9.9	7.3	Once	7.0	11.7
			Twice	2.8	4.4
Nights out with friends			3–5 times	3.1	4.5
None	21.8	18.0	6–10 times	1.8	1.6
Once	21.3	29.8	>10 times	3.0	1.3
Twice	23.5	26.3	*Self-initiated/victim-, witness-related police*		
3–4 times	17.3	17.1	*contacts*		
5+ times	16.2	8.8	Never	70.8	69.9
Spends time on streets			Once	16.1	16.7
Never	32.0	11.8	Twice	6.0	6.7
Rarely	28.7	30.6	3–5 times	5.2	5.1
Often	25.2	31.4	6–10 times	1.3	1.5
Very often	14.1	26.2	>10 times	0.7	1.0

Table 4.A3 Descriptive statistics of continuous independent variables

		Mean	Std. dev.	Min.	Max.
Respondent level					
Age	France	15.0	1.4	12	18
	Germany	14.5	1.1	12	18
Deviant attitudes	France	2.0	0.7	1	4
	Germany	2.0	0.6	1	4
Police trust	France	2.7	0.7	1	4
	Germany	3.1	0.6	1	4
Neighborhood level					
Social disadvantage score	France	0	1	−1.6	3.6
	Germany	0	1	−1.5	3.5
% social housing (HLM)	France	21.7	24.6	0	98.8
	Germany	–	–	–	–
% resident for 5+ years	France	34.3	11.1	0	100
	Germany	32.0	15.8	5.5	99.6
Geometric distance from centre (km)	France	13.7	15.6	0.2	83.6
	Germany	5.8	3.2	0.0	16.6

Table 4.A4a Multilevel nonlinear regression models explaining the incidence of discretionary police controls for boys, French cities

	Model 1		Model 2	
	IRR	CI (95%)	IRR	CI (95%)
L1 – Respondents				
Ethnic background (ref.: native)[a]				
Europe	1.69*	[1.08,2.65]	1.47	[0.96,2.24]
Turkey	2.55**	[1.40,4.63]	1.98*	[1.12,3.51]
Algeria	4.68***	[3.56,6.16]	3.28***	[2.32,4.63]
Other Maghreb/Mid-East	3.37***	[2.19,5.18]	2.66***	[1.60,4.41]
Sub-Saharan Africa	0.95	[0.55,1.62]	1.10	[0.64,1.89]
Rest of world	2.32***	[1.57,3.43]	1.62	[0.98,2.70]
Mixed native/Maghreb	2.48***	[1.70,3.60]	2.10***	[1.35,3.25]
Mixed native/other	1.80***	[1.28,2.54]	1.31	[0.99,1.74]
Age[b]			1.55***	[1.39,1.72]
Family setting incomplete			1.22	[0.99,1.52]
Parent. education high			0.82	[0.66,1.02]
Parental unemployed/welfare (ref.: no)			1	
Yes			1.21	[0.95,1.55]
Unclear			1.74**	[1.17,2.59]
Nights out with friends (ref.: no)			1	1
Once			0.93	[0.62,1.39]
Twice			1.25	[0.86,1.81]
3–4 times			1.96***	[1.35,2.83]
5+ times			2.49***	[1.73,3.58]
Spends time on streets (ref.: no)			1	[1,1]
Rarely			1.48*	[1.08,2.03]
Often			2.18***	[1.64,2.91]
Very often			3.93***	[2.80,5.50]
Has been drunken (ref.: no)			1	[1,1]
1–2 times			1.50*	[1.05,2.15]
3–5 times			1.15	[0.82,1.60]
6+ times			2.12***	[1.50,2.98]
Delinquency last year (ref.: no)			1	[1,1]
1–2 times			2.25***	[1.66,3.05]
3–5 times			3.97***	[2.87,5.50]
6+ times			7.37***	[5.62,9.66]
L2 – Neighbourhoods				
City: Grenoble (ref.: Lyon)	0.75*	[0.59,0.95]	0.61***	[0.50,0.75]
Social disadvantage[b]			1.21**	[1.06,1.38]
Social disadv. X city: Grenoble			0.81*	[0.67,0.99]

Table 4.A4a Continued

	Model 1		Model 2	
	IRR	*CI (95%)*	*IRR*	*CI (95%)*
Constant	0.93	[0.76,1.13]	–2.60	[–3.07,–2.13]
Variance components				
Respondent-level	2.26	[2,17,2.35]	1.47	[1.36,1.57]
Neighborhood-level	0.32	[0.17,0.63]	0.42	[0.29,0.60]
N respondents/neighbourhoods	5,133/464		5,078/464	
AIC	11,836.0		10,537.4	

Notes

IRR: Incidence Rate Ratio (exponentiated coefficients); 95% confidence intervals in brackets.
Neighbourhoods with <10 respondents excluded.

* $p<0.05$;
** $p<0.01$;
*** $p<0.001$.

a missing category included but not reported.
b standardized (mean=0, sd=1).

Table 4.A4b Multilevel nonlinear regression model explaining the incidence of discretionary police controls for boys, German cities

	Model 1		Model 2	
	IRR	CI (95%)	IRR	CI (95%)
L1 – Respondents				
Ethnic background (ref.: native)[a]				
West/South Europe	0.59	[0.33,1.05]	0.54	[0.29,1.01]
Poland	0.86	[0.43,1.73]	0.83	[0.41,1.67]
Ex-Soviet Union	0.99	[0.49,1.98]	0.74	[0.41,1.32]
Other East Europe	0.87	[0.52,1.45]	0.61	[0.37,1.03]
Turkey	0.81	[0.59,1.11]	0.82	[0.60,1.13]
Other Maghreb/Mid-East	1.05	[0.64,1.73]	1.27	[0.80,2.02]
Sub-Saharan Africa	0.74	[0.35,1.55]	0.77	[0.28,2.10]
Rest of world	1.01	[0.55,1.85]	0.74	[0.41,1.31]
Mixed native/Turkey	1.36	[0.57,3.25]	0.70	[0.37,1.32]
Mixed native/other	1.19	[0.86,1.65]	1.04	[0.71,1.52]
Age[b]			1.05	[0.94,1.16]
Family setting incomplete			1.00	[0.79,1.28]
Parent. education high			1.33*	[1.02,1.73]
Parental unemployed/welfare (ref.: no)				
Yes			0.81	[0.62,1.05]
Unclear			0.86	[0.55,1.36]
Time back during weekdays (ref.: before 8 pm)[a]			1	[1,1]
8 p.m.			1.12	[0.73,1.71]
9 p.m.			1.17	[0.75,1.83]
10 p.m.			1.48	[0.96,2.26]
After 10 p.m.			1.61*	[1.03,2.51]
Spends time on streets (ref.: never)[a]			1	[1,1]
Rarely			1.91**	[1.27,2.88]
Often			2.58***	[1.82,3.66]
Very often			3.33***	[2.22,4.99]
Has been drunken (ref.: never)[a]			1	[1,1]
1–2 times			2.09***	[1.48,2.95]
3–5 times			2.10***	[1.54,2.87]
6+ times			2.68***	[1.77,4.06]
Delinquency last year (ref.: none)[a]			1	[1,1]
1–2 times			1.47**	[1.12,1.92]
3–5 times			2.20***	[1.50,3.23]
6+ times			2.44***	[1.70,3.50]

Table 4.A4b Continued

	Model 1		Model 2	
	IRR	CI (95%)	IRR	CI (95%)
L2 – Neighbourhoods				
City: Mannheim (ref.: Cologne)	1.02	[0.80,1.29]	1.07	[0.79,1.46]
Social disadvantage[b]			1.03	[0.88,1.20]
Social disadv. X city: Mannheim			1.14	[0.84,1.56]
Constant	1.00	[0.81,1.23]	0.15	[0.09,0.24]
Variance components				
Respondent-level	1.69	[1.56,1.81]	1.26	[1.12,1.40]
Neighborhood-level	0.09	[0.24,0.32]	0.19	[0.09,0.39]
N	2,540/158		2,509/158	
AIC	6,025.2		5,643.2	

Notes
IRR: Incidence Rate Ratio (exponentiated coefficients); 95% confidence intervals in brackets
Neighbourhoods with < 10 respondents excluded.
* $p<0.05$;
** $p<0.01$;
*** $p<0.001$.
a missing category included but not reported.
b standardized (mean=0, sd=1).

Table 4.A5a Multilevel linear regression models explaining trust in the police, French cities

	Boys		Girls	
	B	CI (95%)	B	CI (95%)
L1 – Respondents				
Ethnic background (ref.: native)[a]				
Europe	0.022	[–0.048,0.091]	0.0085	[–0.050,0.067]
Turkey	–0.12	[–0.25,0.012]	–0.021	[–0.15,0.11]
Algeria	–0.26***	[–0.31,–0.20]	–0.34***	[–0.40,–0.28]
Other Maghreb/Mid-East	–0.27***	[–0.35,–0.20]	–0.29***	[–0.36,–0.22]
Sub-Saharan Africa	–0.28***	[–0.38,–0.19]	–0.25***	[–0.33,–0.16]
Rest of world	–0.17***	[–0.24,–0.098]	–0.13***	[–0.20,–0.052]
Mixed native/Maghreb	–0.10**	[–0.17,–0.041]	–0.18***	[–0.23,–0.13]
Mixed native/other	–0.032	[–0.076,0.012]	–0.053*	[–0.094,–0.011]
Age[b]	–0.035***	[–0.051,–0.019]	–0.064***	[–0.080,–0.049]
Family setting incomplete	–0.046*	[–0.081,–0.011]	–0.040**	[–0.069,–0.010]
Parent. education high	0.021	[–0.013,0.055]	0.021	[–0.0089,0.050]
Parental unemployed/welfare (ref.: no)				
Yes	–0.039	[–0.078,0.0011]	–0.043*	[–0.079,–0.0061]
Unclear	–0.042	[–0.096,0.012]	–0.014	[–0.069,0.042]
Nights out with friends (ref.: none)[a]				
Once	–0.012	[–0.058,0.034]	–0.011	[–0.049,0.026]
Twice	–0.050*	[–0.096,–0.0044]	–0.058**	[–0.098,–0.017]
3–4 times	–0.070**	[–0.12,–0.023]	–0.054*	[–0.099,–0.0089]
5+ times	–0.11***	[–0.17,–0.058]	–0.079**	[–0.13,–0.025]
Spends time on streets (ref.: never)[a]				
Rarely	–0.033	[–0.073,0.0068]	–0.032	[–0.067,0.0034]
Often	–0.056**	[–0.097,–0.014]	–0.067***	[–0.11,–0.028]
Very often	–0.13***	[–0.19,–0.074]	–0.15***	[–0.20,–0.092]
Has been drunken (ref.: never)[a]				
1–2 times	–0.0057	[–0.064,0.053]	–0.036	[–0.087,0.015]
3–5 times	0.040	[–0.020,0.100]	0.0091	[–0.049,0.067]
6+ times	0.055	[–0.010,0.12]	0.037	[–0.034,0.11]
Delinquency last year (ref.: none)[a]				
1–2 times	–0.099***	[–0.14,–0.058]	–0.12***	[–0.16,–0.083]
3–5 times	–0.21***	[–0.28,–0.15]	–0.13***	[–0.19,–0.063]
6+ times	–0.27***	[–0.33,–0.22]	–0.19***	[–0.24,–0.13]
Deviant attitudes[b]	–0.29***	[–0.27,–0.31]	–0.29***	[–0.27,–0.31]
Discretionary police controls (ref.: none)				
Once	–0.046	[–0.098,0.0072]	–0.12***	[–0.18,–0.054]
Twice	–0.19***	[–0.27,–0.10]	–0.26***	[–0.39,–0.13]
3–5 times	–0.23***	[–0.31,–0.16]	–0.37***	[–0.47,–0.26]
6–10 times	–0.32***	[–0.42,–0.22]	–0.46***	[–0.65,–0.27]
>10 times	–0.42***	[–0.50,–0.34]	–0.35***	[–0.54,–0.16]

Table 4.A5a Continued

	Boys		Girls	
	B	CI (95%)	B	CI (95%)
Self-initiated/victim-/witness-related police contacts (ref.: none)				
Once	0.043*	[0.0033,0.082]	0.021	[−0.013,0.055]
Twice	0.054	[−0.0016,0.11]	0.0063	[−0.051,0.064]
3–5 times	0.089*	[0.013,0.16]	0.022	[−0.045,0.089]
6–10 times	0.078	[−0.029,0.18]	−0.032	[−0.17,0.11]
>10 times	0.24**	[0.076,0.41]	0.038	[−0.20,0.27]
L2 – Neighbourhoods				
City: Grenoble (ref.: Lyon)	0.0097	[−0.021,0.041]	0.0085	[−0.019,0.036]
Social disadvantage[b]	−0.041***	[−0.065,−0.018]	−0.057***	[−0.079,−0.035]
Social disadv. X city: Grenoble	0.015	[−0.017,0.048]	0.032*	[0.00018,0.065]
Constant	2.94***	[2.90,2.99]	2.91***	[2.87,2.95]
Variance components				
L1 – respondent	0.26***	[0.25,0.27]	0.23***	[0.22,0.24]
L2 – neighborhood	0.0016***	[0.00021,0.012]	0.0014***	[0.0002,0.0086]
ICC in empty model (%)		8.0		8.0
L1 var. reduction vs. empty model (%)		44.2		38.8
L2 var. reduction vs. empty model (%)		96.0		95.7
N respondents/ neighbourhoods		4,923/464		5,129/463

Notes
B unstandardized coefficient; 95% confidence intervals in brackets.
Neighbourhoods with <10 respondents excluded.
* $p<0.05$;
** $p<0.01$;
*** $p<0.001$.
a missing category included but not reported.
b standardized (mean=0, sd=1).

Table 4.A5b Multilevel linear regression models explaining trust in the police, German cities

	Boys		Girls	
	B	CI (95%)	B	CI (95%)
L1 – Respondents				
Ethnic background (ref.: native)[a]				
West/South Europe	0.0030	[–0.12,0.13]	–0.029	[–0.13,0.066]
Poland	–0.093	[–0.23,0.045]	–0.100	[–0.23,0.030]
Ex-Soviet Union	–0.058	[–0.15,0.033]	–0.053	[–0.15,0.046]
Other east Europe	–0.068	[–0.20,0.064]	–0.063	[–0.14,0.012]
Turkey	–0.090**	[–0.15,–0.030]	–0.023	[–0.073,0.028]
Other Maghreb/Mid-East	–0.054	[–0.17,0.064]	–0.082	[–0.18,0.017]
Sub-Saharan Africa	–0.30*	[–0.55,–0.054]	–0.17*	[–0.35,–0.0014]
Rest of world	–0.11	[–0.23,0.0072]	–0.13**	[–0.21,–0.042]
Mixed native/Turkey	0.014	[–0.12,0.15]	–0.037	[–0.14,0.068]
Mixed native/other	–0.050	[–0.12,0.021]	–0.074*	[–0.14,–0.013]
Age[b]	–0.031**	[–0.054,–0.0083]	–0.016	[–0.036,0.0032]
Family setting incomplete	–0.036	[–0.074,0.0022]	–0.033*	[–0.061,–0.0045]
Parent. education high	–0.045	[–0.096,0.0061]	–0.021	[–0.060,0.018]
Parental unemployed/welfare (ref.: no)				
Yes	–0.038	[–0.086,0.011]	–0.013	[–0.054,0.028]
Unclear	–0.047	[–0.12,0.026]	–0.10*	[–0.18,–0.021]
Time back during weekdays (ref.: before 8p.m.)[a]				
8 p.m.	–0.040	[–0.10,0.021]	0.0039	[–0.041,0.049]
9 p.m.	–0.056	[–0.12,0.0049]	–0.026	[–0.076,0.024]
10 p.m.	–0.11**	[–0.18,–0.041]	–0.048	[–0.11,0.012]
After 10 p.m.	–0.24***	[–0.34,–0.15]	–0.078	[–0.18,0.026]
Spends time on streets (ref.: never)[a]				
Rarely	0.018	[–0.051,0.087]	0.035	[–0.020,0.090]
Often	–0.012	[–0.087,0.062]	0.021	[–0.037,0.079]
Very often	–0.067	[–0.14,0.0091]	0.017	[–0.040,0.073]
Has been drunken (ref.: never)[a]				
1–2 times	–0.038	[–0.10,0.027]	–0.074**	[–0.13,–0.018]
3–5 times	–0.025	[–0.093,0.043]	–0.12**	[–0.19,–0.045]
6+ times	–0.22***	[–0.32,–0.12]	–0.18***	[–0.28,–0.085]
Delinquency last year (ref.: none)[a]				
1–2 times	–0.060**	[–0.11,–0.015]	–0.11***	[–0.17,–0.058]
3–5 times	–0.038	[–0.12,0.043]	–0.067	[–0.17,0.032]
6+ times	–0.21***	[–0.29,–0.12]	–0.23***	[–0.32,–0.13]
Deviant attitudes[b]	–0.27***	[–0.24,–0.29]	–0.25***	[–0.23,–0.27]
Discretionary police controls (ref.: none)				
Once	–0.048	[–0.11,0.018]	–0.022	[–0.075,0.032]
Twice	–0.053	[–0.14,0.033]	–0.023	[–0.11,0.061]
3–5 times	–0.21***	[–0.30,–0.11]	–0.21***	[–0.32,–0.11]
6–10 times	–0.35***	[–0.50,–0.19]	–0.19	[–0.40,0.013]
>10 times	–0.31**	[–0.54,–0.091]	–0.44*	[–0.78,–0.10]

Table 4.A5b Continued

	Boys		Girls	
	B	CI (95%)	B	CI (95%)
Self-initiated/victim-/witness-related police contacts (ref.: none)				
Once	0.014	[−0.040,0.068]	0.041	[−0.0031,0.085]
Twice	0.10**	[0.025,0.18]	0.025	[−0.041,0.091]
3–5 times	0.0046	[−0.085,0.094]	0.019	[−0.071,0.11]
6–10 times	−0.0089	[−0.17,0.16]	0.11	[−0.098,0.31]
>10 times	0.0085	[−0.26,0.27]	−0.50***	[−0.78,−0.21]
L2 – Neighbourhoods				
Mannheim (ref.: Cologne)	0.018	[−0.027,0.063]	−0.043*	[−0.077,−0.010]
Social disadvantage[b]	−0.0041	[−0.023,0.015]	−0.0017	[−0.026,0.023]
Social disadv. X Mannheim	−0.024	[−0.074,0.025]	−0.0043	[−0.047,0.039]
Constant	3.29***	[3.22,3.37]	3.25***	[3.18,3.31]
Variance components				
L1 – respondent	0.24***	[0.22,0.25]	0.17***	[0.16,0.18]
L2 – neighborhood	<0.001	[−,−]	0.00084***	[<0.001,0.012]
ICC in empty model (%)	0.3		0.9	
L1 var. reduction vs. empty model (%)	43.0		38.5	
L2 var. reduction vs. empty model (%)	99.0		67.2	
N respondents/ neighbourhoods	2,468/158		2,754/158	

Notes
B: unstandardized coefficient; 95% confidence intervals in brackets.
Neighbourhoods with < 10 respondents excluded.
* $p<0.05$;
** $p<0.01$;
*** $p<0.001$.
a missing category included but not reported.
b standardized (mean=0, sd=1).

Notes

1 The project has received joint funding from the national funding agencies *Agence nationale de la recherche* (ANR) and *Deutsche Forschungsgemeinschaft (*ANR-DFG Funding Programme for the Humanities and Social Sciences, Call 2008, grant reference: ANR-08-FASHS-19, Pacte research unit, Sciences Po, CNRS, University of Grenoble Alpes, and DFG AL 376–11/1, Max Planck Institute for Foreign and International Criminal Law, Freiburg).

2 According to the definition of the German Federal Statistical Office, a 'migration background' includes immigrants as well as their second- and third-generation descendants (Statistisches Bundesamt 2015). In Mannheim, 38 per cent of the total population and 55 per cent of the population under 18 years had a migration background in 2012 (Stadt Mannheim 2013). In Cologne, the shares were, respectively, 34 per cent and 48 per cent (Stadt Köln 2012). With the lack of official data on ethnicity in France, the

proportion of adolescents from migrant families is difficult to ascertain in Lyon and Grenoble.

3 Except schools for special needs in Germany; in France, only state schools and private schools under state contract.

4 Follow-up questions in the German questionnaire show that $c.12$ per cent of these contacts had taken place earlier than 12 months before the interview, suggesting a telescoping effect.

5 Our consideration of ethnic groups emerged from a mix of theoretical and pragmatic considerations. Ethnic groups of particular analytic interest were examined separately if they were large enough, or if not, as in the case of Sub-Saharan Africans in Germany and Turkish individuals in France, despite small numbers in order to enable a comparison between France and Germany. In cases where the sample of minority groups were small, the groups were combined to include a broader region of origin.

6 In Germany, 7 per cent of respondents were commuting from outside the city boundaries, 5 per cent refused to have their addresses geocoded, and 2 per cent gave invalid information. In France, where administrative city boundaries have not been expanded to include suburban areas around the historic cities, a much larger share of respondents lived outside the municipalities of Lyon and Grenoble. Nevertheless, neighbourhood (IRIS)-level geocodes were recorded for 75 per cent of respondents in Lyon and for 66 per cent of respondents in Grenoble, while the remaining respondents were assigned to smaller municipalities without neighbourhood subdivisions. The administrative units in most cases reflect geographically and historically shaped small areas with a mean population of $c.4,000$ in Germany and 2,500 in France.

7 In France, the official definition of immigrants is restricted to first-generation immigrants that grossly underestimates the share of minority populations, whereas in Germany the definition includes first- to third-generation immigrants. Reflecting the close association of social and ethnic segregation, the correlation between unemployment rate and percentage immigrants is $r=0.84$ in Lyon, 0.82 in Grenoble, 0.76 in Cologne, but only 0.49 in Mannheim where also the unemployment rate is much lower than in the other three cities.

Bibliography

Bayley, D. and Mendelsohn, H. (1969). *Minorities and the Police: Confrontation in America*, New York: Free Press.

Berg, M., Stewart, E., Intravia, J., Warren, P., and Simons, R. (2016). 'Cynical streets: neighborhood social processes and perceptions of criminal injustice', *Criminology*, 54: 520–47.

Billiet, J. and Pleysier, S. (2012). 'Attitudes towards the police in European Social Survey round 5 (2010): comparing Belgium and its neighbours', in E. Devroe, L. Pauwels, A. Verhage, and M. Easton (eds.) *Tegendraadse Criminologie, Liber Amicorum Paul Ponsaers*, Antwerpen: Maklu-Uitgevers, 301–19.

Borooah, V. (2011). 'Racial disparity in police stop and searches in England and Wales', *Journal of Quantitative Criminology*, 27: 453–73.

Bowling, B. and Phillips, C. (2007). 'Disproportionate and discriminatory: reviewing the evidence on police stop and search', *Modern Law Review*, 70: 936–61.

Bowling, B. and Phillips, C. (2008). 'Policing minority ethnic communities', in T. Newburn (ed.) *Handbook of Policing*, Cullompton: Willan, 611–41.

Bradford, B., Jackson, J., and Stanko, E. (2009). 'Contact and confidence: revisiting the impact of public encounters with the police', *Policing and Society*, 19: 20–46.

Bradford, B. and Loader, I. (2016). 'Police, crime and order: the case of stop and search', in B. Bradford, B. Jauregui, I. Loader, and J. Steinberg (eds.) *The SAGE Handbook of Global Policing*, London: Sage, 241–60.

Bradford, B., Murphy, K., and Jackson, J. (2014). 'Officers as mirrors: policing, procedural justice and the (re)production of social identity', *British Journal of Criminology*, 54: 527–50.

Brunson, R. (2007). '"Police don't like black people": African-American young men's accumulated police experiences', *Criminology and Public Policy*, 6: 71–102.

Chainey, S. and Macdonald, I. (2012). *Stop and Search, the Use of Intelligence and Geographic Targeting. Findings from Case Study Research*, London: National Policing Improvement Agency.

De Maillard, J., Hunold, D., Roché, S., and Oberwittler, D. (2016a). 'Different styles of policing: discretionary power in street controls by the public police in France and Germany', *Policing and Society*, online. Available http://dx.doi.org/10.1080/10439 463.2016.1194837 (accessed 21 March 2017).

de Maillard, J., Hunold, D., Roché, S., Oberwittler, D., and Zagrodzki, M. (2016b), 'Les logiques professionnelles et politiques du controle des styles de police différents en France et en Allemagne', *Revue Francaise de Science Politique* 66(2), 271–293.

Delsol, R. and Shiner, M. (2015). *Stop and Search. The Anatomy of a Police Power*, London: Palgrave Macmillan.

Dirikx, A., Gelders, D., and Parmentier, S. (2012). 'Police–youth relationships: a qualitative analysis of Flemish adolescents' attitudes toward the police', *European Journal of Criminology*, 9: 191–205.

Engel, R. and Cohen, D. (2014). 'Racial profiling', in M. Reisig and R. Kane (eds.) *The Oxford Handbook of Police and Policing*, New York: Oxford University Press, 383–408.

European Union Agency for Fundamental Rights (2010a). *EU-MIDIS. European Union minorities and discrimination survey. Data in focus report: police stops and minorities*, online. Available http://fra.europa.eu/sites/default/files/fra_uploads/1132-EU-MIDIS-police.pdf (accessed 10 March 2017).

European Union Agency for Fundamental Rights (2010b). *Towards more effective policing. Understanding and preventing discriminatory ethnic profiling: a guide*, online. Available http://fra.europa.eu/sites/default/files/fra_uploads/1133-Guide-ethnic-profiling_EN.pdf (accessed 10 March 2017).

Fagan, J. (2002). 'Law, social science and racial profiling', *Justice Research and Policy*, 4: 103–30.

Fassin, D. (2013). *Enforcing Order: An Ethnography of Urban Policing*, Cambridge: Polity Press.

Fourquet, J. (2007). 'Présentation des résultats de l'enquête par sondage sur la perception par les habitants des ZUS et hors ZUS des causes et conséquences des violences urbaines', in H. Masurel (ed.) *Rencontres des acteurs de la ville. Violences urbaines, quartiers sensibles et stratégies locales. Rencontre du 18 décembre 2006*, online. Available www.ville.gouv.fr/IMG/pdf/Actesviolences-urbaines17-04-09_cle628388.pdf (accessed 10 March 2017), 34–7.

Gau, J. and Brunson, R. (2010). 'Procedural justice and order maintenance policing: a study of inner-city young men's perceptions of police legitimacy', *Justice Quarterly*, 27: 255–79.

Gauthier, J. (2012). 'Origines controllées. La police à l'épreuve de la question minoritaire à Paris et à Berlin', unpublished Ph.D. thesis, Université Versailles-Saint-Quentin-en-Yvelines and Albert-Ludwigs-Universität Freiburg.

Gelman, A., Fagan, J., and Kiss, A. (2007). 'An analysis of the New York City Police Department's "stop-and-frisk" policy in the context of claims of racial bias', *Journal of the American Statistical Association*, 102: 813–23.

Gesemann, F. (2003). "Ist egal, ob man Ausländer ist oder so jeder Mensch braucht die Polizei." Die Polizei in der Wahrnehmung junger Migranten, In A. Groenemeyer, and J. Mansel, (ed.), *Die Ethnisierung von Alltagskonflikten*, Opladen: Leske + Budrich, 203–28.

Goris, I., Jobard, F., and Lévy, R. (2009). *Profiling Minorities. A Study of Stop-and-Search Practices in Paris*, New York: Open Society Institute.

Hagan, J., Shedd, C., and Payne, M. (2005). 'Race, ethnicity, and youth perceptions of criminal injustice', *American Sociological Review*, 70: 381–407.

Hayle, S., Wortley, S., and Tanner, J. (2016). 'Race, street life, and policing: implications for racial profiling', *Canadian Journal of Criminology and Criminal Justice*, 58: 322–53.

Hunold, D. (2015). *Polizei im Revier. Polizeiliche Handlungspraxis gegenüber Jugendlichen in der multiethnischen Stadt*, Berlin: Duncker und Humblot.

Hunold, D., Oberwittler, D., and Lukas, T. (2016). '"I'd like to see your identity cards please!" Negotiating authority in police–adolescent encounters: findings from a mixed-method study of proactive police practices towards adolescents in two German cities', *European Journal of Criminology*, 13: 590–609.

Hüttermann, J. (2003). 'Policing an ethnically divided neighborhood in Germany: day-to-day strategies and habitus', *Policing and Society*, 13: 381–97.

Jackson, J., Bradford, B., Stanko, E., and Hohl, K. (2013). *Just Authority? Trust in the Police in England and Wales*, London and New York: Routledge.

Koster, N.-S., Kuijpers, K., Kunst, M., and van der Leun, J. (2016): 'Crime victims' perceptions of police behavior, legitimacy, and cooperation: a review of the literature', *Victims and Offenders*, 11: 392–435.

Lewis, P., Newburn, T., and Taylor, M. (2011). 'Rioters say anger with police fueled summer unrest', *Guardian*, online. Available www.guardian.co.uk/uk/2011/dec/05/anger-policefuelled-riots-study (accessed 10 March 2017).

Li, Y., Ren, L., and Luo, F. (2016). 'Is bad stronger than good? The impact of police–citizen encounters on public satisfaction with police', *Policing: An International Journal of Police Strategies and Management*, 39: 109–26.

Lowrey, B., Maguire, E., and Bennett, R. (2016). 'Testing the effects of procedural justice and overaccommodation in traffic stops: a randomized experiment', *Criminal Justice and Behavior*, 43: 1430–49.

MacQueen, S. and Bradford, B. (2015). 'Enhancing public trust and police legitimacy during road traffic encounters: results from a randomised controlled trial in Scotland', *Journal of Experimental Criminology*, 11: 419–43.

Mazerolle, L., Bennett, S., Davis, J., Sargeant, E., and Manning, M. (2013). 'Procedural justice and police legitimacy: a systematic review of the research evidence', *Journal of Experimental Criminology*, 9: 245–74.

Medina Ariza, J. (2014). 'Police-initiated contacts: young people, ethnicity, and the "usual suspects"', *Policing and Society*, 24: 208–23.

Meng, Y., Giwa, S., and Anucha, U. (2015). 'Is there racial discrimination in police stop-and-searches of Black youth? A Toronto case study', *Canadian Journal of Family and Youth*, 7: 115–48.

Mucchielli, L. (2009). 'Autumn 2005: a review of the most important riot in the history of French contemporary society', *Journal of Ethnic and Migration Studies*, 35: 731–51.

Murphy, K., Sargeant, E., and Cherney, A. (2015). 'The importance of procedural justice and police performance in shaping intentions to cooperate with the police: does social identity matter?', *European Journal of Criminology*, 12: 719–38.

Newburn, T. (2016). 'The 2011 England riots in European context: a framework for understanding the "life-cycle" of riots', *European Journal of Criminology*, 13: 540–55.

Norman, J. (2009). 'Seen and not heard: young people's perceptions of the police', *Policing*, 3: 364–72.

Parmar, A. (2011). 'Stop and search in London: counter-terrorist or counter-productive?', *Policing and Society*, 21: 369–82.

Pettersson, T. (2013). 'Belonging and unbelonging in encounters between young males and police officers: the use of masculinity and ethnicity/race', *Critical Criminology*, 21: 417–30.

Police Law Baden-Württemberg (1992). Polizeigesetz in der Fassung vom 13. January 1992, online. Available www.landesrecht-bw.de/jportal/?quelle=jlink&docid=jlr-Pol GBW1992rahmen&psml=bsbawueprod.psml&max=true (accessed 10 March 2017).

President's Task Force on 21st Century Policing (2015). *Final Report of the President's Task Force on 21st Century Policing*, Washington, DC: Office of Community Oriented Policing Services, online. Available https://cops.usdoj.gov/pdf/taskforce/taskforce_finalreport.pdf (accessed 10 March 2017).

Quinton, P. (2015). 'Race disproportionality and officer decision-making', in R. Delsol and M. Shiner (eds.) *Stop and Search. The Anatomy of a Police Power*, London: Palgrave, 57–78.

Republique Francaise (2014). *Rapport relatif aux relations police/citoyens et aux contrôles d'identite*, online. Available www.defenseurdesdroits.fr/sites/default/files/atoms/files/ddd_r_20140515_police_citoyen_controle_identite.pdf (accessed 10 March 2017).

Roché, S. (2010). 'Riots. The nature of rioting: comparative reflections based on the French case study', in M. Evans and S. Dréan-Rivette (eds.) *Transnational Criminology Manual*, Amsterdam: Wolf Legal Publishing, 155–70.

Roché, S. (2016). *De la police en démocratie*, Paris: Grasset.

Roché, S. and de Maillard, J. (2009). 'Crisis in policing: the French rioting of 2005', *Policing*, 3: 34–40.

Schicht, G. (2013). 'Racial profiling bei der Polizei in Deutschland – Bildungsbedarf? Beratungsresistenz?', *Zeitschrift für internationale Bildungsforschung und Entwicklungspädagogik*, 36: 32–37.

Schuck, A., Rosenbaum, D., and Hawkins, D. (2008). 'The influence of race/ethnicity, social class, and neighborhood context on residents' attitudes toward the police', *Police Quarterly*, 11: 496–519.

Schweer, T. and Strasser, H. (2003). '"Die Polizei – Dein Freund und Helfer?!" Duisburger Polizisten im Konflikt mit ethnischen Minderheiten und sozialen Randgruppen', in A. Groenemeyer and J. Mansel (eds.) *Die Ethnisierung von Alltagskonflikten*, Opladen: Leske und Budrich, 229–60.

Sharp, D. and Atherton, S. (2007). 'To serve and protect? The experiences of policing in the community of young people from Black and other ethnic minority groups', *British Journal of Criminology*, 47: 746–63.

Sindall, K., McCarthy, D., and Brunton-Smith, I. (2016). 'Young people and the formation of attitudes towards the police', *European Journal of Criminology*, online. Available http://journals.sagepub.com/doi/pdf/10.1177/1477370816661739 (accessed 21 March 2017).

Skogan, W. (2006). 'Asymmetry in the impact of encounters with police', *Policing and Society*, 16: 99–126.

Slocum, L., Wiley, S., and Esbensen, F.-A. (2016). 'The importance of being satisfied: a longitudinal exploration of police contact, procedural injustice, and subsequent delinquency', *Criminal Justice and Behavior*, 43: 7–26.

Stadt Köln (2012). *Statistisches Jahrbuch Köln* 2012, online. Available http://stadt-koeln.de/mediaasset/content/pdf15/statistisches_jahrbuch_k__ln_2012.pdf (accessed 10 March 2017).

Stadt Mannheim (2013). *Einwohner mit Migrationshintergrund in kleinräumiger Gliederung (Statistische Daten 3/2013)*, online. Available www.mannheim.de/sites/default/files/page/2188/d201303_migrationshintergrund_2012.pdf (accessed 10 March 2017).

Statistisches Bundesamt (2015). *Bevölkerung und Erwerbstätigkeit, Bevölkerung mit Migrationshintergrund, Ergebnisse des Mikrozensus 2012* (Fachserie 1 Reihe 2.2). Wiesbaden: Statistisches Bundesamt.

Stewart, E., Baumer, E., Brunson, R., and Simons, R. (2009). 'Neighborhood racial context and perceptions of police-based racial discrimination among black youth', *Criminology*, 47: 847–87.

Sunshine, J. and Tyler, T. (2003). 'Moral solidarity, identification with the community, and the importance of procedural justice: the police as prototypical representatives of a group's moral values', *Social Psychology Quarterly*, 66: 153–65.

Svensson, J. and Saharso, S. (2015). 'Proactive policing and equal treatment of ethnic-minority youths', *Policing and Society*, 25: 393–408.

Tyler, T. (2011). 'Trust and legitimacy: policing in the USA and Europe', *European Journal of Criminology*, 8: 254–66.

Tyler, T. and Blader, S. (2003). 'The group engagement model: procedural justice, social identity, and cooperative behavior', *Personality and Social Psychology Review*, 7: 349–61.

Tyler, T. and Fagan, J. (2008). 'Legitimacy and cooperation: why do people help the police fight crime in their communities?', *Ohio State Journal of Criminal Law*, 6: 231–75.

Tyler, T. and Wakslak, C. (2004). 'Profiling and police legitimacy: procedural justice, attributions of motive, and acceptance of police authority', *Criminology*, 42: 253–81.

Tyler, T., Fagan, J., and Geller, A. (2014). 'Street stops and police legitimacy: teachable moments in young urban men's legal socialization', *Journal of Empirical Legal Studies*, 11: 751–85.

United Kingdom Ministry of Justice (2013). *Statistics on race and the criminal justice system 2012. A Ministry of Justice publication under Section 95 of the Criminal Justice Act 1991*, online. Available www.gov.uk/government/uploads/system/uploads/attachment_data/file/269399/Race-and-cjs-2012.pdf (accessed 10 March 2017).

Van Steden, R. and Broekhuizen, J. (2015). 'Many disorderly youths, few serious incidents: patrol officers, community officers, and their interactions with ethnic minorities in Amsterdam', *The Police Journal*, 88: 106–22.

Waddington, D. (2010). 'Applying the flashpoints model of public disorder to the 2001 Bradford riot', *British Journal of Criminology*, 50: 342–59.

Weber, L. and Bowling, B. (2013). *Stop and Search. Police Power in Global Context*, Abingdon: Routledge.

Weitzer, R. (1999). 'Citizens' perceptions of police misconduct: race and neighborhood context', *Justice Quarterly*, 16: 819–46.

Weitzer, R. (2014). 'Police race relations', in M. Reisig and R. Kane (eds.) *The Oxford Handbook of Police and Policing*, New York: Oxford University Press, 339–61.

Weitzer, R. and Tuch, S. (2004). 'Race and perceptions of misconduct', *Social Problems*, 51: 305–25.

Wilson, J. (1968). *Varieties of Police Behavior: The Management of Law and Order in Eight Communities*, Cambridge, MA: Harvard University Press.

Wu, Y., Sun, I., and Triplett, R. (2009). 'Race, class or neighborhood context: which matters more in measuring satisfaction with police?', *Justice Quarterly*, 26: 125–56.

5 Police legitimacy and public cooperation

Is Japan an outlier in the procedural justice model?

Mai Sato

Introduction

Police responsibilities – preventing crime, enforcing the law, and generally pro-
tecting the public – are difficult to carry out without public support. Police work
is made possible by various kinds of public cooperation, including reporting
crimes, identifying suspects in police line-ups, and consenting to stops and
searches. Why do people cooperate with the police? Arguably, there are three
main reasons: out of what Hart (1961) referred to as 'the habit of obedience',
obeying without giving it much thought;[1] because they view the police as
effective (utilitarian), which can be described an instrumentalist approach; and
because they perceive the police as fair – a normative (Kantian) approach based
on values and beliefs about what is morally right. The normative explanation is
often termed the procedural justice model of policing and it is the focus of this
chapter.

The procedural justice model argues that people's perception of police fairness is important in shaping their cooperation with the police and compliance
with the law. Public perceptions of fairness have been found to be a better predictor of cooperation with the police than public perception of their effectiveness
(e.g. Jackson *et al.* 2012a; Mazerolle *et al.* 2013; Tyler *et al.* 2007; Tyler 2011).
The benefits of the procedural justice model are described by Myhill and
Quinton (2011: 14) as follows:

> As this model seeks to motivate people to become more cooperative and
> responsible voluntarily, it potentially offers a cost-effective way of prevent-
> ing and reducing crime. Set against the costs of a 'crime control' model
> which attempts to deter crime by increasing the likelihood of detection and
> punishment, the evidence indicates that an approach that encourages greater
> social responsibility could have significant benefits.

The procedural justice model has been shown to explain motivations for
cooperation with the police in the UK (e.g. Jackson *et al.* 2012a, 2012b), United
States (e.g. Sunshine and Tyler 2003), and Australia (e.g. Murphy *et al.* 2009).
These studies argue that when members of the public perceive the police as fair,

they consider them a legitimate authority and, thus, are more likely to cooperate with them. There is growing evidence, however, that the model fails to explain cooperation with the police in some countries outside developed industrialised democracies (see Tankebe 2009 for Ghana; Jackson *et al.* 2014 for Pakistan). Japan is another country where the model did not work as hypothesised (Tsushima and Hamai 2015).

In this chapter, I extend the findings presented by Tsushima and Hamai (2015). Their work demonstrated that the procedural justice model was not applicable in Japan. My contribution in this chapter is, first, to fully explore *why* the procedural justice model did not work there. Why did fairness as well as effectiveness fail to explain cooperation with the police? I also extend my analysis more generally on the sources of legitimacy beyond Japan and evaluate the applicability as well as the limits of the procedural justice model. A theory cannot claim universal applicability if it cannot withstand and accommodate the distinct features of different socio-cultural contexts (Messner 2014). This chapter serves as a corrective to the idea that procedural justice theory will hold in all cultures and countries. Procedural justice theory may be fully applicable only in developed industrialised democracies with traditions of political liberalism. The reason why the model did not work in Japan may be due to its homogeneous society and low crime rate. The lack of racial, ethnic, linguistic, religious, and economic differences and diversity make policing a non-contentious issue. Concepts such as fairness or equal treatment that are used to evaluate the police in the procedural justice model may not be something that can be transported to Japan and are perhaps more applicable to countries with diverse and divided communities.

Japan: cooperation without legitimacy?

The Japanese study mentioned above, carried out in 2011, replicated the questions in Round 5 of the Justice module of the European Social Survey (ESS 2010),[2] which included questions designed to test the procedural justice model of cooperation with the police.[3] The adoption of the ESS questionnaire in the Japanese study makes it possible to compare the relative importance of instrumentalist and normative explanations of cooperation with the police in different countries.

The procedural justice model is operationalised by measuring two linked but separate concepts hypothesised to explain cooperation with the police. Fairness and legitimacy are assumed to have a two-stage link to cooperation. When people trust the police to be fair, this leads them to consider the police as legitimate; when people view the police as legitimate, they are willing to cooperate with the police (e.g. Jackson *et al.* 2012b). Public perception of police *fairness* is measured by asking respondents whether the police treat people respectfully, whether they make fair and impartial decisions, and whether they explain their decisions and actions.[4] Public perception of police *legitimacy* is measured by two sub-concepts – 'duty to obey' and 'moral alignment' – based on David

Beetham's (1991) theory of what constitutes a legitimate authority in the eyes of the governed. Beetham (1991) asserts that an authority commands legitimacy when people feel a moral obligation to obey the authority and feel that they share the same values as the authority.[5] '*Duty to obey*' questions are therefore phrased to capture the degree to which people feel obligations to follow police orders even when they disagree with them.[6] '*Moral alignment*' questions are designed to measure the extent to which respondents consider their values and morals similar to those of the police.[7]

The study shows that the procedural justice model did not work in the Japanese context (Tsushima and Hamai 2015, see Figure 5.1). The paths from 'fairness' to both aspects of legitimacy ('duty to obey' and 'moral alignment') were significant, showing that respondents with higher levels of trust in police fairness were more likely to view the police as legitimate. In particular, there was a strong relationship between perceived fairness and moral alignment. Neither aspect of legitimacy, however, was a significant predictor of cooperation with the police. Thus, the procedural justice model failed: While the first link (between trust in police fairness and legitimacy) worked, the second link (from legitimacy to cooperation) did not. Cooperation was also not explained directly by trust in police fairness. If perceptions of fairness and legitimacy do not explain why people cooperate with the police, did Japanese respondents place more importance on police effectiveness?

Tsushima and Hamai (2015) found that neither the structural equation model (see Figure 5.1), nor a regression model predicting cooperation with the police[8] was explained by trust in police effectiveness. Instrumentalist and normative dimensions of legitimacy did not lead to Japanese cooperation with the police. This leaves us with 'habit' as an alternative source of Japanese police legitimacy.

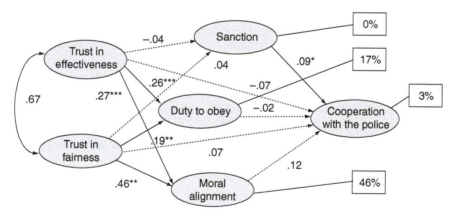

Figure 5.1 Cooperation with the police.

Source: Adapted from Tsushima and Hamai 2015: 220.

Notes
χ^2=218.405, df=69, *p*=0.000, RMSEA=0.042, CFI=0.972, TLI=0.957, *p*<0.05; **p*<0.01; ***p*<0.001.

Unfortunately, habit was not included in the original theoretical model, so it is impossible to determine its importance from the Japanese study.

How do we interpret these results? Do we treat Japan as unique – an exception to the procedural justice (normative) model identified in previous studies for other countries? The following sections extend Tsushima and Hamai's (2015) analysis of why Japan does not fit within this model. They seek to identify not only factors that establish Japan as different but also wider issues related to police legitimacy that are applicable to countries outside of Japan – such as gender identity, position on the individualism-collectivism scale, victimisation, crime levels, and contact with the police.

Individualism versus collectivism: duty to obey

Tsushima and Hamai (2015: 222) offer Japan's low levels of individualism as a possible reason that the procedural justice model did not work there.[9] They argue that 'duty to obey' questions that measure citizen's felt duty to the state did not work because they are designed for 'members of highly civilized societies where individualism is highly valued and praised as a part of citizenship' (Tsushima and Hamai 2015: 222). Putting aside the issue of whether Japan really is a collectivist society (or at least low on individualism), the first question to explore is whether the procedural justice model—and more specifically, the questions used in the ESS (2010) and the Japanese study to test it – are in fact premised on individualism.

Individualism is concerned with the self, and individualists often see themselves as independent beings. Collectivism, on the other hand, is concerned with being part of a group by prioritising collective over private interests. Therefore, individualists value uniqueness and individual achievements, whereas collectivists value cooperativeness and dutifulness (Triandis 1990, 1995).

In the procedural justice model, questions used to measure the sub-concept 'duty to obey' stand out as being collectivist in nature. The questions are designed to capture the degree to which people feel obligations to follow police orders even when they disagree with them. It makes logical sense to measure this by providing respondents with difficult situations where they do not agree with, understand, or like decisions or orders made by the police. However, in addition to (or instead of) felt obligation, these questions may be measuring respondents' position on the individualism-collectivism scale. Respondents who feel obliged to obey the police are willing to sacrifice their internal objections to commit to a collective interest. They are displaying their 'unquestioned attachment' to the police (Triandis 1990: 55).

Japan has long been referred to as a collectivist society, from Benedict's (1946) post-war analysis to Triandis (1990, 1995) in the late twentieth century. The Japanese policing style has also been thought to reflect this collectivism with a strong focus on community policing (Ames 1981; Bayley 1976). Matsumoto and colleagues (1996) argue that Japanese people are in fact more individualistic and less collective. He argues in *The New Japan: Debunking Seven Cultural*

Stereotypes that Japan scores higher on the individualism scale than the US, which is known to score consistently highly on individualism (Matsumoto 2002).

Matsumoto *et al.* (1996) claim that Japan was a collectivist society for a long time. They go back to the sixteenth century, arguing that the scarcity of natural resources coupled with long periods of infighting during the Sengoku Period forced groups of individuals to adopt collectivist patterns of behaviour in order to survive. They also acknowledge that the idea of a collectivist Japan became firmly established internationally due to Japan's rapid economic growth from the 1950s to the 1970s. The economic boom was not possible without 'years of individual sacrifice and social commitment' (Matsumoto 1996: 83). After this successful economic advancement, Matsumoto (1996) argues, the focus on group cohesion, harmony and obedience to elders and those with higher status changed and the younger generation rapidly started displaying individualistic attitudes. This point is echoed by political scientists Inglehart and Welzel (2005), who argue that modernisation – especially economic development – inevitably causes cultural changes that make societies more individualistic. Matsumoto (1996: 85) notes that by the 1990s, Japanese company managers often characterised new graduates as 'being preoccupied with individual reward without the concomitant obligation of individual sacrifice and work ethic that characterized an earlier generation'.

Analyses of the 2010 World Values Survey confirm Matsumoto's (1996, 2002) finding that Japan is in fact more individualistic than the UK, US, Australia, France, and Germany. Questions included self-evaluation of conformity levels, identification of independence and obedience as desirable traits in children, willingness to fight for one's country, and opinion on whether an increase in respect for authority would be a positive change.[10] On all five items, Japan displayed significantly higher levels of individualism. In two items ('fight for your country' and 'respect for authority'), the differences between the Japanese response and the rest were not a matter of degree but at opposite ends of the spectrum. For example, only 5 per cent of Japanese respondents felt 'greater respect for authority' would be a 'good thing'. In contrast, the majority of respondents in the UK (76 per cent), US (55 per cent), and Australia (62 per cent) thought so. It might be possible to interpret Japan's low desire for greater respect for authority as a sign that there already is enough respect and so no

Table 5.1 Individualism-collectivism: World Values Survey (%)

	Japan	UK	US	Australia	France	Germany
Independence	68	59	54	65	37	74
Obedience	5	46	28	28	41	13
Conformity	3	25	14	17	26	10
Fight for your country	15	50	58	64	52	41
Respect for authority	5	76	55	62	85	59

Source: World Values Survey Wave 6; own computations.

more is necessary. When looking at other variables such as 'obedience' (5 per cent regarded 'very much like me') and 'conformity' (3 per cent regarded 'very much like me'), however, they also show significantly lower levels of collectivism in comparison to the US, UK, and Australia. Notably, the procedural justice model has worked in these countries. Correlations between positive attitudes towards the police, trust, and voluntary compliance were also found in France and Germany (see also Oberwittler and Roché, Chapter 4 in this volume). These countries – unlike Japan – show similar results across all items on the individualism-collectivism scale.[11]

Returning to the issue of whether answers to 'duty to obey' questions function as a proxy for the individualism-collectivism scale, I compared Japanese responses to responses from countries that participated in Round 5 of the ESS (2010). While Japan ranks near the middle for most factors measured in the procedural justice model, it ranks near the bottom (26th out of 27 countries) for perceived 'duty to obey'.[12] This demonstrates that Japanese respondents showed strong signs of individualism relative to the other countries. The result is perhaps not surprising after re-establishing modern Japan as highly individualistic. Japan had a similar ranking for frequency of contact with police, which is discussed later. Comparative rankings of survey responses are shown in Table 5.2.

There are groups of countries that behave in a similar manner. Nordic countries consistently rank high on all elements of the procedural justice model, while Eastern European ex-communist countries rank low on most elements, and the UK and Ireland, along with the rest of the Western European countries, rank between these two groups. There are some exceptions to the patterns, driven mostly by responses to the 'duty to obey' questions. Japan is one of these exceptions. Most notable is Israel, which consistently scores low but jumps up to third place for 'duty to obey'.

While the individualism-collectivism link provides an alternative understanding of the felt obligation to obey, other possible sources of legitimacy should also be addressed here. Harkin (2015a) is critical of the idea of the police's capacity to be truly 'democratic', and uses Bittner's (1990) analysis of the police as an executive enforcer of non-negotiable coercive force. He highlights the fact that the police can be undemocratic in applying coercive force, though the opposite is not a completely democratic force but a partially democratic one. The police can be partially democratic by having strict procedural protections or post-hoc accountability structures to limit and monitor their use of force. However, the police will ultimately be the decision-maker on the use of coercive force and 'the public can at best, be a weak advisor to that force' (Harkin 2015a: 739).

When respondents are asked about the 'duty to obey' – applying Harkin's (2015a) analysis of the coercive power held by the police – they do not have a genuine choice even if they live in a partially democratic country. Tankebe (2009) as well as Bottoms and Tankebe (2012) argue that instead of measuring 'true free consent', the 'duty to obey' questions measure strategic or pragmatic

Table 5.2 Procedural justice model – comparison of ESS countries and Japan

Rank	Trust in Effectiveness		Fairness		Legitimacy Duty		Alignment		Cooperation	Contact	
High											
1	Finland	6.2	Denmark	3.1	Denmark	7.8	Finland	2.0	Germany	Finland	50.6
2	Switzerland	5.9	Ireland	3.0	Finland	7.6	Denmark	2.1	Switzerland	Sweden	49.7
3	Spain	5.7	Finland	3.0	Israel	7.3	Norway	2.1	Denmark	Belgium	47.8
4	Germany	5.7	Spain	3.0	Sweden	7.2	Germany	2.1	France	Switzerland	43.0
5	Cyprus	5.5	Switzerland	3.0	Cyprus	6.9	Sweden	2.2	Norway	Netherlands	42.6
6	Czech Republic	5.4	Germany	3.0	Switzerland	6.9	Switzerland	2.2	UK	Estonia	39.1
7	Denmark	5.4	Norway	2.9	Hungary	6.8	Ireland	2.3	Sweden	Spain	38.6
8	Belgium	5.3	UK	2.9	Norway	6.7	Estonia	2.3	Belgium	Cyprus	38.5
9	Poland	5.3	Sweden	2.9	Germany	6.5	Poland	2.3	Finland	Ireland	38.3
10	Slovenia	5.2	Belgium	2.9	Netherlands	6.5	Netherlands	2.3	Netherlands	UK	38.1
11	France	5.2	**Japan**	2.8	Czech Republic	6.5	Spain	2.3	Spain	Norway	38.1
12	UK	5.2	Netherlands	2.8	Poland	6.2	UK	2.3	Slovenia	Croatia	36.8
13	Netherlands	5.2	Estonia	2.7	Portugal	6.2	Belgium	2.3	Greece	Germany	36.7
14	Croatia	5.1	Cyprus	2.7	Belgium	6.0	Portugal	2.4	Cyprus	Hungary	36.5
15	**Japan**	5.1	Croatia	2.7	Slovakia	5.9	Slovenia	2.5	Portugal	Slovenia	35.1
16	Estonia	5.1	Slovenia	2.7	UK	5.9	**Japan**	2.5	**Japan**	Slovakia	35.0
17	Norway	5.0	Hungary	2.6	Spain	5.8	Cyprus	2.5	Ireland	Czech Republic	34.8
18	Hungary	5.0	Czech Republic	2.6	France	5.8	Hungary	2.6	Estonia	France	34.5
19	Ireland	5.0	Portugal	2.6	Ireland	5.7	France	2.6	Hungary	Poland	30.0
20	Sweden	5.0	Poland	2.6	Greece	5.6	Slovakia	2.6	Croatia	Denmark	29.9
21	Slovakia	5.0	France	2.6	Estonia	5.5	Croatia	2.6	Bulgaria	Russia	25.7
22	Greece	4.7	Greece	2.5	Croatia	5.2	Bulgaria	2.6	Czech Republic	Greece	25.1
23	Bulgaria	4.7	Bulgaria	2.5	Bulgaria	4.9	Czech Republic	2.7	Poland	Portugal	24.4
24	Portugal	4.7	Slovakia	2.5	Slovenia	4.5	Greece	2.8	Israel	Ukraine	21.1
25	Russia	4.3	Israel	2.4	Ukraine	4.4	Israel	2.8	Slovakia	Israel	18.5
26	Israel	4.2	Russia	2.3	**Japan**	4.1	Russia	3.0	Russia	**Japan**	18.2
27	Ukraine	3.8	Ukraine	2.0	Russia	4.0	Ukraine	3.1	Ukraine	Bulgaria	16.1
Low											

Source: European Social Survey Round 5 Data; own computations.

Notes

The table presents a ranking of averages for ESS participating countries and Japan. Effectiveness scores ranges from 0 to 10; fairness ranges from 0–10; alignment from 1–5; cooperation from 1–4; duty from 0–10; alignment from 1–4; and contact shows the proportion of those who had contact.

consent based on self-interest or fear of authority. Jackson *et al.* (2016) empirically tested the current 'duty to obey' questions and argued that they do, in fact, capture true free consent rather than one based on coercion or self-interest. The article acknowledges, however, that their experiment may not have universal application. They explain that Scotland – where the experiment was carried out – is a country with relatively low crime rates and little history of tense and fraught police–citizen relationships (Jackson *et al.* 2016).

Therefore, if respondents live in a country where the police are authoritarian and are accustomed to them using coercive force frequently, their felt obligation to obey the police may be automatic or pressured rather than a matter of choice. In countries that scored low on 'fairness' or 'moral alignment' but high on 'duty to obey', high levels of police legitimacy may be due simply to habit or self-interest (e.g. avoidance of trouble), which is more consistent with Weber's (1947) idea of legitimacy than with Beetham's normative idea of legitimacy, upon which the questions are based.

Gender identity

Finding that the attitudinal data did not fit the procedural justice model, Tsushima and Hamai (2015) turn to demographic variables, arguing that people in certain groups – males, younger people, people who are married or living with a partner, people who have some higher education, or have resided at their current address for a shorter time – are more likely to cooperate with the police (Tsushima and Hamai 2015: 221). Among the statistically significant demographic variables, they focused on gender, by running separate models for men and women. While men were more likely to cooperate with the police, the procedural justice variables could not predict cooperation with the police for both genders. Cooperation with the police for women was not explained by *any* procedural justice variables but explained by other demographic variables (e.g. being married and higher educated). Similarly, for men none of the procedural justice variables – such as fairness, moral alignment, and felt duty to obey – was a statistically significant predictor of cooperation. Perceived sanction (whether people think they will be caught and punished for non-compliance) was the only statistically significant attitudinal variable aside from demographics.

After establishing the limited role procedural justice variables played in explaining cooperation with the police for both genders, Tsushima and Hamai (2015) turn to the possible reasons why men are still more likely to cooperate with the police by stating that gender role expectations in Japan relate to cooperation with the police. Contacting or cooperating with the police is 'traditionally seen as a male role in Japan' and 'unfavourable behaviour for women' (Tsushima and Hamai 2015: 223). While they offer no data to support their claim, according to Wave 6 of the World Values Survey, carried out between 2010 and 2014, traditional gender roles feature quite markedly. When respondents were asked whether men should have a greater right to a job than women when jobs are scarce, only 14 per cent of Japanese respondents disagreed, compared to 73 per cent in Australia and 69 per cent in the US.[13] Japanese women also seem to embrace the idea with only 5 percentage points difference between women (17 per cent) and men (12 per cent) who disagreed with the statement.

Tsushima and Hamai (2015: 223) further point out that the low representation of women in the police force – 8 per cent according to recent figures (Japanese National Police Agency 2015) – could account for women's reluctance to cooperate with the police. Interviews conducted with organisations that provide rape and sexual assault aftercare in Japan revealed that female victims often find the attitude of the police 'unsympathetic at best and "shocking" at worst' and that the Japanese police were perceived to be treating female victims as no more than a tool for investigating crime (McLean and L'Heureux 2007: 245).

Research on ethnic minority attitudes outside Japan has found that unfair and discriminatory treatment is detrimental to police legitimacy because the police send an implicit message about how members of an ethnic group are valued (Bradford *et al.* 2014; Murphy 2013; Murphy and Cherney 2011; Roux *et al.* 2011; Sunshine and Tyler 2003; Tyler and Blader 2003). Ethnic profiling, for example, will leave those targeted feeling stigmatised 'via the application of a negative group stereotype to them based not on what they are doing, but on their race, gender, or age' (Tyler and Blader 2003: 359). Bradford *et al.* (2014) found that if members of the public perceive police officers to share their values and morals, it helps them to legitimise their authority and identify with them. Research in Australia has found that it is not membership in an ethnic minority as such that diminishes willingness to cooperate with the authorities but strong identification with a subordinate group and not with the superordinate group (Murphy *et al.* 2015: 17).

Applying these findings on ethnicity, if women in Japan are acutely aware of and identify with their gender role, the fact that a police force is almost entirely male may well discourage women from cooperating with the police. Female crime victims, for example, may hesitate to report crime. While training police officers to treat women in a procedurally just manner may improve the legitimacy of the police for women, this should be done alongside increasing female representation in the police force.

Contact with the police: what happened to community policing?

In a systematic review, Mazerolle *et al.* (2013) summarise four key elements of procedural justice: participation, neutrality, dignity, and respect. These elements require a style of policing – often referred to as community policing – where police officers are known to the public and work in close partnership with citizens to deal with community problems. Policing based on informal mechanisms of social control, as opposed to a reactive enforcement-based policing, is considered to improve police–community relations and reduce levels of crime and disorder (Newburn 2003: 85). The history of policing in England and Wales illustrates a decline as well as a revival of community policing. In the 1970s, the number of foot patrol officers – *bobbies on the beat* – were reduced so that officers in card could react more quickly to crime, which weakened ties between the police and communities (Newburn 2003). The Brixton riots[14] and the police investigation into the murder of Stephen Lawrence[15] highlighted the strained relationship between the police and the community. These events influenced the re-introduction of various community policing strategies such as police community support officers.

Community policing is an ideal way to incorporate principles of procedural justice theory due to its citizen-focused approach. Japan is widely known for community policing (Ames 1981; Bayley 1976). The fact that the procedural justice model did not work there and the negative police encounters with victims of sexual abuse described in the previous section may, therefore, come as a surprise. Community policing in Japan is based on a system of *koban*, dating back to 1971. In this system, small neighbourhood police units patrol the streets, make home visits to establish links, receive feedback on community safety, and respond to crime reports. They also deal with non-crime-related work such as handling lost and found items, and providing local knowledge and direction to those who are lost. As of April 2004, there were 14,101 *koban* across Japan (Japanese National Police Agency 2004).

The description of *koban* resonates with many key elements of the procedural justice model, but public views of *koban*, according to a survey carried out in 2004 by the Japanese National Police Agency, expose the police as a detached and poorly integrated organisation.[16] While 82 per cent of respondents knew the location of a nearby *koban*, their satisfaction with *koban* was low – only 21 per cent said they were either 'very satisfied' or 'satisfied' with the services provided (Japanese National Police Agency 2004).[17] The main reason for dissatisfaction was the lack of police officers patrolling the streets, indicating the desire for police officers to be out in the community rather than staffing the *koban* (Japanese National Police Agency 2004). In a survey carried out in 2007, 42 per cent of respondents said they had not seen any police officers on the street in the last month, 13 per cent had initiated contact with a *koban*, and 94 per cent had not been stopped by the police in the last year (Nikkoso Research Foundation for Safe Society 2007). Johnson (2003), for example, has looked beyond the *koban* model of policing and questioned the integrity of the force by exposing high levels of corruption. Miyazawa (1992), in his book *Policing in Japan: A Study on Making Crime*, describes the range of questionable and illegal police actions to secure the famous 99.9 per cent conviction rate. These findings suggest a gap between the idea of Japanese community policing based around the *koban* system, and the reality of every day Japanese policing.

The above findings reaffirm the result of Tsushima and Hamai's (2015) study, in which only 18 per cent of all respondents had contact with the police in the past two years.[18] This level of contact, compared to the results of the ESS (2010), is extremely low (Sato 2013). With an overall average of 34 per cent having contact with the police in the ESS, Japan's contact rate is only 2 percentage points higher than that of Bulgaria, which had the lowest level of contact of any ESS country (see Table 5.2). Tsushima and Hamai (2015) observe that low levels of contact are associated with large portions of respondents selecting 'don't know'-answers to attitude-related questions.[19]

They further argue that low contact led the majority of Japanese respondents to answer questions not based on their own experience but purely on their image of the police, which may have contributed to the model not working in Japan (Tsushima and Hamai 2015: 222–3). Previous research has shown that experience of police contact is a key in explaining cooperation and compliance with the police. In Australia, Murphy *et al.* (2015: 12–13) argue that increased personal contact indicates a greater willingness to cooperate,[20] whereas the opposite was true in the UK (Bradford *et al.* 2009) and the US (Skogan 2006). Poor quality contact may reduce citizens' confidence in the police (Myhill and Bradford 2012). What is clear from these findings is the existence of contact where 'a shared moral position is communicated to citizens by the police through the quality of their behaviour in specific interactions' (Hough *et al.* 2010: 4–5). Yet, proponents of the procedural justice model argue that

> procedural justice is not just connected to people who have direct encounters with officers. Even people without direct experience of the police have opinions about whether the police would treat them fairly, if they were to come into contact.
>
> (Jackson *et al.* 2012b: 8)

To argue that direct experience is irrelevant for having an opinion about police procedures is questionable. If you have not been stopped by the police, contacted them or seen a police officer patrolling the streets, it is difficult to answer questions such as whether you think the police explain their actions or decisions, whether you think they make fair decisions, and whether you think you would obey the police when you disagree with them.

Low crime rate: the felt need for a police force

The low level of victimisation in Japan may also explain why the procedural justice model did not work. People may have views about the police – even if they have not had any personal contact with them – if they live in a country where crime is an issue. Compared to countries where the procedural justice model has worked, Japan stands out for its low crime rate. According to the International Crime Victimisation Survey, which asked about 11 types of crime, the prevalence of those victimised in Japan was 15 per cent, compared with 30 per cent in Australia, 26 per cent in England and Wales, and 21 per cent in the US (van Kesteren *et al.* 2000).[21] The same pattern is true for homicide rates recorded by the United Nations Office on Drugs and Crime with 0.3 per 100,000 people in Japan, compared to 3.9 in the US, 1 in Australia and 0.9 in the UK.[22]

Japan's low crime levels may indicate a lack of deep public concern about policing. As noted earlier in the chapter, the Japanese study shows that police effectiveness does not explain cooperation with the police. This probably means that Japanese people do not appreciate the necessity of crime control or think much about police work (Tsushima and Hamai 2015: 223). In high-crime countries such as Pakistan, where homicide rates reached 7.8 per 100,000 in 2012 (United Nations Office on Drugs and Crime n.d.) – 26 times higher than Japan – research has shown that the public perception of police effectiveness was a stronger predictor of trust in the police than perceptions of police procedural fairness (Jackson *et al.* 2014). Similar results have been shown in the case of Ghana, where willingness to cooperate with the police was based on the expectations of a minimum threshold of police effectiveness (Tankebe 2008: 1281).

In sum, there may be certain thresholds that need to be met for the procedural justice model to work. Experience of contact with the police may be one of them. When contact levels are so low, questions may be too abstract for people to grasp and appreciate their spirit. The questions used to measure the importance of procedural justice might be misunderstood by respondents. As for victimisation, people in high-crime countries place greater emphasis on effectiveness than fairness. For countries with a moderate level of crime, and a democratic, well-functioning police force, people may be more likely to judge the police based on fairness rather than effectiveness. Last, for countries with very low levels of crime, police legitimacy may have little to do with consequential or normative considerations. Due to the police's limited relevance, perceptions of legitimacy may no longer be based on fairness or effectiveness. In the Japanese case, it could be argued that neither contact nor victimisation levels have reached the minimum threshold where concerns about police fairness or effectiveness affect people's willingness to cooperate with the police.[23]

Discussion

Why do people cooperate with the police in Japan? We know that willingness to cooperate cannot be explained by the procedural justice model. The chapter offered possible explanations why the model did not work. First, Japanese citizens' level of contact with the police was very low, despite the Japanese policing model of close police–citizen contact based on *koban*. The low level of contact included reporting a crime, being stopped or seeing a police patrol on the street. This may have made it impossible for Japanese respondents to form concrete views on the importance of police fairness. Even though the procedural justice model asks about perceptions of the police rather than actual contact, there may be a threshold where it becomes difficult to have a clear impression of the police. This leaves open the possibility that if the Japanese police fully commit to community policing and police presence increases, the procedural justice model may work in the future. However, for now, low levels of contact combined with low levels of crime may have broken the obvious link between community safety and policing, whether the focus is on effectiveness or procedural fairness.

Second, the low crime rate may have been another reason why the procedural model did not work. The Japanese study also showed that police effectiveness did not explain cooperation with the police. This points to the possibility that Japanese people do not appreciate that crime control by the police is necessary. In contrast, it is notable that in high-crime countries such as Pakistan and Ghana, police *effectiveness* was a stronger predictor of trust in the police than fairness (Jackson *et al.* 2014; Tankebe 2008).

Third, I have argued that there may have been problems in the operationalisation of the 'duty to obey' questions. I have used the World Value Survey Wave 6 (2010–2014) results to show that Japan is actually no less individualistic than Western countries, if not more, and that the 'duty to obey' questions may have acted as a proxy for the individualism-collectivism scale. 'Duty to obey' questions posed problems in Ghana and Pakistan. It has been argued that where policing practices are coercive and authoritarian, citizens may obey the police not because they embrace their authority but simply as the option of disagreeing with the police is not practical or smart (e.g. Tankebe 2009). This is unlikely to be the case in Japan, but the very low level of felt obligation to obey the police hints that the questions were not directly transferrable to the Japanese context.

Finally, there may be differences between countries regarding the importance of how *fair* the police are. Jackson *et al.* (2014) and Tankebe (2009) argue that in the UK, in the US, and in Australia, where the procedural justice model worked, there are shared beliefs about the basic social utility of the police and an understanding of the limits of what the police can do to prevent and control crime. Based on the shared understanding of the limits of police *effectiveness*, these countries may focus instead on the procedural fairness of the police. In addition, the UK, the US, and Australia are countries with substantial ethnic and religious diversity, and this may heighten their citizens' sensitivity to equal treatment by state organisations. As noted above, the 2016 shooting of Black men such as Philando Castile in the US, and the 2011 shooting of Mark Duggan in the UK, highlights the tension between police and Black and ethnic minority groups.

In contrast, police misconduct or discrimination has not been discussed extensively in Japan. The 2015 census data show that only 1.7 per cent of Japan's population are foreign nationals (Statistics Bureau Japan 2017). This makes Japan a homogenous country in terms of nationality and language. Religion has also not been a divisive topic with the majority of Japanese people being *mushukyo*, which refers to a lack of specific religious beliefs while fusing Shinto, Buddhism, and Christianity into a hybrid form of spirituality (Ama 2004). Income inequality has also remained comparatively low: The share of wealth held by the richest tenth of Japanese people is lower than Norway or Sweden, both countries known for being egalitarian (*The Economist* 2015). Racial, ethnic, linguistic, religious, and economic differences and divisions often provoke tensions between those in authority and the governed. People in homogenous countries like Japan, however, may start with the assumption that all are equal and the expectation of a shared morality and may be less sensitive to issues of fairness and equal treatment. This is not to say that the police in Japan *are* fair or provide equal treatment to its citizens. It simply means that police (mis)conduct is not an issue that has been associated with discrimination in a homogenous country like Japan.

So far, this chapter has examined why the procedural justice model did not work in Japan. If not fairness, then what are the sources of police legitimacy? Beetham's (1991) idea of legitimacy based on normative considerations is narrower than Weber's, where close evaluation of the ruler is not necessary (Harkin 2015b). Weber (1947) understands legitimacy as the public having 'faith' in the ruler and offers three sources of legitimacy: tradition, charisma, and legality. While charisma may not be directly applicable to a police force, as it is made up of various individuals, tradition and legality could be useful concepts. People could also have faith in police legitimacy as they trust its legality and respect the rule of law. They may regard a police force as legitimate purely because it has existed for a long time. A police force newly established after a country's democratisation, for example, may not be perceived as legitimate due to its lack of history; whereas even if *koban* principles are not properly upheld, people may still regard the *koban* system as legitimate due to its long history.

As noted at the beginning of this chapter, habit could also explain cooperation with the police (Hart 1961; Weber 1947). Young (1979: 24) argues that habit could explain cooperation if certain conditions are met: marginal importance, frequent recurrences, and little change over time. Those who are exposed to regular stops and searches may consider such events of marginal importance and may believe that discriminatory police practice will not change. For such people, there may be high levels of cooperation based on habit and irrespective of police fairness. This represents a challenge to the commonly held view that if we engage in an action, it must be 'intentional' and can be explained in logical, rational or moral terms (Pollard 2006). Yet, our lives are filled with habits where we act without much deliberation (Pollard 2006; Wikström *et al.* 2012).

In order to better understand the sources of police legitimacy, researchers should extend their focus beyond the normative explanation of subjective legitimacy. The attractiveness of the normative hypothesis is clear: As noted by Myhill and Quinton's (2011: 14) quotation at the beginning of this chapter, it provides a cost-effective and, generally speaking, ethical framework to foster cooperation with the police. In reality, however, growing evidence suggests that effectiveness is sometimes more important than fairness as in Pakistan and Ghana. We also know from looking at Japan that we need to look beyond normative and instrumental sources of police legitimacy. The *usefulness* of normative methods in securing cooperation with the police, however, should not cause police practice to undermine the importance of fair and respectful treatment of the public. The police should provide fair and respectful treatment with minimum levels of coercion without being influenced by its possible instrumental benefits. In this sense, procedural justice has intrinsic value, but it is increasingly clear that the current procedural justice model does not have universal applicability.

Notes

1 Per-Olof Wikström and his colleagues (2012) look – in their Peterborough Adolescent and Young Adult Development Study – the importance of a habit as an explanatory factor for offending. Their work based on situational action theory showed that while morality prevents majority of young people from engaging in criminal activity, young people who were 'crime-prone' tended to be impulsive and habit played a large role (Wikström *et al.* 2012).

2 The Japanese study was carried out in 2011 by Masahiro Tsushima and Koichi Hamai at Ryukoku University, Japan. Two-stage stratified sampling was used in 136 cities across Japan. The survey consisted of a combination of home visits and self-administered questionnaires. The resulting sample was made up of 1,251 respondents aged 15 and over (response rate: 63 per cent). The original ESS survey was fielded in 28 European countries at the end of 2010. Each country organised its own translation and fieldwork to standards specified by the ESS Core Scientific Team. Face-to-face interviews were conducted in people's homes.

3 'Cooperation with the police' was measured by 4-point Likert-type questions. Respondents were asked:

> Imagine that you were out and saw someone push a man to the ground and steal his wallet. How likely would you be to call the police? Would you be ... not at all likely, not very likely, likely or very likely?

'How willing would you be to identify the person who had done it? Would you be ... not at all willing, not very willing, willing, or very willing?'; 'How willing would you be to give evidence in court against the accused? Would you be ... not at all willing, not very willing, willing, or very willing?'. 'Effectiveness' was measured by three questions on perceptions of the effectiveness of the police in preventing violent crimes and catching people who commit burglaries and of the time police take to arrive at the scene of a violent crime. 'Sanction' was measured by three questions on the perceived likelihood of being caught when making an exaggerated or false insurance claim, buying stolen goods or committing a traffic offence.

4 'Fairness' was measured by three 4-point Likert-type questions. Respondents were asked: 'How often would you say the police generally treat people in [name of country] with respect?'; 'About how often would you say the police make fair, impartial decisions in the cases they deal?'; and 'When dealing with people in [name of country], how often would you say the police generally explain their decisions and actions when asked to do so?'.

5 Beetham's idea of legitimacy had a third component, 'legality' – perceived institutional commitment to the rule of law – which was included in the Japanese study but dropped from the analysis in line with the decision taken in Jackson *et al.* 2012b which analysed the ESS questions looking at the UK.

6 'Duty to obey' was measured by three 11-point Likert-type questions. Respondents were asked to what extent they felt it was their duty to 'back the decisions made by the police even when you disagree with them'; 'do what the police tell you even if you don't understand or agree with the reasons'; and 'do what the police tell you to do even if you if you don't like how they treat you'.

7 'Moral alignment' was measured by three 4-point Likert-type questions. Respondents were asked to what extent they agreed with these statements: 'The police generally have the same sense of right and wrong as I do'; 'The police stand up for values that are important to people like me'; and 'I generally support how the police usually act'.

8 In the regression model, all the latent variables shown in Figure 5.1 and demographic variables (gender, age, marital status, education, and years of residence) were included as independent variables in predicting cooperation with the police (see Tsushima and Hamai 2015: 221). That model is not discussed in this chapter.

9 Tsushima and Hamai (2015) refer to 'civic individualism'. They argue that 'the Japanese do not have a sense of citizenship as Western people do, partly because Japanese society did not go through a "people's revolution" such as the French revolution or the American War of Independence' (Tsushima and Hamai 2015: 222). If civic individualism does explain why the Japanese respondents scored low on 'duty to obey' questions, it should still be noted that the UK, which has also not gone through a people's revolution, scored much higher than Japan, and two ranks higher than France, on 'duty to obey' (see Table 5.1).

10 The World Values Survey was carried out in 2010 in Japan, 2005 in the UK, 2011 in the US, 2012 in Australia, 2013 in Germany, and 2006 in France. 'Independence' and 'obedience': Respondents who selected the quality in response to the question 'Here is a list of qualities that children can be encouraged to learn at home. Which, if any, do you consider to be especially important?'. 'Conformity': Respondents who selected 'very much like me', on a 6-point Likert-type scale, in response to the statement 'It is important to this person to always behave properly; to avoid doing anything people would say is wrong.' 'Fight for your country': Respondents who answered 'yes' to the question 'Of course, we all hope that there will not be another war, but if it were to come to that, would you be willing to fight for your country?' 'Respect for authority': Respondents who chose 'a good thing' in the category 'greater respect for authority' in response to the following:

> I'm going to read out a list of various changes in our way of life that might take place in the near future. Please tell me for each one, if it were to happen, whether you think it would be a good thing, a bad thing, or don't you care?

11 Another possible explanation of the World Value Survey is that Japanese respondents might comprehend the survey questions in a totally different way to Western respondents. Messner (2014) argues that there are different constructions of 'self' depending on socio-cultural context and provides an example of 'independent self' (personal social identity) versus an 'interdependent self' (relational social identify).

12 Care should be taken when carrying out international comparisons of this kind without knowing how the police function in each country. They nonetheless provide a useful reference point in positioning Japan, or any other country, in a cross-country comparison.

13 Respondents had three options: agree, disagree, and neither agree nor disagree.

14 The 1981 Brixton riot occurred between the Metropolitan Police and protesters in London resulting in almost 280 injuries to police and 45 injuries to members of the public. High unemployment, poverty, racial tensions, and poor relations with police are considered to be the causes of the riot.

15 Stephen Lawrence, an 18-year-old student, was attacked and killed in London in 1993. The Macpherson report, which reviewed the handling of the case, found flawed police investigation and institutional racism. The report contributed to the move in creating a more representative police force and strategies to work with London's diverse communities.

16 This was a nationwide survey using a two-stage stratified random probability sample of 2,148 respondents (response rate: 72 per cent).

17 Another 57 per cent answered 'cannot say', and 23 per cent answered 'very unsatisfied' or 'unsatisfied' (Japanese National Police Agency 2004).

18 This question was phrased as '[i]n the past 2 years, did the police in [country] approach you, stop you or make contact with you for any reason?'.

19 The highest proportion of 'don't know'-answers, 44 per cent, responded to the question of whether the police explain their decisions and actions.

20 It should be noted, however, that Murphy *et al.* (2015) do not specify the type of contact (e.g. police-initiated contact or citizen-initiated contact) with the police.

21 The survey was carried out in 2000 and asked about people's experience in 1999 of car theft, theft of items from a car, car vandalism, motorcycle theft, bicycle theft, burglary, attempted burglary, robbery, theft of personal property, and threatened or actual sexual assault.

22 The Australian and Japanese data are from 2014; the US and UK data are from 2013.

23 What I am proposing is similar to what has been identified with regard to respect for democracy, such as transparency and corruption (Tankebe 2009; Jackson *et al.* 2014). High levels of police corruption were found to undermine police legitimacy in Pakistan and Ghana (Jackson *et al.* 2014; Tankebe 2009). In political philosophy, according to Buchanan (2002), state organisations cannot be legitimate unless they are democratic, regardless of their instrumental value.

References

Ama, T. (2004). *Why are the Japanese Non-religious? Japanese Spirituality: Being Non-religious in a Religious Culture*, Lanham, MD: University Press of America.

Ames, W. (1981). *Police and community in Japan*, Berkley, CA: University of California Press.

Bayley, D. (1976). *Forces of Order: Police Behavior in Japan and the United States*, Berkeley, CA: University of California Press.

Beetham, D. (1991). *The Legitimation of Power*, London: Macmillan.

Benedict, R. (1946). *The Chrysanthemum and the Sword: Patterns of Japanese Culture*, Boston, MA: Houghton Mifflin.

Bittner, E. (1990). *Aspects of Police Work*, Boston, MA: Northeastern University Press.

Bottoms, A. and Tankebe, J. (2012) 'Beyond procedural justice: a dialogic approach to legitimacy in the criminal justice system', *Journal of Criminal Law and Criminology*, 102: 119–70.

Bradford, B., Jackson, J., and Stanko, E. (2009). 'Contact and confidence: revisiting the impact of public encounters with the police', *Policing and Society*, 19: 20–46.

Bradford B., Murphy K., and Jackson J. (2014). 'Officers as mirrors. Policing, procedural justice and the (re)production of social identity', *British Journal of Criminology*, 54: 527–50.

Buchanan, A. (2002). 'Political legitimacy and democracy', *Ethics*, 112: 689–719.

The Economist (2015, February 12). 'The secure v the poor' [Editorial], online. Available www.economist.com/news/finance-and-economics/21643202-problem-not-super-rich-secure-v-poor (accessed 3 March 2017).

European Social Survey Round 5 Data (2010). NSD – Norwegian Centre for Research Data, Norway – Data Archive and distributor of ESS data for ESS ERIC.

Harkin, D. (2015a). 'Simmel, the police form and the limits of democratic policing', *British Journal of Criminology*, 55: 730–46.

Harkin, D. (2015b). 'Police legitimacy, ideology and qualitative methods: a critique of procedural justice theory', *Criminology and Criminal Justice*, 15: 1–19.

Hart, H. (1961). *The Concept of Law*, Oxford: Oxford University Press.

Hough, M., Jackson, J., Bradford, B., Myhill, A., and Quinton, P. (2010). 'Procedural justice, trust, and institutional legitimacy', *Policing*, 4: 203–10.

Inglehart, R. and Welzel, C. (2005). *Modernization, Cultural Change, and Democracy: The Human Development Sequence*, New York: Cambridge University Press.

Jackson, J., Asif, M., Bradford, B., and Zakar, M. (2014). 'Corruption and police legitimacy in Lahore, Pakistan', *British Journal of Criminology*, 54: 1067–88.

Jackson, J., Bradford, B., Hough, M., Myhill, A., Quinton, P., and Tyler, T. (2012a). 'Why do people comply with the law? Legitimacy and the influence of legal institutions', *British Journal of Criminology*, 52: 1051–71.

Jackson, J., Bradford, B., MacQueen, S., and Hough, M. (2016, September 3) 'Truly free consent? Clarifying the nature of police legitimacy', *SSRN*, online. Available https://ssrn.com/abstract=2620274 (accessed 03 March 2017).

Jackson, J., Hough, M., Bradford, B., Hohl, K., and Kuha, J. (2012b). *Policing by consent: topline results (UK) from Rounds 5 of the European Social Survey*, ESS Country Specific Topline Results Series, online. Available www.europeansocialsurvey.org/docs/findings/ESS5_gb_toplines_policing_by_consent.pdf (accessed 3 March 2017).

Japanese National Police Agency (2004). *White paper on crime*, online. Available www.npa.go.jp/hakusyo/h16/hakusho/h16/index.html (accessed 3 March 2017).

Japanese National Police Agency (2015). *White paper on crime*, online. Available www.npa.go.jp/hakusyo (accessed 3 March 2017).

Johnson, D. (2003). 'Above the law? Police integrity in Japan', *Social Science Japan Journal*, 6: 19–37.

Matsumoto, D. (2002). *The New Japan: Debunking Seven Cultural Stereotypes*, Yarmouth, ME: Intercultural Press.

Matsumoto, D., Kudoh, T., and Takeuchi, S. (1996). 'Changing patterns of individualism in the United States and Japan', *Culture and Psychology*, 2: 77–107.

Mazerolle, L., Bennett, S., Davis, J., Sargeant, E., and Manning, M. (2013). *Legitimacy in Policing: A Systematic Review*, Oslo: The Campbell Collaboration.

McLean, I. and L'Heureux, S. (2007). 'Sexual assault aftercare services in Japan and the UK', *Japan Forum*, 19: 239–356.

Messner, S. (2014) 'When West meets East: generalising theory and expanding the conceptual toolkit of criminology', *Unpublished Keynote Address at the 6th Annual Conference of the Asian Criminological Society*, Osala, Japan.

Miyazawa, S. (1992). *Policing in Japan: A Study on Making Crime*, New York: University of New York Press.

Murphy, K. (2013). 'Policing at the margins: fostering trust and cooperation among ethnic minority groups', *Journal of Policing, Intelligence and Counter Terrorism*, 8: 184–99.

Murphy, K. and Cherney, A. (2011). 'Fostering cooperation with police: how do ethnic minorities in Australia respond to procedural justice-based policing?', *Australian and New Zealand Journal of Criminology*, 44: 235–57.

Murphy, K., Sargeant, E., and Cherney, A. (2015). 'The importance of procedural justice and police performance in sharing intentions to cooperate with the police: does social identity matter?', *European Journal of Criminology*, 12: 719–38.

Murphy, K., Tyler, T., and Curtis, A. (2009). 'Nurturing regulatory compliance: is procedural justice effective when people question the legitimacy of the law?', *Regulation and Governance*, 3: 1–26.

Myhill, A. and Bradford, B. (2012). 'Can police enhance public confidence by improving quality of service? Results from two surveys in England and Wales', *Policing and Society*, 22: 397–425.

Myhill, A. and Quinton, P. (2011). *It's a fair cop? Police legitimacy, public cooperation, and crime reduction*, National Policing Improvement Agency, online. Available https://static-2.socialgo.com/cache/79864/assets/files/5044962a00023-79864-FairCopFull Report.pdf (accessed 3 March 2017).

Newburn (2003). *Handbook of policing*, Cullompton: Willan.

Nikkoso Research Foundation for Safe Society (2007). *Patororu Katsudou [Survey on Patrol]*, online. Available www.syaanken.or.jp/?p=951 (accessed 3 March 2017).

Pollard, B. (2006). 'Explaining actions with habits', *American Philosophical Quarterly*, 43: 57–69.

Roux, G., Roché, S., and Astor, S. (2011). *Minorities and Trust in the Criminal Justice. French Case Study*, Grenoble: University of Grenoble.

Sato, M. (2013). 'Keisatsu ni taisuru shinrai to seitousei' [Trust in the police and legitimacy], *Kyosei Koza [Journal of Correctional Issues]*, 33: 13–25.

Skogan, W. (2006). *Police and Community in Chicago; A Tale of Three Cities*, Oxford: Oxford University Press.

Statistics Bureau Japan (2017). *Japan Statistical Yearbook 2017*, Ministry of Internal Affairs and Communication.

Sunshine, J. and Tyler, T. (2003). 'The role of procedural justice and legitimacy in public support for policing', *Law and Society Review*, 37: 513–48.

Tankebe, L. (2008). 'Public cooperation with the police in Ghana: does procedural fairness matter?', *Criminology*, 47: 1265–93.

Tankebe, J. (2009). 'Self-help, policing and procedural justice: vigilantism and the rule of law in Ghana', *Law and Society Review*, 43: 245–69.

Triandis, H. (1990). 'Cross-cultural studies of individualism and collectivism', in J. Berman (ed.), *Nebraska Symposium on Motivation*, Lincoln, NE: University of Nebraska Press, 41–133.

Triandis, H. (1995). *Individualism and Collectivism*, Boulder, CO: Westview Press.

Tsushima, M. and Hamai, K. (2015). 'Public cooperation with the police in Japan: testing the legitimacy model', *Journal of Contemporary Criminal Justice*, 31: 212–28.

Tyler, T. (2011). *Why People Cooperate: The Role of Social Motivations*, Princeton, NJ: Princeton University Press.

Tyler, T. and Blader, S. (2003). 'The group engagement model: procedural justice, social identity, and cooperative behavior', *Personality and Social Psychology Review*, 7: 349–61.

Tyler, T., Braga, A., Fagan, J., Meares, T., Sampson, R., and Winship, C. (2007). 'Legitimacy and criminal justice: international perspectives', in T. Tyler (ed.), *Legitimacy and Criminal Justice*, New York: Russell Sage Foundation, 9–28.

United Nations Office on Drugs and Crime (no date). *Statistics on Crime*, online. Available https://data.unodc.org/ (accessed 30 March 2017).

Van Kesteren, J., Mayhew, P., and Nieuwbeerta, P. (2000). *Criminal Victimisation in Seventeen Industrialised Countries: Key-findings from the 2000 International Crime Victims Survey*, The Hague: Ministry of Justice, WODC.

Weber, M. (1947). *The Theory of Social and Economic Organization*, New York: The Free Press.

Wikström, P.-O., Oberwittler, D., Treiber, K., and Hardie, B. (2012). *Breaking Rules: The Social and Situational Dynamics of Young People's Urban Crime*, Oxford: Oxford University Press.

World Values Survey Wave 6 (2010–2014). Official Aggregate v.20150418. World Values Survey Association. Aggregate File Producer: Asep/JDS, Madrid, Spain.

Young, O. (1979). *Compliance and Public Authority: A Theory with International Applications*, New York: Resources for the Future.

6 Why do Nigerians cooperate with the police?

Legitimacy, procedural justice, and other contextual factors in Nigeria[1]

Oluwagbenga Michael Akinlabi

Introduction

Current theorizations of legitimacy have shown that legitimacy is often built on the perceptions of legal authorities during their encounters with the public, whether they are seen as fair, just, and effective (Sunshine and Tyler 2003; Tyler 1990; Tyler and Huo 2002). Specifically, Tyler and his colleagues have argued that people primarily assess the fairness of legal authorities like police, judges, and prison officers on whether they employ fair procedures during their own encounters with them. While police effectiveness is important, Tyler suggests procedural justice is a more important consideration shaping legitimacy judgements (Tyler 1990). Perceptions or judgements about the fairness of procedures ultimately have a strong influence on how the public ascribe legitimacy to legal authorities, and whether legitimacy, in turn, will influence people's voluntary compliance and their expressed willingness to cooperate with the directives of legal authorities (Sunshine and Tyler 2003; Tyler 1990; Tyler and Huo 2002).

Similar studies, particularly those conducted in developed Western societies (e.g. the United States, the United Kingdom, and Australia), consistently find this to be true: When making judgements about police, procedural justice is more important than police effectiveness (Bradford 2014; Murphy *et al.* 2014; Sunshine and Tyler 2003; Tyler 2006). Beyond police studies, evidence shows that procedural justice can also motivate compliance among offenders (Murphy *et al.* 2016), reduce misconduct among prison inmates (Reisig and Meško 2009), and encourage young people to support police (Murphy 2015; Reisig *et al.* 2012). These studies support the general arguments encapsulated in Tyler's procedural justice model, that when legal authorities are procedurally just, people are more inclined to ascribe legitimacy to them and more willing to comply with their directives. What remains largely underexplored, however, is whether procedural justice bears the same influence in African societies, especially in a country like Nigeria where police–public relations are often fragile and sometimes volatile.

This chapter presents a number of significant contributions to the legitimacy and procedural justice literature. Specifically, it explores whether perceptions of procedural justice are more influential than perceptions of police effectiveness in determining Nigerians' legitimacy assessments and expressed willingness to cooperate with police. In addition, this study extends existing police legitimacy scholarship by examining additional variables (e.g. predatory policing, police corruption, and police colonial origin) that might predict public perceptions of police legitimacy and self-reported willingness to cooperate with police in Nigeria.

Legitimacy, normative issues, and cooperation with police

Several studies from some developed Western societies – with important exceptions being Murphy and Cherney (2011) and Sargeant et al. (2014) – have consistently confirmed that procedurally just policing is more important to assessments of legitimacy and compliance than judgements about police effectiveness (Hough et al. 2010; Hinds and Murphy 2007; Tyler 1990; Tyler and Fagan 2008). However, empirical investigations on procedural justice and police legitimacy in African societies, especially Nigeria, are scarce. Given widespread police corruption and distrust of police in Nigeria, there is reason to believe that procedural justice may be less relevant in such contexts.

The few studies that have examined the impact of procedural justice and police effectiveness on perceptions of police legitimacy in developing nations show inconsistent results. Some studies report that procedural justice is a stronger predictor of police legitimacy than police effectiveness (e.g. Akinlabi 2015; Bradford et al. 2014; Kochel et al. 2013; Murphy and Cherney 2011; Tankebe 2009b), while others do not (e.g. Brockner et al. 2001; Tankebe, 2009a). For example, Tankebe (2009a) has shown that in Ghana, instrumental factors are far more important at predicting public perceptions of police legitimacy than perceived procedural justice. Tankebe based his study on general survey data from 405 households located in Accra, Ghana. The results showed a lack of empirical validity to Tyler's procedural justice model, but indicated that perceptions of police legitimacy and public cooperation with the police in Ghana were most strongly predicted by instrumental factors, such as perceptions of police effectiveness in fighting crime.

In a South African study, Bradford et al. (2014) considered whether the link between perceptions of procedural fairness and police legitimacy 'travelled' to the often-fraught context of policing in South Africa. Bradford and colleagues found that procedural fairness judgements did in fact play a key role in legitimacy assessments, but that South Africans tended to place greater emphasis on police effectiveness (and concerns about crime). Most recently, Akinlabi (2015) compared the strength of procedural justice with other police behaviours considering the perspectives of young people in Nigeria. The results substantiate the procedural justice hypothesis outside developed Western democracies, confirming that procedural justice is a more important predictor of police legitimacy than police effectiveness.

However, even in developed Western democracies, the generalizability of the procedural justice model has been questioned. In a survey of 1,204 Australians, Murphy and Cherney (2011) tested whether procedurally fair policing enhanced perceptions of police legitimacy and fostered cooperation with Australian police. Their findings revealed that perceived procedural justice predicted perceptions of police legitimacy more so than instrumental factors for both minority and majority group members. However, for ethnic minorities living in Australia, perceived procedural justice was less effective at fostering self-reported willingness to cooperate with police.

Similarly, Sargeant *et al.* (2014) examined the relationship between perceived procedural fairness, perceptions of police performance, trust in the police, and the self-reported willingness to cooperate with police among the general population and two ethnic minority groups in Australia (i.e. those with Vietnamese and Indian ancestry). They found that perceptions of procedural justice were less important for trust and self-reported willingness to cooperate with police among ethnic minority groups. Such findings suggest that procedural justice may bear varying influence on the attitudes and behaviours of different groups.

The findings discussed above reveal the limits to the procedural justice model when applied in other socio-cultural contexts, such as Nigeria. Without sufficiently accounting for the socio-cultural differences of developing countries, the procedural justice model may not provide an adequate explanation for why people perceive the police as legitimate, why they voluntarily comply with the law, or why they cooperate with police. Hence, it is important to address whether perceived procedural justice dominates public concerns about police legitimacy in countries such as Nigeria, where police corruption is often rife.

Studies have shown that in contexts where police legitimacy is judged to be low or non-existent, citizens are less likely to obey the law (see Agbiboa 2015; Akinlabi 2016; Alemika 2013); in these contexts, police officers often cannot rely on citizens' normative commitment to obey the law (Bradford *et al.* 2014). The result is that policing in these contexts may become arbitrary, coercive, and repressive (Akinlabi 2016). It has also been shown that when people experience coercion, abuse, or repressive policing, procedural justice may become inconsequential (Akinlabi 2016; Alemika and Chukwuma 2003; Gerber and Mendelson 2008). This in turn diminishes legitimacy and people's expressed willingness to cooperate with police (Anderson and Tverdova 2003; Tankebe 2010).

Given the historical antecedents of modern policing in Africa, the repertoire of colonial repression and the co-optation of police to suppress colonial African states (see Alemika 1993; Tamuno 1970, Tankebe 2008), one may ask whether such a history of malfeasance has altered public perceptions of modern policing and whether legitimacy deficits persist in post-colonial Africa. The current study is oriented towards broadening readers' understanding of police legitimacy in Africa, with a particular focus on the historical and popular discontents of colonial policing in Nigeria. Presenting these accounts may better situate Nigerians' definitions legitimacy and how (if at all) they ascribe it to the police.

Africa in context: tradition, colonialism, and popular discontent

Before colonization, traditional systems of maintaining law and order existed in Africa (Baker 2010; Dike 1956; Tamuno 1970). The African people had typically policed themselves through local customs, beliefs in deities, religious practices, rituals, and traditional values (Davidson *et al.* 1966; Onyeozili 1998, 2005; Tamuno 1970). These traditional systems were potent enough to deter and control crime and deviance and maintain compliance with the laws, mores, and traditions of the community (Davidson *et al.* 1966; Nzimiro 1972; Oli 1985; Tamuno 1970).

The religious practices governed by beliefs in deities had a strong influence on how Africans interpreted laws and adjudicated disputes (Oli 1985). Pre-colonial Africans frequently shared entrenched beliefs regarding the omniscience of deities and spirits. This conviction was so often internalized that people were willing to confess 'secret offences' to avoid the wrath of the spirits or deities. Generally, offenders were punished only after a hearing at the elders' councils. Depending on the gravity of the crime, in certain instances, those who violated the law were made to undergo the appropriate rituals to appease a particular deity or spirit, and some offenders could be banished from their communities (Otu 1999).

The belief in instant judgement was deeply ingrained in the people and passed down from one generation to another. The concept of the god, Amadioha among the Igbo people, is similar to Ṣàngó among the Yorubas. This god was believed to strike offenders with a 'thunderbolt', thereby meting out instant judgement (see Dierk 2011; Johnson 1921). Amadioha was generally referred to as the 'god of justice'. Traditions and cultural practices invariably dictated the ways of life and law, and served as the very fabric of existence to Africans before colonialization.

In the pre-colonial era, military and para-military institutions served more as a vehicle to advance the community's territorial expansionist interests and political dominations than for social interests. They played an important role in controlling the power struggles of neighbouring 'city-states' and communities, thereby ensuring territorial safety and diplomacy (Onyeozili 1998). Among the numerous palace officials in the centralized emirates of the North and the Yoruba and Edo kingdoms of Western Nigeria were those who performed the role of police (Vaaseh and Ehinmore 2011). In the Northern Emirates, these officials were known as *dogarai* (Nadama 1977; Smith 1960).

Smith notes that the dogarai were entrusted with the capture and discipline of offenders, and the prevention and detection of crime and punishment (Fika 1978; Smith 1960; Ubah 1973). The Yoruba leaders had a recognized 'traditional police', popularly referred to as ilari (in Oyo), emese (in Ife, Ijesa, and Ekiti kingdoms) and agunren in Ijebu-Ode (see Ahire 1991; Alemika 2010; Falola and Adebayo 1985; Rotimi 2001; Vaaseh and Ehinmore 2011). Though little is known about the pre-colonial policing system among the Igbo in Eastern Nigeria, available evidence suggests that a body of men known as umuokorobia, who were drawn mainly from youth groups, performed policing duties in many communities of Eastern Nigeria (Isichei 1978; Okafor 2007).

It should be noted that this strong belief in traditional processes of adjudication still exists in some communities in modern-day Nigeria as well as other African countries (Tade and Olaitan 2015). For instance, in some rural Nigerian settings, regardless of region or ethnicity, some traditional rulers still control the affairs of local 'police' who carry out duties such as 'arrest' of offenders and keeping people in line with the cultures, traditions, and norms of their communities. Also, there are courts in which traditional rulers have elders' councils, where they adjudicate on matters in their communities with little or no governmental interference. Tradition and cultural practices permeate every aspect of the society, making it difficult to separate the secular from the religious life. As such, religion has become part and parcel of the customary laws.

As the European conquest of Africa unfolded at the end of the nineteenth century, Britain, France, Belgium, Spain, Germany, Portugal, and Italy staked claims to almost all the territories in Africa (Jones 2015; Meredith 2011). With the emergence of colonialism, the drive to keep the conquered colonies in check became paramount. At this point, policing was introduced by the various European powers. The colonial police were introduced not to serve but to subjugate the cultural values of the indigenous people for the sake of the political and economic interests of the colonialists (Ahire 1991; Tankebe 2008). According to Tamuno (1970), the major purpose of policing in Africa was to enforce colonial laws and to extract resources. In other words, policing was formed to protect colonial interests, not the African people.

During this period, policing in the African states was very different to that of Europe. For example, the nine 'Peelian Principles' of policing in England and Wales were never introduced in the British Protectorates in Africa (Ahire 1991; Akinlabi 2016; Tamuno 1970; Tankebe 2008). Rather than promoting the 'Peelian Principles' of accountability, impartiality, and consent, colonial policing was done through armed raids, arrests, and the detention of any opposition to the British Crown (Ahire 1991; Tankebe 2008). Consequently, the relationship between the police and the public was often strained (McCracken 1986; Onoge 1993; Tamuno 1970; Tankebe 2008) and without regard for procedural fairness (Deflem 1994; McCracken 1986; Onoge 1993). Thus, a sensibility emerged that police should be avoided at all cost.

The popular perception of policing is overwhelmingly negative. It has been argued that historical experiences of police abuse can have lingering impacts on perceptions of modern policing, especially when these issues continue unabated (see Johnson *et al.* 2014). Although, as earlier asserted, these problems were not isolated to any one country in Africa, this study, however, is focused on Nigeria as a case study for wider post-colonial policing.

Following the British conquest, colonial rule was consolidated through a system that undermined the existing traditional and informal method of maintaining law and order. Colonialists introduced new laws, which replaced or seriously threatened the efficacy of native laws and customs, traditional religions, and other sanctions, as well as indigenous tribunals and justice (Carter 1981, Onoge 1993; Onyeozili 2005; Tamuno 1970). When certain African communities were reluctant to accept the 'new ways', colonial 'masters' tasked the military with punishing that community to set an example for others who may be contemplating resistance (Onyeozili 2005).

In 1861, the first major step towards establishing the colonial police was taken by William McCoskry, a Briton and the Acting Governor of Lagos Colony (Ahire 1991; Onyeozili 2005; Tamuno 1970). McCoskry established the foundation for the first police force – a Hausa constabulary of 30 men (Ahire 1991; Tamuno 1970;). This formation of the Hausa constabulary consisted mainly of Hausa-speaking ex-slaves from Sierra Leone (Ahire 1991), which meant that they were not Yorubas or citizens of Lagos colony. This contributed to the pervasive belief that nineteenth-century police in Nigeria were alien organizations established by foreigners. Policing duties were delegated to the Hausas, who were rivals to the Yoruba people. In 1862, the size of the constabulary was increased from 30 to 100 men, forming the 'Armed Police Force'. At the same time, a battalion of the West Indian Regiment was moved from another colony, The Gambia, to Lagos to complement the new police force (Ahire 1991; Onyeozili 2005; Tamuno 1970). One year later, in October 1863, the Armed Police Force had increased to 600 men and earning the new name, 'The Armed Hausa Police Force'.

No sooner had the police force been established than they were employed in a series of colonial government atrocities. In April 1865, 118 police constables were deployed alongside 18 British marines from HMS *Investigator* and HMS *Handy* to attack the Egba force (a sovereign force from the Old Oyo Empire) that besieged Ikorodu – a suburb of Lagos, which the British considered a 'friendly town'. Hardly four months later, in August 1865, another 62 constables were deployed to attack a nearby village, 'Edinmo' for disturbing the peace of the neighbourhood (Ahire 1991; Tamuno 1970).

However, as a result of incessant agitation by the people of Lagos, on the 27 December 1895, Police Ordinance No. 10 was enacted to establish a civil police force called 'The Lagos Police' as an organization distinct to the existing Hausa constabulary. Unlike the previous police arrangement, the Lagos Police consisted of indigenous Yoruba people. In the view of Onyeozili (2005), this was the year for the 'civilization' of Nigeria Police, as well as the basis for the professionalization of the force.

Between 1895 and the mid-1900s, several developments and administrative restructurings took place in the British protectorate later designated Nigeria, one of which was the police force. It was not until 1930, however, that a national Nigerian Police Force was established.

Abuse of power, problems of legitimacy, and policing in modern Nigeria

Nigeria eventually declared its independence from Britain on 1 October 1960. At the dawn of independence in 1960, Nigerians hoped for an indigenous national police force that would provide just, fair, and effective policing for its citizens (Baker 2004; Hills 2008; Onyeozili 2005). However, 56 years after independence, the Nigerian state still fails to provide a democratically accountable and publicly supported police force. The successive government administrations have prioritized regime stability and sectional interests at the expense of police reform and public safety (Hills 2008). Even when police reform is discussed, it is often under pretext and at the aim of political expediency, such as for improving the country's international human rights rating or defusing media criticism (Akinlabi 2016; Baker 2010; Hills 2008). It often seems appropriate to conclude that the successive post-independence governments are guilty of malevolent indifference in their continuous neglect of police reform (Akinlabi 2016; Alemika and Chukwuma 2003; Smith 2007).

The years of neglect by successive government administrations, in addition to the rapid and uncoordinated expansion of Nigeria's civilian administrations, has rendered the police largely unaccountable (Agbiboa 2015; Akinlabi 2013; Alemika 2010). The Nigeria police have 'impressive' records of corruption, arbitrariness, abuse of power, extorting motorists, use of excessive force, extrajudicial killings, beating detainees, colluding with criminals, and several other forms of misconduct (Agbiboa 2015; Alemika and Chukwuma 2000; Hills 2008). As a result of this history of abuse and lack of effective relationship between the police and public, it is not uncommon to witness members of the public avoiding contact with the Nigerian police (Agbiboa 2015). Despite the bold police insignias that proclaim 'police are your friend', Nigerians are still reluctant to trust police. A pervasive joke exists among Nigerians that, 'it would be better to trust an armed robber than to rely on a police officer' (Akinlabi 2013, 2016).

There is also a gross disparity between how police treat the general public and how they respond to the more influential members of society (Agbiboa 2015; Akinlabi 2016; Alemika 2013). On many occasions, police officers have committed extrajudicial killings, beaten crime suspects, and arbitrarily arrested and detained those not found guilty of any offence (Alemika 2013; Human Rights Watch 2010). These recurring crises between the police and the public have generated significant deficits of legitimacy for the Nigerian police.

Studies have consistently demonstrated that every encounter an individual has with police is 'teachable', either building or undermining perceptions of legitimacy (Crawford and Hucklesby 2012; Skogan 2005). That is, every contact provides an opportunity for members of the public to learn about the police and how to interact with police in the future (Akinlabi 2016). Seen this way, the ways in which Nigerian police exercise their authority and treat citizens should have a significant influence on citizens' perceptions of police legitimacy and their willingness to cooperate (Akinlabi 2015, 2016).

Moreover, deference and public support for the police can contribute in meaningful ways to the effective and equitable day-to-day functions of the police (Shearing and Stenning 2016). It has been frequently noted that the felt duty to call officers, report crime, and provide police with information to identify criminals lies with citizens (Skogan 2004), and that crime control and social order maintenance by the police are facilitated when citizens are willing to voluntarily provide information or report crimes to the police (Johnson *et al.* 2014; Tyler and Darley 2000).

Whereas many studies have shown that friendly and constructive relations between police and public tend to be the norm in developed Western societies (see Bradford *et al.* 2014; Skogan 2005; Sunshine and Tyler 2003), police in Nigeria frequently abuse their powers, thereby undermining affective links with the public (Akinlabi 2013; Alemika and Chukwuma 2003; Tyler and Fagan 2008). These issues raise, then, the question of whether Nigerians will cooperate with police in a context where the perceived legitimacy of the police is extremely low. The following sections address this question by analysing a population survey on Nigerians' attitudes towards the police.

Method

Data and participants

The data for the present study was collected in a cross-sectional survey of 600 participants from the six states that comprise the southwest geopolitical zone of Nigeria. To draw the sample for this study, capitals of each of the six states were used. These parameters were based on the fact that police activity and citizen contact is much more common in the capital cities than in rural communities, where there is little or no police presence.

The researcher was not granted access to the 2006 Census Enumeration Area Data from the National Population Commission. As a result, a 'captive audience' approach was used in each of the state capitals through churches, mosques, and institutions of higher education to obtain the sample of survey participants. In each state capital, a list of all major religious institutions (mosques and churches) and institutions of higher education (universities and polytechnics) was created from which a set of two mosques, two churches, and two institutions of higher education was then randomly drawn.

For each selected institution, permission was sought from either the senior pastor, chief Imam, or the lecturers in charge of the settings. Access was granted to all selected institutions. After this, I addressed the 'captive audience' in each institution by explaining the purpose of the research and what was required from each participant. Consent forms were handed out to the willing participants and upon reading the consent form, those who were willing to participate were given the survey.

A total of 702 people were addressed and invited to participate in the survey and 638 indicated a willingness to participate. The surveys were given to the willing participants with a two-week deadline to be returned to padlocked boxes (marked with 'research project') in designated locations. After two weeks of administering the questionnaires, 611 completed questionnaires were returned to the various locations. However, during the data coding process, only 600 questionnaires (85.5 per cent of the invited persons) were retained for this study. It is important to note that the research was conducted with ethics approval from Griffith University's Human Research Ethics Committee.

Table 6.1 presents the demographic characteristics of the sample. It is important to note that the sample is strongly biased towards highly educated respondents. Unsurprisingly, this survey sample is an approximation of the literacy level in Southwest Nigeria. In a 2012 UNESCO Action Plan on Literacy, literacy rates in the six states of the Southwest geo-political zone ranged between 63 to 92 per cent of the population. However, this bias needs to be taken into account when interpreting the findings, as prior research in Western countries has found that highly educated individuals tend to be more trusting of police (Skogan 2006).

Table 6.1 Demographic structure of the sample

Demographics	Range	Per cent		Range	Per cent
Age (Mean=32.70, SD=7.52)	20–62		*Education*		
			No schooling		3.8
			Primary		1.2
			Secondary		5.5
			University		64.3
			Postgraduate		24.8
Gender			Number of children	0–7	
Male		49.0			
Female		51.0			
Marital status			*Employment status*		
Single		45.2	Unemployed		24.5
Married		52.7	Full housewife		1.7
Divorced/separated		1.8	Self employed		23.8
			Employed full time		35.5
			Employed part time		13.5
			Retired		0.5
Religion			*Monthly income (Naira)*		
No religious affiliation		1.8	0–5,000		13.8
Muslim		19.3	6,000–10,000		9.5
Catholic		7.3	11,000–20,000		14.7
Protestant/Pentecostal		47.2	21,000–30,000		13.2
Anglican		15.3	41,000–50,000		15.7
Traditional practice		0.3	50,000–100,000		12.8
Others		8.2	100,000–200,000		2.3
			300,000–400,000		1.3
			Above 500,000		0.8
Ethnicity					
Yoruba		72.0			
Hausa		10.5			
Igbo		16.8			

Measures

This study utilized a range of measures to address the issues at hand. The full wordings of the items, showing the mean values, standard deviations, and percentages of each item are presented in Table 6.2. The individual variables and their relevance to this study are described below.

Cooperation with police

Willingness to cooperate with police was measured using a four-item scale adapted from existing literature (Murphy et al. 2010; Tankebe 2009a). The scale used a five-point Likert-type response ranging from 1 (strongly disagree) to 5 (strongly agree); a higher score on this scale reflected greater levels of self-reported cooperation. The cooperation with police scale was found to be very reliable (Cronbach's $\alpha=0.87$; Mean$=3.61$; SD$=1.06$).

Police legitimacy

Public perceptions of police legitimacy were measured using a five-item scale based on Murphy et al. (2010). The scale measured the beliefs citizens held about the normative appropriateness of what they perceive as 'right' or 'wrong' about police behaviour. Items in the police legitimacy scale were measured on a five-point Likert-type response ranging from 1 (strongly disagree) to 5 (strongly agree); higher mean scores indicate stronger perceptions of legitimacy (Cronbach's $\alpha=0.86$; Mean$=2.14$; SD$=0.91$).

Procedural justice

The procedural justice scale was adapted from Tyler (2006), Tankebe (2009a), and Murphy et al. (2010). The scale has five items which measured four major components of procedural justice: (1) neutrality, (2) fairness, (3) voice, and (4) respect. Items were measured using a five-point Likert-type response ranging from 1 (strongly disagree) to 5 (strongly agree); a higher mean score on the scale indicated more favourable assessments of procedural justice (Cronbach's $\alpha=0.88$; Mean$=2.50$; SD$=0.92$).

Police effectiveness

Police effectiveness refers to the extent to which police achieve their proper, officially sanctioned duties and goals. This scale was administered using a six-item scale. These items were measured using a five-point Likert-type response ranging from 1 (strongly disagree) to 5 (strongly agree); a higher score on this scale indicated greater perceptions of police effectiveness (Cronbach's $\alpha=0.92$; Mean$=2.55$; SD$=1.10$).

Predatory policing

Predatory policing is best described as police activities mainly devoted to the personal enrichment and self-preservation of the police themselves or the systematic subjugation of subordinate and vulnerable groups (Gerber and Mendelson 2008). The predatory policing scale was constructed using a seven-item scale developed by Akinlabi (2013). The items used to construct the scale were measured using a five-point Likert-type response ranging from 1 (strongly disagree) to 5 (strongly agree), a higher score on this scale indicated high prevalence of policing activities that are considered predatory in nature (Cronbach's $\alpha=0.90$; Mean$=3.68$; SD$=0.94$).

Police corruption

Police corruption in this research project was measured using a six-item scale adapted from Tankebe (2010) and Akinlabi (2011, 2015). It focused mainly on perceptions of police corruption rather than the actual experience of corruption. This scale incorporates items about bribe-taking, extortion, and the use of familial connections to influence the police in order to turn a blind eye to law-breaking. The police corruption scale was measured using a five-point Likert-type response ranging from 1 (strongly disagree) to 5 (strongly agree); a higher score on this scale indicated greater perceptions of police corruption (Cronbach's $\alpha=0.88$; Mean$=3.98$; SD$=0.84$).

Police colonial origin

A police colonial origin scale was developed using a six-item scale with five-point Likert-type responses ranging from 1 (strongly disagree) to 5 (strongly agree) (e.g. 'Nigerian police represent British colonialism'). The scale assessed perceptions of the colonial origin of the police and how this perception affected attitudes towards the police and policing activities (Cronbach's $\alpha=0.86$; Mean$=3.14$; SD$=1.07$).

Results

The present study seeks to assess Nigerians' perceptions of procedural justice and police effectiveness, and whether police can utilize procedural justice to improve legitimacy and cooperation. This analysis also incorporates other factors that may be unique to Nigerians and their socio-cultural environment into the understanding of police legitimacy in Nigeria. Table 6.2 presents the mean and standard deviation of each key construct measured in this study. Table 6.3 presents the Pearson's bivariate correlations between the constructs, Table 6.4 presents a hierarchical multiple regression analysis with police legitimacy as the outcome variable, and Table 6.5 presents a hierarchical multiple regression analysis with cooperation with police as the outcome variable.

Table 6.2 Means and standard deviation of each variable items

	Variable items	Mean	SD
	Cooperation with Police (Mean=3.61; SD=1.06) (I am willing ...)		
CP1	to help police find someone suspected of committing a crime	3.47	1.33
CP2	to report dangerous or suspicious activities to police	3.75	1.17
CP3	to assist police, if asked	3.56	1.22
CP4	to call police to report a crime	3.66	1.26
	Police Legitimacy (Mean=2.14; SD=0.91)		
PL1	Even if police are doing the wrong thing, I still feel a moral obligation to obey police	2.27	1.16
PL2	One should always obey police even if it goes against what you think is right	2.28	1.16
PL3	My own feelings about what is right and wrong usually agree with police rules and policies	2.06	1.11
PL4	The police share the same values of ordinary citizens like me	1.96	1.12
PL5	People should accept the decisions of police even if they think they are wrong	2.13	1.12
	Procedural Justice (Mean=2.50; SD=0.92)		
PJ1	If you are treated unfairly by the police, it is easy to get your complaint heard	2.59	1.31
PJ2	Overall, I am satisfied with how police treat people and handle problems in my community	2.37	1.22
PJ3	Police treat all people fairly and equally.	2.20	1.20
PJ4	Police give people the opportunity to express their views before decisions are made	2.68	1.30
PJ5	Police treat people with dignity and respect	2.50	1.29
PJ6	Police listen to people before making decisions	2.70	1.29
PJ7	Police are always polite when dealing with people	2.39	1.16
PJ8	Police make decisions based on facts, not their personal biases or opinions	2.56	1.26
	Police Effectiveness (Mean=2.55; SD=1.10)		
PEF1	The police respond promptly to calls about crime	2.64	1.39
PEF2	The police are always ready to provide satisfactory assistance to victims of crime	2.50	1.26
PEF3	The police are always able to provide the assistance the public need from them	2.50	1.32
PEF4	The police are doing well at controlling violent crime	2.60	1.32
PEF5	Overall, the police are doing a good job in my neighbourhood	2.55	1.29
PEF6	When the police stop people they usually handle the situation well	2.50	1.26
	Predatory Policing (Mean=3.68; SD=0.94) (The police are known for ...)		
PP1	planting evidence or setting up people for offences they did not commit	3.71	1.22
PP2	shooting innocent citizens	3.75	1.14
PP3	killing offenders without normal judicial process	3.63	1.16
PP4	subjecting anyone who disobeys their directives to harsh treatment	3.74	1.18
PP5	prowling around in the shadows/hidden places so as to arrest people	3.63	1.20
PP6	stopping people randomly for questioning	3.51	1.23
PP7	mounting checkpoints in order to extort money from citizens	3.84	1.19

Table 6.2 Continued

	Variable items	Mean	SD
	Police Corruption (Mean=3.98; SD=0.84) (Nigeria Police …)		
PC1	take bribes	4.21	1.01
PC2	is known to deliberately provide false evidence to the courts	3.88	1.08
PC3	use more force than is legally allowed when making arrests	4.00	0.99
PC4	are often bribed to overlook unlawful behaviour	4.01	1.06
PC5	often refuse to investigate, arrest, or prosecute people because they are related to a police officer	3.82	1.06
PC6	often refuse to investigate, arrest, or prosecute people because they know influential citizen(s)	3.92	1.06
	Police Colonial Origin (Mean=3.14; SD=1.07)		
CO1	The best form of policing in Nigeria is the traditional system such as OPC, Arewa, Egbesu, Agaba Boys, etc.	3.21	1.38
CO2	Nigeria police is a conception of the British colonialist	3.05	1.34
CO3	Nigeria police should have been scrapped after independence in favour of the traditional police	3.32	1.42
CO4	I see Nigeria police as alien to the Nigerian value system	3.30	1.37
CO5	I would rather trust the traditional police than the Nigeria Police	2.96	1.43
CO6	I would rather obey the traditional police than the Nigeria Police	3.01	1.45

Note
Responses ranged from strongly disagree (1) to strongly agree (5).

It is evident from Table 6.2 that the results for cooperation with police are on average positive, indicated by mean values above the neutral mid-point of the scale (3.0). Thus, it seems the public is generally more inclined to cooperate with police than to disobey. A closer look at the predatory policing, police corruption, and police colonial origin scales also reveal mean values above the neutral mid-point. This means that there are generally widespread perceptions of predatory policing, police corruption, and police colonial origin. Procedural justice, police effectiveness, and particularly police legitimacy, all have mean values below 3.0, indicating generally unfavourable assessments of key dimensions of public trust in the police. It is worth again noting that these descriptive findings are from a sample of highly educated respondents who, in the context of developed Western societies, typically appraise police more favourably than the general population.

In Table 6.3, Pearson product-moment correlations are presented to indicate the relationships between the variables in the study. Significant relationships were established between some of the important variables and the results were also in the expected directions.

Specifically, a significant positive bivariate relationship was established between cooperation with police and police legitimacy ($r=0.117$, $p<0.01$), procedural justice ($r=0.288$, $p<0.01$), and police effectiveness ($r=0.216$, $p<0.01$). This indicates that those who perceive police as legitimate, use fair procedures, and are effective in providing security and controlling crime, are more likely to cooperate with police. A high bivariate relationship was also established between predatory policing and police corruption ($r=0.452$, $p<0.01$). This indicates that

Table 6.3 Bivariate correlations of survey scales

	1	2	3	4	5	6	7
(1) Cooperation with police	1	0.117**	0.288**	0.216**	0.018	0.009	0.005
(2) Police legitimacy	–	1	0.069	0.142**	–0.068	–0.026	–0.098*
(3) Procedural justice	–	–	1	0.494**	–0.139**	–0.227**	–0.028
(4) Police effectiveness	–	–	–	1	–0.248**	–0.315**	–0.106**
(5) Predatory policing	–	–	–	–	1	0.452**	0.043
(6) Police corruption	–	–	–	–	–	1	0.098*
(7) Police colonial origin	–	–	–	–	–	–	1

Notes

$N=600$;

* $p<0.05$;

** $p<0.01$.

those who perceived the police to be predatory in their activities are likely to see them as corrupt.

It is important to note that procedural justice is negatively related to predatory policing ($r=-0.139$, $p<0.01$) and police corruption ($r=-0.227$, $p<0.01$), but not to police legitimacy. However, significant positive relationships were established between police effectiveness and police legitimacy ($r=0.142$, $p<0.01$). A low but significant correlation was also identified between police legitimacy and perception of police colonial origin ($r=-0.098$, $p<0.05$).

These results show that those who perceive police as corrupt and predatory are more likely to see the police as not fair during encounters with the public. Similarly, those who perceive the police as effective are more likely to ascribe them legitimacy. Conversely, those who see police as an alien organization, established by the British colonial regime, are more inclined to perceive the police as illegitimate.

Hierarchical multiple regression

Two hierarchical regression analyses were conducted to examine the relevance of Tyler's procedural justice model in Nigeria. The first used eleven variables to predict Nigerians' perceptions of police legitimacy. The second used the twelve variables to predict willingness to cooperate with police.

Predicting police legitimacy

A three-step hierarchical multiple regression analysis was performed in Table 6.4 to investigate public perceptions of police legitimacy. In the first step of the analysis, six demographic variables (age, gender, marital status, education, ethnicity, and religion) were entered. This model was statistically significant with 2.2 per cent of the variation in police legitimacy explained. Two demographic

Table 6.4 Hierarchical multiple regression model predicting police legitimacy

Variables	β	T	R	R^2	ΔR^2	F
Step 1	–	–	0.148	0.022	0.022	2.194*
Age	−0.158***	−3.051	–	–	–	–
Gender	0.019	0.450	–	–	–	–
Marital status	0.148***	2.867	–	–	–	–
Education	−0.010	−0.238	–	–	–	–
Ethnicity	0.004	0.091	–	–	–	–
Religion	−0.046	−1.104	–	–	–	–
Step 2	–	–	0.181	0.033	0.011	2.191*
Age	−0.146**	−2.820	–	–	–	–
Gender	0.018	0.444	–	–	–	–
Marital status	0.141**	2.729	–	–	–	–
Education	−0.010	−0.232	–	–	–	–
Ethnicity	0.003	0.067	–	–	–	–
Religion	−0.039	−0.935	–	–	–	–
Predatory policing	−0.066	−1.443	–	–	–	–
Police corruption	0.017	0.366	–	–	–	–
Police colonial origin	−0.084*	−2.033	–	–	–	–
Step 3	–	–	0.219	0.048	0.015	2.670***
Age	−0.142**	−2.753	–	–	–	–
Gender	0.020	0.493	–	–	–	–
Marital status	0.136**	2.635	–	–	–	–
Education	−0.005	−0.127	–	–	–	–
Ethnicity	0.009	0.208	–	–	–	–
Religion	−0.039	−0.933	–	–	–	–
Predatory policing	−0.063	−1.380	–	–	–	–
Police corruption	0.028	0.599	–	–	–	–
Police colonial origin	−0.084*	−2.034	–	–	–	–
Police effectiveness	0.134**	2.749	–	–	–	–
Procedural justice	0.057	1.349	–	–	–	–

Notes
* $p<0.05$;
** $p<0.005$;
*** $p<0.001$.

variables, age ($\beta=-0.158$; $p<0.005$) and marital status ($\beta=0.148$; $p<0.001$) were significant predictors of police legitimacy.

In the second step of the analysis, predatory policing, police corruption, and perceptions of police colonial antecedents were added to the model. The result showed that one of the newly added variables (police colonial origin) and the two significant demographic variables (age and marital status) from the first model step were significant in the second step. These results show that younger and married respondents are more inclined to perceive the police as legitimate, and, conversely, those who perceive the police as originating from the British colonial legacy are less likely to perceive the police as legitimate.

In the final step of the analysis, police effectiveness and procedural justice were added to the model. The result showed that procedural justice was not a significant predictor of police legitimacy. However, a statistically significant relationship was established between police effectiveness and police legitimacy; those who believed police were more effective viewed police as more legitimate.

Predicting cooperation with police

In Table 6.5, a three-step hierarchical multiple regression analysis was performed to investigate Nigerians' willingness to cooperate with police. In the first step of the analysis, six demographic variables (age, gender, marital status, education, ethnicity, and religion) were entered into the model. Individually, two demographic variables, gender ($\beta=-0.156$; $p<0.001$) and marital status

Table 6.5 Hierarchical multiple regression model predicting cooperation with police

Variables	B	T	R	R^2	ΔR^2	F
Step 1	–	–	0.178	0.032	0.032	3.197**
Age	−0.027	−0.527	–	–	–	–
Gender	−0.156***	−3.803	–	–	–	–
Marital status	0.103*	2.015	–	–	–	–
Education	0.051	1.223	–	–	–	–
Ethnicity	−0.012	−0.294	–	–	–	–
Religion	−0.022	−0.543	–	–	–	–
Step 2	–	–	0.179	0.032	0.000	2.142*
Age	−0.029	−0.559	–	–	–	–
Gender	−0.156***	−3.785	–	–	–	–
Marital status	0.105*	2.034	–	–	–	–
Education	0.051	1.215	–	–	–	–
Ethnicity	−0.012	−0.291	–	–	–	–
Religion	−0.024	−0.573	–	–	–	–
Predatory policing	0.006	0.131	–	–	–	–
Police corruption	0.003	0.065	–	–	–	–
Police colonial origin	0.015	0.374	–	–	–	–
Step 3	–	–	0.370	0.137	0.105	7.684***
Age	0.003	0.058	–	–	–	–
Gender	−0.143***	−3.655	–	–	–	–
Marital status	0.069	1.405	–	–	–	–
Education	0.073	1.842	–	–	–	–
Ethnicity	0.017	0.421	–	–	–	–
Religion	−0.014	−0.368	–	–	–	–
Predatory policing	0.040	0.914	–	–	–	–
Police corruption	0.078	1.740	–	–	–	–
Police colonial origin	0.031	0.784	–	–	–	–
Police effectiveness	0.113*	2.422	–	–	–	–
Procedural justice	0.251***	5.563	–	–	–	–
Police legitimacy	0.091*	2.302	–	–	–	–

Notes
* $p<0.05$;
** $p<0.005$;
*** $p<0.001$.

($\beta=0.103$; $p<0.05$) significantly predict willingness to cooperate with police. This indicates that when people make decisions whether to cooperate with the police, their gender and marital status are very important precursors to this decision; men and married participants are more cooperative.

In the second step, three variables (predatory policing, police corruption, and police colonial origin) were added to the model. The new variables showed no significant contribution to the model (R^2 change$=0.000$), however, significant relationships were maintained by gender ($\beta=-0.156$; $p<0.001$) and marital status ($\beta=0.105$; $p<0.05$).

In the final step of the analysis, police effectiveness, procedural justice, and police legitimacy were added to the model. Four variables predicted cooperation with police in the final step: gender ($\beta=-0.143$; $p<0.001$), police effectiveness ($\beta=0.113$; $p<0.05$), procedural justice ($\beta=0.300$; $p<0.001$), and police legitimacy ($\beta=-0.102$; $p<0.05$) respectively. These results show that those who identified as male, who perceived police as effective and procedurally fair during police–public encounters, and those who believe police are legitimate are more likely to cooperate with police.

Discussion

The purpose of this study was to assess Nigerians' perceptions of procedural justice and police effectiveness, and whether police could utilize procedural justice to improve perceptions of police legitimacy and willingness to cooperate. This study also incorporated other context-specific factors, such as the perceptions of predatory policing, police corruption, and police colonial origin, to broaden our understanding of whether these factors will hinder or enhance perceptions of police legitimacy and willingness to cooperate.

The result of the analysis found significant effects of the perceived effectiveness of police on legitimacy judgements but not of perceived procedural justice. This result is highly incongruent with findings from developed Western democracies where perceptions of police legitimacy are primarily determined by procedural justice evaluations, not police effectiveness evaluations (see Mazerolle *et al.* 2013; Sunshine and Tyler 2003; Tyler and Huo 2002). This indicates that procedurally just policing in Nigeria is unlikely to be the solution for addressing Nigeria's police legitimacy crisis. It should be noted that this finding deviates from a previous study in Nigeria where procedural justice was a more important predictor of police legitimacy than police effectiveness among Nigerian adolescents (Akinlabi 2015). But these findings align with Bradford *et al.*'s (2014) South African study. While Bradford and his colleagues found procedural justice played a key role in predicting police legitimacy, South Africans placed greater emphasis on police effectiveness.

The question that remains, however, is why Nigerians place a greater emphasis on perceptions of police effectiveness than on perceptions of procedural justice when making judgements about police legitimacy? One important explanation may be the strong emphasis on crime control. In Nigeria today, crime is on the rise and the general public expects the police to guarantee the safety of lives and property. Whenever this expectation is not met, people tend to view or perceive police as ineffective.

It should be noted that this study has identified a significant negative effect of perceptions of police colonial origin on police legitimacy. The origin of modern policing and its history of malfeasance have created a schism and climate of alienation among the public. The consequence of this in Nigeria today is that the legacy of colonialism remains largely unforgotten. This means that people might still associate the modern police with a repressive and dictatorial colonial origin. As noted by Alemika and Chukwuma (2000), the struggle for independence from colonial rule was predicated upon the belief that self-governance would ameliorate or bring an end to colonial oppression and exploitation. Unfortunately, almost six decades after independence, this expectation has not been met.

The current analysis also revealed that cooperation with police was predicted by multiple factors, such as perceptions of police effectiveness, procedural justice, and police legitimacy. The analysis also showed that gender and marital status had significant effects on self-reported willingness to cooperate with police. These results are predicated upon the idea that the two antecedent factors – the first being perceptions of procedural justice and the second, perceived police effectiveness – are applicable when Nigerians make judgements about their willingness to cooperate with police. In fact, the current study aligns with a growing number of studies that reveal that perceptions of police effectiveness can be very relevant in some contexts when people make decisions about whether to voluntarily cooperate with the police (see Murphy and Cherney 2010; Sargeant *et al.* 2014; Tankebe 2009a).

Specifically, in a similar study in Africa, Tankebe (2009a) found that perceived police effectiveness was the main factor determining self-reported willingness to cooperate with police among Ghanaians. In New York, Sunshine and Tyler (2003) found that perceptions of police effectiveness were also related to self-reported willingness to cooperate with police in the first wave of data collections before the September 11 terror attacks; however, in the second wave, the effect was not found. Similarly, in a recent study in London, Bradford (2014) found that perceived police effectiveness and perceptions of procedural justice were both correlates of willingness to cooperate with police. Finally, Sargeant *et al.* (2014) found that for some ethnic minority groups in Australia, police effectiveness was more important than procedural justice in their decision to cooperate with police.

It is worth noting that in the current study, public perceptions of police legitimacy were found to influence willingness to cooperate with police. This legitimacy-based approach to cooperating with the police relies on the assumption that people are more willing to cooperate with the police when they perceive it as legitimate. That is, if police are perceived as legitimate, people are more likely to report crime and victimization, and are more likely to serve as a witness in police investigations. Despite perennial problems between the police and the public (see Agbiboa 2015; Alemika 2013; Akinlabi 2015, 2016; Smith 2007), the police in Nigeria do appear to retain some support among public in terms of legitimacy judgements and expressed willingness to cooperate. Yet, procedural justice does not appear to be a predictor of legitimacy judgements.

Conclusion

The overarching aim of this study was to explore whether perceptions of procedural justice are more influential than perceptions of police effectiveness in determining Nigerians' legitimacy judgements and expressed willingness to cooperate with police. In addition, this current study sought to extend existing police legitimacy scholarship by examining additional variables (e.g. predatory policing, police corruption, and colonial antecedents of the police) that might predict public assessments of police legitimacy and self-reported willingness to cooperate with police. The results indicated that public perceptions of procedural justice were not relevant in fostering public perceptions of police legitimacy in Nigeria. The research established a more important role for perceived police effectiveness in predicting perceived police legitimacy.

However, public perceptions of procedurally just policing, in addition to perceived police effectiveness, were found to be relevant in predicting Nigerians' self-reported willingness to cooperate with police. This emerged despite Nigeria being a country riddled with corruption and police abuse. These results confirmed both the robustness and limits of the procedural justice model in developing contexts. Most illuminating is that, compared with previous research, the current findings reinforce the argument that there is significant variation in the influence of procedural justice on perceptions of police legitimacy and self-reported willingness to cooperate with police across different contexts.

Note

1 This research was supported by Griffith University Postgraduate Research Scholarship and Griffith University Publication Assistance Scholarship.

Bibliography

Agbiboa, D. (2015). ' "Policing is not work: it is stealing by force": corrupt policing and related abuses in everyday Nigeria', *Africa Today*, 62: 94–126.

Ahire, P. (1991). *Imperial Policing: The Emergence and Role of the Police in Colonial Nigeria, 1860–1960*, Milton Keynes: Open University Press.

Akinlabi, O. (2011). *Legitimacy, Corruption and Delinquency: A Study of Adolescents' Perceptions and Behaviour in Nigeria*, Cambridge: University of Cambridge.

Akinlabi, O. (2013). 'Predatory policing in Nigeria: public experiences of police corruption, brutality and its implication on police legitimacy', *Australia and New Zealand Society of Criminology Conference*. Brisbane.

Akinlabi, O. (2015). 'Young people, procedural justice and police legitimacy in Nigeria', *Policing and Society*, 1–20, online. Available http://dx.doi.org/10.1080/10439463.2015.1077836 (accessed 13 February 2017).

Akinlabi, O. (2016). 'Do the police really protect and serve the public? Police deviance and public cynicism towards the law', *Criminology and Criminal Justice*, 1–17, online. Available http://journals.sagepub.com/doi/pdf/10.1177/1748895816659906 (accessed 13 February 2017).

Alemika, E. (1993). 'Colonialism, state and policing in Nigeria', *Crime, Law and Social Change*, 20: 187–219.

Alemika, E. (2010). 'History, context and crises of the police in Nigeria. Repositioning the Nigeria police to meet the challenges of the policing a democratic society in the twenty-first century and beyond', *Unpublished Presentation at the Biennial Retreat of the Nigeria Police Service Commission*, Uyo, Nigeria.

Alemika, E. (2013). 'Criminal victimization, policing and governance in Nigeria', *CLEEN Foundation Monographe*, 18: 1–81.

Alemika, E. and Chukwuma, I. (2000). *Police–Community Violence in Nigeria*, Nigeria: Centre for Law Enforcement Education and National Human Rights Commission and National Human Rights Commission.

Alemika, E. and Chukwuma, I. (2003). *Civilian Oversight and Accountability of Police in Nigeria*, Lagos: Centre for Law Enforcement Education.

Anderson, C. and Tverdova, Y. (2003). 'Corruption, political allegiances, and attitudes toward government in contemporary democracies', *American Journal of Political Science*, 47: 91–109.

Baker, B. (2004). 'Protection from crime: what is on offer for Africans?', *Journal of Contemporary African Studies*, 22: 165–88.

Baker, B. (2010). *Security in Post-Conflict Africa: The Role of Nonstate Policing*, Boca Raton, FL: CRC Press.

Bradford, B. (2014). 'Policing and social identity: procedural justice, inclusion and cooperation between police and public', *Policing and Society*, 24: 22–43.

Bradford, B., Huq, A., Jackson, J., and Roberts, B. (2014). 'What price fairness when security is at stake? Police legitimacy in South Africa', *Regulation and governance*, 8: 246–68.

Brockner, J., Ackerman, G., Greenberg, J., Gelfand, M., Francesco, A., Chen, Z., Leung, K., Bierbrauer, G., Gomez, C., and Kirkman, B. (2001). 'Culture and procedural justice: the influence of power distance on reactions to voice', *Journal of Experimental Social Psychology*, 37: 300–15.

Carter, H. (1981). 'Prospects for the administration of justice in Nigeria: courts, police, and politics', *Journal of Opinion*, 11: 29–34.

Crawford, A. and Hucklesby, A. (2012). *Legitimacy and Compliance in Criminal Justice*, Oxford: Routledge.

Davidson, B., Buah, F., and Ade-Ajayi, J. (1966). *A History of West Africa to the Nineteenth Century*, New York: Doubleday and Co. Inc.

Deflem, M. (1994). 'Law enforcement in British colonial Africa: a comparative analysis of imperial policing in Nyasaland, the Gold Coast and Kenya', *Police Studies: The International Review of Police Development*, 17: 45–68.

Dierk, L. (2011). 'Yoruba origins and the lost tribes of Israel', *Anthropos*, 106: 579–95.

Dike, K. (1956). *Trade and Politics in the Niger Delta, 1830–1885: An Introduction to the Economic and Political History of Nigeria*, Oxford: Clarendon Press.

Falola, T. and Adebayo, A. (1985). *Pre-Colonial Nigeria: North of the Niger-Benue. Nigerian History and Culture*, Hong Kong: Longman Group (FE) Ltd.

Fika, A. (1978). *The Kano Civil War and British Over-Rule, 1882–1940*, Oxford: Oxford University Press.

Gerber, T. and Mendelson, S. (2008). 'Public experiences of police violence and corruption in contemporary Russia: a case of predatory policing?', *Law and Society Review*, 42: 1–44.

Hills, A. (2008). 'The dialectic of police reform in Nigeria', *Journal of Modern African Studies*, 46: 215–34.

Hinds, L. and Murphy, K. (2007). 'Public satisfaction with police: using procedural justice to improve police legitimacy', *Australian and New Zealand Journal of Criminology*, 40: 27–43.

Hough, M., Jackson, J., Bradford, B., Myhill, A., and Quinton, P. (2010). 'Procedural justice, trust, and institutional legitimacy', *Policing: A Journal of Policy and Practice*, 4: 203–10.

Isichei, E. (1978). *Igbo Worlds: An Anthology of Oral Histories and Historical Descriptions*, Philadephia: Institute for the Study of Human Issues.

Johnson, D., Maguire, E., and Kuhns, J. (2014). 'Public perceptions of the legitimacy of the law and legal authorities: evidence from the Caribbean', *Law and Society Review*, 48: 947–78.

Johnson, S. (1921). *History of the Yorubas: From the Earliest Times to the Beginning of the British Protectorate*, London: Routledge.

Jones, J. (2015). 'The Portuguese in Africa in the 19th Century', *West Chester University*, online. Available http://courses.wcupa.edu/jones/his312/lectures/portugal.htm (accessed 1 July 2016).

Kochel, T., Parks, R., and Mastrofski, S. (2013). 'Examining police effectiveness as a precursor to legitimacy and cooperation with police', *Justice Quarterly*, 30: 895–925.

Mazerolle, L., Antrobus, E., Bennett, S., and Tyler, T. (2013). 'Shaping citizen perceptions of police legitimacy: a randomized field trial of procedural justice', *Criminology*, 51: 33–63.

McCracken, J. (1986). 'Coercion and control in Nyasaland: aspects of the history of a colonial police force', *The Journal of African History*, 27: 127–47.

Meredith, M. (2011). *The Fate of Africa: A History of the Continent Since Independence*, New York: PublicAffairs.

Murphy, K. (2015). 'Does procedural justice matter to youth? Comparing adults' and youths' willingness to collaborate with police', *Policing and Society*, 25: 53–76.

Murphy, K., Bradford, B., and Jackson, J. (2016). 'Motivating compliance behavior among offenders: procedural justice or deterrence?', *Criminal Justice and Behavior*, 43: 102–18.

Murphy, K. and Cherney, A. (2010). *Policing Ethnic Minority Groups with Procedural Justice: An Empirical Study*, Geelong: Alfred Deakin Research Institute.

Murphy, K. and Cherney, A. (2011). 'Fostering cooperation with the police: how do ethnic minorities in Australia respond to procedural justice-based policing?', *Australian and New Zealand Journal of Criminology*, 44: 235–57.

Murphy, K., Mazerolle, L., and Bennett, S. (2014). 'Promoting trust in police: findings from a randomised experimental field trial of procedural justice policing', *Policing and Society*, 24: 405–24.

Murphy, K., Murphy, B., and Mearns, M. (2010). *'The 2009 Crime, Safety and Policing in Australia Survey': Survey Methodology and Preliminary Findings*, Geelong: Alfred Deakin Research Institute, Deakin University.

Nadama, G. (1977). 'The rise and collapse of a Hausa State: a political and social history of Zamfara', unpublished Ph.D. thesis, Ahmadu Bello University.

'Nigeria: Corruption Fueling Police Abuses' [Editorial], (2010, August 17), *Human Rights Watch*, online. Available www.hrw.org/news/2010/08/17/nigeria-corruption-fueling-police-abuses (accessed 10 February 2017).

Nzimiro, I. (1972). *Studies in Ibo Political Systems: Chieftancy and Politics in Four Nigerian States*, Berkeley, CA: University of California Press.

Okafo, N. (2007). 'Law enforcement in postcolonial Africa: interfacing indigenous and English policing in Nigeria', *International Police Executive Symposium Working Paper Number 7*, online. Available http://ipes.info/WPS/WPS%20No%207.pdf (accessed 13 February 2017).

Oli, I. (1985). 'Crime and social control in Nigeria: growth of a quandary', unpublished Ph.D. thesis, City University of New York.

Onoge, O. (1993). *Social Conflicts and Crime Control in Colonial Nigeria. Policing Nigeria: Past, Present and Future*, Lagos: Malthouse Press Ltd.

Onyeozili, E. (1998). 'An examination of social control and policing in Nigeria: a theoretical and evaluative analysis', unpublished Ph.D. thesis, Florida State University.

Onyeozili, E. (2005). 'Obstacles to effective policing in Nigeria', *African Journal of Criminology and Justice Studies*, 1: 32–54.

Otu, N. (1999). 'Colonialism and the criminal justice system in Nigeria', *International Journal of Comparative and Applied Criminal Justice*, 23: 293–306.

Reisig, M. and Meško, G. (2009). 'Procedural justice, legitimacy, and prisoner misconduct', *Psychology, Crime and Law*, 15: 41–59.

Reisig, M., Tankebe, J. and Meško, G. (2012). 'Procedural justice, police legitimacy, and public cooperation with the police among young Slovene adults', *Journal of Criminal Justice and Security*, 14: 147–64.

Rotimi, K. (2001). *The Police in a Federal State: The Nigerian Experience*, Ibadan: College Press.

Sargeant, E., Murphy, K., and Cherney, A. (2014). 'Ethnicity, trust and cooperation with police: testing the dominance of the process-based model', *European Journal of Criminology*, 11: 500–24.

Shearing, C. and Stenning, P. (2016). 'The privatization of security: implications for democracy', in R. Abrahamsen and A. Leander (eds.), *Routledge Handbook of Private Security Studies*, Oxford: Routledge, 140–48.

Skogan, W. (2004). *Community Policing: Can it Work?*, Belmont, CA: Wadsworth/Thomson Learning.

Skogan, W. (2005). 'Citizen satisfaction with police encounters', *Police Quarterly*, 8: 298–321.

Skogan, W. (2006). 'Asymmetry in the impact of encounters with police', *Policing and Society*, 16: 99–126.

Smith, D. (2007). *A Culture of Corruption: Everyday Deception and Popular Discontent in Nigeria*, Princeton, NJ: Princeton University Press.

Smith, M. (1960). *Government in Zazzau, 1880–1950*, London: Oxford University Press.

Sunshine, J. and Tyler, T. (2003). 'The role of procedural justice and legitimacy in shaping public support for policing', *Law and Society Review*, 37: 513–48.

Tade, O. and Olaitan, F. (2015). 'Traditional structures of crime control in Lagos, Nigeria', *African Security Review*, 24: 138–52.

Tamuno, T. (1970). *The Police in Modern Nigeria, 1861–1965: Origins, Development and Role*, Ibadan: Ibadan University Press.

Tankebe, J. (2008). 'Colonialism, legitimation, and policing in Ghana', *International Journal of Law, Crime and Justice*, 36: 67–84.

Tankebe, J. (2009a). 'Public cooperation with the police in Ghana: does procedural fairness matter?', *Journal of Criminology*, 47: 1265–93.

Tankebe, J. (2009b). 'Self-help, policing, and procedural justice: Ghanaian vigilantism and the rule of law', *Law and Society Review*, 43: 245–69.

Tankebe, J. (2010). 'Public confidence in the police testing the effects of public experiences of police corruption in Ghana', *British Journal of Criminology*, 50: 296–319.

Tyler, T. (1990). *Why People Obey the Law: Procedural Justice, Legitimacy, and Compliance*, New Haven, CT: Yale University Press.

Tyler, T. (2006). *Why People Obey the Law*, Princeton, NJ: Princeton University Press.

Tyler, T. and Darley, J. (2000). 'Building a law-abiding society: taking public views about morality and the legitimacy of legal authorities into account when formulating substantive law', *Hofstra Law Review*, 28: 707–39.

Tyler, T. and Fagan, J. (2008). 'Legitimacy and cooperation: why do people help the police fight crime in their communities', *Ohio State Journal of Criminal Law*, 6: 231–75.

Tyler, T. and Huo, Y. (2002). *Trust in the Law: Encouraging Public Cooperation with the Police and Courts*, New York: Russell Sage Foundation.

Ubah, C. (1973). 'Administration of Kano Emirate under the British, 1900–1930', unpublished Ph.D. thesis, University of Ibadan.

Vaaseh, G. and Ehinmore, O. (2011). 'Ethnic politics and conflicts in Nigeria's first republic: the misuse of Native Administrative Police Forces (NAPFS) and the Tiv Riots of Central Nigeria, 1960–1964', *Canadian Social Science*, 7: 214–22.

Part III

Societal cleavages and legitimacy

Minorities and religions

7 Policing marginalized groups in a diverse society

Using procedural justice to promote group belongingness and trust in police[1]

Kristina Murphy and Adrian Cherney

Introduction

Police play an important role in society. They are charged with enforcing the law and they work hard to detect and prevent crime. Without the support of the public, however, police cannot be fully effective in their fight against crime. Police rely heavily on members of the public to tell them about social disorder in their neighbourhood, and they rely on members of the public to report incidents of crime and victimization. But not all members of society wish to engage with police, and police often struggle to encourage members of the public to collaborate with them (AIFS 2014; Weitzer 2010). We also know from the criminology literature that many incidents of crime and victimization go unreported (Skogan 1977).

The reluctance of some members of society to engage with police can often be traced to low levels of trust in police (Murphy *et al.* 2014; Stoutland 2001; Tyler and Huo 2002; Weitzer 2010). Distrust in police can be particularly salient in some communities (van Craen 2013; Weitzer 2010). These communities are often characterized by high levels of economic and social disadvantage, high levels of perceived or experienced violent crime, and a high density of ethnic and racial minority residents (Weitzer 2010). In these communities, individuals also report often being subjected to biased or overly punitive policing practices (Weitzer 2010). For immigrants in these communities, past experiences with highly corrupt police in their countries of origin can also add to their distrust of police (Murphy 2013; Tyler 2001). The challenge for police agencies, therefore, is to identify strategies that can foster public trust in police among all members of society.

The present study examines the role that *procedural justice policing* can play in promoting public trust in police. We are interested in the effects of procedural justice as prior research has shown that procedural justice policing can have a number of positive effects on people's attitudes towards police and their willingness to work collaboratively with police (e.g. McCluskey 2003; Murphy *et al.* 2008; Sunshine and Tyler 2003; for a review see Murphy *et al.* 2014). Given that police agencies globally are identifying procedural justice as an important way of improving engagement and public confidence in their roles and functions

(Mazerolle *et al.* 2014; Task Force 2015), being able to identify and better understand the conditions where procedural justice policing might have the most beneficial effect (or counter-productive effect) across different population groups and policing contexts is important.

In this study, we examine whether procedural justice policing is effective in promoting trust in police in Australia's diverse population. We are particularly interested in whether procedural justice works effectively for those who feel a lower sense of 'belonging' in society. 'Policing has always been implicated in processes of social inclusion and exclusion' (Bradford 2014: 22). Hence, we explore whether feelings of 'group belongingness' can be influenced by procedural justice policing and, importantly, whether it can moderate the effect of procedural justice on citizens' trust in police.[2]

The symbolic nature of policing and group belongingness

People have a natural desire to form and maintain social bonds with others. Baumeister and Leary (1995) suggest this drive to affiliate with others is known as the need to belong. Feeling connected to people and feeling accepted by others in a group is what is termed 'group belongingness' (Baumeister and Leary 1995; van Prooijn *et al.* 2004). Scholars suggest that exclusion from valued social groups ranks as one of the most aversive of human experiences, with exclusion linked to poor self-esteem, anxiety, depression, disengagement, aggression, and loneliness (Gardner *et al.* 2000; Nezlek *et al.* 1997).

The concern for legal authorities is how feeling excluded might influence peoples' willingness to engage with police and with other members of society. We suggest that procedural justice policing might prove effective in fostering feelings of belonging, and we also argue that belonging may be related to people's trust in authorities, with those feeling a greater sense of belonging being more likely to trust legal authorities. Why do we think this? Scholars suggest that feelings of group belonging are related to acts of fairness and unfairness. According to Tyler and Lind's (1992) Group Value Model of *procedural justice*, for example, people value fair interpersonal treatment from group authorities for symbolic reasons. It has been suggested that procedural justice 'signals to recipients that they are valued members of a social group, and consequently enhances their sense of belonging' (Lind and Tyler 1988: 92).

Police officers, as a consequence of their position as societal representatives, play a potentially important role in promoting feelings of belonging because police have the power to define who is and who is not recognized and included in society. Police also have the power to act on these definitions through the type of treatment they impart to citizens (Blackwood *et al.* 2013; Bradford 2014; Hopkins *et al.* 1997). Specifically, the way in which police exercise their power communicates to people how society views them. Treat people with procedural justice and it signals that they are valued members of society (i.e. that they are accepted and belong); treat them unfairly, however, and it signals marginalization. In other words, people derive important information about their membership in groups, and their level of belongingness in that group, partly from the way that group authorities treat them.

Police officers demonstrate procedural justice when they treat individuals with respect and dignity, when they communicate to people that they have their best interests at heart, when they are unbiased in their decision-making, and when they provide people the opportunity to air concerns and grievances (i.e. voice) before decisions are made. Research consistently reveals that if police officers use these four elements of procedural justice (i.e. respect, trustworthiness, neutrality, and voice), this leads to a number of positive outcomes: greater public trust in police, greater perceptions that the police are legitimate and entitled to be obeyed, greater satisfaction with police contact, greater willingness to comply and cooperate with police directives, and greater willingness to work collaboratively with police (e.g. Hinds and Murphy 2007; Jackson *et al.* 2012; Mazerolle *et al.* 2012a; McCluskey 2003; Murphy *et al.* 2008, 2014; Sunshine and Tyler 2003; Tyler 2006). In fact, Tyler (2006) specifically argues that when procedural justice policing works well, society benefits from a more 'engaged' community and a reduction in crime.

How might group belongingness influence reactions to procedural justice?

We suggest that feelings of group belongingness may have consequences for people's reactions to police. Group belongingness may either diminish or amplify the effect of procedural justice policing on people's trust in police. We draw on a number of published studies to predict how citizens might react to procedural justice policing when they feel they do not belong. Findings from these studies typically support the predictions made by Tyler and Lind's (1992) *Group Value Model*. An important premise of the model is that people's relationships to groups should *moderate* the importance they place on how they are treated by group authorities. Given that fair treatment conveys relational information about people's value to a group, Tyler and Lind argue that such information should be particularly important to people when they are dealing with an authority that represents a valued in-group (i.e. a group to which they identify strongly with). Studies indeed support this suggestion (see Huo *et al.* 1996; Smith *et al.* 1998; Stahl *et al.* 2004; van Prooijen *et al.* 2004). For example, both Smith *et al.* (1998) and Stahl *et al.* (2004) found that procedural justice had stronger effects on people's reactions to authorities if procedural justice was provided by an in-group authority, as opposed to an out-group authority. Huo *et al.* (1996) also found that people who identified more strongly with the group that the authority represented were affected more so by procedural justice than those who identified weakly with the group (for similar findings in the policing context see Bradford 2014; Bradford *et al.* 2014; Huo 2003; Sargeant *et al.* 2014).

Similarly, Murphy and her colleagues recently revealed that procedural justice policing can have variant effects across different population groups and policing contexts (see also Tankebe's 2009 work in Ghana). Murphy revealed that procedural justice had stronger effects for (a) ethnic minorities who identify weakly with Australia (Murphy 2013) or who report being disengaged from police (Madon *et al.* 2017); (b) youth (Murphy 2015); and (c) some crime victims (Murphy and Barkworth 2014). Together, these findings seem to contradict those presented earlier and suggest that marginalized individuals may be more attune to messages that they are being treated fairly by group authorities.

How might we explain these contradictory findings? Social psychological research has revealed that feelings of 'uncertainty' can increase people's need to belong to social groups (Hogg and Abrams 1993; Hogg and Mullin 1999). The notion of uncertainty has been included in social-cognitive models of procedural justice, such as Van den Bos' *Uncertainty Management Model* (see Lind and Van den Bos 2002; Van den Bos 2001; Van den Bos and Lind 2002). This model, for example, suggests that procedural justice should be particularly important to people in situations where they feel uncertain about their position in a group. Status uncertainty leaves people feeling anxious about what to expect in interactions with authorities, so they focus on how they are being treated. Being treated with respect, being given voice in decision-making, and experiencing unbiased procedures communicates to these people that they are valued members of the group, which reduces their feelings of uncertainty. We suggest similar effects may be operating in the context of police–citizen interactions, and that these effects may explain why procedural justice can be more effective for individuals who feel marginalized in society.

Present study

Our study examines how feelings of 'group belongingness' and 'trust in police' can be promoted with procedural justice policing. We also examine how group belongingness may affect people's reactions to procedural justice policing. Before setting out our hypotheses, however, we should make one important point. Many of the studies cited above use measures of social identity (e.g. identification with one's nation or ethnic group) to examine how procedural justice can either promote or interact with identity. We propose that social identity and group belongingness are distinct constructs and should each be studied in their own right. For example, one might identify strongly with a group but feel little sense of belongingness in that group (i.e. 'I identify strongly with Australia, but others in Australia do not accept me so I don't feel I belong'). On the other hand one might feel accepted and feel they belong in a community but don't identify strongly with that group. This might apply to a person who lives in Australia but is not Australian. How identity moderates the effect of procedural justice policing has already been well established in the literature. How group belongingness moderates the effect of procedural justice policing has not. It is for this reason that the current study focuses on group belongingness. Based on our review of the literature presented above, we propose three hypotheses:

1   procedural justice policing will promote people's feelings of group belongingness;
2   procedural justice policing will promote people's trust in police; and
3   feelings of group belongingness will moderate the effect of procedural justice policing on people's trust in police.

In predicting how group belongingness will moderate the effect of procedural justice policing on people's trust in police, the group value model predicts that procedurally fair treatment from police might be more important to those who report higher levels of group belongingness. In contrast, the uncertainty management model predicts the opposite; procedural justice should be more important to those who report lower levels of group belongingness. Psychology research tells us that all people wish to be accepted and wish to belong in their community (Baumeister and Leary 1995). Hence, we argue that those low on group belongingness will look for external cues that they are valued members of that community. We therefore expect that procedural justice will have a more beneficial effect in promoting trust for those low on group belongingness.

Australia in context

Australia has seven state police forces (Western Australia Police, New South Wales Police, Victoria Police Force, Queensland Police Service, South Australia Police, Northern Territory Police, and Tasmania Police) and one federal police force that also provides policing services to the Australian Capital Territory. Australia is a Western-democratic nation where multiculturalism is valued and promoted; approximately 27 per cent of Australian residents are born overseas and 46 per cent of residents are either born overseas or have at least one parent born overseas (ABS 2012a). These immigrants are drawn from countries all around the world.

To test our three hypotheses, we draw on Australian survey data. The Australian Community Capacity Survey (ACCS) is an Australian study of residents living in two major Australian cities: Brisbane and Melbourne. At the time of data collection in 2011, Brisbane had a population of approximately two million residents (ABS 2012a), and Melbourne had approximately four million residents (ABS 2012b). Australia's population was approximately 21.5 million in 2011 (ABS 2013). The ACCS involves both a large-scale sample of 9,420 residents from the general population and an additional booster sample of 1,300 people from Arabic-speaking, Vietnamese and Indian backgrounds. People from Vietnamese and Indian backgrounds represent prominent minority ancestral groups in Australia. Migrants from India and Vietnam make up approximately 2.5 per cent of the Australian population, and are among the top five country of birth groups according to the Australian Bureau of Statistics. People from an Arabic-speaking background are one of the fastest growing immigrant groups in Australia and comprise about 2 per cent of the population (ABS 2012c).

These three minority groups were selected as important groups to study in the context of Australian policing because each has had problematic relationships with Australian police and each group comprises a significant portion of the Australian population (Mason 2009; Meredyth *et al.* 2010; Poynting 2006). Australia has a unique immigration history that has lent itself to distinctive patterns of perceived police bias. Prior to the 1970s, Australia's population was predominately composed of Caucasian migrants from the UK (Gerstenfeld 2013). This was due to the Australian policies of the time prohibiting immigration from non-Western countries. The abolition of the 'White Australia Policy' in 1973, however, brought a large number of immigrants from Asian countries. The end of the Vietnam War coincided with this change in immigration policy, and Vietnamese immigrants constituted the first large-scale wave of non-Caucasian immigrants to Australia. Settlers from other non-Western countries have since migrated to Australia. Australia is now considered one of the most ethnically diverse countries in the world.

The first wave of Asian immigrants in the 1970s brought new and specific concerns regarding police bias. Asians were very different culturally to previous immigrants and were viewed with scepticism by many Australians. The integration of Asian youth was a particular challenge. Due to the lack of opportunities for many immigrants, a significant number of Vietnamese youth joined Asian Street gangs and became involved in drug dealing and crime (Dixon and Maher 2002). This attracted heavy-handed policing tactics to bring the problem under control, resulting in perceived police-bias from the Vietnamese community (Meredyth *et al.* 2010).

Indian and Arabic-speaking immigrants have similarly experienced problematic relationships with police in Australia. For example, in 2009, a series of violent attacks on Indian students occurred in Sydney and Melbourne. Investigating police agencies claimed the attacks were not racially driven and were perpetrated by opportunistic criminals (Verghis 2009). The Indian population criticized police as being racially biased for not taking their safety concerns seriously (Mason 2009). These incidents had a significant impact on the number of Indian students choosing to study and settle in Australia. Finally, Sentas (2014) argues that while counter-terrorism laws on the surface appear neutral, their practical application by police and security agencies often conflates Islam with the risk of terrorism. As a result, many within the Arab and Muslim communities feel that they receive disproportionate and biased attention from police agencies (Poynting and Perry 2007; Cherney and Murphy 2016). While we have discussed perceived bias among these three minority communities, examples of overt police bias against other ethnically and racially diverse groups in Australia have also occurred.

Method

Participants and procedure

We use survey data from 10,720 respondents. For the primary sample (N=9,420), households were randomly selected from within 298 randomly selected suburbs in the Brisbane and Melbourne Statistical Divisions. The electronic telephone directory and Random Digit Dialing was then used to select the resulting sample. Participants were selected from a household if they had most recently celebrated a birthday and were over 18 years of age. Interviews were conducted by telephone using Computer Assisted Telephone Interviewing (Mazerolle *et al.* 2012b).

The ethnic minority booster sample was selected using a surname-based method, as Random Digit Dialing is unviable for a small target population. A list of common surnames for Indian, Vietnamese, and Arabic-speaking people was collated and the list of names was employed in combination with the electronic telephone directory and post-code matching to select a sampling pool of 10,800 households. Participants in this pool were randomly contacted by phone and were selected if they were over 18 years of age and were next to celebrate a birthday. An assisted interview was then arranged and conducted face-to-face, using pen-and-paper surveys in the participant's preferred language (Murphy *et al.* 2012). For the primary sample the response rate was 50 per cent, while the ethnic minority booster response rate was 43 per cent.

Participants in the combined sample were aged between 18 and 99 (Mean age=50.07 years; SD=15.82). 40 per cent were male, 68 per cent were married or in a cohabiting relationship, 39 per cent had a university education, 59 per cent worked either full- or part-time, and 30 per cent were born overseas (the proportion of overseas born respondents did not differ between the primary and ethnic minority samples). The median household income was AU$60,000–79,999.

Questionnaire and scale construction

The ACCS contained hundreds of survey questions. For the purposes of the current chapter, however, only those items relevant to procedural justice policing, trust in police, group belongingness, and demographic/control characteristics were used (see the Appendix for survey questions). The procedural justice and trust scales were both based on the work of policing scholars in the US (Sunshine and Tyler 2003); these measures have been widely validated in previous studies. The 'group belongingness' scale was drawn from the work of Hipp (2010) and Sampson *et al.* (1999) and was designed to measure feelings of belongingness in one's community. These three scales were each measured on a 1 = strongly disagree to 5 = strongly agree Likert scale; with higher scores indicating greater general perceptions of procedural justice, trust in police, and feelings of group belongingness, respectively.

The 'procedural justice policing' scale comprised five items (see Appendix). When answering these items, respondents were asked to think about how they thought police treated residents in their local community (Mean=3.76; SD=0.64). As such, the procedural justice scale was a general perception measure, rather than a measure of personal experience of fair treatment. As can be seen in Table 7.1, fewer than half our respondents had personal contact with police in the preceding 12 months. Hence, attitudes regarding police are typically built through vicarious experience. As such, this study used a general perception measure to assess procedural justice perceptions. To measure 'trust in police', respondents were asked two questions about how much they trusted and had confidence in police in their local community (Mean=3.94; SD=0.66). The 'group belongingness' scale comprised five items and assessed respondents' level of attachment and feelings of belonging in their local community; higher scores indicate greater feelings of group belongingness (Mean=3.88; SD=0.65).

Demographic and other control variables were also measured. These additional variables were used in this study because prior research has shown these items to influence people's attitudes and reactions to police (Skogan 2006). These measures were age, gender (0=female; 1=male), education (1=no schooling to 7=post-graduate qualifications), employment (0=employed; 1=unemployed), prior contact with police (0=no contact; 1=has had prior contact with police), ethnicity (0=non-minority; 1=ethnic minority), and language (0=speaks English at home; 1=speaks a language other than English at home).

The ethnicity variable was created by coding respondents' self-reported ancestry. All respondents were asked to indicate their country of birth and their country of ancestry. Respondents who indicated they were either born in, or originated from, Africa, the Middle East, Asia, or Oceania were categorized as coming from an ethnic minority background (N=1,686; 15.9 per cent of the sample), while those born in, or from, Australia, Europe, and the Americas were categorized as coming from a non-ethnic minority background. While this method of classifying people into an ethnic minority or non-minority group is not perfect, it does give a rough guide of the ethnic minority status of respondents. The ethnicity variable was strongly correlated with the language variable (r=0.57, $p<0.001$), suggesting that those who spoke a language other than English at home were more likely to be classified as an ethnic minority group member.

Also measured were a 'perceived crime' scale and a question asking respondents to gauge the level of ethnic diversity in their neighbourhood ('Can you tell me the percentage of people in your community from a non-Anglo-Saxon background?'). The 'perceived crime' scale comprised four items measured on a 1 = never to 4 = often Likert scale. This scale measured the perceived violent crime problem in a respondent's local neighbourhood; higher scores indicate a greater perceived violent crime problem in one's neighbourhood.

Results

Descriptive results

Table 7.1 presents the means, standard deviations, and Cronbach alpha reliability coefficients for each of the scales and variables used in this study. Also presented is the proportion of respondents falling into each demographic category, and the bivariate correlations between all measures. Table 7.1 shows that the four scales used (procedural justice, group belongingness, trust in police, perceived crime) are highly reliable, with the lowest Cronbach alpha score being 0.76.

Table 7.1 Mean, standard deviation, and Cronbach alpha scores for each measure; also reported are the bivariate correlations between measures

Scale/variable	Mean/%	SD	1	2	3	4	5	6	7	8	9	10	11	12
1 Procedural Justice	3.76	0.64	(0.86)	0.28*	0.63*	0.08*	-0.06*	-0.04*	0.05*	-0.05*	-0.06*	0.00	-0.10*	-0.06*
2 Group belongingness	3.88	0.65	—	(0.76)	0.31*	0.11*	0.01	-0.03	-0.01	-0.08*	-0.12*	-0.01	-0.21*	-0.19*
3 Trust in police	3.94	0.66	—	—	(0.89)	0.06*	-0.05*	-0.07*	0.03*	-0.6*	-0.06*	-0.01	-0.10*	-0.05*
4 Age	50.07	15.82	—	—	—	—	-0.20*	0.02	0.39*	-0.29*	-0.30*	-0.11*	-0.14*	-0.13*
5 Education	4.89	1.39	—	—	—	—	—	0.08*	-0.25*	0.13*	0.16*	0.09*	0.03*	-0.02
6 Gender (0=female)	59.8	—	—	—	—	—	—	—	-0.11*	0.07*	0.07*	0.07*	0.01	-0.03*
7 Employment (0=employed)	59.2	—	—	—	—	—	—	—	—	-0.08*	-0.07*	-0.10*	-0.06*	-0.04*
8 Language (0=English)	77.9	—	—	—	—	—	—	—	—	—	0.57*	-0.09*	-0.01	0.20*
9 Ethnicity (0=non-minority)	84.1	—	—	—	—	—	—	—	—	—	—	-0.07*	-0.01	0.14*
10 Contact with police (0=no)	58.2	—	—	—	—	—	—	—	—	—	—	—	0.13*	0.02
11 Perceived crime problem	1.57	0.65	—	—	—	—	—	—	—	—	—	—	(0.79)	0.20*
12 Perceived ethnic diversity	27.76	25.90	—	—	—	—	—	—	—	—	—	—	—	—

Notes

* Indicates a significant relationship at $p < 0.01$. All scales measured on a 1 to 5 scale: higher scores indicate greater levels of procedural justice, group belongingness, trust in police, perceived crime, and percentage of ethnic minorities living in their community, respectively. A higher score on the age and education variables represents a greater age and a higher level of education. The perceived ethnic diversity measure reflects the estimated perceived percentage of minorities living in the community. Figures in parentheses are Cronbach alpha coefficients. Percentage figures for the other variables are provided for the 0 category.

The correlations show that procedural justice was related to all of the variables, except contact with police. This suggests that those who perceive the police as treating citizens in their community with procedural justice are more likely to feel higher levels of belonging and have greater trust in police. Those with higher procedural justice scores were also less likely to see a violent crime problem in their community. Older participants were also more likely to view police as procedurally fair, so too were women, while those from an ethnic minority background and those who spoke a language other than English at home, were less likely to view police as procedurally just. Greater belonging was also associated with greater trust in police.

Regression analyses

Two Ordinary Least Squares (OLS) regression analyses were undertaken to answer our three research hypotheses. The first regression analysis (see Table 7.2) used the demographic and control variables, as well as procedural justice to predict respondents' feelings of group belongingness. This regression enabled us to test if procedural justice policing was associated with enhanced feelings of belongingness. The second regression used the demographic and control variables, as well as the procedural justice and group belongingness variables to predict trust in police (see Table 7.3). In addition, in the third step of the second regression analysis, an interaction term between the procedural justice and group belongingness variables was included. This interaction term allowed us to examine whether group belongingness moderated the effect of procedural justice on trust in police.

Predicting group belongingness

As can be seen in Step 1 of Table 7.2, older respondents and those who were more educated felt a greater sense of belongingness in their local community, while men, those not employed, and those who came from an ethnic minority background were less likely to feel they belonged in their local community. Further, those who felt there was more violent crime in their neighbourhood or who felt there was greater ethnic diversity in their neighbourhood were less likely to feel they belonged. All but one of these relationships continued to predict group belongingness after the procedural justice policing variable was entered into the model at Step 2 (the ethnicity variable became insignificant at Step 2).

Importantly, procedural justice was the strongest predictor of group belongingness at Step 2. Those respondents who felt police use procedural justice when dealing with members of their community were also more likely to feel a greater sense of group belongingness in their local community. This positive and significant relationship suggests that police have the potential to positively influence feelings of belongingness in communities.

Table 7.2 OLS regression analysis showing how control variables and procedural justice predict group belongingness

Predictor	Step 1			Step 2		
	B	SE_B	β	B	SE_B	β
Constant	4.09	0.04	–	3.08	0.06	–
Age	0.00	0.00	0.08***	0.00	0.00	0.07***
Education	0.02	0.01	0.04***	0.03	0.01	0.05***
Gender (0=female)	–0.06	0.01	–0.05***	–0.05	0.01	–0.04***
Employment (0=employed)	–0.07	0.02	–0.06***	–0.08	0.02	–0.06***
Language (0=English)	–0.01	0.03	–0.01	–0.01	0.02	–0.01
Ethnicity (0=non-minority)	–0.06	0.03	–0.02*	–0.04	0.03	–0.02
Contact with police (0=no)	0.04	0.01	0.03**	0.03	0.01	0.02*
Perceived ethnic diversity	–0.01	0.00	–0.18***	–0.01	0.00	–0.17***
Perceived crime problem	–0.18	0.01	–0.18***	–0.15	0.01	–0.16***
Procedural justice	–	–	–	0.26	0.01	0.26***
R^2	–	–	0.09	–	–	0.16
R^2 change	–	–	0.09	–	–	0.07
F change	–	–	84.81***	–	–	610.63***
df	–	–	97,761	–	–	17,760

Notes
* $p<0.05$;
** $p<0.01$;
*** $p<0.001$.

Predicting trust in police

As can be seen in Step 1 of Table 7.3, five control variables were significant predictors of trust in police. Those who were older were more likely to trust police, while those who were less educated, who were male, and who came from ethnic minority backgrounds were less likely to trust police. Those who indicated their neighbourhood had a more serious crime problem were also less likely to trust police. These specific findings support prior research (see Skogan 2006). In Step 2, the procedural justice and group belongingness variables were entered into the model. Both variables were significant and positive predictors of trust in police; those who felt police were more procedurally fair were more likely to trust police, and those who felt a stronger sense of belonging in their community were also more likely to trust police. Procedural justice was the stronger predictor of the two, however. Interestingly, most of the demographic and control variables ceased to predict trust in police on entry of these two variables; again, the ethnicity variable ceased to be significant. Finally, the interaction term in Step 3 was negative and significant, albeit weak. This suggests that procedural justice is slightly more likely to have a positive effect on trust in police for those low on group belongingness. Figure 7.1 illustrates this weak interaction effect.

Table 7.3 OLS regression analysis showing how control variables, procedural justice and group belongingness predict trust in police

Predictor	Step 1			Step 2			Step 3		
	B	SE_B	β	B	SE_B	β	B	SE_B	β
Constant	4.17	0.05	–	4.03	0.04	–	4.03	0.04	–
Age	0.00	0.00	0.04**	0.00	0.00	-0.01	0.00	0.00	-0.01
Education	-0.01	0.01	-0.03*	-0.00	0.00	-0.01	-0.00	0.00	-0.01
Gender (0 = female)	-0.10	0.02	-0.07***	-0.05	0.01	-0.04***	-0.05	0.01	-0.04***
Employment (0 = employed)	-0.01	0.02	-0.01	-0.01	0.01	-0.01	-0.01	0.01	-0.01
Language (0 = English)	-0.02	0.03	-0.01	-0.03	0.02	-0.01	-0.03	0.02	-0.01
Ethnicity (0 = non-minority)	-0.06	0.03	-0.03*	-0.01	0.02	-0.00	-0.01	0.02	-0.00
Contact with police (0 = no)	0.03	0.02	0.02	0.00	0.01	0.00	0.00	0.01	0.00
Perceived ethnic diversity	-0.01	0.00	-0.02	0.00	0.00	0.02*	0.00	0.00	0.02*
Perceived crime problem	-0.10	0.01	-0.10***	-0.02	0.01	-0.02*	-0.02	0.01	-0.02
Procedural justice	–	–	–	0.63	0.01	0.62***	0.63	0.01	0.62***
Group belongingness	–	–	–	0.14	0.01	0.13***	0.14	0.01	0.13***
PJ x group belongingness	–	–	–	–	–	–	-0.05	0.01	-0.04***
R^2	–	–	0.02	–	–	0.46	–	–	0.46
R^2 change	–	–	0.02	–	–	0.44	–	–	0.01
F change	–	–	17.91***	–	–	3,145.14***	–	–	18.48***
df	–	–	97,752	–	–	27,750	–	–	17,749

Notes
* $p<0.05$;
** $p<0.01$;
*** $p<0.001$.

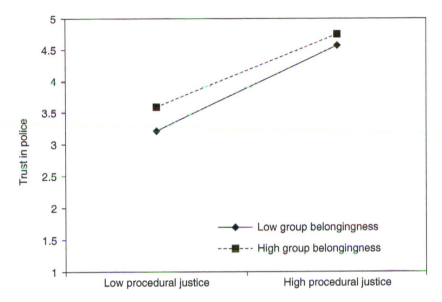

Figure 7.1 Interaction between procedural justice and group belongingness predicting trust in police.

Discussion

The objective of the current study was twofold. First, to test whether procedural justice policing could foster peoples' sense of belonging in their local community. Second, to examine whether procedural justice policing enhanced public trust in police, particularly among people who reported feeling more marginalized in their local community.

We found that procedural justice was positively associated with feelings of group belongingness; those who perceived police to be treating citizens in their community more fairly were more likely to report stronger feelings of belonging (Hypothesis 1 supported). As expected, we also found procedural justice to be related to people's trust in police; those who perceived police as more procedurally just with their community were also more likely to say they trusted local police. This finding supports Hypothesis 2 and also supports prior research in the procedural justice field (see Tyler and Huo 2002; Murphy *et al.* 2014).

We also found that a number of demographic and control variables predicted people's trust in police, although to a lesser extent than procedural justice. For example, those who lived in communities that were perceived to have high rates of violent crime were less likely to trust police. Those from an ethnic minority background were less likely to trust police, so too were men and younger respondents (thus supporting prior criminology research; Skogan 2006; Weitzer 2010). However, many of these demographic and control variables ceased being significant predictors of trust after procedural justice perceptions or feelings of belongingness were taken into account. Of particular note is the fact that 'ethnicity' was no longer a significant predictor of belongingness or trust in police when procedural justice was accounted for. This finding is inconsistent with research from other countries, which typically reveals that ethnicity/race is a major predictor of people's attitudes toward police (see Skogan 2006). Australia's strong emphasis on multiculturalism may explain why ethnicity was a less important variable in our study. Multiculturalism focuses on the recognition and active support of group differences. Here, cultural differences within society are seen as valuable and worthy of being preserved and immigrants are encouraged to practice their customs in Australia. In contrast, many other Western nations emphasize assimilation over multiculturalism. Here, immigrants are strongly encouraged to assimilate and take on the identity of their new country above all else. Some individuals do not, however, perhaps resulting in greater variability in feelings of belonging and greater distrust of social institutions in those countries.

Turning to some of our other findings, we also demonstrated that group belongingness was positively related to trust in police. Those respondents with stronger feelings of group belongingness were more likely to report greater trust in police. We also found that feelings of group belongingness had important consequences for people's reactions to procedural justice policing. Specifically, group belongingness moderated the effect of procedural justice on respondents' trust in police. Many previous studies (most in non-policing contexts) have found procedural justice effects are typically stronger under conditions of high inclusiveness (e.g. strong identification, high belongingness, when imparted by in-group authorities or in within-group interactions). However, we found procedural justice policing had a slightly stronger, positive impact on building trust in police for those low on group belongingness (i.e. those more marginalized individuals). While this particular finding supports Hypothesis 3, it does contradict previous findings in the literature (although see Madon *et al.* 2017).

Together, our findings suggest that procedural justice policing has the potential to be particularly effective if used with individuals who feel marginalized in society. The findings are significant because they support Bradford's (2014) assertions that police officers can play an important role in fostering feelings of social inclusion in local communities (see also Blackwood *et al.* 2013; Murphy 2013; Murphy *et al.* 2015; Madon *et al.* 2017).

Implications for theory and police practice

Our findings have implications for both procedural justice theories and for police practice more broadly. The first implication is that our findings contradict the main predictions made by Tyler and Lind's (1992) Group Value Model. They also contradict many of the results reported in previous studies in the literature. Tyler and Lind's model predicts that those who feel less identified with their community should be less responsive to procedural justice policing. The model suggests that procedural justice should carry more weight when imparted by an authority that represents a group one identifies strongly with (e.g. Huo 2003).

Our findings suggest that marginalized individuals may in fact benefit more when receiving procedural justice from legal authorities. We found that those low on feelings of group belongingness were more strongly affected by procedural justice than those scoring high on group belongingness. While procedural justice promoted trust in police for those who were both low and high on group belongingness, it had a slightly stronger effect for those low on group belongingness. This pattern of results supports the predictions made by Van den Bos' (2001) Uncertainty Management Model.

The Uncertainty Management Model proposes that procedurally fair treatment will be more salient to people who feel uncertain about their status within groups or how they will be treated by group authorities. Members of racial and ethnic minority groups often highlight how their status within society is tenuous (Weitzer 2010; Wolfe *et al.* 2016). We propose that fair treatment from important group authorities can serve to allay their concerns that they are viewed differently to others in society, and communicates to them that they do belong. In other words, procedural justice reduces their feelings of status uncertainty.

Of course, one of the major assumptions of the uncertainty management model is that those recipients of procedural justice actually want to identify with, or be members of, a specified group (i.e. their local community in our study). It is possible that we may obtain different results if our respondents do not *want* to belong to their local community. An important direction for future research therefore may be to explore how our interaction effect plays out as a function of in-group and out-group membership. Whatever the case, our findings provide support for the predictions made by the uncertainty management model.

Our findings also have implications for police practice. Police can struggle to gain the trust of marginalized communities and can struggle to promote their willingness to collaborate in crime control efforts. Such marginalized groups can include ethnic and racial minority groups, new immigrants, youth, and victims of crime. Our findings suggest that procedural justice policing may offer significant promise for enhancing feelings of belonging and trust in diverse and marginalized communities. But what might this procedurally just treatment look like in practice?

On a daily basis, police officers encounter different types of situations in their policing duties. These situations range from being called to a domestic dispute or the scene of a crime, having to stop people committing a traffic offence, arresting an offender, and dealing with drunk and disorderly people. Each situation is likely to require a different policing response. We argue that whatever the policing response may be, procedural justice elements can be used in each encounter to impart symbolic messages of respect and value. We know from previous research in the domestic violence context that offenders arrested by police were less likely to reoffend if they perceived the arresting officer to be using procedural justice (Paternoster *et al.* 1997). We also know from a randomized controlled trial that young ethnic minority drivers were more likely to trust police if procedural justice was communicated by police during a traffic stop (Murphy and Mazerolle 2016). If treatment imparted by an officer is procedurally just – through the display of neutrality, fairness, respect and voice – then this can have positive benefits for police.

In the context of policing, the procedural justice element of 'neutrality' relates to whether police are seen to be acting in a neutral fashion during encounters with members of the public. For example, racial profiling or excessive force against minority group members often signals to certain members of the public that they are being treated differently to others (Tyler and Wakslak 2004). 'Fairness' relates to the view that authorities are benevolent in their actions towards individuals; that they demonstrate to people that they have their best interests at heart when making a decision. Police officers who display concern for an individual or explain to them the reasons for their decisions can demonstrate fairness. People are also extremely sensitive to signs that authorities in power treat them with 'respect'. Respectful and dignified treatment communicates to people that the authority values them. Police officers can display respect by being polite during interactions with all members of the public. In the case of policing ethnic minority communities, for example, displaying knowledge and respect for particular cultural and religious practices can be a demonstration of respectful treatment. In the case of an offender, treating them in a dignified manner during an arrest also demonstrates respect. Finally, people value the opportunity to have a say in situations that affect them. Being able to 'voice' one's concerns during an encounter with a police officer, and seeing that a police officer is taking those concerns into account in the decision-making process, is viewed positively by citizens.

Limitations of this study

Before we conclude, we should acknowledge a number of limitations of our study. Future studies may wish to address these limitations to ascertain whether our findings can be replicated in different policing contexts and in different types of communities. First, we should note that our procedural justice and trust scales were highly correlated. This is common in the procedural justice policing literature. Although we did not have any issues with multicollinearity between these measures, it may be the case that our effects would not have been obtained had we used a procedural justice measure that captured perceptions of a specific encounter with police. Second, many of the regression coefficients reported in Table 7.2 and 7.3 were small; the interaction effect was particularly small. The sample size was extremely large (thus providing more power to detect subtle differences) and this could have led to significant results that did not really exist. Third, the data used was collected at one point in time. The causal relationships between our variables could therefore not be ascertained. We cannot be certain whether procedural justice leads to enhanced feelings of belonging or trust. Longitudinal survey data or experimental methods could be used in future research to tease apart the causal relationships between our variables (for example see Murphy *et al.* 2014). Fourth, our group belongingness variable pertained to feelings of belonging in one's local community. It could be that individuals feel differing senses of belongingness to different communities. Our study revealed that one's feelings of belongingness at the neighbourhood level could moderate the effect of procedural justice policing. Whether it can do so for other types of group belongingness remains to be seen, and this may prove a worthwhile avenue for future research. Finally, we used the uncertainty management model to explain our results. Our study did not actually measure feelings of status uncertainty. We simply measured 'group belongingness' to one's community. Future studies may wish to examine how group belongingness and status uncertainty measures correlate and interact to predict trust in police.

Conclusion

To conclude, our study has added to our understandings of group membership in procedural justice research by showing that the level of belonging one feels in their local community can moderate procedural justice policing effects. Specifically, procedural justice policing can be used to enhance public trust in police, particularly for those who feel marginalized in their local community. Importantly, police cannot control the level of ethnic diversity in a community, nor can they always control the level of crime in that community. What they can do is ensure that all interactions with the public are imparted in a procedurally fair manner. This is important because we know that police will be able to better promote public cooperation if people feel they belong and if they have trust in police.

Appendix

Survey items used to assess concepts of interest in this study. Reverse coded items are marked as (R).

Procedural justice

The following questions ask about your views of policing and police in your community. Recall that by community, we mean your local suburb.

- Police treat people fairly.
- Police treat people with dignity and respect.
- Police are always polite when dealing with people.
- Police listen to people before making decisions.
- Police make decisions based upon facts, not their personal biases or opinions.

Trust in police

The following questions ask about your views of policing and police in your community. Recall that by community, we mean your local suburb.

*   I trust the police in my community.
*   I have confidence in the police in my community.

Group belongingness

*   I feel that I belong to this local community.
*   I would like to be living in this local community in three years' time.
*   I am proud to live in this local community.
*   This is a close-knit community.
*   Some people in this community have been excluded from social events because of their skin colour, ethnicity, race or religion. (R)

Perceived violent crime problem

Please indicate whether the following events have happened in this community during the past 12 months:

*   A robbery or mugging.
*   A sexual assault or rape.
*   A violent argument between neighbours.
*   A fight in which a weapon was used.

Notes

1 This work was supported by the Australian Research Council [Grant Number DP10939360 and DP170101149].
2 In Australia, Markus (2014) argues that socially inclusive communities comprise a large number of members who (1) feel a sense of belonging in the community; (2) feel there is equity and they receive social justice; (3) participate in the workforce; (4) feel accepted and free from discrimination; and (5) feel generally satisfied with life. Group belongingness as measured in the current study, therefore, is only one component of the broader conceptualization of social inclusion.

Bibliography

Australian Bureau of Statistics (ABS) (2012a). *Queensland*, online. Available www.abs.gov.au/ausstats/abs@.nsf/Products/3235.0~2011~Main+Features~Queensland?OpenDocument (accessed 17 May 2013).
Australian Bureau of Statistics (ABS) (2012b). *Victoria*, online. Available www.abs.gov.au/ausstats/abs@.nsf/Products/3235.0~2011~Main+Features~Victoria?OpenDocument (accessed 17 May 2013).

Australian Bureau of Statistics (ABS) (2012c). *Australia's population by country of birth*, online. Available www.abs.gov.au/ausstats/abs@.nsf/Products/84074889D69E738CCA 257A5A00120A69?opendocument (accessed 17 May 2013).

Australian Bureau of Statistics (ABS) (2013). *Census community profiles by location*, online. Available www.censusdata.abs.gov.au/census_services/getproduct/census/2011/ quickstat/0?opendocument&navpos=220 (accessed 22 August 2013).

Australian Institute of Family Studies (AIFS) (2014). *Facts and figures*, online. Available https://aifs.gov.au/projects/sexual-violence-research (accessed 2 March 2015).

Baumeister, R. and Leary, M. (1995). 'The need to belong: desire for interpersonal attachments as a fundamental human motive', *Psychological Bulletin*, 117: 497–529.

Blackwood, L., Hopkins, N., and Reicher, S. (2013). 'Turning the analytic gaze on "us": the role of authorities in the alienation of minorities', *European Psychologist*, 18: 245–52.

Bradford, B. (2014). 'Policing and social identity: procedural justice, inclusion and cooperation between police and the public', *Policing and Society*, 24: 22–43.

Bradford, B., Murphy, K., and Jackson, J. (2014). 'Officers as mirrors: policing, procedural justice and the (re)production of social identity', *British Journal of Criminology*, 54: 527–50.

Cherney, A. and Murphy, K. (2016). 'Police and community cooperation in counterterrorism: Evidence and insights from Australia', *Studies in Conflict and Terrorism*, published online 27 October 2016, doi: 10.1080/1057610X.2016.1253987.

Dixon, D. and Maher, L. (2002). 'Anh Hai: policing, culture and social exclusion in a street heroin market', *Policing and Society*, 12: 93–110.

Gardner, W., Pickett, C., and Brewer, M. (2000). 'Social exclusion and selective memory: how the need to belong influences memory for social events', *Personality and Social Psychology Bulletin*, 26: 486–96.

Gerstenfeld, P. (2013). *Hate Crimes: Causes Controls, and Controversies*, Thousand Oaks, CA: Sage Publications.

Hinds, L. and Murphy, K. (2007). 'Public satisfaction with police: using procedural justice to improve police legitimacy', *Australian and New Zealand Journal of Criminology*, 40: 27–42.

Hipp, J. (2010). 'What is the "neighbourhood" in neighbourhood satisfaction? Comparing the effects of structural characteristics measured at the micro-neighbourhood and tract levels', *Urban Studies*, 47: 2517–36.

Hogg, M. and Abrams, D. (1993). 'Towards a single-process uncertainty-reduction model of social motivation in groups', in M. Hogg and D. Abrams (eds.), *Group Motivation: Social Psychological Perspectives*, Hempel Hempstead: Harvester Wheatsheaf, 173–90.

Hogg, M. and Mullin, B. (1999). 'Joining groups to reduce uncertainty: subjective uncertainty reduction and group identification', in D. Abrams and M. Hogg (eds.), *Social Identity and Social Cognition*, Oxford: Blackwell, 249–79.

Hopkins, N., Reicher, S., and Levine, M. (1997). 'On the parallels between social cognition and the "new racism"', *British Journal of Social Psychology*, 36: 305–29.

Huo, Y. (2003). 'Procedural justice and social regulation across group boundaries: does subgroup identity undermine relationship-based governance?', *Personality and Social Psychology Bulletin*, 29: 336–48.

Huo, Y., Smith, H., Tyler, T., and Lind, E. (1996). 'Superordinate identification, subgroup identification, and justice concerns: is separatism the problem; is assimilation the answer?', *Psychological Science*, 7: 40–5.

Jackson, J., Bradford, B., Stanko, E., and Hohl, K. (2012). *Just Authority? Trust in the Police in England and Wales*, Oxford: Routledge.

Lind, E., and Tyler, T. (1988). *The Social Psychology of Procedural Justice*, New York: Springer.

Lind, E. and Van den Bos, K. (2002). 'When fairness works: toward a general theory of uncertainty management', *Research in Organizational Behavior*, 24: 181–223.

Madon, N., Murphy, K., and Sargeant, E. (2017). 'Promoting police legitimacy among disengaged minority groups: does procedural justice matter more?', *Criminology and Criminal Justice*. Online first 16 February 2017, doi: 10.177/1488958176928349.

Markus, A. (2014). *Mapping Social Cohesion*. Scanlon Foundation: Monash University.

Mason, G. (2009). 'Violence against Indian students in Australia: a question of dignity', *Current Issues in Criminal Justice*, 21: 461–5.

Mazerolle, L., Bennett, S., Antrobus, E., and Eggins, E. (2012a). 'Procedural justice, routine encounters and citizen perceptions of police: main findings from the Queensland Community Engagement Trial (QCET)', *Journal of Experimental Criminology*, 8: 343–67.

Mazerolle, L., Sargeant, E., Cherney, A., Bennett, S., Murphy, K, Antrobus, E., and Martin, P. (2014). *Procedural Justice and Legitimacy in Policing*, Switzerland: Springer Briefs.

Mazerolle, L., Wickes, R., Cherney, A., Murphy, K., Sargeant, E., and Zahnow, R. (2012b). *Community Variations in Crime: A Spatial and Ecometric Analysis Wave 3*, ARC Centre of Excellence in Policing and Security, Brisbane.

McCluskey, J. (2003). *Police Requests for Compliance: Coercive and Procedurally Just Tactics*, USA: LFB Scholarly Publishers.

Meredyth, D., McKernan, H., and Evans, R. (2010). 'Police and Vietnamese-Australian communities in multi-ethnic Melbourne', *Policing*, 4: 233–40.

Murphy, K. (2013). 'Policing at the margins: fostering trust and cooperation among ethnic minority groups', *Journal of Policing Intelligence and Counter Terrorism*, 8: 184–99.

Murphy, K. (2015). 'Does procedural justice matter to youth? Comparing adults' and youth's willingness to collaborate with police', *Policing and Society*, 25: 53–76.

Murphy, K. and Barkworth, J. (2014). 'Victim willingness to report crime to police: does procedural justice or outcome matter most?', *Victims and Offenders*, 9: 178–204.

Murphy, K., Cherney, A., Wickes, R., Mazerolle, L., and Sargeant, E. (2012). *The Community Capacity Survey – Face to face Ethnic Minority Interviews: Methodology and Preliminary Findings*, ARC Centre of Excellence in Policing and Security, Brisbane.

Murphy, K., Hinds, L., and Fleming, J. (2008). 'Encouraging cooperation and public support for police', *Policing and Society*, 18: 136–55.

Murphy, K. and Mazerolle, L. (2016). 'Policing immigrants: using a randomized control trial of procedural justice policing to promote trust and cooperation', *The Australian and New Zealand Journal of Criminology*. Available https://doi.org/10.1177/0004 865816673691 (accessed 3 July 2017).

Murphy, K., Mazerolle, L., and Bennett, S. (2014). 'Promoting trust in police: findings from a randomized experimental field trial of procedural justice policing', *Policing and Society*, 24: 405–24.

Murphy, K., Sargeant, E., and Cherney, A. (2015). 'The importance of procedural justice and police performance in shaping intentions to cooperate with the police: does social identity matter?', *European Journal of Criminology*, 12: 1–20.

Nezlek, J., Kowalski, R., Leary, M., Blevins, T., and Holgate, S. (1997). 'Personality moderators of reactions to interpersonal rejection: depression and trait self-esteem', *Personality and Social Psychology Bulletin*, 23: 1235–44.

Paternoster, R., Brame, R., Bachman, R., and Sherman, L. (1997). 'Do fair procedures matter? The effect of procedural justice on spouse assault', *Law and Society Review*, 31: 163–204.

Poynting, S. (2006). 'What caused the Cronulla riot?', *Race and Class*, 48: 85–92.

Poynting, S. and Perry, B. (2007). 'Climates of hate: media and state inspired victimisation of Muslims in Canada and Australia since 9/11', *Current Issues in Criminal Justice*, 19: 151–71.

Sampson, R., Morenoff, J., and Earls, F. (1999). 'Beyond social capital: spatial dynamics of collective efficacy for children', *American Sociological Review*, 64: 633–60.

Sargeant, E., Antrobus, E., Murphy, K., Bennett, S., and Mazerolle, L. (2014). 'Social identity and procedural justice in police encounters with the public: results from a randomized controlled trial', *Policing and Society*, 26: 789–803.

Sentas, V. (2014). *Traces of Terror: Counter Terrorism Law, Policing and Race*, Oxford: Oxford University Press.

Skogan, W. (1977). 'Dimensions of the dark figure of unreported crime', *Crime and Delinquency*, 23: 41–50.

Skogan, W. (2006). 'Asymmetry in the impact of encounters with police', *Policing and Society*, 16: 99–126.

Smith, H., Tyler, T., Huo, Y., Ortiz, D., and Lind, E. (1998). 'The self-relevant implications of the group value model: group membership, self-worth, and treatment quality', *Journal of Experimental Social Psychology*, 34: 470–93.

Stahl, T., van Prooijen, J., and Vermunt, R. (2004). 'On the psychology of procedural justice: reactions to procedures of ingroup vs. outgroup authorities', *European Journal of Social Psychology*, 34: 173–89.

Stoutland, S. (2001). 'The multiple dimensions of trust in resident/police relations in Boston', *Journal of Research in Crime and Delinquency*, 38: 226–56.

Sunshine, J. and Tyler, T. (2003). 'The role of procedural justice and legitimacy in shaping public support for policing', *Law and Society Review*, 37: 513–48.

Tankebe, J. (2009). 'Public cooperation with the police in Ghana: does procedural fairness matter?', *Criminology*, 47: 1265–93.

Task Force (2015). *Final Report for the President's Task Force on 21st Century Policing*, Washington, DC: Office of Community Oriented Policing Services.

Tyler, T. (2001). 'Public trust and confidence in legal authorities: what do majority and minority group members want from the law and legal institutions?', *Behavioral Sciences and the Law*, 19: 215–35.

Tyler, T. (2006). *Why People Obey the Law*, Princeton, NJ: Princeton University Press.

Tyler, T. and Huo, Y. (2002). *Trust in the Law: Encouraging Public Cooperation with the Police and Courts*, New York: Russell Sage Foundation.

Tyler, T. and Lind, E. (1992). 'A relational model of authority in groups', in M. Zanna (ed.), *Advances in Experimental Social Psychology*, San Diego, CA: Academic Press, 115–292.

Tyler, T. and Wakslak, C. (2004). 'Profiling and police legitimacy: procedural justice, attributions of motive and acceptance of police authority', *Criminology*, 42: 253–82.

Van Craen, M. (2013). 'Explaining majority and minority trust in police', *Justice Quarterly*, 30: 1042–67.

Van den Bos, K. (2001). 'Uncertainty management: the influence of human uncertainty on reactions to perceived fairness', *Journal of Personality and Social Psychology*, 80: 931–41.

Van den Bos, K. and Lind, E. (2002). 'Uncertainty management by means of fairness judgments', in M. Zanna (ed.), *Advances in Experimental Social Psychology*, San Diego, CA: Academic Press, 1–60.

Van Prooijen, J., Van den Bos, K., and Wilke, H. (2004). 'Group belongingness and pro-cedural justice: social inclusion and exclusion by peers affects the psychology of voice', *Journal of Personality and Social Psychology*, 87: 66–79.

Verghis, S. (2009, September 10). 'Australia: attacks on Indian students raise racism cries', *TIME*, online. Available http://content.time.com/time/world/article/0,8599,192 1482,00.html?iid=sr-link1 (accessed 27 September 2016).

Weitzer, R. (2010). 'Race and policing in different ecological contexts', In S. Rice and M. White (eds.), *Race, Ethnicity, and Policing*, New York: New York University Press, 118–39.

Wolfe, S., Nix, J., Kaminski, R., and Rojek, J. (2016). 'Is the effect of procedural justice on police legitimacy invariant? Testing the generality of procedural justice and com-peting antecedents of legitimacy', *Journal of Quantitative Criminology*, 32: 253–82.

8 Adolescents' divergent ethnic and religious identities and trust in the police

Combining micro- and macro-level determinants in a comparative analysis of France and Germany

Sebastian Roché, Anina Schwarzenbach,
Dietrich Oberwittler, and Jacques De Maillard

Introduction

Even in the highly developed and stable democracies of Europe, legitimacy and trust in the police are still – or are increasingly – an issue of concern. Unemployment, migration patterns, the constitution and perseverance of large minority communities, exacerbated by social and ethnic segregation and exclusion, are high on the political agenda and remain important electoral themes in many European nations. These processes often create social friction and can jeopardize a sense of national cohesion. In particular, tensions between adolescents and the police, primarily in the poorer districts of large cities and among minority populations, can serve as an indicator of social disintegration, especially if they escalate into violent protests (Moran and Waddington 2016; Newburn 2016; Roché 2010). The increasing threat of Islamist radicalization in recent years has added a new and much more sinister dimension to this topic. Against this backdrop, comparing two European countries with different experiences of riotous violence can help to shed light on the sources and mechanisms that shape the legitimacy of police among adolescents.

Adolescents' attitudes to and relations with police can and have been analysed on many different levels. Researchers have often studied various features that are specific to adolescents, such as their tendencies towards increased levels of deviancy or rebelliousness, or their daily routines which can put them in public places and expose them to the risks of street crimes and deviant peer groups more frequently (see Oberwittler and Roché, Chapter 4 in this volume). Other studies have combined the peculiarities of age with other key social dimensions, such as race, ethnicity, socio-economic status, or neighbourhood cohesion (Brick *et al.* 2009; Nix *et al.* 2015). The POLIS study on which the following analysis is based uses the macro-level differences between two neighbouring European countries to enhance the analytical power to detect influences that may explain the degree of contentiousness of adolescent-police relations.

The recent history of France has been pockmarked by several, serious youth riots since the 1980s, while Germany has not had any.[1] Our study can shed light on important differences across the two countries with respect to the experience of everyday police work and the wider contexts of social, religious, and political integration of minorities. Social and political integration is important because it fundamentally entails the feeling that an authority is legitimate, a feature on which police work necessarily rests.

In this chapter, we want to contribute to answering to two overarching questions: what are the conditions under which adolescent trust in the police emerges in France and Germany; and to what extent do the factors which foster or diminish trust differ between these countries? While far from offering a comprehensive picture, we still attempt to implement a more complex approach of combining the micro-level of adolescents' actual experiences of policing with the meso-level of neighbourhood conditions and the macro-level of cross-national differences. Thus, by extending the levels and dimensions of analyses, The POLIS study can contribute many critical aspects to this debate:

1   Most studies focus on differences between groups in a given society, while only a small minority of research compares attitudes across nations. Very few studies try to understand the differences between groups across nations.
2   Most studies incorporate a major social division (race or ethnicity, typically), but few studies try to deal with two divisions (e.g. ethnicity and religion) simultaneously.
3   Some studies focus on neighbourhood effects, others on cross-national differences, but few combine the meso- and the macro-level in one analysis.

Theoretical discussion and research hypotheses

The primacy given to legitimacy and trust as the foundations for positive police–citizen relations largely stems from two fundamental notions: that force is not sufficient for obtaining obedience, and that the justification for obedience lies in what is shared between rulers and subjects. According to Max Weber (1964), legitimacy is a 'feeling of duty' – a definition that is still used in most studies today. It may be the case that trust engenders legitimacy (understood as the moral right to demand obedience), or conversely that legitimacy generates trust. Either way, trust is a critical element to how a city or a country may be governed: it either is legitimacy with a different tag or it has a status of cause of the causes.

Trust will be theoretically assessed as a relationship (here between youth and the police) and in relation to achieving a performance, in line with the framework proposed by Hardin (2000: 26) who claims that trust can be expressed as 'A trusts B to do X'. Here, we will measure trust in police as getting protection, obtaining respect, and fair treatment for all, and produce a construct called 'relational trust in police'.

Social and political scientists have long been interested in macro-level, societal differences in trust as well as its causes (e.g. Bjørnskov 2006; Herreros 2012; Rothstein and Stolle 2008). We know from cross-national research that generalized trust, political trust, and trust in police and the judicial system are all closely linked (Lappi-Seppälä 2008; Marien and Hooghe 2011, see Kääriäiäen, Chapter 13 in this volume). Disparities in trust on a global level are massive, but gulfs may also be found between countries of similar polity, as within the EU (Grönlund and Setälä 2012; Jackson *et al.* 2014) or within culturally similar regions as Taiwan and China (Lai *et al.* 2010). Countries of comparable size and economic wealth, or of shared continental legal tradition may differ considerably in their levels of trust, as in the case of France and Germany. In recent cross-national surveys, Germany has consistently scored higher in trust in the police and other state institutions than France has (Billiet and Pleysier 2012; Marien and Hooghe 2011). Yet, in police studies and academic research, a focus on individual conditions, experiences and attitudes, and on local contexts prevails. While this perspective should not be ignored, it misses out on relevant larger-scale societal and state-level conditions.

Our aim is not to account for all of the possible macro-level causes of trust, nor will our data from just two countries allow for this. Rather, we intend to explore some specific relevant dimensions, the interplay between macro-, meso- and micro-levels of analysis, and between individual attributes (e.g. ethnicity), and societal factors, based on the existing literature. Inspired by a micro-macro approach to the study of the sources of legitimacy (Mishler and Rose, 2001), we categorize a series of macro- and meso-level sources of trust:

* nation-state: historical experience and institutional features (e.g. state-religion relations);
* government and policy outcomes: public policy targets, police agents' behaviours;
* socio-demographic composition of the population (socio-economic status, ethnicity in city or neighbourhood level).

All these dimensions meet and interact with individual propensities and socio-political attitudes which vary between people, and in themselves are partly shaped by different national contexts.

Most importantly, national and local contexts are relevant for both majority and minority populations but may have different meanings and evoke different reactions. Building on social identity theory (Tajfel and Turner 1986), we suggest that positive bonds to a social group are an important part of the identity and self-esteem of every individual. The formation of national identity is defined as a process by which individuals develop attachments and build loyalty to the national political community, not just its geographical territory, but also its traditions and symbols, such as the national football teams (Druckman 1994).

The importance of the national community for 'system support' or 'political support', or the 'psychological orientation' towards the acceptance of 'the legitimacy of the state to govern', has long been empirically documented since Easton's work in the mid-1960s (Norris 2017: 20). A feeling of attachment creates a 'reservoir of goodwill', which to use Easton's words, builds 'more lasting bonds to the nation-state, as exemplified by feelings of national pride and identity' (Norris 2017, 21).

Applied to police–adolescent relations, social identity theory highlights the importance of the attachment to society for fostering police trust and legitimacy (Bradford *et al.* 2014; Oliveira and Murphy 2015; Roché 2016; Tyler and Blader 2003). By contrast, the French riots of 2005, by far the largest in Europe, have been regarded as an expression of failed integration of minority communities into the French society. Some have argued that failures of social and economic integration have led to stronger levels of frustration in France than in Germany because there are more unmet promises for equality (Loch, 2009; Tucci 2010).

Issues of social and national identity in France and Germany are further complicated by religion, especially for the largest minority group of Muslim faith, specifically Maghrebian in France and Turkish in Germany. Religion and religiosity can have a strong role in adolescents' development (Trommsdorff and Chen 2012). While Christian youth have typically become more secular over time (Lambert and Michelat 1992), Muslim adolescents have maintained strong religious orientations across generations in Western countries (Jacob and Kalter 2013). As a consequence, European societies today are characterized by large differences in religious beliefs, varying between agnosticism and low levels of religiosity among majority populations, and often very strong religiosity for Muslim minorities (Alba and Foner 2015; Güngör *et al.* 2013; Koopmans 2015). Several studies have demonstrated that both ethnic and religious (e.g. Muslim) identities are associated with a sense of weakened legitimacy of the norms and public institutions of the host society, such as the police (Bradford 2014; Murphy *et al.* 2015).

What are the constitutive elements of macro-level analysis that may explain the tension between a sense of belonging to a nation and a religious community? McConnell accounts for this dilemma by noting that religious believers have an 'allegiance to an authority outside of the commonwealth' (McConnell 2000: 91). The notion of having dual allegiance is not new and has been recognized as an important idea in understanding how believers negotiate their identity in society, even after modern democracies severed the connection between citizenship and religion. The concrete institutional arrangements regarding the relations between the state and the church might help to understand the contrasts between France and Germany. Although increasing secularization is a reality for both countries, as it is for the Western world, historically, the church-state relationship has typically been more antagonistic in Catholic than in Protestant nations. Anti-clericalism was central to the Catholic Church but not to the Protestant one, McLeod (2000) explains. Secular liberals had positive perceptions of Protestants in Germany unlike Catholics in France. Secularization was systemic in France while for Protestants in Germany, close ties between the church and the state existed until 1918, McLeod writes. Stein Rokkan further expanded this point, arguing that the Protestant Church did not stand in direct opposition to the nation-builders in the way the Roman Catholic Church did (Flora *et al.* 1999). In other words, the division between church and state often has a more hostile character in some countries than in others. Thus, depending on the national context, religiosity may or may not be seen to oppose national identification (Alba and Foner 2015; Schnabel and Hjerm 2014). In this vein, France and Germany have been portrayed as opposite paradigms (Brubaker 1992), partly due to the institutionalization of state relations with religious communities and education policies (Campbell 2006; Wilde 2005). Based on an international study of adolescents, Béraud, Massigon and Mathieu (2008) argued that in France, the ideal of 'laïcité' is at odds with religious diversity, a situation quite distinct from Germany where religious education is a regular school subject (Knauth 2008).

Following these theoretical considerations and previous research on trust in police and the influence of ethnic and religious identities, and taking into account existing evidence about differences between France and Germany, we make the following claims to guide our empirical analysis: First, we propose that trust in the police is higher in Germany than in France, and second that the gap in trust between majority and minority populations is larger in France. We suggest that this gap may be partly explained by differences in the ethnic/national identities and religious feelings of minority adolescents. Minority adolescents who identify with the host society should have more trust in the police. The impact of religion may make adolescents feel a conflict of allegiance – i.e. in the case of Muslim faith – and will be more pronounced in France than in Germany due to the more antagonistic character of secularism in France.

In addition to our focus on macro-level contexts and their bearing on national and religious identities, we also include micro- and meso-level influences on trust that are regularly considered in research on police–adolescent relations. Many studies have shown that actual experiences with the police, in particular in the form of police-initiated contact, can have a negative impact on adolescents' trust in the police (Berg *et al.* 2016; Sindall *et al.* 2016; Tyler *et al.* 2014; Weitzer and Tuch 2004; see Oberwittler and Roché, Chapter 4 in this volume). Possibly biased and aggressive police practices, such as 'stop and search', form part of the individual everyday experience of policing for many adolescents, but as policing styles are shaped by organizational and political contexts on regional or national levels, these daily experiences, too, reflect macro-level influences and are expected to differ between countries. We will therefore control for the exposure to police-initiated contact.

Finally, adolescents' daily lives in socially and ethnically segregated cities are shaped by their different neighbourhood contexts. Research primarily from the US, where levels of ethnic and social segregation often exceeds those of European cities, has found that adolescents living in disadvantaged neighbourhoods trust the police significantly less than adolescents in other urban areas (Schuck 2013; Stewart *et al.* 2009; Wu *et al.* 2009). In France, the concentrated disadvantage and poor living conditions of the 'banlieues' has been well documented since the 1980s and is seen as a major cause of collective youth violence

(Lapeyronnie 2008; Roché and de Maillard 2009). Almost no systematic comparisons of urban segregation in France and Germany exist, but levels of concentrated disadvantage seem to be less acute in Germany (Lichter *et al.* 2016). We therefore suggest that neighbourhood effects on trust in the police are more pronounced in France than in Germany.

Data

We use school survey data collected during 2011 and 2012 as part of the comparative research project 'Police and Adolescents in Multi-Ethnic Societies' (POLIS) (see Oberwittler and Roché, Chapter 4 in this volume, for a more detailed description).[2] The survey was conducted in secondary schools in Lyon and Grenoble in France and in Cologne and Mannheim in Germany, four cities with large minority populations. The school-level response rate was 69 per cent in Grenoble, 37 per cent in Lyon, 68 per cent in Cologne and 93 per cent in Mannheim. Within schools in France, 698 classes from eighth to eleventh grade were randomly selected, yielding a total sample of 13,679 respondents (response rate within selected classes was 82 per cent). In Germany, 351 classes from eighth to tenth grade were randomly selected, yielding a total sample of 6,948 respondents (response rate within selected classes was 78 per cent).

Dependent variable: relational trust in police

The subject of our analysis is adolescents' trust in the police. We use the term 'relational trust in police' as the focus is on the assessment of the officers' behaviour during interactions with adolescents represented by three items ('police protects adolescents', 'police disrespects adolescents', and 'police treat foreigners worse than French [Germans]'), plus one item on general trust ('overall the police can be trusted'). The response categories ranged from 1 'don't agree at all', 2 'don't agree', 3 'agree', to 4 'completely agree'. Table 8.1 shows that more adolescents in France than in Germany felt that the police treat foreigners worse (53 per cent vs. 31 per cent), and less adolescents in France than in Germany generally trusted the police (55 per cent vs. 73 per cent). Cronbachs' $\alpha=0.73$ suggests a sufficient reliability of this scale. For the analyses, we used scores computed in polychoric confirmatory factor analysis (Holgado-Tello *et al.* 2010).

Independent variables

Ethnicity or migrant background (which will be used interchangeably in this chapter) was established by asking respondents for their country of birth, as well as that of their parents and grandparents. Respondents were labelled as having a migrant background if they had two parents or more than two grandparents born abroad. They were categorized as 'native' only if both parents and most of their grandparents were born in Germany or France. Otherwise, they were categorized as coming from mixed native/migrant families. For the analyses in this chapter, we concentrate on the largest minority group in each respective country (Turkish in Germany, Maghrebian in France) and combine all other ethnic origins to large residual groups. In the German sample, 48 per cent of respondents were native Germans, and 19 per cent belonged to the Turkish minority (Table 8.1). Likewise, in France the distinction was between native French adolescents (49 per cent) and adolescents of Maghrebian origin, i.e. Morocco, Tunisia and Algeria (15 per cent).

We were particularly interested in the effects of religiosity and national identification on trust in the police. Respondents were asked to rate the *importance of religion* in their life (1 'very important', 2 'important', 3 'less important', and 4 'not important at all'). As reported in Table 8.2, the importance of religion varied greatly across ethnic groups. Whereas for most respondents of native background in Germany and France religion played a minor role in their lives ('less' or 'not important at all' for 71 per cent of native German and 75 per cent of native French respondents), the opposite was true for the largest minority groups in both countries, which are predominantly Muslim. The vast majority of adolescents of Turkish descent in Germany (89 per cent) and of Maghrebian descent in France (94 per cent) felt that religion plays an 'important' or 'very important' role in their lives.

Ethnic/national identification was measured by a single question directed only towards minority respondents: 'All in all, do you feel rather as French [German] or as a member of your group of origin?' with the answer categories 'I feel …' '… completely French [German]', 'Rather French [German]', 'partly', 'rather as member of the group of origin', and 'completely as member of the group of origin'. Answer categories were recoded to three groups of adolescents: rather or completely leaning towards either the host society, or the society of origin, and a third group of undecided or split identities. As reported in Table 8.2, around 12 per cent of the respondents of Turkish background in Germany identified with German society, and slightly more, around 18 per cent of the respondents of Maghrebian background in France felt attached to French society. But almost half of the Turkish respondents in Germany (48 per cent) and around a third of the Maghrebian respondents in France (33 per cent) identified with their countries of origin.

Table 8.1 Distribution of migrant backgrounds in German and French samples

	Germany (%)	France (%)
Native	48.5	49.4
Turkish (DE) or Maghrebian (FR)	18.8	15.2
Other migration background	21.2	16.6
Mixed native and Turkish (DE)/Maghrebian (FR)	1.6	5.8
Mixed native and other	9.5	11.3
Missing	0.4	1.7
Total	100	100
N=	6,948	13,679

Table 8.2 Ethnic/national identification and religiosity by ethnic origins in Germany and France (mixed backgrounds excluded)

	Native German (N = 3,369) (%)	Turkish (N = 1,307) (%)	Other background (N = 1,475) (%)
Germany			
National identification			
Host	–	12.4	23.1
Divided	–	37.3	40.4
Origin	–	47.6	34.2
Missing	–	2.7	2.3
Total	–	100	100
Importance of religion			
Not important at all	30.7	2.6	12.5
Less important	40.6	6.9	25.2
Important	22.3	24.7	30.7
Very important	5.7	64.3	30.0
Missing	0.7	1.5	1.5
Total	100	100	100

	Native French (N = 6,760) (%)	Maghrebian (N = 2,074) (%)	Other background (N = 2,269) (%)
France			
National identification			
Host	–	18.1	24.2
Divided	–	45.9	42.4
Origin	–	33.0	31.1
Missing	–	2.9	2.2
Total	–	100	100
Importance of religion			
Not important at all	42.8	2.0	13.6
Less important	32.5	3.1	18.1
Important	16.4	20.1	27.5
Very important	6.4	73.5	38.9
Missing	1.9	1.3	1.9
Total	100	100	100

Related to ethnic/national identification, we asked respondents about the proportion of their friends who were of foreign origin, with the answer categories 'all', 'more than half', 'around half', 'less than half', and 'none'. The answers were recoded into a dummy variable which indicated whether an adolescent had only friends of ethnic minority background (0), or also native French [German] friends (1). Research has shown that interethnic bonds to native peers foster identification with the host society (Verkuyten and Fleischmann 2017), and beyond this may also foster trust to its institutions.

For socio-demographic control variables, we used gender, age, family structure, parental educational status, and parental employment. In addition, the analyses account for several variables measuring delinquency, as well as experiences with police.

Self-reported delinquency was measured by asking the respondents whether, and if yes how often, they had committed seven criminal offences in the last 12 months (vandalism, vehicle theft, shoplifting, break in, use of drugs, selling of drugs, and assault).

To measure victimization, respondents were asked whether, and if yes how often, during the last 12 months they had been victim of four types of violent offences (assault, robbery, threatening/extortion, and cyberbullying).

To measure police-initiated contact the respondents were asked if they had been contacted by the police (and if so, how often) in their home city during the last 12 months for one of the following reasons: 'As a suspect of a criminal offence (e.g. shoplifting)', 'As a traffic participant (e.g. on a bike ride)', and 'I was approached or checked (stopped and searched) on the street/in a park/on a public square'.

The residential locations of respondents were geocoded by looking up the ID numbers of small administrative units in address directories. We used official data from the French National Statistical Office (INSEE) and from the city statistical offices in Cologne and Mannheim to measure neighbourhood socio-economic conditions. 'Concentrated disadvantage' is a factor score combining the rate of unemployment with the percentage of immigrants, computed separately for the two countries. For multilevel regression analyses, we excluded neighbourhoods with less than 15 respondents.

Results

We used stepwise OLS regression to analyse the factors predicting relational trust in the police, and to identify relevant differences between Germany and France. We ran separate models for the French and German samples, using the same predictors.

The analysis consists of three regression models for each country and follows a block-wise approach according to the theoretical assumptions about the influence of identities, exposure to discriminatory police contact, and involvement in delinquency. Once all attitudinal and behavioural predictors are included, the R-square values show that for Germany 21 per cent, and for France 30 per cent of the variance can be explained.

Model 1 includes only the socio-demographic variables and reports a substantial and significant effect of ethnic minority background on the respondents' relational trust in the police. In France, compared to native all migrant adolescents express less trust in the police, especially those of Maghrebian descent whose trust is half a scale unit lower (Table 8.4, B = −0.54, $p < 0.001$). This effect size is halved once ethnic/national identification and religiosity are introduced into the analysis but remains significant (Table 8.4, B = −0.23, $p < 0.001$ in

Table 8.3 Linear regression of relational trust in the police in Germany

	Model 1		Model 2		Model 3	
Female (ref = boy)	0.17***	(10.1)	0.15***	(9.0)	0.07***	(4.0)
Age	−0.11***	(−10.3)	−0.10***	(−10.3)	−0.07***	(−7.0)
Parental unemployment (ref = no)						
Yes	−0.05	(−1.9)	−0.05	(−1.8)	0.00	(0.1)
Unclear	−0.07	(−1.9)	−0.08*	(−2.2)	−0.09*	(−2.5)
Parental educational level (ref = no degree)						
Below Bac/Abi	−0.00	(−0.1)	−0.01	(−0.3)	−0.00	(−0.1)
Bac/Abi	0.01	(0.4)	0.01	(0.2)	0.01	(0.3)
Above Bac/Abi	−0.03	(−0.8)	−0.03	(−1.0)	−0.02	(−0.8)
Family structure (ref = complete)	−0.12***	(−6.4)	−0.11***	(−5.5)	−0.05**	(−2.7)
Migration background (ref = native)						
Turkish	−0.13***	(−5.5)	−0.08*	(−2.3)	−0.07	(−1.9)
Other background	−0.13***	(−5.6)	−0.07*	(−2.5)	−0.06*	(−2.2)
Mixed native/Turkish	−0.03	(−0.5)	0.01	(0.1)	0.02	(0.4)
Mixed native/other	−0.11***	(−3.6)	−0.05	(−1.2)	−0.02	(−0.6)
National identification (ref = host country)						
Divided	–	–	−0.09*	(−2.6)	−0.06	(−1.6)
Country of origin	–	–	−0.27***	(−8.3)	−0.20***	(−6.6)
Importance of religion (ref = not important)						
Less important	–	–	0.17***	(6.0)	0.11***	(4.1)
Important	–	–	0.28***	(10.8)	0.22***	(7.8)
Very important	–	–	0.27***	(7.5)	0.22***	(6.8)
Police–initiated contacts (ref = no)						
1–2 contacts	–	–	–	–	−0.10***	(−4.7)
3–5 contacts	–	–	–	–	−0.30***	(−5.6)
>5 contacts	–	–	–	–	−0.41***	(−6.7)
Victimization (ref = no)	–	–	–	–	−0.06**	(−3.3)
Self–reported delinquency (ref = no)						
1–2 offenses	–	–	–	–	−0.20***	(−7.6)
3–5 offenses	–	–	–	–	−0.33***	(−9.8)
>5 offenses	–	–	–	–	−0.53***	(−18.3)
Native friends (ref = no)						0.14***	(5.6)
Constant	2.87***	(88.4)	2.74***	(77.1)	2.82***	(54.0)
Adjusted R–squared	0.07	–	0.09	–	0.21	–
BIC	13,451	–	13,300	–	12,455	–

Notes
N=6,716, *t* statistics in parentheses.
* $p<0.05$;
** $p<0.01$;
*** $p<0.001$.
Missing categories are included in the analysis but not reported.

Table 8.4 Linear regression of relational trust in the police in France

	Model 1		Model 2		Model 3	
Female (ref = boy)	0.10***	(5.2)	0.10***	(5.7)	0.00	(0.1)
Age	–0.11***	(–9.3)	–0.11***	(–10.6)	–0.05***	(–5.6)
Parental unemployment (ref = no)						
Yes	–0.09***	(–5.2)	–0.07***	(–3.6)	–0.03	(–1.9)
Unclear	–0.15***	(–5.3)	–0.10***	(–3.6)	–0.08**	(–3.2)
Parental educational level (ref = no degree)						
Degree below Bac/Abi	0.15***	(3.5)	0.11**	(2.7)	0.05	(1.4)
Bac/Abi	0.16***	(4.3)	0.11**	(2.9)	0.06	(1.7)
Above Bac/Abi	0.24***	(5.9)	0.15***	(3.8)	0.10**	(2.6)
Family structure (ref = complete)	–0.10***	(–6.4)	–0.09***	(–5.6)	–0.06***	(–4.4)
Migration background (ref = native)						
Maghrebian	–0.54***	(–22.8)	–0.25***	(–8.3)	–0.23***	(–7.9)
Other migration background	–0.19***	(–6.9)	0.03	(0.9)	–0.01	(–0.2)
Mixed native and Maghrebian	–0.26***	(–7.3)	–0.13***	(–4.0)	–0.12***	(–3.6)
Mixed native and other	–0.13***	(–6.1)	–0.04*	(–2.0)	–0.02	(–0.7)
National identification (ref = host country)						
Divided	–	–	–0.24***	(–9.8)	–0.18***	(–8.1)
Country of origin	–	–	–0.46***	(–14.4)	–0.32***	(–11.3)
Importance of religion (ref = not important)						
Less important	–	–	0.07***	(3.5)	0.04*	(2.4)
Important	–	–	0.06*	(2.1)	0.04	(1.7)
Very important	–	–	–0.11***	(–3.4)	–0.12***	(–4.0)
Police-initiated contacts (ref = no)						
1–2 contacts	–	–	–	–	–0.12***	(–6.2)
3–5 contacts	–	–	–	–	–0.35***	(–11.1)
>5 contacts	–	–	–	–	–0.47***	(–16.8)
Victimization (ref = no)	–	–	–	–	–0.00	(–0.2)
Self-reported delinquency (ref = no)						
1–2 offences	–	–	–	–	–0.24***	(–12.0)
3–5 offences	–	–	–	–	–0.31***	(–11.4)
>5 offences	–	–	–	–	–0.44***	(–16.3)
Native friends (ref = no)	–	–	–	–	0.23***	(8.0)
Constant	2.50***	(66.1)	2.58***	(64.7)	2.64***	(54.3)
Adjusted R-squared	0.13	–	0.18	–	0.30	–
BIC	24,779	–	24,203	–	22,355	–

Notes
N=11,881, *t* statistics in parentheses.
*   *p*<0.05;
**   *p*<0.01;
*** *p*<0.001.
Missing categories are included in the analysis but not reported.

model 3). Although a negative effect of minority status on trust is reported for the German sample, too, it is much smaller than in France (Table 8.3, B=−0.13, $p<0.001$ in model 1) and is fully mediated in model 3. Other socio-demographic effects of age, gender, family structure, and low social status are comparable in the two countries, and are largely mediated by the attitudinal and behavioural predictors in later models.

Model 2 tests the core theoretical assumptions of the effects of ethnic/national identification and religiosity on relational trust in the police (Tables 8.3 and 8.4). Empirical evidence is provided for a substantial effect of ethnic/national identifi- cation in both countries. Compared to youths who identify with the German or French host society, those that identify with their countries of origin trust the police less, especially in France (Germany: B=−0.27, $p<0.001$, France: B=−0.46, $p<0.001$). Related to the effect of ethnic/national identification, ado- lescents who have at least one native friend trust the police significantly more than those who have only friends with a migrant background (model 3, for Germany: B=0.14, $p<0.001$, for France: B=0.23, $p<0.001$), findings which both support our theoretical assumptions.

The effect of religiosity on relational trust in the police differs for Germany and France (Tables 8.3 and 8.4, Figure 8.1). In Germany, highly religious ado- lescents assess the police more positively (B=0.27, $p<0.001$), while in France the opposite is true (B=−0.11, $p<0.001$). We found a curvilinear effect in France as moderate religiosity slightly increases but strong religiosity decreases trust. In contrast, the effect is linear in Germany yet there is no difference between the categories 'important' and 'very important'. In both countries, the effects of religiosity remain significant even when controlling for delinquency and police contact in model 3.

We elaborated the role of ethnic/national identification and religiosity further by testing for differential effects by ethnic groups with the help of multiplicative interaction terms between migration background and these predictors.[3] No dif- ferential effects were found for ethnic/national identification: identifying with one's country of origin is associated with a decrease in relational trust in the police equally for both the largest ethnic minority groups and the other migrant groups (native adolescents were not asked about their national identification). In contrast, religiosity shows differential effects by ethnic groups in the French sample (but not in the German sample), which are plotted in Figure 8.1. Adoles- cents of Maghrebian descent who claim that religion is 'important' or 'very important' in their lives show a significantly stronger decline in trust the police compared to other adolescents. Also, while native French adolescents report slightly increasing trust in the police up to the category 'important', all migrant groups show a decreasing trend starting from a lower level of religiosity.

Regression models 3 also show very strong negative effects of self-reported delinquency and police-initiated contact in both countries. Trust diminishes with more frequent contact with police, and is lowest for those with more than five encounters with police (for Germany: B=−0.41, $p<0.001$, for France: B=−0.47, $p<0.001$; see Oberwittler and Roché, Chapter 4 in this volume).

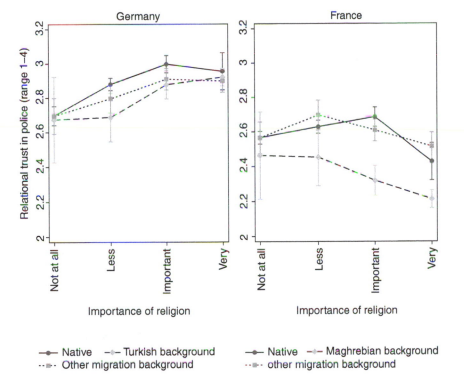

Figure 8.1 Interaction effects of religiosity and migrant background on relational trust in police, Germany and France.

Note
Predictions from regression models.

Table 8.5 Intraclass correlation coefficients (ICC) of neighbourhood contexts of relational trust in the police in Germany and France

	Germany	France
Empty model	0.011	0.061
Conditional model controlling for socio-demographic composition	0.005	0.019
Model with all level 1 covariates	–	0.007
Model with level 2 variable	–	0.004

In order to detect potential influences of neighbourhood conditions on trust in the police, we ran multilevel models which included the same level 1 variables as the previous linear regression models.[4] A look at the intraclass correlation coefficients (ICCs), first in empty models without predictors, show that only 1 per cent of the variance in Germany but 6 per cent of the variance in France is between neighbourhoods, which is a preliminary indication of potential area differences. After controlling for socio-demograpic composition, the ICC is considerably reduced to 0.5 per cent in Germany and to 2 per cent in France. Thus, controlling for ethnicity and social status, adolescents who live in the same neighbourhood in France are slightly more likely to share similar relational trust in the police, whereas in Germany relational trust in the police is not specific to a neighbourhood. A full multilevel model for France shows that neighbourhood concentrated disadvantage is associated with a minor but significant drop in respondents' relational trust in the police (B$=-0.04$, $p<0.001$).

Discussion: cross-national variations in the effects of national and religious identities

In this chapter we intended to make progress on two fronts that might help better clarify the effects of national context on relational trust in police. Trust is about a relationship and a context. National effects on trust consist of two main types: First, those factors that turn various groups into a political community through institutional arrangements and legal traditions, i.e. how majority and minority groups are politically and culturally integrated into a nation, and, second, those that relate to the performance of the government policies, in our study the actions of police officers which bring adolescents into contact with the police.

The first lesson from our findings pertains to the organization of various groups into a political community and about societal integration. Citizens have multiple affiliations to various infra- or supra-national groups. Comparative studies allow us to explore how a national feeling is grounded on other group allegiances, and how all these affiliations influence trust in the police. We show that the effect of ethnic background is of subordinate importance in Germany, and youth of Turkish origin, who form the largest minority group, do not substantially differ from native youth in their levels of trust in the police. Conversely, in France, the largest minority, adolescents of Maghrebian descent, are substantially less inclined to trust in the police compared to the natives. And this remains the case even after controlling for a whole set of variables (e.g. the religious and national identification, police-initiated contact, and past delinquency). Extant research has shown that while race or ethnicity can be a major divide (for example in the US, see Weitzer, Chapter 2, and in Turkey, see Roché, Özaşçılar, and Bilen, Chapter 10 in this volume), in other cases, no substantial ethnic differences have been found and thus this notion cannot be generalized (Bradford, Jackson, and Hough, Chapter 3 in this volume). In our study, the members of the respective largest minority groups, the Turkish in Germany and the Maghrebian in France, have comparable positions in the socio-economic structure (lower levels of education, socio-economic status, and residence in poorer parts of the cities) and share a similar religious denomination (Sunni Muslims), yet they display different attitudes towards the police. These findings suggest that their disadvantaged group status in society is not the sole key variable at play for explaining trust.

We suggest that national identification underpins the state's legitimate political rule and assessments of police's daily interactions on the streets. Such a fundamental feeling is a sense of belonging to a superordinate group, an 'imagined community' (Anderson 2006). In both countries, the POLIS surveys shows, attachment to the host national community has a significant effect on the levels of trust among minority groups. Interestingly, the level of identification with country of origin is higher among adolescents of Turkish descent in Germany (47.6 per cent, see Table 8.2) than among adolescents of Maghrebian descent in France (33 per cent). Yet, for Maghrebians, not identifying with their host country France has a stronger negative effect on trust in police than it does for the Turkish in Germany. We interpret this as a difference between the prevalence of status (here an ethnic one) and its social expression (the fact that it is activated and has social effects).

Integration of minorities into the larger society, and trusting the police, may also depend on the local integration into cities, and on the political model of integration. In Germany, with its apparently less contentious model of policing minorities, we found no substantial difference in attitudes towards police across neighbourhoods, from the most disadvantaged to the most advantaged. Shifting the country modifies this contextual influence, albeit not with a large effect size. Still, adolescents living in deprived neighbourhoods in France have significantly lower levels of trust in the police. The fact that neighbourhood effects are found in France but not in Germany may stem from the culture of the 'banlieues', which are deprived neighbourhoods at the periphery of large cities where minority groups have developed a specific sense of identity. Individuals may not simply reside in a banlieue, they belong to it, and this creates an 'ethnoterritorial' identity, as suggested by focus group research (Roux and Roché 2016). The important finding here is that ethnic identity impacts trust in police differently based on national context, and that structural neighbourhood conditions also have variable consequences on trust in police in different national contexts. Macro-contextualization of variables operating at lower levels seems an essential dimension to be considered for explaining trust in police.

Because the largest minority groups in both countries are predominantly Muslim, closely examining levels of religiosity may shed additional light on the hypothesis that the national structuring of lower-level variables impacts trust in the police. Here, we show that religious faith and religiosity predict attitudes towards the police (their degree of fairness or protective aims); and moreover, that an identical individual characteristic (being more religious) may have opposite effects for the same ethno-religious group (from a Muslim country) in two countries that belong to the same region and have comparable level of socio-economic development. Religion and religiosity have not received much attention in studies on attitudes to the police. Empirical evidence has often shown that religiosity provides opportunities to engage in civic life and civic arguments, in particular for the underprivileged it can be a means for the 'realization of citizenship' (Weithman 2002). In the US, religiosity is positively correlated with trust in police, as is also the case in Germany (Cao and Zhao 2005).

According to the POLIS study, in Germany, higher religiosity is associated with more trust in the police for all ethnic groups, be it adolescents of Turkish background (i.e. Muslim) or native adolescents (i.e. Christians). However, in France, the most religious adolescents express significantly less support to the police compared to the less religious. This effect of religiosity is particularly strong among the adolescents of Maghrebian descent (i.e. Muslims). It seems that the religious convictions are, in certain contexts, a source of tension with police officers as an embodiment of the state. Research has already shown that faith puts limits on trust and legitimacy of public organizations (Skitka *et al.* 2009) and that the intention to cooperate with the police lessens for those who 'place a great deal of emphasis on retaining a separate culture' (Oliveira and Murphy 2015: 16), of which strong religiosity could be a proxy.

Second, national differences in trust in the police can also be associated with differences in the performance of their task in different policing strategies. The extent to which proactive control and checks of citizens (i.e. stop and search) is used, and its disproportionate application across ethnic groups is clearly distinct in France and Germany (see Oberwittler and Roché, Chapter 4, in this volume for more details). The explanation of such a difference lies in the policing policies in a broad sense (training of agents, definition of performance targets, consideration given to population diversity, monitoring of agents' work; on some of these aspects see Lukas and Gauthier 2011). Adolescents who unwillingly interact more with the police see the police less often as trustworthy, even after controlling for lifestyle and delinquent behaviour. In both Germany and France, police-initiated contact deteriorates relational trust in police, in line with previous research (e.g. Skogan 2006; Tyler *et al.* 2014). Thus it may be not only the biased use of stop and search which distinguishes France from Germany, but also the propensity of French police to use stops more aggressively (de Maillard *et al.* 2016; Hunold *et al.* 2016) that impacts on all forms of support to police. We suggest that a more peaceful policing style, and consequently more harmonious relations with adolescents in Germany, tends to foster positive attitudes towards police, but also to decrease intergroup differences (i.e. being male or female, of high or low social status, living in well-off or deprived areas, or, being of native or foreign origin). In order to further explore the effects of policing policies, it would be necessary to study the interactions between all the experiences of police and the feeling of national integration.

Conclusion

Trust towards the police and state institutions in general is a critical element of social and political stability, and a vital prerequisite of police work. The cross-national comparative study of attitudes towards the police is a fruitful but challenging task as nations-states are different on several dimensions. The POLIS study is an attempt to uncover national differences by collecting data in four cities in two countries using standardized methodologies. Yet, if the results of data analyses differ between the two countries, as it is the case for trust in police, it still is a challenge for researchers to disentangle the causes of these differences. Specifically, national variations may be a result of differences in the political system, the religious traditions, or the composition of the population (in terms of ethnicity), to name just a few. Even in the case of Germany and France, two neighbouring countries with a great deal of commonalities in terms of shared history, socio-economic structure and development, type of welfare system, political stability, and the composition of ethnic minorities (in both cases originating from Sunni Muslim tradition countries), differences in police trust cannot easily be attributed to a single major cause. In order to move forward in disentangling the sources of national differences, and ultimately the sources of trust in the police, we argue that a more finely grained exploration and a combined micro-macro analysis of individual and contextual effects is needed. Certain predictors of trust worked in a similar direction in the two countries (such as age, gender, social status, delinquency and the experience of a police-initiated contact), while identity-related variables did not display such consistency across countries. Effects of key variables, such as ethnicity and religiosity, varied between France and Germany. Political systems frame collective meanings of ethnicity and religiosity and modify their relations to a sense of belonging to a community in unique ways, reflecting the specific development of socio-economic and political cleavages in different societies.

Notes

1 With the exception of more confined left-wing extremist street-fighting and right-wing xenophobic violence which cannot compare with the large-scale riots seen in French or UK cities.
2 The project has received joint funding from the national funding agencies *Agence nationale de la recherche* (ANR) and *Deutsche Forschungsgemeinschaft* (ANR-DFG Funding Programme for the Humanities and Social Sciences, Call 2008, grant reference: ANR-08-FASHS-19, Pacte research unit, Sciences Po, CNRS, University of Grenoble Alpes, and DFG AL 376–11/1, Max Planck Institute for Foreign and International Criminal Law, Freiburg).
3 The models with interaction effects are not presented in tabular form, but can be requested from the authors.
4 The models are not presented in tabular form, but can be requested from the authors.

Bibliography

Alba, R. and Foner, N. (2015). *Stranger No More: Immigration and the Challenges of Integration in North America and Western Europe*, Princeton, NJ: Princeton University Press.

Anderson, B. (1983). *Imagined Communities: Reflections on the Origin and Spread of Nationalism*, London and New York: VERSO.

Béraud, C., Massigon, B., and Mathieu, S. (2008). 'French students, religion and school: the idea of Laïcité at stake with religious diversity', in: Knauth, T., Jozsa, D.-P., Bertram-Troost G., *et al.* (eds.), *Encountering Religious Pluralism in School and Society*, Münster: Waxmann, 51–80.

Berg, M., Stewart, E., Intravia, J., Warren, P., and Simons, R. (2016). 'Cynical streets: neighborhood social processes and perceptions of criminal injustice', *Criminology*, 54: 520–47.

Billiet, J. and Pleysier, S. (2012). 'Attitudes towards the police in European Social Survey round 5 (2010): comparing Belgium and its neighbours', in: Devroe, E., Pauwels, L., Verhage, A., Easton, M., and Cools, M. (eds.) *Tegendraadse Criminologie. Liber Amicorum Paul Ponsaers*, Antwerp: Maklu, 301–19.

Bjørnskov, C. (2006). 'Determinants of generalized trust: a cross-country comparison', *Public Choice*, 130: 1–21.

Bradford, B. (2014). 'Policing and social identity: procedural justice, inclusion, and cooperation between police and public'. *Policing & Society*, 24: 22–43.

Bradford, B., Murphy, K., and Jackson, J. (2014). 'Officers as mirrors: policing, procedural justice and the (re)production of social identity', *British Journal of Criminology*, 54: 527–50.

Brick, B., Taylor, T.J., and Esbensen, F.-A. (2009). 'Juvenile attitudes towards the police: the importance of subcultural involvement and community ties'. *Journal of Criminal Justice*, 37: 488–95.

Brubaker, R. (1992). *Citizenship and Nationhood in France and Germany*, Cambridge, MA: Harvard University Press.

Campbell, E. (2006). 'What is education's impact or civic and social engagement?' in: Desjardins, R. and Schuller, T. (eds.), *Measuring the Effects of Education Health and Civic Engagement: Proceeding of the Copenhagen Symposium*, Paris: OECD, 25–126.

Cao, L. and Zhao, J.-S. (2005) 'Latin America versus the US: confidence in the police in Latin America', *Journal of Criminal Justice*, 33: 403–12.

De Maillard, J., Hunold, D., Roché, S., and Oberwittler, D. (2016). 'Different styles of policing: discretionary power in street controls by the public police in France and Germany', *Policing & Society*, online. Available http://dx.doi.org/10.1080/10439463.2016.1194837 (accessed 21 March 2017).

Druckman, D. (1994). 'Nationalism, patriotism, and group loyalty: a social psychological perspective', *Mershon International Studies Review* 38: 43–68.

Flora, P., Stein, K., and Derek, U. (1999). *State Formation, Nation-building and Mass Politics in Europe: The Theory of Stein Rokkan Based on his Collected Works*. New York: Oxford University Press.

Güngör, D., Fleischmann, F., Phalet, K., and Maliepaard, M. (2013). 'Contextualizing religious acculturation: cross-cultural perspectives on Muslim minorities in Western Europe', *European Psychologist*, 18: 203–14.

Grönlund, K. and Setälä, M. (2012). 'In honest officials we trust: institutional confidence in Europe', *The American Review of Public Administration*, 42: 523–42.

Hardin, R. (2000). 'Do we want trust in government?', in Warren, M.E. (ed.), *Democracy and Trust*, Cambridge: Cambridge University Press, 22–41.

Herreros, F. (2012). 'The state counts: state efficacy and the development of trust'. *Rationality and Society*, 24: 483–509.

Holgado-Tello, F.P., Chacón-Moscoso, S., Barbero-García, I., and Vila-Abad, E. (2010). 'Polychoric versus Pearson correlations in exploratory and confirmatory factor analysis of ordinal variables', *Quality & Quantity* 44: 153–66.

Hunold, D., Oberwittler, D., and Lukas, T. (2016). '"I'd like to see your identity cards please!" Negotiating authority in police-adolescent encounters: findings from a mixed-method study of proactive police practices towards adolescents in two German cities', *European Journal of Criminology*, 13: 590–609.

Jackson, J., Asif, M., Bradford, B., and Zakar, M. Z. (2014). 'Corruption and police legit-imacy in Lahore, Pakistan'. *British Journal of Criminology*, 54: 1067–88.

Jacob, K. and Kalter, F. (2013). 'Intergenerational change in religious salience among immigrant families in four European countries', *International Migration*, 51: 38–56.

Knauth, T. (2008). 'Better together than apart: religion in school and lifeword of students in Hamburg', in: Knauth, T., Jozsa, D.-P.; Bertram-Troost G., *et al.* (eds.), *Encountering Religious Pluralism in School and Society*, Münster: Waxmann, 207–45.

Koopmans, R. (2015). 'Religious fundamentalism and hostility against out-groups: a comparison of Muslims and Christians in Western Europe', *Journal of Ethnic and Migration Studies*, 41: 33–57.

Lai, Y.-L., Cao, L., and Zhao, J.-S. (2010). 'The impact of political entity on confidence in legal authorities: a comparison between China and Taiwan', *Journal of Criminal Justice*, 38: 934–41.

Lambert, Y. and Michelat, G. (1992). *Crépuscule des religions chez les jeunes*, Paris: l'Harmattan.

Lapeyronnie, D. (2008). *Ghetto urbain. Ségrégation, violence, pauvreté en France aujourd'hui*, Paris: Robert Laffont.

Lappi-Seppälä, T. (2008). 'Trust, welfare, and political culture – explaining differences in national penal policies', *Crime and Justice*, 37: 313–87.

Lichter, D.T., Parisi, D., and de Valk, H. (2016). 'Residential segregation', in *Pathways*, special issue "State of the Union, The Poverty and Inequality Report", online, 65–74. Available http://inequality.stanford.edu/sites/default/files/Pathways-SOTU-2016-Residential-Segregration-3.pdf (accessed 22 March 2017).

Loch, D. (2009). 'Immigrant youth and urban riots: a comparison of France and Germany.' *Journal of Ethnic and Migration Studies*, 35: 791–814.

Lukas, T. and Gauthier, J. (2011). 'Warum kontrolliert die Polizei (nicht)?' *Soziale Probleme*, 22: 174–206.

Marien, S. and Hooghe, M. (2011). 'Does political trust matter? An empirical investigation into the relation between political trust and support for law compliance', *European Journal of Political Research*, 50: 267–91.

McConnell, M.W. (2000). 'Believers as equal citizens', in Rosenblum, N.L. (ed.), *Obligations of Citizenship and Demands of Faith: Religious Accommodation in Pluralist Democracies*, Princeton, NJ: Princeton University Press, 90–110.

McLeod, H. (2000). *Secularisation in Western Europe, 1848–1914*, London, Macmillan Press.

Mishler, W. and Rose, R. (2001). 'What are the origins of political trust? Testing institutional and cultural theories in post-communist societies', *Comparative Political Studies*, 34: 30–62.

Moran, M. and Waddington, D.P. (2016). *Riots: An International Comparison*. London: Palgrave Macmillan.

Murphy, K., Sargeant, E., and Cherney, A. (2015). 'The importance of procedural justice and police performance in shaping intentions to cooperate with the police: does social identity matter?' *European Journal of Criminology*, 12: 719–38.

Newburn, T. (2016). 'The 2011 England riots in European context: a framework for understanding the 'life-cycle' of riots, *European Journal of Criminology*, 13: 540–55.

Nix, J., Wolfe, S. E., Rojek, J., and Kaminski, R. J. (2015). 'Trust in the police: the influence of procedural justice and perceived collective efficacy', *Crime & Delinquency*, 61: 610–40.

Norris, P. (2017). 'The conceptual framework of political support', in Zmerli, S. and van der Meer, T. (eds.), *Handbook on Political Trust*, Cheltenham: Edward Elgar Publishing: 19–32.

Oliveira, A. and Murphy, K. (2015). 'Race, social identity, and perceptions of police bias', *Race and Justice*, 5: 259–77.

Roché, S. (2010). 'Riots. The nature of rioting. Comparative reflexions based on the French case study', in Herzog-Evans, M. (ed.) *Transnational Criminology Manual*, Oisterwijk: Wolf Legal Publishers: 155–70.

Roché, S. (2016). *De la police en démocratie*, Paris: Grasset.

Roché, S. and de Maillard, J. (2009). 'Crisis in policing: the French rioting of 2005.' *Policing*, 3: 34–40.

Rothstein, B. and Stolle, D. (2008). 'The state and social capital: an institutional theory of generalized trust', *Comparative Politics*, 40: 441–59.

Roux, G, and Roché, S. (2016). 'Police et phénomènes identitaires dans les banlieues: entre ethnicité et territoire. Une étude par focus groups', *Revue française de science politique*, 66: 729–50.

Schnabel, A. and Hjerm, M. (2014). 'How the religious cleavages of civil society shape national identity', *SAGE Open*, 4: 1–14.

Schuck, A.M. (2013). 'A life-course perspective on adolescents attitudes to police: DARE, delinquency, and residential segregation', *Journal of Research in Crime and Delinquency*, 50: 579–607.

Sindall, K., McCarthy, D., and Brunton-Smith, I. (2016). 'Young people and the formation of attitudes towards the police', *European Journal of Criminology*, online. Available http://journals.sagepub.com/doi/pdf/10.1177/1477370816661739 (accessed 21 March 2017).

Skitka, L.J., Bauman, C., and Lytle, B. L. (2009). 'Limits on legitimacy: moral and religious convictions as constraints on deference to authority', *Journal of Personality and Social Psychology*, 97: 567–78.

Skogan, W. (2006). 'Asymmetry in the impact of encounters with the police', *Policing and Society* 16: 99–126.

Stewart, E., Baumer, E., Brunson, R., and Simons, R. (2009). 'Neighborhood racial context and perceptions of police-based racial discrimination among black youth', *Criminology*, 47: 847–87.

Tajfel, H. and Turner, J. (1986). 'The social identity theory of intergroup behavior', in: Worchel, S. and Austin, W. (eds.), *Psychology of Intergroup Relations*. Chicago, IL: Nelson Hall, 7–24.

Trommsdorff G. and Chen, X. (eds.) (2012). *Values, Religion, and Culture in Adolescent Development*. Cambridge: Cambridge University Press.

Tucci, I. (2010). 'Les descendants de migrants maghrebins en France et turcs en Allemagne: deux types de mise à distance sociale?', *Revue française de sociologie*, 51: 3–38.

Tyler, T. and Blader, S. (2003). 'The Group Engagement Model: procedural justice, social identity, and cooperative behavior', *Personality and Social Psychology Review*, 7: 349–61.

Tyler, T., Fagan, J., and Geller, A. (2014). 'Street stops and police legitimacy: teachable moments in young urban men's legal socialization', *Journal of Empirical Legal Studies*, 11: 751–85.

Verkuyten, M. and Fleischmann, F. (2017). 'Ethnicity, religion and nationality: group identifications among minority youth', in: Rutland, A., Nesdale, D., and Spears Brown,

C. (eds.), *Handbook of Group Processes in Children and Adolescents*, Oxford: Wiley, 23–46.

Weber, Max (1964). *The Theory of Social and Economic Organization*, New York: Free Press.

Weithman, Paul J. (2002). *Religion and the Obligations of Citizenship*, Cambridge: Cambridge University Press.

Weitzer, R. and Tuch, S. (2004). 'Race and perceptions of misconduct', *Social Problems*, 51: 305–25.

Wilde, S. (eds.) (2005). *Political and Citizenship Education, International Perspectives*, Wallingford, UK: Symposium Books.

Wu, Y., Sun, I., and Triplett, R. (2009). 'Race, class or neighborhood context: which matters more in measuring satisfaction with police?', *Justice Quarterly*, 26: 125–56.

9 The impact of the Ferguson, MO police shooting on Black and Nonblack residents' perceptions of police

Procedural justice, trust, and legitimacy

Tammy Rinehart Kochel

Introduction

When White Ferguson Police Officer Darren Wilson shot and killed African American suspect Michael Brown on August 9, 2014, it seemed to trigger a tidal wave. The public response to his shooting death was emotional, especially among minorities, vigorously displaying frustration with police through protests as well as violence and looting. The police response to the public was equally dramatic. The challenges faced by police of delivering procedurally just and effective policing in the face of an angry and sometimes violent public played out internationally on news and social media. However, this chapter examines the nature of the police response through the eyes of the residents living in the area, assessing how experiencing the shooting, the subsequent civil unrest, and the police response to the civil unrest, along with intense media coverage, affected residents' assessments about police aggressiveness, procedural justice, legitimacy, and their willingness to cooperate with police.

Few prior studies have assessed how high-profile critical incidents affect public opinions about police. What is especially unique in this case is that a prior study in St. Louis County, where Ferguson, Missouri is located, asked residents to report their views about police, and provides a baseline of data from which to assess this impact. I subsequently took the public temperature among the same residents in the immediate aftermath of the shooting, but also nearly one year later, to document changing views among residents in the height of the unrest and after sufficient time had passed to allow hope for some recovery of any damage done to police–community relations.

The focus of the research is on assessing Black and Nonblack residents' reactions, with a goal toward understanding what may lead to differences in perspective by race. This chapter will first synthesize what happened in Ferguson, Missouri in August 2014; briefly outline why it is important to understand the effects of Ferguson on residents' views about police, including any differences by race; describe the data on which this study is based; present the results of the short and long-term impact study; and consider the implications of the findings.

What happened in Ferguson, Missouri

On August 9, 2014, 28-year-old, White police officer Darren Wilson stopped 18-year-old, African American Michael Brown and a friend as they walked down a residential street, because they matched the description of individuals who had just robbed a convenience store. During the encounter, Wilson and Brown had a physical encounter and the result was that Officer Wilson shot and killed Brown. Initially, little specific information about the circumstances of the shooting was provided by police to the public, but the news and social media broadcast images of Brown lying in the street for hours accompanied by claims of citizen witnesses who questioned the reasonableness of the use of fatal force. Weeks of large protests, rioting, and looting followed the shooting incident. Police responded with fortified vehicles, riot gear, skirmish lines, beanbag bullets, and tear gas. The heaviest period of civil unrest lasted from August 9 and into September, with an additional "Weekend of Resistance" in October, and additional unrest when the grand jury decided against indicting Officer Wilson at the end of November 2014.

What is known about fatal police encounters in the U.S.

Deaths of police suspects that are caused by police are not well tracked in the U.S., but we know that this outcome is extremely rare relative to the number of police–citizen encounters. Nationally, official records are not kept on police shootings, but recently, news organizations have begun keeping their own records, based on news reports. The *Guardian* newspaper documented 1,146 people killed by police in 2015 in their database 'The Counted' (The Counted 2016), while the *Washington Post* tracked nearly 990 people shot and killed by police over the same timeframe ('990 people shot dead by police in 2015' 2015). These estimates are certainly tragic. Put into perspective, however, they reflect the unfortunate outcome of a minute fraction of police and citizen interactions. The most recently available official estimates on police–public contact in the U.S. found that over 62.9 million residents aged 16 or older (26 percent of the population aged 16 and up) had at least one contact with police in the preceding 12 months (Langton and Durose 2013), so the ratio of those killed compared to those engaging with police can be estimated at fewer than 16 fatalities per one-million people that U.S. police encounter each year in a variety of circumstances. In spite of the infrequency with which these events occur, it is apparent, given the public reaction to Brown's police shooting death in Ferguson, that the impact on the public of even one suspect fatality has the potential to be profound and is important to understand.

The value of understanding the effects of Ferguson on residents' views

Understanding the specific impact on the public is important, because in a democracy, police rely on the support and cooperation of the public to be able to co-produce order and apply minimal use of force (Bittner 1970). Citizens who perceive that police are fair and have legitimate authority tend to comply with the law and follow police directives because they feel they ought to do so (Fagan and Tyler 2004; Kochel et al. 2013; Lind and Tyler 1988; Murphy et al. 2008; Reisig et al. 2007; Sunshine and Tyler 2003; Tyler 1990; Tyler and Fagan 2008). Police rely on diffuse support from the public to adopt effective strategies such as community policing, problem solving, third party policing, hot spots policing, etc. that rely on input and involvement from the public to reduce crime and disorder problems. Thus, it is important to measure public assessments of police and to strive to sustain positive views.

Even under ordinary conditions, minority residents hold more negative views about police. Evidence supports that views among minority residents in the U.S. tend to be less positive than White residents (Brown and Benedict 2002; Kirk and Papachristos 2011; Sunshine and Tyler 2003). African American residents trust police less and hold lower assessments of police legitimacy (Dunham and Alpert 1988; Jefferis et al. 1997; Oliveira and Murphy 2015; Van Craen 2012; Van Craen and Skogan 2015; Weisburd et al. 2000; Weitzer 1999; Weitzer and Tuch 2005a). Recent research by the Reason Foundation shows that African Americans also believe that police are quick to use lethal force and that police use of force is increasing (Ekins 2014). This more disapproving perspective may derive from the disproportionate amount of interaction that African American residents have with police in enforcement situations. For instance, while 12 percent of drivers across the U.S. are stopped by police in a year, the rate for minorities is 24 percent (Engel and Calnon 2004). African Americans are more likely to be searched during traffic stops, although fewer searches result in contraband being seized (Engel and Johnson 2006). While African Americans compose 13.6 percent of the U.S. population in the 2010 U.S. Census, in the same year, the FBI reported that they represent 32 percent of drug arrests in the U.S. (Engel et al. 2012; Federal Bureau of Investigation 2010; Rastogi et al. 2011). Even taking into account other circumstances about the situation, African American residents are more likely to be arrested than White residents (Kochel et al. 2011).

One concern is that the Ferguson incident will amplify minority residents' distrust and respect for police authority and willingness to cooperate with police. Race seemed especially salient in this case, as the "Black Lives Matter" campaign became a central theme in the public outcry. Feeling marginalized or experiencing repeated accumulated negative experiences with police may contribute to a different perspective among African Americans than other residents.

Consistent with this concern over minority residents' views, Blodorn et al. (2016) found that race affected residents' perceptions about the motives of government officials handling Hurricane Katrina. They found that African

American residents of New Orleans perceived more racism in the government response to Hurricane Katrina than White residents. Feeling that one's ethnicity was central to his/her identity also contributed to residents' assessments of racism in the government response. Therefore, it is practical and advantageous to understand the impact of Ferguson's events on public views, and to assess whether that impact differs by race, as it did in the government response to handling Hurricane Katrina.

The data

Prior to August 2014, St. Louis County Police Department, the county in which Ferguson, Missouri is located, had been monitoring public opinion of police, investigating how various strategies implemented in disadvantaged, high-crime hot spots in the county might differently affect how the public views them. To this end, three waves of community surveys had been conducted by the research partner in the two years immediately preceding the shooting incident, returning to the same individuals over time to show a trend. Having these baseline measures allowed for a rigorous examination of the effects of the events surrounding the shooting on these residents—taking a measure of their views in September and October 2014 and then again in May through July 2015—and comparing these opinions to the attitudes held prior to the shooting.

The first three survey waves were conducted in March–May 2012, November 2012–January 2013, and May–July 2013. Addresses for wave 1 were randomly sampled from a list of all addresses within each of 71 crime hot spots. The adult resident who answered the door was asked to participate. Cooperation rates for the pre-Ferguson waves ranged from 38–45 percent. Waves 2 and 3 strived to interview the same respondents from the early wave(s), but allowed for address level substitution, if the wave 1 respondent was still in the same household. Additionally, we randomly sampled new addresses to supplement the wave 1 sample. Most surveys during the first three waves were in-person, but in later waves, residents who provided phone numbers and preferred to be surveyed by phone were accommodated.

The cooperation rate for the short-term follow-up in September–October 2014 was 48 percent. All of the wave 4 surveys were conducted by telephone as a precaution for interviewer safety, because chaos and violence in the area was ongoing. Additionally, this part of the project did not have Federal or Foundation funding, and thus only used the resources provided by the University of the researcher. In-person surveys were deemed cost and safety prohibitive. Residents had to report that they continued living in St. Louis County to be eligible to complete the survey.

The long-term follow-up cooperation rate in May–July 2015 was 28 percent. Most of these surveys were conducted by telephone, although a very small portion was conducted in-person. By this time, residents had grown weary of responding to the survey, particularly without a new incident to motivate an interest in speaking with us. Examining descriptive statistics for the sample over time, however, suggests no major shifts in the nature of the sample. Clearly as we aimed to interview the same sample over time, we would expect slight increases in age and time at residence. Some may also gain home ownership, education, and income. As we suffer from attrition, the proportion of home-owners would also likely decrease (because homeownership may increase stability at the specific address whereas renters would be able to move with less effort). Table 9.1 shows a similar distribution in race/ethnicity, marital status, education, and income across the waves. Residents in the later waves are older, have lived at their address longer, a higher proportion owns their homes, and slightly fewer are males.

Table 9.1 Survey demographics by Wave

	Wave 1 Mar.– May 12	Wave 2 Nov. 12– Jan. 13	Wave 3 May– July 13	Wave 4 Sep.– Oct. 14	Wave 5 May– July 15
Male (%)	40	40	38	39	36
Average age	38	42	41	45	46
Police officer (%)	2	2	1	0	1
Average years at address	5.5	7.2	6.8	8.8	10.7
Own (%)	21	25	26	33	36
Race/Ethnicity					
African American (%)	75	71	70	70	70
Asian/Pacific Island (%)	0	1	1	0	0
Multi-racial (%)	2	1	2	5	not measured
White (%)	20	22	20	24	25
Other (%)	3	3	5	3	7
Hispanic (%)	1	2	1	1	0
Marital status					
Married (%)	22	23	23	24	27
Never married (%)	56	47	50	44	46
Divorced (%)	15	20	18	22	18
Widowed (%)	5	6	5	10	8
Education					
College degree (%)	11	17	15	18	23
Some college (%)	43	43	45	49	43
High school GED/ diploma (%)	31	29	30	28	29
Less than high school degree (%)	9	9	6	5	5
Income					
No income (%)	11	11	10	7	9
$1–$15,000 (%)	21	20	19	18	18
$15,000–$24,999 (%)	21	18	18	23	21
$25,000–$34,999 (%)	17	16	18	18	19
$35,000–$49,000 (%)	13	12	13	19	19
$50,000–$74,999 (%)	7	7	7	10	11
$75,000 or more (%)	1	2	2	5	4

Variables

The study examines four outcomes: perceived frequency police use aggressive tactics (stopping people without good reason, more force than needed under the circumstances, insulting language); trust and procedural justice (police act fairly, impartially and respectfully); police legitimacy (police authority is valid and should be respected); and a resident's willingness to cooperate with police by providing information and reporting crime and suspicious behaviors. The measures were first formed using confirmatory factor analysis, and upon identifying good model fit and good reliability, whereby factor loadings were within 0.1 of each other and low rates of missing data (less than 10 percent), I converted the scores to percent of maximum possible scores (POMP). This allows for easier comparison across studies and meaningful interpretation of the scores.[1] For each outcome measure, I averaged across non-missing indicators for each case and applied the POMP formula below. Scores range 0 through 100.

$$POMP = \frac{(\text{Observed minus the Minimum in the scale})}{(\text{Maximum minus Minimum scale score})} \times 100 \qquad (9.1)$$

Race is binary (African American = 1). Fewer than 4 percent of the sample did not identify as at least part White or Black. Only 1 percent identified as Hispanic, so using a dichotomy is not expected to impact the findings. Given past research that suggests Hispanic respondents tend to have views that fall between Black and White residents, if anything, this operationalization would slightly diminish the size of a measured race effect.

Analysis strategy

I use mixed effects regression, modeling the fixed and random effects, for both the short and long-term impact studies. Random effects account for the nested sample, including repeated measures over time.[2] The short-term impact study compares the change in views of African American residents versus Nonblack residents immediately following the shooting compared to views prior to the shooting (the change in views from waves 1–3 to wave 4). The short-term impact study sample includes only respondents who were surveyed at wave 4 and at least one time prior to that ($N=390$). The long-term impact analysis compares African Americans' versus Nonblack residents' change in views from wave 4 to wave 5 and controls for views prior to Ferguson, including the change in views from waves 1–3 to wave 4. The long-term impact study sample includes only respondents who were surveyed at least once before and after the shooting ($N=472$). Missing data is addressed with maximum likelihood estimation.

Qualitative data are coded using open coding to identify themes (Corbin and Strauss 2015). At wave 4, three open-ended questions address views about the police and public responses to Brown's shooting death. Coded responses were compared to components of accumulated experiences theory and the group position/conflict perspective as potential reasons contributing to residents' views.

At wave 5, two open-ended questions address observed and preferred changes in policing. For wave 5, particular attention was paid to the proportion of responses that may indicate reasons for improved, worsened, or stable views of police (e.g., change in police presence or nature of behaviors with citizens in neighborhoods).

Short-term impact

Table 9.2 provides the results of the short-term impact study. The results show a significant difference by race in how the events in Ferguson affected African American versus Nonblack residents' views about police for three of the four outcomes. African Americans' views worsened and Nonblack residents' views remained fairly stable. The coefficients for wave 4 X Black are statistically

Table 9.2 Short-term impact

	Model 1: Frequency of aggressive tactics (n = 383)	Model 2: Trust and procedural justice (n = 390)	Model 3: Police legitimacy (n = 388)	Model 4: Willingness to cooperate (n = 388)
Predictive margins				
African American				
Percent change	+20.8[a]	−25.5[a]	−8.2[a]	+2.6
Score before shooting	50.8 [b]	61.5	66.7	88.2
Score after shooting	61.4 [b]	45.8[b]	61.2[b]	90.5[b]
Nonblack				
Percent change	+5.1	+1.5	+1.4	+4.8[a]
Score before shooting	36.1	67.9	70.0	90.7
Score after shooting	37.9	69.0	71.1	95.1
Fixed effects	*b (se)*	*b (se)*	*b (se)*	*b (se)*
Intercept	35.07 (2.43)*	68.68 (2.91)*	69.31 (2.86)*	90.32 (2.21)*
Wave 4 (vs. prior)	1.88 (2.34)	1.01 (1.65)	1.03 (2.25)	4.39 (1.70)*
Black	13.85 (2.94)*	−5.76 (3.09)	−4.01 (3.13)	−2.80 (2.46)
W4 X black	8.72 (2.99)*	−16.70 (2.38)*	−6.46 (2.88)*	−2.08 (2.21)
North county	3.36 (2.46)	−2.50 (2.55)	2.40 (2.86)	1.25 (1.75)

Notes
Random effects are included in the analysis, but not displayed. For aggressive tactics, insufficient variation existed to model the random effects across hot spots, so for Model 1, random effects only model the repeated measures within person.
n reflects the number of individuals, not the number of observations.
* $p \leq 0.05$.
a Refers to a significant difference ($p < 0.05$) *within race* in the scores prior to versus after the shooting event, based on pairwise comparisons of the margins.
b Refers to a significant difference ($p < 0.05$) in scores between African American and Nonblack residents at that time point (prior or after the shooting), based on pairwise comparisons of the margins.

significant and negative for trust and procedural justice ($b=-16.70$, $p<0.001$) and for legitimacy ($b=-6.46$, $p=0.025$) and significant and positive for perceived frequency of aggressive tactics ($b=8.72$, $p=0.004$). The coefficient for willingness to cooperate with police was not statistically significant ($b=-2.08$, $p=0.346$). Both African American and Nonblack residents saw a slight increase in willingness to cooperate, although Nonblack residents reported a slightly larger, but not significantly larger improvement. This uptick is likely to follow from the increased use of force by police during that time, which promotes compliance.

Predictive margins based on these analyses suggest that prior to the shooting, there were not significant differences between African American and Nonblack residents' assessments about procedural justice and trust, police legitimacy, or the willingness to cooperate, although even prior to Brown's death in Ferguson, African American residents assessed the frequency of aggressive policing much higher than Nonblack residents (African American=50.8, Nonblack=36.1, $p<0.001$). Following the events in Ferguson, African Americans' views about procedural justice and trust declined by 26 percent while Nonblack residents' views about procedural justice and trust remained stable, a nonsignificant uptick of only 1.5 percent. Similarly, African Americans' legitimacy assessments declined by 8.2 percent, while Nonblack residents' assessments remained stable. Perceived frequency of aggressive policing tactics increased by 21 percent among African American residents, but Nonblack residents saw a nonsignificant 5 percent increase. In spite of relatively similar views across race prior to Ferguson, during the immediate aftermath of Ferguson, there were significant differences in the predicted margins scores by race for all four outcomes. Figure 9.1 depicts the predictive margins for African American versus Nonblack residents over each survey time point and visually shows that while African American and Nonblack residents followed similar trends prior to the Ferguson events, the trends depart following Ferguson for three of the four outcomes.

Explaining residents' short-term reactions

As important as it is to document the impact of the events in Ferguson on public views about police, it is even more valuable to try to understand the potential explanations for the way opinions about police were affected. Certainly, prior to the incident, the trend was that African American residents' assessments were lower than Nonblack residents (see Figure 9.1), albeit not significantly so, other than assessments of the frequency police use aggressive tactics. Given that diffuse support was not quite as strong among minority residents, diminished support can make that group vulnerable to large shifts in opinion following a significant incident (Kaminski and Jefferis 1998).

Examining the qualitative data from the wave 4 (short-term impact) survey shows that in the immediate aftermath of the shooting, the qualitative data parallels the quantitative results, depicting a sharp divide by race in how residents felt

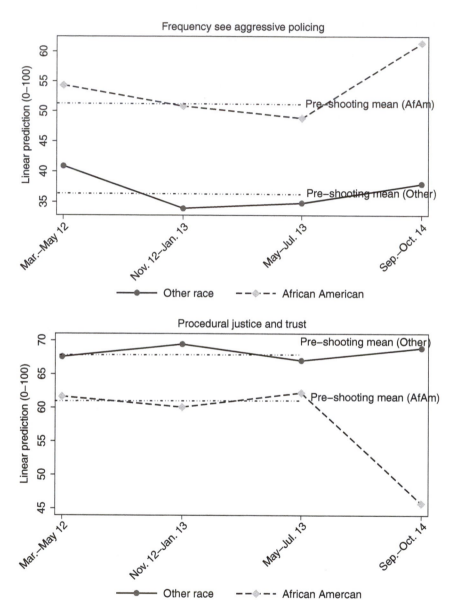

Figure 9.1 Views about police by race over time waves 1–4.

Notes
(*n*=390); adapted from Kochel (2017).

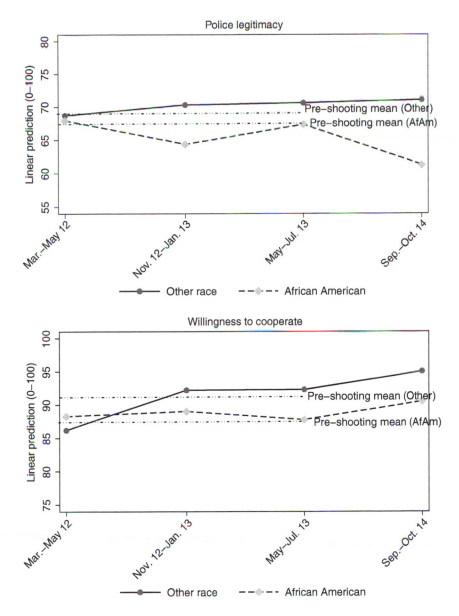

Figure 9.1 Continued

about the incident and the public and police response to it. The comments conveyed that the incident felt personally relevant among many African American residents. One 57-year-old female explained, "[t]his happens a lot to the Black community, this is nothing new. It happens a lot.... As a mother of four sons, I am touched by it deeply. I can certainly feel for the mother of Michael Brown." Comments about how similar use of force events happened to their own family members, cousins, and acquaintances in the past paint a picture of a long series of accumulated experiences. The shooting triggered a desire among a group that felt marginalized to take action to disrupt what they saw as a trend in discrimination. One 38-year-old African American male explained,

> [w]e need the protests to get attention and be heard. People need to know what is going on. I'm sorry about the businesses, but shootings have happened hundreds of times over. We finally stood up to the police, who treat the value of an African American male as very low on the stock exchange.

Three-quarters of African American residents said that they disagreed with the police response, citing that it was too harsh (32 percent), that police should not use "military tactics" (26 percent), or disagreement with the use of tear gas (19 percent) or rubber bullets (3 percent).[3] Some African American residents more generally just reported that the response was not the correct one (10 percent) or that it made the situation worse (12 percent).

The shooting of Brown appeared symbolic for his racial group, as evidenced by the "Black Lives Matter" movement that became a central part of the public response to the shooting. African American residents viewed the incident as part of a series of discriminatory behaviors by police against African Americans (e.g., "Police always discriminating on us"—21-year-old African American female; "[t]hey have always treated us that way…"—58-year-old African American female) and sought to raise public awareness about this racial tension. African Americans' assessment of the response by police to the public protests, looting, and riots certainly highlights this racial tension.

Conversely, Nonblack residents' comments paint a very different perspective about the events in Ferguson. Nonblack residents' comments lacked a connotation that the shooting incident was personal to them and did not include references to the incident as part of a series of discrimination. Nonblack residents were much more likely to view the incident in isolation and promote use of the courts to ensure justice. Numerous remarks by Nonblack residents condemned the public's use of looting, non-peaceful protests, and disregard for due process. One 74-year-old female's remark makes the perspective clear, "[i]t goes against everything that I was taught as a child, which is to respect the police. If the policeman was wrong in shooting Michael Brown, the court should settle it, not the people." While two-thirds of African Americans supported the public response, two-thirds of Nonblack residents condemned the public response. While three-quarters of African American residents disagreed with the police response to the shooting and civil unrest, two-thirds of Nonblack residents agreed with it. Those Nonblack residents who agreed with the police response saw the situation as challenging and felt that appropriate tactics were used or that "they did what was needed."

Apparent in the divergent sentiments expressed along racial lines is support that group identity played an important role in interpreting events. Nonblack, predominantly White, residents mostly supported the status quo, their diffuse support for police did not waiver, and they valued the existing justice system as an appropriate means for addressing the shooting, restoring order, and gaining justice. As a group, African American residents tended to see meaning in the race of Michael Brown. They associated his experience with their own accumulated experiences and what they have heard from other minority group residents. Social media and the intense network media coverage provided a unique opportunity to increase and validate the sense of shared discrimination and provided an opportunity to raise awareness about racial tension in policing and to instigate change.

What is perhaps especially interesting to note is that as part of the survey, we asked residents to rate the types of strategies that may be able to help restore confidence and trust in police, and residents tended to agree on the best approaches, even across racial lines. The strongest support was for strategies designed to increase the transparency of policing and increase the engagement and interaction between the police and the public. Greatest support was found for the use of body/dash cameras (83 percent supported) and police organizing focus groups of community members to discuss police practices (80 percent supported). Residents also supported increasing patrols (71 percent), increasing the proportion of minority officers (69 percent—albeit significantly more support among African American respondents), officers participating in community events (68 percent—with stronger support among Nonblack residents), sharing statistics with the public about the racial breakdown of stops and arrests (58 percent), and using social media to share information with the public (55 percent). Following the initial response to the shooting and unrest, St. Louis County Police did take steps to hold meetings with the public, increase the use of body cameras, use social media to proactively share information with the public, and re-intensify efforts to hire more minority officers (although this is a significant challenge in the wake of the Ferguson unrest) (Chief Jon Belmar, personal communication September 28, 2015).

Long-term impact

Thus, it was important to re-assess public views once some time had passed and some initial strategies had been implemented to improve police–community relations. Table 9.3 provides the long-term impact results, both the fixed effects and predicted margins. Assessments of the long-term impact, measured 9 to 11 months following the shooting incident, show that the only significant difference in trends by race between waves 4 and 5 is for procedural justice and trust ($b = 12.87$, $p < 0.001$). African Americans saw a 19 percent improvement while

Table 9.3 Long-term impact

	Model 1: Frequency aggressive tactics (n = 470)	Model 2: Trust and procedural justice (n = 473)	Model 3: Police legitimacy (n = 472)	Model 4: Willingness to cooperate (n = 472)
Predictive margins				
African American				
% change W4–5	–6.1	+18.8[a]	+10.7[a]	–2.4
Wave 4 score	60.6 [b]	46.8[b]	61.5[b]	90.4[b]
Wave 5 score	56.9 [b]	55.6	68.1	88.2
Nonblack				
% change W4–5	+8.0	–6.1	+2.0	–5.0[a]
Wave 4 score	37.5	67.6	71.1	95.7
Wave 5 score	40.5	63.5	72.5	90.9
Fixed Effects	*b (se)*	*b (se)*	*b (se)*	*b (se)*
Intercept	37.5 (1.83)*	67.61 (1.29)*	70.27 (2.72)*	95.34 (0.94)*
Wave 1–3 (to 4)	–2.86 (4.46)	–0.74 (0.07)	–0.86 (2.30)	–4.00 (1.56)*
Wave 5 (from 4)	2.99 (4.19)	–4.07 (1.51)*	1.40 (2.96)	–4.78 (1.43)*
Black	23.10 (0.69)*	–20.85 (0.74)*	–10.41 (3.22)*	–5.59 (1.48)*
W1–3 X black	–8.13 (5.08)	17.15 (0.15)*	–7.13 (2.87)*	1.57 (2.03)
W5 X black	–6.65 (8.09)	12.87 (2.10)*	5.22 (3.46)	2.63 (2.22)
North county	–	–	3.01 (2.25)	1.20 (1.52)

Notes

Random effects are included in the analysis, but not displayed. For aggressive tactics, insufficient variation existed to model the random effects across hot spots, so for Model 1, random effects only model the repeated measures within person.

n reflects the number of individuals, not the number of observations.

* $p \leq 0.05$.

a Refers to a significant difference ($p < 0.05$) *within race* between scores at Wave 4 versus Wave 5, based on pairwise comparisons of the margins.

b Refers to a significant difference ($p < 0.05$) in scores between African American and Nonblack residents at that time, based on pairwise comparisons of the margins.

Nonblack residents' views about procedural justice and trust declined by 6 percent between the short- and long-term impact measurements. This is not to suggest that views did not change considerably within race between waves 4 and 5, especially among African Americans, but rather that the changes reported between waves 4 and 5 among African American residents did not *significantly* differ from those reported by Nonblack residents for police legitimacy ($b = 5.22$, $p = 0.132$), aggressive policing ($b = -6.65$, $p = 0.411$), and willingness to cooperate with police ($b = 2.63$, $p = 0.236$). However, some of the nonsignificant differences are worth noting. For instance, among Nonblack residents, the trend for police legitimacy remained fairly stable between waves 4 and 5, although African American residents scores improved by nearly 11 percent. Willingness to cooperate with police showed slight declines among Nonblack residents and an even smaller decline among African American residents. It is easy to see that the trends during this period are more positive among African American residents than Nonblack residents—showing some movement toward recovery.

Predictive margins scores derived from the analyses show that while African American and Nonblack residents' scores for all four outcomes differed significantly from one another at wave 4, by wave 5 the only remaining significant difference in the predictive margins scores by race is for the frequency of aggressive policing tactics (which were also different from one another prior to Brown's shooting death). Although African Americans saw a 6 percent decline while Nonblack residents saw an 8 percent increase in the frequency of aggressive policing following wave 4, compared to each other at wave 5, the scores still differ by 16 points (African Americans=56.9, Nonblack=40.5, $p=0.009$). The remaining scores for African American versus Nonblack residents were not significantly different by wave 5 (police legitimacy: African American=68.1, Nonblack=72.5, $p=0.715$; procedural justice: African American=55.6, Nonblack=63.5, $p=0.155$; cooperation: African American=88.3, Nonblack=90.9, $p=0.424$).

The graphs in Figure 9.2 depict the predicted margins scores by race over time. It is clear from these figures that among African American residents, who experienced the most dramatic impact on perceptions of police immediately following the events in Ferguson, recovery of views is ongoing, particularly for procedural justice and trust. Assessments of police across race are becoming more similar again in wave 5.

Explaining the long-term impact

In the long term, several reasons may explain why African American residents reported slightly improved opinions about police while Nonblack residents' views fairly remained stable. Past research by Ron Weitzer (2002) into public opinion following four high-profile police incidents in Los Angeles (e.g., beatings, a shooting, an exposed scandal in one division) found that public attitudes toward police that were initially drastically reduced following events tended to eventually recover to approximately pre-incident levels. In Los Angeles, he postulates that the recovery may have been because memories fade, a tendency to regress to the mean, or due to reforms by the Los Angeles Police Department designed to improve police–community relations—including replacing Chief Daryl Gates following the Rodney King incident with African American Chief Willie Williams.

In St. Louis County, similar reasons may explain the improvement among African Americans in their trust for police and to a lesser extent police legitimacy. Memories about the incident may have faded or at least hold a reduced priority or urgency as time has passed, views may have regressed to their mean as a statistical matter, or changes in policing may have led to improved police–community relations. Additionally, since the grand jury decision not to indict Officer Wilson was made and released in November 2014, this

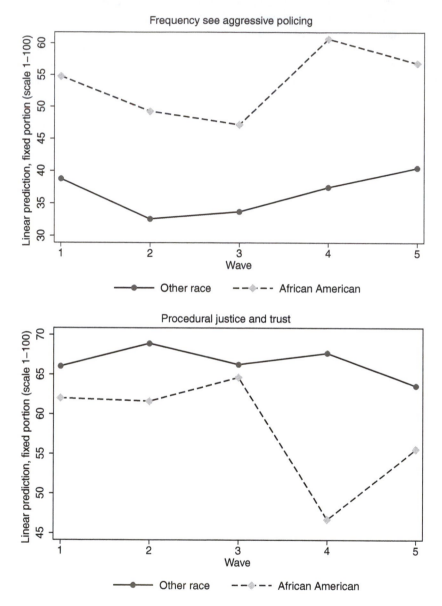

Figure 9.2 Views about police by race over time waves 1–5.

Note

(*n*=423).

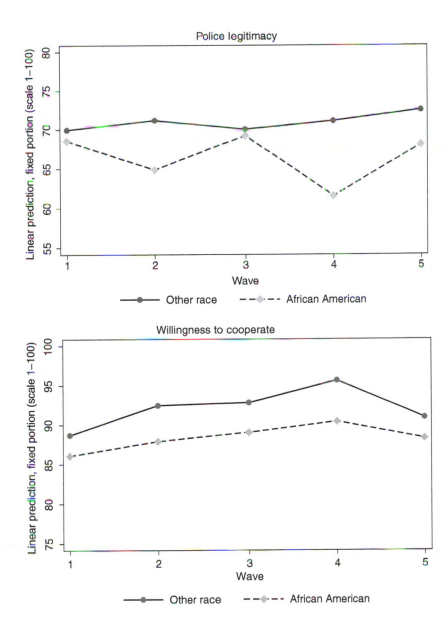

Figure 9.2 Continued

212 T. R. Kochel

additional information about the circumstances of the original incident and exoneration for Officer Wilson from being prosecuted for legal wrongdoing may have affected public opinions. It may also be the case that the number of police stops of African American residents declined in the time following Ferguson, thus potentially leading to fewer accumulated encounters perceived as negative by residents and fewer negative consequences. If time passes with fewer perceived negative encounters with police, this may help promote improved attitudes toward police (Kochel 2012; Reisig and Parks 2000; Skogan 2006). Additionally, media coverage depicting police negatively as using excessive force or misconduct, which can influence residents' perceptions of police (Chermak et al. 2006; Weitzer and Tuch 2005b) faded following the grand jury decision not to indict.

While each of these explanations may play a role in influencing residents' views following Ferguson, one explanation for which data is available points to the reduction in negative police encounters and in fact a general reduction in police presence in the areas where these residents live. Both police self-reported data on stops and other outcomes as well as the wave 5 survey data provide some support for a reduction in negative police–citizen encounters as one mechanism that may have allowed for some recovery of views (see Table 9.4). Police self-reported activity data show that across the county overall, and comparing the eight months leading up to the shooting in Ferguson (January–August 2014) to the eight months that followed (September 2014–April 2015), officers reported less self-initiated activity, fewer stops, fewer moving and nonmoving citations, fewer Driving While Intoxicated stops, and fewer felony and misdemeanor arrests. Declines in potentially negative outcomes for citizens ranged from 21 percent to 41 percent countywide. However, the declines within North County, where Ferguson is located, were particularly evident. In North County, stops declined by 40 percent, moving citations declined by 50 percent, as did summons in lieu of citations, field investigations, and guns seized. Comparing these data to experiences reported by citizens, the proportion of residents stopped at both waves 4 and 5 are lower than in each of the waves measured before Michael Brown's death. An assessment of the frequency that citizens reported seeing police in their neighborhoods showed significant declines between waves 4 and 5, and African Americans reported steeper declines than Nonblack residents (wave 5 X African American $b=-15.31$, s.e. $=4.01$, $p<0.001$) (see Figure 9.3).[4] At wave 4, on average (examining predictive margins), African Americans reported seeing police in their neighborhood several times each week while Nonblack residents reported seeing police between once a week and several times each week. By wave 5, both African American and Nonblack residents, on average, reported seeing police in their neighborhoods less than once each month.

Table 9.4 Police activity: citizen and police data

Citizen-self reports during surveys	Wave 1 (%)	Wave 2 (%)	Wave 3 (%)	Wave 4 (%)	Wave 5 (%)
Proportion of respondents stopped	31.8	23.1	19.6	9.5	16.5
% black stopped	34.4	26.4	20.6	10.8	18.9
% nonblack stopped	23.2	14.2	16.7	6.6	10.8
Disparity index % black/% nonblack	1.48	1.86	1.23	1.64	1.75

Self-report police activity data	Countywide			North County		
	January–August 14	September 14–April 15	Percent change	January–August 14	September 14–April 15	Percent change
Self-initiated activities	141,782	121,640	−14.2	29,513	21,479	−27.2
Stops	42,412	30,152	−28.9	6,256	3,761	−39.9
Moving violation citations	14,097	8,960	−36.4	2,241	1,114	−50.3
Nonmoving violation citations	22,767	15,072	−33.8	5,267	2,941	44.2
Summons in lieu of citation	6,793	4,248	−37.5	1,462	693	−52.6
Felony arrests	3,739	2,963	−20.8	999	749	−25.0
Misdemeanor Arrests	9,173	6,370	−30.6	2,503	1,522	−39.2
Driving while intoxicated	567	395	−30.3	57	40	−29.8
Guns seized	700	414	−40.9	361	160	−55.7

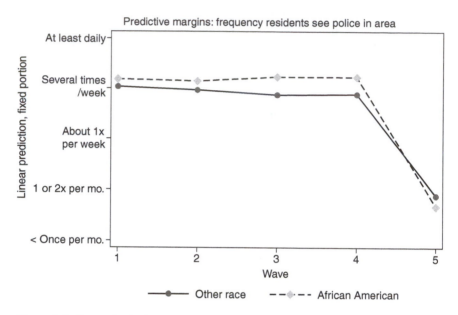

Figure 9.3 Change in the frequency residents report seeing police.

Implications for police–community relations

This is not to suggest that the answer to handling the negative consequences to police–community relations following a high-profile police incident is for police to "back off." In this case, both police and the public may have benefited from initial reductions in adversarial encounters. Yet, this is not the only change that was made, as previously mentioned. One major shift is that St. Louis County Police became concerned about and attentive to public image, being more thoughtful about what they wear, what tools are used to achieve outcomes, and that lack of timely information sharing with the public can generate misconceptions that are subsequently difficult to change. Thus, they have changed tactical uniforms, increased the use of body cameras, are more cautious about the deployment of canines, fortified vehicles, and assault style weapons—focusing on being tactically available and alert, but without being so visible or "in the face" of the public. A key change was hiring someone who specifically manages communications via social media. She shares both positive police–community interactions and events as well as aims to quickly share accurate information about incidents before someone without firsthand knowledge takes control of the message or tone (Chief Jon Belmar, personal communication September 28, 2015).

The lessons learned from the Ferguson incident that can be applied to police–community relations appear to be consistent with these efforts to increase transparency, information sharing and engagement. Furthermore, as minority residents tend to hold worse views than majority residents in many contexts over time (Brown and Benedict 2002; Oliveira and Murphy 2015; Reisig and Parks 2000; Sampson and Bartusch 1998; Van Craen 2012), a concerted effort to improve those experiences as well as diffuse support for police should include advancing procedurally just tactics and aiming to reduce accumulated negative experiences with police. In fact, qualitative comments at wave 5 (long-term impact survey) revealed that 27.3 percent of residents still wanted to see better police–citizen interactions, suggesting a desire for respectful, friendly, and professional interactions that incorporate empathy. Furthermore, 12.7 percent stated that they wanted to see better interactions with minority residents specifically, to create a sense that all races are treated equally. Additionally, 12.4 percent reported wanting more community engagement and collaboration, while 11.6 percent said that they wanted less police aggression. It should also be recognized that in response to a question asking what changes that they would like to see police make, 12 percent stated that police are doing a good job. To conclude, at the time of the long-term impact survey, recovery of police–community relations was underway, but further improvements may be possible with an additional focus on policing in ways that limit accumulated negative experiences among minority residents, focusing on procedural justice, and promoting information sharing, transparency, and inclusiveness.

This research highlights the importance of measuring public attitudes toward police and being able and willing to adjust policing policies and practices in an effort to maximize police–community relations. Police efforts to proactively promote positive police–citizen relations within marginalized communities and to minimize their experiences and perceptions of discriminatory practices could eventually lay a foundation of support (much like the Nonblack residents sampled) that may provide an opportunity to investigate the necessity of and culpability within high-profile situations before the public passes judgement. Improving the foundation of trust and police legitimacy among marginalized groups is inherently valuable, but weaknesses in these views and reduced diffuse support for police can generate significant consequences for police and communities when rare yet high-profile and impactful events occur, as observed in Ferguson.

Notes

1 See Cohen et al. (1999) for a detailed discussion of the value of POMP as a meaningful measurement unit for the social sciences.
2 The full random effects model includes the repeated measures over time, people nested in addresses, addresses in hot spots, and hot spots nested in North County or not (this was part of the blocked sampling design of the original study). However, in the event of insufficient variation to model the random effects at a particular level, it was removed. If that level is North County/not, it was modeled as a direct effect.
3 Although the St. Louis Post Dispatch (2014) reported that police used rubber bullets, SLCPD states that they do not have nor did they or other police agencies have access to or use rubber bullets.
4 This post-hoc analysis is a mixed effect regression of a question asking how frequently residents saw police in the area over the preceding 6 months.

Bibliography

Bittner, E. (1970). *The Functions of the Police in Modern Society*, Chevy Chase, MD: U.S. National Institute of Mental Health, Center for Studies of Crime and Delinquency.

Blodorn, A., O'Brien, L., Cheryan, S., and Vick, S. (2016). 'Understanding perceptions of racism in the aftermath of Hurricane Katrina: the roles of system and group justification', *Social Justice Research*, 29: 139–58.

Brown, B. and Benedict, W. (2002). 'Perceptions of the police: past findings, methodological issues, conceptual issues and policy implications', *Policing: An International Journal of Police Strategies and Management*, 25: 543–80.

Chermak, S., McGarrell, E., and Gruenewald, J. (2006). 'Media coverage of police misconduct and attitudes toward police', *Policing: An International Journal of Police Strategies and Management*, 29: 261–81.

Cohen, P., Cohen, J., Aiken, L., and West, S. (1999). 'The problem of units and the circumstance for POMP', *Multivariate Behavioral Research*, 34: 315–46.

Corbin, J. and Strauss, A. (2015). *Basics of Qualitative Research: Techniques and Procedures for Developing Grounded Theory*, Thousand Oaks, CA: SAGE Publications.

Dunham, R. and Alpert, G. (1988). 'Neighborhood differences in attitudes toward policing: evidence for a mixed-strategy model of policing in a multi-ethnic setting', *The Journal of Criminal Law and Criminology*, 79: 504–23.

Ekins, E. (2014, October 9). 'Poll: Americans want congress to vote on military force before midterms, say an Ebola outbreak is likely and kids should be required to get vaccinations', *Reason Foundation*, online. Available http://reason.com/poll/2014/10/09/october-2014-reason-rupe-poll (accessed January 17, 2017).

Engel, R. and Calnon, J. (2004). 'Examining the influence of drivers' characteristics during traffic stops with police: results from a national survey', *Justice Quarterly*, 21: 49–90.

Engel, R. and Johnson, R. (2006). 'Toward a better understanding of racial and ethnic disparities in search and seizure rates', *Journal of Criminal Justice*, 34: 605–17.

Engel, R., Smith, M., and Cullen, F. (2012). 'Race, place, and drug enforcement', *Criminology and Public Policy*, 11: 603–35.

Fagan, J. and Tyler, T. (2004). 'Policing, order maintenance and legitimacy', in G. Mesko, M. Pagon, and B. Dobovsek (eds.), *Policing in Central and Eastern Europe: Dilemmas of Contemporary Criminal Justice*, Maribor: University of Maribor, Faculty of Criminal Justice, 91–102.

Federal Bureau of Investigation (2010). *Crime in the United States: 2010*, Washington, DC: U.S. Government Printing Office.

Jefferis, E., Kaminski, R., Holmes, S., and Hanley, D. E. (1997). 'The effect of a videotaped arrest on public perceptions of police use of force', *Journal of Criminal Justice*, 25: 381–95.

Kaminski, R. and Jefferis, E. (1998). 'The effect of a violent televised arrest on public perceptions of the police: a partial test of Easton's theoretical framework', *Policing: An International Journal of Police Strategies and Management*, 21: 683–706.

Kirk, D. and Papachristos, A. (2011). 'Cultural mechanisms and the persistence of neighborhood violence', *American Journal of Sociology*, 116: 1190–233.

Kochel, T. (2012). 'Can police legitimacy promote collective efficacy?', *Justice Quarterly*, 29: 384–419.

Kochel, T. (2017). 'Explaining racial differences in Ferguson's impact on local residents' trust and perceived legitimacy', *Criminal Justice Policy Review*, Online First. Available http://journals.sagepub.com/doi/abs/10.1177/0887403416684923 (accessed July 11, 2017).

Kochel, T., Parks, R., and Mastrofski, S. (2013). 'Examining police effectiveness as a precursor to legitimacy and cooperation with police', *Justice Quarterly*, 30: 895–925.

Kochel, T., Wilson, D., and Mastrofski, S. (2011). 'Effect of suspect race on officers' arrest decisions', *Criminology*, 49: 473–512.

Langton, L. and Durose, M. (2013). *Police Behavior During Traffic and Street Stops 2011*, Washington, DC: U.S. Department of Justice Office of Justice Programs.

Lind, E. and Tyler, T. (1988). *The Social Psychology of Procedural Justice*, New York: Springer.

Murphy, K., Hinds, L., and Fleming, J. (2008). 'Encouraging public cooperation and support for police', *Policing and Society*, 18: 136–55.

Oliveira, A. and Murphy, K. (2015). 'Race, social identity, and perceptions of police bias', *Race and Justice*, 5: 259–77.

Rastogi, S., Johnson, T., Hoeffel, E., and Drewery, M. (2011). *The Black Population*, Washington, DC: U.S. Department of Commerce, Economics and Statistics Administration, U.S. Census Bureau.

Reisig, M., Bratton, J., and Gertz, M. (2007). 'The construct validity and refinement of process-based policing measures', *Criminal Justice and Behavior*, 34: 1005–28.

Reisig, M. and Parks, R. (2000). 'Experience, quality of life, and neighborhood context: a hierarchical analysis of satisfaction with police', *Justice Quarterly*, 17: 607–30.

Sampson, R. and Bartusch, D. (1998). 'Legal cynicism and (subcultural) tolerance of deviance: the neighborhood context of racial difference', *Law and Society Review*, 32: 777–804.

Skogan, W. (2006). 'Asymmetry in the impact of encounters with police', *Policing and Society*, 16: 99–126.

Sunshine, J. and Tyler, T. (2003). 'The role of procedural justice and legitimacy in shaping public support for policing', *Law and Society Review*, 37: 513–48.

The Counted (2016). 'The Counted. People killed by police in the US', *Guardian*, online. Available www.theguardian.com/us-news/ng-interactive/2015/jun/01/the-counted-police-killings-us-database (accessed September 20, 2016).

Tyler, T. (1990). *Why People Obey the Law*, New Haven, CT: Yale University Press.

Tyler, T. and Fagan, J. (2008). 'Legitimacy and cooperation: why do people help the police fight crime in their communities?', *Ohio State Journal of Criminal Law*, 6: 231–75.

Van Craen, M. (2012). 'Determinants of ethnic minority confidence in the police', *Journal of Ethnic and Migration Studies*, 38: 1029–47.

Van Craen, M. and Skogan, W. (2015). 'Differences and similarities in the explanation of ethnic minority groups' trust in the police', *European Journal of Criminology*, 12: 300–23.

Weisburd, D., Greenspan, R., Hamilton, E., Williams, H., and Bryant, K. (2000). *Police Attitudes Toward Abuse of Authority: Findings from a National Study*, Washington, DC: U.S. Department of Justice, Office of Justice Programs, National Institute of Justice.

Weitzer, R. (1999). 'Citizens' perceptions of police misconduct: race and neighborhood context', *Justice Quarterly*, 16: 819–46.

Weitzer, R. (2002). 'Incidents of police misconduct and public opinion', *Journal of Criminal Justice*, 30: 397–408.

Weitzer, R. and Tuch, S. (2005a). 'Determinants of public satisfaction with the police', *Police Quarterly*, 8: 279–97.

Weitzer, R. and Tuch, S. (2005b). 'Racially biased policing: determinants of citizen perceptions', *Social Forces*, 83: 1009–30.

'990 people shot dead by police in 2015', (2015), *Washington Post*, online. Available www.washingtonpost.com/graphics/national/police-shootings/ (accessed September 20, 2016).

10 Why may police disobey the law?

How divisions in society are a source of the moral right to do bad: the case of Turkey

Sebastian Roché, Mine Özaşçılar, and Ömer Bilen

Introduction: the legitimacy to act beyond the law

According to Machiavelli (1513: Chapter 15), governing often entails acting in accordance with the situation at the expense of morality: 'Hence it is necessary for a prince wishing to hold his own [power] to know how to do wrong, and to make use of it not according to necessity.' This idea might be something the governed not only understand or empathize with, but actually agree with. The purpose of the following chapter is to explain a specific type of attitude towards the police, an unusual kind of support: the acceptance of the necessity of unlawful and even violent behaviour – what we term 'extra-legal' behaviour or 'police deviance'. This topic relates directly to legitimacy, not in terms of voluntary obedience and the free acceptance of authority on the part of the public, but rather in terms of granting a 'moral right' to police to compel citizens to comply with all means necessary, or as Bensman (1979: 330) suggests 'naked coercion'. This idea is not new within the field of policing. As early as 1970, Gamson and McEvoy (1970) were interested in support for police violence during protests in the US and more recently, attitudes towards misconduct have been studied as the main focus (Weitzer and Tuch 2004) or as part of a satisfaction index (Howell *et al.* 2004). Bradford *et al.* (2016) and Kochel (Chapter 9) have analysed UK and US data on the public acceptance of police use of force. Studies generally concentrate on the extent to which members of the public view select types of misconduct as a problem. The underlying assumption is that misconduct is considered a problem for the public, and an eradication of such behaviour would improve police relations with the public and the overall efficiency of police. 'In other words, it is in the interest of every police department to not only reduce officer misconduct but to also be perceived as doing so, because this makes police work less contentious and more effective' (Weitzer and Tuch 2004: 399). That is, it is as if there is a 'need [for police] to act in a procedurally fair manner' and that such behaviour is the foundation for police legitimacy (Bradford *et al.* 2016: 2). This is a broad assumption that raises many major questions that, in the authors' view, remain largely open to interpretation. In fact, we argue that it is theoretically and empirically risky to assume that all the people, *everywhere* want the police to be fair with *everyone* or to always expect and obtain voluntary compliance (i.e. policing *without* the use of force). It is possible that some people support police acting as a 'stick' and that they are not (if at all) disturbed by overt violence, even if illegal. These individuals might even distrust police who do not use force or who appear to be overly concerned with the law and its potential constraints. The existence of these public preferences would explain the apparent paradox that police departments do not necessarily see their interests well served in the total ban of misconduct. The reason is simple: enforcing a ban on police use of force could potentially deprive the police of support and legitimacy from certain sections of the public. It may be against their interest in fact, for police to always act peacefully and lawfully. Indeed, we should not assume that all political systems are consensual. Based on the moral and political standards of a country and its societal cleavages, it is possible that police deviance might be more or less supported.

In this chapter, we introduce a necessary distinction between the police (an enforcing authority) and the law. The two should not be conflated and we will endeavour to empirically disentangle them. We will analyse the determinants of why an enforcing authority (i.e. police) is given a right to dictate behaviour outside of the law (by force and illegal means). Certain groups of citizens believe that when police behave violently or outside the bounds of the law, they are within their rightful limits. Based on a secondary analysis of a 2014 TESEV survey in Turkey, we seek to determine who makes up such groups and why they hold these attitudes, and we highlight the importance of politics and societal level cleavages.

Theoretical background

From a theoretical perspective, a reason for condoning police deviance may be that police are perceived as the 'ally' of a certain group in a conflict situation, a partisan instrument or a combination of the two. This idea forms the bedrock of our thesis. Political tension is at the core of this interpretation and it has attracted surprisingly little attention from scholars (although see above). Still, justification of power and of how it is used may well depend on politics. We contend that the relationships citizens share with the police are part of a more general relationship to the state. A first justification why relations to the state need to be considered is as simple as it is essential: The police derive their authority from the state and answer directly to state officials. A second justification is the relationship between social groups, which is the starting point for the 'group position thesis' (Weitzer and Tuch 2004). Here we stretch the concept beyond racial group position to incorporate identification with a group sharing ideological preferences for explaining specific attitudes towards the police (Gamson and McEvoy 1970; Gerber and Jackson 2016; Roché and Roux 2017; Stack and Cao 1998). Preference for a political party does not constitute a social group comparable to an ethnic group. The latter is based on kinship, a place of origin, language, physical appearance, among other factors, and is largely ascribed. Party alignment, on the other hand, results from a set of values or to political issues and is changeable.

For a long time, political scientists have studied these fault lines in society and have found importance for the fact that those divides crystalize at the political level, that they are expressed in the political sphere by various means (vote, protests, and sometimes violence). A political majority is often based on, but does not necessarily fully correspond to, religious and ethnic cleavages.

The politically driven reading is referred to as the 'socio-political cleavages thesis'. It points towards the relationship between the citizen and the state in three ways. First, the state is conquered and owned by a political majority. Assessment of services obtained from the state and understood as a set of bureaucracies (school, hospital) impacts on the support that is granted to the incumbent leadership (for a comparative study, see Kutnjak Ivkovic 2008). Paul Benson (1981) used 'political alienation' to describe the feeling of disillusionment characterized by a belief that authorities are not concerned by neighbourhood needs or that contacting public officials is useless. He also used this concept to explore attitudes towards the police. Second, since elections are a fundamental element of democracy and elected governments reflect voters' adherence to a certain ideology or organized set of beliefs (such as nationalism, or support for aggressive policing), policies pursued by any government will inevitably resemble the preferences of some citizens, while being dissimilar to others. Therefore, a broader relation to political institutions must be taken into account, in particular, political alignment with the ruling party and general perceptions of public trust in national institutions. Of course, some political systems are more consensus-based than others. Trust in institutions is important to explain the support of police not only in cases of polarized societies (Marenin 1985) but also in very egalitarian Nordic states (Kääriäinen 2007, cf. Kääriäinen, Chapter 13 in this volume). Third, a state refers to a nation from which it emanates. However, the definition of the nation itself is complex and varies from country to country. It can refer to a historical legacy or culture, to religious or ethnic unity or even to ideology (adherence to a set of values as declared in the constitution, for example). It can also refer to past and current policy orientations by political authorities, and precisely how the latter regards various groups (ethnic, cultural, religious, regional, political) and envisage their symbolic inclusion into an imagined nation, 'the people'. Socio-political cleavages determine how group positions are experienced and individual judgements are made. We already have evidence that when a citizen feels part of the national community, it enhances their sense of representation by the state and their trust in the police (Murphy and Cherney 2011; Oliveira and Murphy 2015; Roché and Roux 2017). Conversely, when citizens feel estranged, they may feel less represented.[1] If people have collective grievances against the state, the distance to the national community should be maximum.

These three dimensions of the relationship between citizens and 'the state' (here, defined as the assessment of policing policies, trust in institutions/political party preference, and state definition of 'the people') are neither identical nor independent from each other. Our aim here is to take into account some dimensions of the citizens' relationship to the nation-state (within the limits of our data), together with citizens' daily experience of policing, and other socio-economic control variables in order to understand the extent to which these have an influence on public opinions of police unlawfulness and violence in Turkey.

Societal dividing lines are expected to reflect on attitudes towards police deviance. We presume when citizens position themselves alongside the state it increases support for police deviance. We use the term 'positioning' to describe: the proximity to the ruling party and affiliation to the religious majority, the largest ethnic group, and residing in the most prosperous part of the country. Specifically, we anticipate that voting for the incumbent majority, and belonging to a majority group (religious or ethnic) ultimately gives police wider latitude to use illegal courses of action. We further hypothesize that ideological proximity with the government will have a positive impact on the public's attitudes towards police deviance.

Based on a 2014 survey commissioned by TESEV, a Turkish independent think tank (Kirmizidag 2015), we seek to determine if variables that relate to possible sources of division (i.e. political preferences, ethnicity, religion, geographic region) are important for Turkish citizens to thereby grant police a great latitude in carrying out their duties, even if unlawfully. In this study, we do not use direct measures of police deviance, such as participant observations or a police national repository; and we did not ask respondents whether they have had direct experience of police deviance. Instead, we attempt to understand the public attribution of the right to act with violence and without respect for the law – what is often referred to as police misconduct in the police literature. A *belief* that the police are tough or neglect certain aspects of the law can be essential. These opinions matter at both a material and symbolic level. Perceptions of policing styles can impact political and ethnic-religious tensions in a city or a country, and polarize beliefs about the legitimacy of the national and local government, as well as the police departments across the country. Citizens' beliefs and expectations may translate into public support for aggressive policing strategies and votes for political leaders that advocate for them. Such beliefs might also influence citizens' demeanour in encounters with police, as they might anticipate rough interactions, or are prepared to comply with an officer's demands even if they are not, or do not seem to be legal. It is also probable that if one is ready to grant moral power to police to use force, especially illegal, it means that one might be willing to assist the police by reporting crimes and serve as a witness, even when such testimonies or acts fall outside of the law. Legitimacy may well hide darker sides, such as a type of partisan policing which prioritizes certain groups' interests at the expense of others (Bradford *et al.* 2016; Harkin 2015) and of the law.

Turkey: a brief review of the context and extant research about attitudes towards police

Turkey is a country currently in transition from military rule to a democracy facing recurrent military coups (some more successful than others, the last one as recent as July 2016) and enduring intense domestic armed tensions despite robust economic development. Under the martial-law regime and the constitution promulgated in the aftermath of the 1980 coup, Turkish citizens suffered a serious curtailment of their rights. In 1983, parliamentary elections were held and the government gradually lifted restraints on individual liberties. Nevertheless, the conduct of the Turkish police has been the subject of persistent criticism for violations of human rights (e.g. torture during questioning, detention, politically motivated disappearances, 'mystery killings', and excessive use of force; see IBP 2015) and corruption (Cengiz *et al.* 2014). Police violence has received growing international and domestic attention. Successive governments have repeatedly promised to curb abuses by the internal security forces, and starting in 2005, the Justice and Development Party (AKP), has started to implement new policies (e.g. increasing the level of education for selected police officers, instituting a 'zero tolerance policy' against torture, community policing, civilian oversight of the internal security sector among others). The latest development in Turkey for the years 2016 and 2017 are not relevant with regards to our data set.

Over the last decade, citizens' attitudes towards police in Turkey has become a more important issue. The issue of fairness, equality before the police, and of lawfulness has only been addressed in two studies. Research has found that, as in most countries, when measured with general phrases such as 'do you trust the police?', citizens' attitudes towards police are generally positive. Studies on the comparison of trust in police and other public institutions demonstrated that the Turkish National Police (TNP), excluding Traffic Units, ranked as the third most trusted institution in the country, after the military and schools (Adaman *et al.* 2009; MetroPoll 2012). Adaman *et al.* (2009) show that from 2000 until 2008 there has been an increase in trust in police from around 7.7 to 8.3/10 based on a national data set. European Social Survey (ESS) (Cao and Burton 2006; Delice and Duman 2012) and World Value Survey (WVS) data confirm modest increases in trust from 1990 to 2000, and from 1996 to 2011, respectively. This positive trend corresponds to the period of consolidation of the civilian government and later the rise of the AKP, between 2002 and 2016, and more generally to the transition from a military to a civilian government.

Placed in an international context, a survey in 2014 (ICOISS 2015a) asked 'how good a job' the police were doing in their neighbourhood, which was then compared to other participant countries in the 2010 round of the ESS (EU countries, Israel, Russian Federation, and Ukraine). Turkey stands well below the leading EU nations like the Nordic countries, and lower still from average nations like France, Poland, and the Netherlands. It is however, above Greece and the ex-Communist countries such as Russia and the Ukraine. Findings about police making 'fair and impartial decisions' were consistent: Nordic and Western European countries were clearly above Turkey, and the post-Communist countries below Turkey. According to a national survey (ICOISS 2015a), Gendarmerie area residents have higher trust in gendarmerie then police area residents have in police. This is supported by another set of local studies conducted in selected Turkish districts (ICOISS 2015b).

Hypotheses: testing the effect of socio-political fractures

We will first consider political divides in Turkey. According to the 'representation hypothesis', people 'feel represented' by the bureaucracy. In England and Wales, colleagues have proposed that public support for police stems from identifying with 'a category the police might plausibly be said to represent' (Bradford et al. 2016: 2). Although we do not dispute that people look for similarities with police, we emphasize identification with the government more generally, as 'masters of the police' (Anderson and Tverdova 2001; Curini et al. 2016). Hence, we formulate the representation hypothesis differently, taking into account the hierarchical dependence of police vis-à-vis the centralized government. Because Turkish police report to the central government, police intentions may be inferred from those of the central government. We contend that political representation through elections and ideological proximity with the central government in Turkey drive attitudes towards police and the sense that the national police have discretion to act forcefully and even illegally. Furthermore, we argue that police embody the government, and when people support the government, the chances that they will condone police violence is higher. This is aligned with 'systems justification' theory in social psychology (Van Der Toorn et al. 2015), which proposes that those already possessing or identifying with political power holders will support and justify its action.

Second, social status and social identity are critical in shaping attitudes towards police. Group conflict theory and group position theory (Blumer 1958) are among the most cited interpretive frameworks for the study of policing. Aspects of group position theory have been re-considered to include race (Weitzer and Tuch 2004). It has been applied to explain the inter-country differences in the EU (Bradford et al. Chapter 3 in this volume). The group position theory as an explanatory framework for the racial divisions in the US has been widely used. However, there are other salient societal divisions in European countries (Belgium, France, and the UK, to name a few), which are well documented: opposition between groups may be of an ethnic and racial nature, but also religious. In France, for example, the majority worldview is one of atheism or agnosticism. It is not a surprise that adolescents with that worldview are more supportive of the police than those who believe in God. Catholicism is the largest majority religion and is conducive to positive attitudes towards police, while the largest minority religion, Islam, is not (Roché et al. Chapter 8 this volume). Individuals do not form opinions in a vacuum, disconnected from their various social identities. This is especially true in extremely divided societies (i.e. Northern Ireland, Israel), in some case with apartheid (South Africa). Social polarization between Turks and Kurds (Saraçoğlu 2009; Yılmaz 2014), for example, (Saraçoğlu 2009; Yılmaz 2014) or Sunnis and Alevis has heightened throughout the 1990s (Shankland 2003, cited in Akbaş 2010; Çelik et al. 2016). Recent research has demonstrated that Turks have stronger negative attitudes towards Kurds than others, including Alevis and Armenians (Bilali et al. 2014; Sarıgil and Karakoç 2016). Given the importance of regional identities in certain parts of the world, including Turkey, we consider this an important variable when understanding attitudes towards police. In other words, we argue that societal divisions will impact on how police are perceived, and possibly the extent to which police can be granted a moral right to act beyond the law.

Third, we need to consider that socio-economic status (SES), here operationalized as income and level of educational attainment, may also be a relevant factor. There are mixed findings about SES and attitudes towards police in general. A higher level of education may correlate with an increased knowledge of one's rights (and the transgression of them). Others find more education is linked to lower expectations in terms of protection (Regulus *et al.* 2001: 194). Within the Turkish literature, there has been a well-documented negative relationship between educational attainment and favourable attitudes towards the police, using a variety of measures for attitudes towards police, including confidence, trust, and satisfaction (see Çakar 2015; Delice and Duman 2012; Doğan and Bağış 2011; Karakuş *et al.* 2011). In Turkey, studies have yielded inconsistent results on citizens' income as a predictor of attitudes towards police. A municipal study in Şanlıurfa, a city in South Eastern Anatolia, found that citizens with lower incomes were more likely to report negative attitudes towards police (Doğan and Bağış 2011), while a different national study suggested that lower income individuals were more likely to view police positively (Karakuş *et al.* 2011). In other countries, there are also inconsistencies with regards to SES, with some finding the black middle-class as more critical than lower SES Blacks (Weitzer and Tuch, 2004). Given the mixed findings, we do not anticipate any strong effect.

The nature and type of contact with police are key determinants in shaping what individuals think about policing. A particularly important distinction has been drawn between citizen-initiated contact and police-initiated contact. The first type seems to matter very little in explaining a person's attitudes towards police (although sometimes they can prompt positive attitudes, as evidenced by a study in Sivas, a Central Anatolian city, which found that citizen-initiated contact with the police was positively correlated with favourable attitudes towards police) (Taslak and Akın 2005). The second type, police-initiated contact, is regularly found to have an adverse effect. Being stopped by police has been correlated to decreased levels of satisfaction, trust, or acknowledgment that police are fair (Oberwittler and Roché, Chapter 4 in this volume). This might be because people *decide* to seek service from police, but encounters such as an identity check are *imposed* on them, and thus can be perceived as an intrusion on one's privacy (associated with body search). And, finally, negative experiences are proven to have a stronger effect than positive ones. A negativity bias is found when it comes to police as for other cases. Research has shown that the subjective assessment of an interaction as 'good' (when people are satisfied) or 'bad' (when they are not) matters, but no such variable is available in our data set.

As an additional step, it is important to acknowledge that the above hypotheses may interact with each other. There is evidence that social identity

(Murphy and Cherney 2011; Oliveira and Murphy 2015) or cultural cognition (Kahan 2013) play a role. In order to test some of the possible links between them (and the theories that follow), a number of interactions are included in our regressions. The perception of police deviance during a police-initiated contact may be dependent on the mental frame or structural context of individuals, their proximity with the ruling party, with religious and ethnic identity, and with the region in which they live.

Finally, a number of socio-demographic variables are used as controls. Prior research has shown the importance of age and gender (Web and Marshall 1995), in particular when they are combined since young males have the most hostile opinions of the police (especially if they are a minority). Younger Turks are more likely to hold unfavourable attitudes towards police than older (Arslan and Olgun 2009; Doğan and Bağış 2011; Delice and Duman 2012; Hasta and Arslantürk 2013; Şahin 2014). In regards to gender, research findings are contradictory: some studies indicate that men are more likely to hold positive attitudes towards police (Delice and Duman 2012), and others find the opposite (national data from Life Satisfaction Surveys (LSS) 2004 and 2012; ICOISS 2015a). Regarding the effect of living in an urban area, LSSs have found that rural residents have a more positive perception of law enforcement agencies (i.e. gendarmerie vs. police) (Karakuş *et al.* 2011; Muş *et al.* 2014). Since residing in urban places is often associated with higher crime rates and fear of crime, citizens in these areas might express a stronger desire for protection vis-à-vis crime and condone aggressive policing. Because only urban area of residence, educational attainment, and income were significant in our survey, we dropped other variables.

The survey: data and constructs

Data used for this analysis originate from a nation-wide survey commissioned by a think tank, the Turkish Economic and Social Studies Foundation (TESEV). Sample design and data collection were performed by an opinion poll company, the Social Research Center (SAM) in 2014. The probability sample ($n=3,207$) is representative of the Turkish population aged 18 and over in metropolitan areas with a population over 37,000 (for methods, see TESEV's report: Kirmizidag 2015).

The study examines attitudes towards 'unlawfulness and use of force by police' or 'police deviance' – the two expressions will be used interchangeably. A construct for police deviance was created using nine statements as 'Police can from time to time act against the law for the public benefit' (see Table 10.A1, appendix, for the complete list of items and descriptive results).[2] Responses for each item is measured by 5-point Likert-type scale, ranging from (1) never/strongly disagree/strongly disapprove to (5) always/strongly agree/strongly approve. Higher scores indicated a higher approval of police force and unlawfulness. The scale reliability is high (Cronbach's alpha=0.83). These items' responses were summed and averaged to create an overall scale ranging from 1 to 5. The mean score on this index is 2.47, i.e. slightly below the mid-point (SD=0.95).

Independent variables are included in the model as categorial variables. Respondents' income is measured by a question asking the household's average income per month in Turkish Liras (TL). A question asked the respondent's highest educational degree, with 'illiterate, literate but no schooling, primary school, secondary school' as the base category. Respondents' geographic location was coded based on information (municipality, district, and street) recorded by the interviewer. Metropolitan areas (urban only) were distinguished from mixed urban/rural areas. As regions of residence, we distinguish Istanbul, the main economic centre with 16 million inhabitants, Western and Mediterranean (Marmara, Aegean, West Anatolia, Central Anatolia, and Mediterranean areas) as another relatively wealthy region, and two less well-off areas, one with, and the other without, armed conflict. The Black Sea coastal region (including the North East of Turkey) is exempt of major conflict. South Eastern and Eastern Anatolian regions are poorer and have a long history of conflict between the state's army and the Kurdistan Workers' Party (PKK) considered a terrorist organization by the UE and the US as well as Turkey.

Considering the importance of ethnic background and religion as a possible source of conflict, the current questionnaire included self-declared ethnic background and religion ('Which ethnic group do you mostly identify with?'; 'Which best describes your religious affiliation?'). Respondents' ethnic background was recoded in three categories: Turkish, Kurdish, and other (including Arabic, Bushnak, Circassian, Armenian, Laz, Assyrian, Greek, and no response). Most of the respondents were Turkish (80.6 per cent), and 14.7 per cent were Kurdish. Religion was categorized into four categories: (1) Muslim/Sunni/Shafi/Hanefi/Shia, (2) Alevi/Bektashi, (3) others with a religion, including Catholics, Jewish, or else, and (4) no response/Atheists/no religion. There is a lower representation of religious minority groups in the sample compared with the general population census. For example, there are 4.9 per cent of Alevi/Bektashi among the respondents compared to 8 per cent of the general population in 2013.

Political party preference was measured asking 'which political party will you vote for if there were a general election now?' (Justice and Development party AKP=1, Republican's People Party CHP=2, Nationalist Action Party MHP=3, Peace and Democracy Party BDP-left-wing HDP-Independents=4, no answer, no vote=5). Less than half of the survey respondents (42.8 per cent) said that they would vote for the AKP. The AKP, the ruling party since 2002, is an Islamic or religious conservative party (Yılmaz 2014). CHP, the largest opposition party gathering both social and secular nationalists (Bardakçı 2016), was selected by 15.7 per cent of the survey respondents, and the ultra-nationalist and rightist MHP by 9.7 per cent of the survey respondents. The BDP, which is 'organically' linked to the Kurdish nationalist movement (Çelik *et al.* 2016), joined the HDP in 2014. The HDP, formally established in 2012, is the most recent of left-wing political parties, aimed to establish itself not only as a pro-Kurdish party but also as a secular and left-wing party (Grigoriadis 2016). Of the respondents, 5.6 per cent reported that they would vote for it.

The study included police–citizen contacts, captured by two questions. The first was 'during the last year were you ever in contact with the police?' There were 469 (14.6 per cent) respondents who had had contact with police. For these respondents, police-initiated contact was distinguished from citizen-initiated contact and both coded yes (1) or no (0). Police-initiated contact occurred for 5.7 percent of survey respondents (and 39.4 per cent of those with at least one contact) and consisted of stop and search, road check, asked for a testimony by police, attending protest, respondent reported by someone to the police. Citizen-initiated contact occurred for 8.9 per cent of respondents (and 60.6 per cent of those with at least one contact) and occurred mostly at the police station. It comprised several items: to report someone as a suspect of a crime, to visit a police relative, as a crime witness, as a victim of property crime, to apply for passport or driving license, and was coded as yes (1) or no (0).

Analysis: attitudinal correlates and determinants of support to police deviance

We conducted theoretically driven hierarchical regression. At each new step, all the previously used variables are preserved and new ones are added. The first block is about individual characteristics: income, level of education, and residing in an urban or mixed environment. The second block introduces the last experience with police, police-initiated contact, and citizen-initiated contact. The third consists of variables that make up social identity: ethnic, religious, and geographical regions. In the fourth block, political party preference was added. During the last step, the interactions between police-initiated contact and several variables were tested (political party preference, region, ethnicity, religion).

Correlations dimensions of attitudes towards police: police deviance, trust, and compliance

A series of two additional classic attitudes towards police indexes were built (not presented here), and correlated with the measure of support for police deviance. Correlations (Pearson's r) with police deviance were positive and significant with trust ($0.37, p<0.01$), and felt an obligation to obey ($0.45, p<0.01$). The correlation between trust and accepted police deviance indicates that trust, understood as reasonable certainty about the ends pursued by the use of force, is enough to grant the police a moral right to use violence when they see fit, and ignore legal boundaries. The correlation between conceded unlawfulness and felt moral obligation to obey, an indicator pointing at legitimacy, indicates that when oneself 'freely' feels an obligation to obey police, one equally tends to think that others should obey even unwillingly, and for that purpose can be scrutinized, subjected to constraints, without due oversight of the law, and ultimately that their rights may be curtailed.

Regressions: looking for determinants of attitudes towards police deviance

Table 10.1 presents the determinants of attitudes towards police use of force and unlawfulness. First, respondents' individual characteristics were tested (model 1). With the exception of the highest income group (2,500 TL and over), all other variables were significant ($p<0.05$). Respondents who lived in metropolitan areas (compared to mixed rural-urban areas) and had middle incomes (between 1,501 and 2,500 TL, compared to base, i.e. low income,) were more likely to approve of the use of force and unlawful acts by the police. Compared to those without at least primary school education, respondents with a university degree or high school degree were more likely to disapprove of police use of deviant behaviour. Model 1 had a R^2 value of 0.03. After adding citizen-initiated and police-initiated contacts (model 2), the latter being negatively correlated with police use of force and acceptance of unlawfulness, explained variance (R^2) increased to 0.04.

In model 3, we added religion, ethnic background, and geographical region. All minority worldviews (all denominations, and having no religion) compared to base (Sunni Islam), and all minority ethnic backgrounds compared to base (Turks) were significant, and negatively correlated with acceptance of police deviance ($p<0.05$). Compared with the more urbanized, wealthy, and educated Istanbul region (base), citizens residing in the Black Sea and North Eastern Anatolia areas were more likely to endorse police use of force and unlawful acts. In all other regions, respondents were less likely to approve police deviance, in particular West-Mediterranean (strongest $\beta=-0.12$, $p<0.05$). The explained variance (R^2) for model 3 increased to .12.

In model 4, we added political party preference. Compared to the base (AKP, ruling party), all other affiliations were significantly and negatively correlated with the approval of police deviance ($p<0.05$): CHP (the main opposition party), MHP (nationalist party), BDP-others (Kurdish based) and 'no to vote or no response', were less likely to approve of police force and unlawful acts of police. The significance of correlations with other variables remains unchanged. The explained variance increases to 0.17.

Model 5 included all independent variables plus interactions between police-initiated contact and party alignment, religion, ethnic background, and region of residence. Interactions effects are plotted in Figure 10.1. Regarding political party preferences, for CHP (main opposition party) the experience of a police-initiated contact is associated with a decreased toleration for police deviance (significant at <0.06 only). The same effect (however non-significant with $p>0.10$ and above) is found among would-be voters of the other opposing party HDP. Affiliation with the nationalist party, as well as those with no political preference, are insensitive to police-initiated contact, in line with AKP voters (base category). It appears that political distance to the ruling party moderates the effect of contact with police (cf. Figure 10.1, upper left plot). Regarding world vision, we observed that persons with an Alevi religious denomination

Table 10.1a Determinants of acceptance of police deviance

Independent variables	Model 1 β	Model 1 Sig.	Model 2 β	Model 2 Sig.	Model 3 β	Model 3 Sig.	Model 4 β	Model 4 Sig.	Model 5 β	Model 5 Sig.
Income (ref.: Low)										
Middle (1501–2500 TL)	0.06***	0.00	0.06***	0.00	0.02	0.15	0.03*	0.08	0.03*	0.07
High (2500 over TL)	0.01	0.44	0.01	0.38	-0.01	0.56	-0.01	0.93	0.00	0.93
No answer	-0.10***	0.00	-0.10***	0.00	-0.11***	0.00	-0.10***	0.00	-0.10***	0.00
Education (ref.: Primary)										
Secondary school degree	-0.09***	0.00	-0.08***	0.00	-0.09***	0.00	-0.05***	0.00	-0.06***	0.00
University and higher degree	-0.10***	0.00	-0.10***	0.00	-0.09***	0.00	-0.06***	0.00	-0.06***	0.00
Metropolitan area (ref.: urban)	0.04**	0.01	0.04**	0.01	0.09***	0.00	0.09***	0.00	0.09***	0.00
Police contact (ref.: no contact)										
Police-initiated contact	—		-0.07***	0.00	-0.06***	0.00	-0.05***	0.00	0.02	0.56
Citizen-initiated contact	—		-0.02	0.13	-0.02	0.11	-0.02	0.13	0.16	
Religion (ref.: Sunni)										
Alevi–Bektashi	—		—		-0.07***	0.00	-0.02	0.24	-0.03*	0.06
Others	—		—		-0.00	0.82	-0.00	0.90	0.00	0.72
No religion, no response	—		—		-0.04**	0.01	-0.03**	0.04	-0.03*	0.09
Ethnic background (ref.: Turkish)										
Kurdish	—		—		-0.05***	0.00	-0.02	0.27	-0.02	0.16
Others	—		—		0.01	0.38	0.01	0.26	0.02	0.23
Region (ref.: Istanbul)										
West, Mediterranean	—		—		-0.12***	0.00	-0.10***	0.00	-0.09***	0.00
Black Sea	—		—		0.15***	0.00	0.13***	0.00	0.14***	0.00
South/east Anatolia	—		—		-0.11***	0.00	-0.12***	0.00	-0.12***	0.00
Political affiliation (ref.: AKP)										
CHP	—		—		—		-0.21***	0.00	-0.21***	0.00
MHP	—		—		—		-0.06***	0.00	-0.06***	0.00
BDP–HDP	—		—		—		-0.16**	0.03	-0.15***	0.00
No response, no vote	—		—		—		-0.06***	0.00	-0.06***	0.00

Table 10.1b Determinants of acceptance of police deviance (continued)

Independent variables – interactions	Model 1		Model 2		Model 3		Model 4		Model 5	
	β	Sig.	β	Sig.	β	Sig.	β	Sig.	β	Sig.
Police–init. contact – pol. affiliation (ref.: AKP)										
CHP	–	–	–	–	–	–	–	–	−0.04*	0.06
MHP	–	–	–	–	–	–	–	–	0.00	0.83
HDP	–	–	–	–	–	–	–	–	−0.02	0.34
No response, no vote	–	–	–	–	–	–	–	–	−0.00	0.93
Police–init. contact – religion (ref.: Sunni)										
Alevi–Bektashi	–	–	–	–	–	–	–	–	0.04**	0.01
Others	–	–	–	–	–	–	–	–	−0.00	0.79
No religion, no response	–	–	–	–	–	–	–	–	−0.00	0.73
Police–init. contact – geogr. region (ref.: Istanbul)										
West, Mediterranean	–	–	–	–	–	–	–	–	−0.07**	0.02
Black Sea, South/east Anatolia	–	–	–	–	–	–	–	–	−0.04**	0.03
South/east Anatolia	–	–	–	–	–	–	–	–	−0.00	0.76
Police–init. contact – ethnic background (ref.: Turkish)										
Kurdish	–	–	–	–	–	–	–	–	0.01	0.46
Others	–	–	–	–	–	–	–	–	−0.00	0.78
Constant	2.47*	–	2.49*	–	2.56*	–	2.68*	–	2.67*	–
R^2	0.035	–	0.041	–	0.119	–	0.168	–	0.173	–
F	19.03	–	16.89	–	26.74	–	32.03	–	20.66	–

Notes
* Significant at the level $p < 0.10$;
** Significant at the level $p < 0.05$;
*** Significant at the level $p < 0.01$.

Table 10.2 Correlations

	Equal treatment	Police deviance	Felt obligation to obey	Police trust	Coerced obedience	Police respect during police-initiated contact	Police respect during citizen-initiated contact	Cooperation	Police efficacy
Equal treatment	1	–	–	–	–	–	–	–	–
Police deviance	0.48*	1	–	–	–	–	–	–	–
Felt obligation to obey	0.66*	0.44*	1	–	–	–	–	–	–
Police trust	0.69*	0.37*	0.58*	1	–	–	–	–	–
Coerced obedience	0.48*	0.31*	0.62*	0.43*	1	–	–	–	–
Police respect during police-initiated contact	0.66*	0.35*	0.54*	0.66*	0.38*	1	–	–	–
Police respect during citizen-initiated contact	0.69*	0.40*	0.58*	0.67*	0.41*	0.66*	1	–	–
Cooperation	0.54*	0.30*	0.46*	0.50*	0.37*	0.44*	0.49*	1	–
Police efficacy	0.72*	0.46*	0.61*	0.68*	0.47*	0.62*	0.65*	0.59*	1
Police service	0.78*	0.43*	0.65*	0.79*	0.48*	0.74*	0.75*	0.54*	0.76*

Note
* Significant at the level $p < 0.01$.

tend to have a greater acceptance of police deviance, even if subjected to police contact, than the base category (Sunni) and all other groups (Figure 10.1, lower right plot). Since Alevi who had a contact with police represent a very small number of individuals ($n=13$) we have excluded them from Figure 10.1. In terms of ethnicity, all groups seem to react similarly to police contact and no inter-action reaches the significance level of <0.10. Finally, contrary to the base region (Istanbul), respondents of two regions react negatively to police contacts, with a significant interaction for the upper middle income West-Mediterranean Anatolia

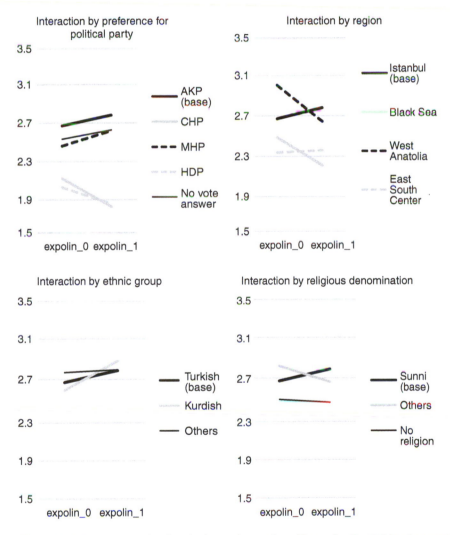

Figure 10.1 Acceptance of police deviance: interaction effects of police-initiated contact with socio-demographic and political variables.

Note
Alevi excluded due to lack of police contact ($n=13$).

region and lower-income Black Sea regions ($p<0.05$). In the Eastern part of Turkey (South East and Central East), contrary to expectations that an armed conflict ridden region might form a context prompting resentment towards police-initiated contacts and therefore a tendency to restrict the right to act beyond the law to police, we don't record any effect of individual encounters with police (Figure 10.1, upper right plot).

Overall, the strongest predictors of reluctance to accept police deviance were strong disagreements with the ruling party (i.e. preference for CHP or BDP), region of residence (West-Mediterranean and South East), and to a lesser extent, being Kurdish, and religiously speaking, Alevi, or agnostic. While police-initiated contact was important and increased reluctance to condone police deviance, the interactions show that it is moderated by other variables (e.g. in the case of alignment with the main opposition party and residing out of Istanbul, contact decreases the moral right to police deviance).

Discussion: the importance of society level cleavages and experience of police

Would anyone support more police violence and less legal protection if it were detrimental to one-self? As a consequence, attitudes towards police deviance will be affected by societal divisions if the police are perceived to be a prot-agonist. Our hypotheses have been based on the assumption that some societies are divided along a series of fault lines, and that the acceptability of police viol-ence and unlawfulness will be brokered along them. These dividing lines may be of ideological (i.e. political and religious), identity (i.e. ethnic, geographic), or socio-economic (i.e. related to income or education) nature. Respondents evaluate if they might be targeted by police as a member of a group, and if so they condemn deviant means of police action. Similarly, if respondents feel that another group different from their own will suffer from police violence, they might be more inclined to condone it. In addition, guided by a cultural cognition framework, our empirical endeavour here has consisted of testing interactions between, on the one hand, the ideological or social identity-based variables and, on the other hand, contact with police (the relational foundation of attitudes towards police).

First, at the ideological level, we argue that identification with the political authority under which the police work might prompt respondents to grant police the moral right to do bad. Here we use 'bad' because we don't neces-sarily think respondents have lost their moral sense, but only that acting force-fully or illegally can be acceptable, if directed towards others. Because in Turkey police answer to the central government, proximity with the party in power is predicted to explain attitudes towards police. This differs from other nations with a decentralized police system, such as the US (Walker and Katz 2007), or Switzerland or even Germany. Our findings affirm our hypothesis: compared to AKP voters (if elections were held now), no other group is as highly prepared to endorse police deviance. The major opposition party, the

Kemalist and secular CHP, which gathers respondents most distant from AKP, as well as BDP, are the most reluctant to think that police can work outside the constraints of law.

Statistically, party proximity in Turkey is one of the strongest contributors to the explained variance among all other variables. It is a good example of how politics expresses latent identifications. Although the Turkish republic which was founded on strict secularist principles, political Islam has gained significant political power during recent decades with AKP, built on Sunni Islamist heritage (Bardakçı 2016), promoting its religious reinterpretation of Turkish national identity (Keyman 2007). Policy towards the South East region has contributed to the polarization of society along ethnic-nationalist lines, opposing Kurds and Turks (Kıbrıs 2014; Yavuz and Özcan 2006). Marenin (1985: 103) has suggested, based on a literature review, that there generally exists a 'much less neutral role of the rule of law' contrary to what conventional theories of the state would impute. This is an important observation. In transitional and divided societies, such as Turkey, people's loyalty to the state, i.e. to the ruling party, will impact on their relations with the police more deeply than in other contexts. It must also be noted that conservative voters tend to trust the police more (Gameson and McEvoy 1970; Roché and Roux 2017; Stack and Cao 1998), and AKP is a socially conservative party. Their supporters and voters therefore are more comfortable with granting the police the moral right to work outside of the boundaries of the law. If police forces usually claim their duty to be essentially apolitical, this is not how attitudes of the public towards their work is structured. Taken together, the research findings suggest that attitudinal effects (adherence to conservative values) combine with the proximity to the government, making conservatives voters more prepared to give police carte blanche when their preferred party is in power. For them, deviant policing is not seen as a threat to citizens since it serves a good cause.

Second, being part of a religious, ethnic, or regional group constitutes a person's social identity. When introduced as a block in the regression analysis, all these dimensions of social identity matter. Compared to Sunni Muslims, Alevi and other non-Muslim religions ('others') were the most prone to disapproved of extra-legal police behaviour, slightly more than agnostics. Empirically, the divide is as strong between Muslim groups (Sunni versus Alevi) than it is across the majority Sunni group and the non-Muslims religions. Together, all these minority groups represent only a small fraction of the population of Turkey in our survey (6.2 per cent). Alevi have experienced discrimination and violence as the result of Turkification and Islamization policies emphasizing the Sunni Muslim values. During the Republic, massacres of Alevi occurred for example in Dersim (in 1937–1938) composed of Alevi majority, or in Gazi (in 1995), Maraş (in 1978), Çorum (in 1980), and finally in Sivas (in 1993). In 2007, the leading party, AKP, embarked on Turkey's democratization project, called 'Alevi openings'. It produced changes of little significance between the state and Alevi, and ultimately came to an end in 2011 – a year considered a turning point in the relations between Alevi and the state. Some scholars have interpreted subsequent 2013 events in that perspective when, during the Gezi park protests, AKP leaders blamed Alevi for taking part in the movement (Lord 2016). Because the incumbent ruling party leaders have repeatedly emphasized the importance of the Sunni religion as an expression of their party's identity, willingness to give more leeway to police is unsurprising.

The effect of religion on attitudes towards police is not much studied and not well known. However, in Latin America (Cao and Zhao 2005) and France (Roché et al. Chapter 8 this volume), a similar effect of world view on attitudes towards police is found: belonging to the majority faith (together with a high level of religiosity) predicts a lower level of criticism and greater general approval for police. Police legitimacy increases, in different national religious contexts, for the majority group compared to the minority groups. This gap exists irrespective of religious denomination, the largest faith group has the most favourable attitudes to police (e.g. Sunni Muslim in Turkey; atheists in France). This gives credence to the idea that attitudes towards police is associated with a larger sense of integration, or 'belonging', to the wider society. Possibly, majority religion works as a link (and minority religion as a wall) between the individual and the government when it uses religion for defining the political community.

Ethnic identity (i.e. being Turkish, Kurdish, or part of another ethnic group) has an additional effect on attitudes towards police. Compared to Turks, Kurds are more reluctant to allow police misbehaviour, probably because they anticipate that they may suffer from it. Negative attitudes towards police among minority groups is one of the most replicated findings in the US (where a history of racial and ethnic conflict has contributed to negative attitudes towards police for African-Americans; see Feagin 1991), as well as Australia and Europe. In addition, the strength of ethnic attachment has been found to reinforce a feeling of police discrimination (even for juvenile offenders see Lee et al. 2010) and is linked to distrust in institutions more generally (Warren 2011). Fewer studies have been done in other parts of the world. In Turkey, Kurds, the second largest ethnic group, have a strong sense of identity, with their own cultural traditions and language. The group's identity has been maintained, despite its separation across several neighbouring states following the 'Sykes–Picot' or 'Asia Minor' agreement in 1916, which foiled the Kurdish project of forming a sovereign Kurdistan, and despite the assimilation policy of the new regime in 1921 (Yegen 2009). The tension escalated after the military coup when their language was banned in media and Kurdish names for children were banned as part of a 'Turkification' process. While the ban on use of the Kurdish language was repealed in 1991 and other steps towards peace were taken between 2002 and 2014, there is still a great deal of tension. It is possible that police in these contexts are perceived as 'ethnic police' more than a law enforcement body, despite officers' attempts for positive relationships. Such a strained relationship between Kurds and the state might explain reluctance to condone the use of extra-legal means by police. However, given the history of Turkey, one can be surprised of the limited effect size of the ethnic variable.

The residential region appears to bear great significance. We grouped regions into four large blocks, with the South East of Turkey (composed of South East, East Marmara, Central Eastern Anatolia) in notable contrast. Compared to the reference category (Istanbul), it has the greatest resistance to extra-legal and violent policing. The Black Sea and North East of the country, which are conservative areas with modest support for AKP, on the other hand, is the most accepting of police misconduct. These geographic disparities reflect: (1) the political geography of Turkey, with CHP support confined to Western and Southern cities and coastal areas, while the Independent party is strong in the South Eastern Kurdish majority provinces (Özen and Kalkan 2016), and (2) the divide between regions more acutely affected by the Kurdish-Turkish conflict and those that are not. It is noteworthy that in addition to the ethnic disparity between Turkish and Kurdish individuals, geographic region substantially influences responses: the variance explained by the regional variable is among the two highest. This finding likely underscores the importance of the historical development of a region scarred by years of conflict. Police (and gendarmerie) in such cases are not only symbols of the central state, but also the tools necessary to exert its power. The tension between Kurds and the state turned into open conflict with the army and the gendarmerie after the founding of the PKK in 1978 as a clandestine organization focused on 'national liberation' (Gunes and Zeydanlioglu 2014: 4). Since then the population has been displaced and villages emptied, martial law ruled from 1987 until 2002. The insurgency and counterinsurgency has led to an estimated 40,000 casualties on both sides.

Two more important messages from this research need to be underscored. The first one is about the effect of contacts with police and how they interact with the above discussed variables (ideology and identity). In line with research elsewhere, exposure to undesired police contact is associated with less positive attitudes towards police (e.g. Brunson and Miller 2005; Cheurprakobkit 2000; Weitzer and Tuch 2004). Even after controlling for SES, educational attainment, urbanization, political ideology, and group belonging, we found evidence of this correlation. This is a classic finding, explained by a negativity bias that seems to be applicable in the context of Turkey. In addition, we also hypothesized interaction effects based on the notion of cultural cognition. Behavioural economist Dan Kahan (2013) has studied whether the use of reason aggravates or reduces partisan beliefs. He found that people use their faculties in such a way that they disregard facts and are likely to take a strong position that aligns with their political group. Here, we study how people experience police-initiated contact in interaction with a series of variables, in particular political party preference and region of residence. Members of parties in strong opposition (CHP, HDP) with the ruling one (AKP) experience police-initiated contact in a parallel and negative manner (interaction significant for CHP only). AKP, MHP, and those with no political preference were less likely to be affected by encounters with police. Experience of police seem to be filtered by distance to the ruling party and the state, and tend to reinforce people's inclination to condone police unlawfulness.

Conclusion: cleavages and the risk of depriving others of the right to disobey

Legitimacy translates into obeying a law because one feels that the legitimate authority has the right to govern and to dictate behaviour, Weber wrote. Here, we explored the darker side of legitimacy, the feeling that the police have a moral right to dictate behaviour through violence and illegal means.

We found that trust in police and voluntary obedience to police were positively correlated with condoning police deviance. These findings illustrate the notion that there might be types of 'just violence' for people, or that 'bad' actions might be considered necessary to achieve a greater good. Findings from Turkey challenge the assumption that the public expects police to be procedurally fair, and trust them on that basis. Precisely, our findings suggest that public trust and voluntary obedience may be converted into a police moral right to ignore human rights. Acceptance of police deviance is tantamount to agreeing to obtain obedience through naked coercion, another classic, and too often forgotten, source of authority. The felt obligation to obey may increase granting of a moral right to police deviance, and the obvious risk would be to deprive others of their legal rights. Those two aspects need to be investigated before concluding that there are many advantages to voluntary obedience and no costs to it.

Why should people agree that bad policing is good? Isn't legitimacy, despite its nature of a normative commitment, instrumental to a societal confrontation? This chapter aims to bring some of the societal aspects of attitudes towards police to the forefront of discussions of police legitimacy by focusing on police deviance. First, direct individual experiences of police, such as stop and search, are not necessarily the main basis by which people form their judgements of police. Second, when thinking about policing, it is useful to remember what police forces are in most countries: organizations that take their orders from the executive branch of government. Hence, legitimacy granted by the public depends on the political party values and policy goals of the government. Third, as a consequence, party alignment is a critical aspect of explaining the police's 'right' to be deviant. We believe that politics has been accorded insufficient attention relative to other forms of collective identity since it crystallizes cleavages in society. When latent social identities are expressed through political processes, that they can form a societal divide. Together, social identities and political cleavages are the main basis along which legitimacy to use deviant means is granted to police.

Appendix

Table 10.A Composition of acceptance of police deviance index

	Strongly Disagree N %	Disagree N %	Neither agree nor disagree N %	Agree N %	Strongly Agree N %
Police can use wire taping without legal authorization if it may prevent a possible illegal activity	851 (27.3)	437 (14)	561 (18)	645 (20.7)	621 (19.9)
Police can track online posts and messages to find potential offenders	593 (19.2)	435 (14.1)	638 (20.7)	776 (25.1)	646 (20.9)
Police can resort to torture if it may prevent a possible illegal activity	1,756 (55.7)	481 (15.3)	380 (12.1)	311 (9.9)	222 (7)
Violent behaviour of police officers is legitimate when there is a threat against public order	1,197 (38.5)	561 (18.1)	527 (17)	461 (14.8)	362 (11.6)
Police can use violence against protestors when taking them into custody	1,774 (56.1)	555 (17.5)	392 (12.4)	287 (9.1)	157 (5)
Beating up a criminal at the police station is not crime	315 (10)	244 (7.7)	386 (12.2)	734 (23.2)	1,482 (46.9)
Police can illegally – without legal authorization – search my bag to maintain the safety at the public transportation vehicles (e.g. bus, metro etc.)	1,068 (33.8)	469 (14.9)	612 (19.4)	572 (18.1)	435 (13.8)
Police can respond to protests at the university with tear gas	1,517 (48.4)	497 (15.9)	481 (15.3)	349 (10.9)	291 (9.1)
Police can from time to time act against the law for the public benefit	1,015 (33.1)	567 (18.5)	526 (17.1)	494 (16.1)	468 (15.2)

Notes

1 The complexity of the relation between belonging to social groups and to the state cannot be discussed here in detail. However, it is clear that not all group allegiances have the same effect in all contexts, for example, religious belonging and national identification are not correlated in the US but it can be positively or negatively correlated in some EU states.
2 The translation of the items is our own, based on the original questionnaire, and slightly departs from the one in the English version of the TESEV report.

Bibliography

Adaman, F., Carkoğlu, A., and Senatalar, B. (2009). 'Hanehalkı Gözünden Kamu Hizmetleri ve Yolsuzluk', *TEPAV*, online. Available www.tepav.org.tr/tur/admin/dosyabul/upload/kamuhizmetleri.pdf (accessed 18 December 2016).

Akbaş, G. (2010). 'Social identity and intergroup relations: the case of Alevis and Sunnis in Amasya', unpublished M.A. thesis, Middle East Technical University Ankara.

Anderson, C. and Tverdova, Y. (2001). 'Winners, losers, and attitudes about government in contemporary democracies', *International Political Science Review*, 22: 321–38.

Arslan, M. and Olgun, A. (2009). 'Üniversite Öğretim Elemanları ve Öğrencilerinin Polis ve Polislik Mesleği ile İlgili Algıları: Erciyes Üniversitesi Örneklemi', *Polis Bilimleri Dergisi/Turkish Journal of Police Studies*, 11: 107–34.

Bardakçı, M. (2016). '2015 parliamentary elections in Turkey: demise of revival of AKP's single-party rule', *Turkish Studies*, 17: 4–18.

Bensman, J. (1979). 'Max Weber's Concept of Legitimacy: an evaluation', in A. Vidich and R. Glassman (eds.), *Conflict and Control. Challenge to Legitimacy of Modern Governments*, London: Sage, 325–71.

Benson, P. (1981). 'Political alienation and public satisfaction with police services', *The Pacific Sociological Review*, 24: 45–64.

Bilali, R., Celik, B., and Ok, E. (2014). 'Psychological asymmetry in minority-majority relations at different stages of ethnic conflict', *International Journal of Intercultural Relations*, 43: 253–64.

Blumer, H. (1958). 'Race prejudice as a sense of group position', *Pacific Sociological Review*, 1:3–7.

Bradford, B., Milani, J., and Jackson, J. (2016). 'Identity, legitimacy and "making sense" of police violence', *Oxford Legal Studies Research Paper No. 41/2016*, online. Available https://papers.ssrn.com/sol3/papers.cfm?abstract_id=2793818&download=yes (accessed 24 March 2017).

Brunson, R. and Miller, J. (2005). 'Young Black men and urban policing in the United States', *British Journal of Criminology*, 46: 613–40.

Cao, L. and Burton, V. (2006). 'Spanning the continents: assessing the Turkish public confidence in the police', *Policing: An International Journal of Police Strategies and Management*, 29: 451–63.

Cao, L. and Zhao, J. (2005). 'Confidence in the police in Latin America', *Journal of Criminal Justice*, 33: 403–12.

Çakar, B. (2015). 'Factors affecting trust in police in Turkey', *International Journal of Social Sciences*, 12: 1381–93.

Çelik, A., Bilali R., and Iqbal, Y. (2016). 'Patterns of "othering" in Turkey: a study of ethnic, ideological, and sectarian polarisation', *South European Society and Politics*, online. Available http://dx.doi.org/10.1080/13608746.2016.1250382 (accessed 24 March 2017).

Cengiz, Z., Yenigün-Dilek, P., Özhabeş, H., Tarhan, B., Üstünel-Yırcalı, A., and Zeytinoglu, C. (2014). 'Corruption assessment report Turkey', *TESEV*, online. Available http://seldi.net/fileadmin/public/PDF/Publications/CAR_Turkey/CAR_Turkey_English_Final.pdf (accessed 24 March 2017).

Cheurprakobkit, S. (2000). 'Police–citizen contact and police performance: attitudinal differences between Hispanics and non-Hispanics', *Journal of Criminal Justice*, 18: 365–91.

Curini, L., Jou, W., and Memoli, V. (2016). *Why Policy Representation Matters: The Consequences of Ideological Proximity*, London: Routledge.

Delice, M. and Duman, A. (2012). 'Toplum Destekli Polislik Kapsamında Halkın Polis Algısının Ölçülmesi: Erzurum ili örneği', *Polis Bilimleri Dergisi/Turkish Journal of Police Studies*, 14: 1–31.

Doğan, Z. and Bağış, M. (2011). 'Toplumun Polisten Beklenti ve Düşüncelerine Etkili Olan Faktörlerin Likert Ölçekli Sorularla Belirlenmesi', *Atatürk Üniversitesi İktisadi ve İdari Bilimler Dergisi*, 25: 207–23.

Feagin, J. (1991). 'The continuing significance of race: anti-black discrimination in public places', *American Sociological Review*, 56: 101–16.

Gamson, W. A. and McEvoy J (1970). Police violence and its public support, *The Annals of the American Academy of Political and Social Science*; 391–97.

Gerber M. and Jackson, J. (2016). 'Justifying violence: legitimacy, ideology and public support for police use of force, psychology', *Crime and Law*, 23: 79–95.

Grigoriadis, I. (2016). 'The People's Democratic Party (HDP) and the 2015 elections', *Turkish Studies*, 17: 39–46.

Gunes, C. and Zeydanlioglu, W. (2014). *The Kurdish Question in Turkey: New Perspectives on Violence, Representation, and Reconciliation*, London and New York: Routledge.

Harkin, D. (2015). 'Police legitimacy, ideology and qualitative methods: a critique of procedural justice theory', *Criminology & Criminal Justice*: 1–19.

Hasta, D. and Arslantürk, G. (2013). 'Polislik Mesleğine Yöenlik İç-Grup Yanlılığı ve Tutumlar', *Türk Psikoloji Dergisi*, 16: 60–70.

Howell, S. E., Huey, L., and Perry, M. V. (2004). Black cities/White cities: evaluating the police, *Political Behavior*, 26: 45–68.

IBP (2015). *US–Turkey Economic and Political Cooperation Handbook*, Washington: International Business Publications.

ICOISS (2015a). *The measurement of the trust and satisfaction in police and gendarmerie based on international instruments. Findings from a national opinion poll in Turkey*, online. Available www.sivilgozetim.org.tr/Source/Publication/en/16_national_SURVEY.p1.pdf (accessed 24 March 2017).

ICOISS (2015b). *Polis ve Jandarmaya Duyulan Güven ve Memnuniyetin. Uluslararası Yöntemlerle ölçülmesi: Yerel kamuoyu yoklaması sonuçları*, online. Available www.sivilgozetim.org.tr/Source/Publication/piar/15_polis_jandarma.p1.pdf (accessed 24 March 2017).

Kääriäinen, J. (2007). 'Trust in the police in 16 European countries: a multilevel Analysis', *European Journal of Criminology*, 4: 409–35.

Kahan, D. (2013). 'Ideology, motivated reasoning, and cognitive reflection', *Judgment and Decision Making*, 8: 407–24.

Karakuş, O., McGarrell, E., and Basibuyuk, O. (2011). 'Public satisfaction with law enforcement in Turkey', *Policing: An International Journal of Police Strategies and Management*, 34: 304–25.

242   *S. Roché* et al.

Keyman, F. (2007). 'Modernity, secularism and Islam: the case of Turkey', *Theory, Culture and Society*, 24: 215–34.

Kıbrıs, A. (2014). 'The polarisation trap', *Studies in Conflict and Terrorism*, 37: 492–522.

Kirmizidag, N. (2015). *Research on Public Trust in the Police in Turkey*, Istanbul: TESEV.

Kutnjak, Ivkovic, S. (2008). 'A comparative study of public support for the police', *International Criminal Justice Review*, 18: 406–34.

Life Satisfaction Surveys (LSS) by the Turkish Statistical Institute, online. Available www.turkstat.gov.tr/PreHaberBultenleri.do?id=21518 (accessed 24 March 2017).

Lee, J., Steinberg, L., and Piquero, A. (2010). 'Ethnic identity and attitudes toward the police among African American juvenile offenders', *Journal of Criminal Justice*, 38: 781–9.

Lord, C. (2016). 'Rethinking the Justice and Development Party's "Alevi openings"', *Turkish Studies*, online. Available http://dx.doi.org/10.1080/14683849.2016.1257913 (accessed 24 March 2017).

Machiavelli, N. (1513). *The Prince*, online. Available www.cliffsnotes.com/literature/p/the-prince/summary-and-analysis/chapter-15/chapter-15-1 (accessed 22 March 2017).

Marenin, O. (1985). 'Police performance and state rule', *Comparative Politics* 18: 101–22.

MetroPoll (2012). 'Liderlerin İmajı ve Kurumlara Güven – Aralık 2011', online. Available www.metropoll.com.tr/arastirmalar/siyasi-arastirma-9/1710 (accessed 12 December 2016).

Murphy, K. and Cherney, A. (2011). 'Fostering cooperation with the police: how do ethnic minorities in Australia respond to procedural justice-based policing?', *The Australian and New Zealand Journal of Criminology*, 44: 235–57.

Muş, E., Köksal, T., and Yeşilyurt, H. (2014). 'Türkiye'de Güvenlik Hizmetlerinin Vatandaş Memnuniyeti Açısından Değerlendirilmesi', *International Journal of Human Sciences*, 11: 559–81.

Oliveira, A. and Murphy, K. (2015). 'Race, social identity, and perceptions of police bias', *Race and Justice*, 5: 259–77.

Özen, I. and Kalkan, K. (2016). 'Spatial analysis of contemporary Turkish elections: a comprehensive approach', *Turkish Studies*, online. Available http://dx.doi.org/10.1080/14683849.2016.1259576 (accessed 24 March 2017).

Regulus, T., Taylor, R., and Jackson, J. (2001). 'The structure of Black Americans' attitudes toward the police', *African American Research Perspectives*, 7: 185–206.

Roché, S. and de Maillard, J. (2009). 'Crisis in policing: the French rioting of 2005', *Policing*, 3: 34–40.

Roché, S. and Roux, G. (2017). 'The "silver bullet" to good policing: a mirage. An analysis of the effects of political ideology and ethnic identity on procedural justice', *Policing: An International Journal*.

Şahin, N. (2014). 'Legitimacy, procedural justice and police–citizen encounters: a randomized controlled trial of the impact of procedural justice on citizen perceptions of the police during traffic stops in Turkey', unpublished Ph.D. thesis, Rutgers University of New Jersey, USA.

Saraçoğlu, C. (2009). 'Exclusive recognition: the new dimensions of the question of ethnicity and nationalism in Turkey', *Ethnic and Racial Studies*, 32: 640–65.

Sarigil, Z. and Karakoç, E. (2016). 'Inter-ethnic (in)tolerance between Turks and Kurds: implications for Turkish democratisation', *South European Society and Politics*, online. Available http://dx.doi.org/10.1080/13608746.2016.1164846 (accessed 24 March 2017).

Stack, S. and Cao, L. (1998). 'Political conservatism and confidence in the police: a comparative analysis', *Journal of Crime and Justice*, 21: 71–6.

Taslak, S. and Akın, M. (2005). 'Örgüt İmajı Üzerinde Etkili Olan Faktörlere Yönelik Bir Araştırma: Yozgat İli Emniyet Müdürlüğü Örneği', *Sosyal Bilimler Enstitüsü Dergisi*, 19: 263–94.

Van der Toorn, J., Feinberg, M., Jost, J., Kay, A., Tyler, T., Willer, R., and Wilmuth, C. (2015). 'A sense of powerlessness fosters system justification: implications for the legitimation of authority, hierarchy, and government', *Political Psychology*, 36: 93–110.

Walker, S. and Katz, C. (2007). *The Police in America*, New York: McGraw-Hill.

Warren, P. (2011). 'Perceptions of police disrespect during vehicle stops: a race-based analysis', *Crime and Delinquency*, 57: 356–76.

Web, V and Marshall, C (1995). 'The relative importance of race and ethnicity on citizen attitudes toward the police', *American Journal of Police*, 14: 45–56.

Weitzer, R. and Tuch, S. (2004). 'Race and perceptions of police misconduct', *Social Problems*, 51–3: 305–25.

Yavuz, H. and Özcan, N. (2006). 'Kurdish question and Turkey's Justice and Development Party', *Middle East Policy*, 13: 102–19.

Yegen, M. (2009). 'Prospective Turks or pseudo citizens: Kurds in Turkey', *Middle East Journal*, 63: 597–615.

Yılmaz, H. (2014). *Identity in Turkey, Kurdish question and reconciliation process: perceptions and positions*, online. Available http://aciktoplumvakfi.org.tr/pdf/reconciliation_process_perception_survey_summary.pdf (accessed 31 January 2017).

Part IV

Procedural justice as cause and consequence

11 Stop-and-frisk and trust in police in Chicago[1]

Wesley G. Skogan

Introduction

This chapter examines some of the consequences of stop-and-frisk as a law enforcement strategy. This is important because stop-and-frisk has become the crime prevention strategy of choice in American policing. Stop-and-frisk embodies the theory of general deterrence. The idea is that a relentless focus on presumably "hot people" concentrated in crime "hot spots" increases the risks involved in carrying drugs or weapons. This, in turn, will deter crimes that stem from holding contraband, including shootings and drug dealing. In this view, stop-and-frisk increases the perception among potential offenders that they face a high risk of being apprehended if they commit a crime or are provisioned to do so, and thus reduces offending.

Of course, there may be collateral consequences of turning to an aggressive stop-and-frisk style of policing, and that is the focus of this chapter. One possible consequence is that—from the point of view of the citizens involved—these stops may seem unwarranted. Even in crime hot spots, most people, most of the time, are just going about their daily lives. The ability of the police to accurately select suitably hot people from among them is very limited, further reducing the "hit rate" for seizing contraband and making arrests. These rates are typically quite low, so the risk of unwarranted intrusion into people's lives seems a real one.

Another collateral consequence is that stops may be unfairly distributed. The vision of stop-and-frisk underlying the law and decisions of courts in the United States is that they are preceded by careful surveillance and a nuanced analysis of the situation by experienced officers who are wise to criminal opportunities near the scene and the ways of those who are up to no good there. This was the understanding of policing evidenced by the US Supreme Court in one of its leading endorsements of stop-and-frisk, *Terry* v. *Ohio* (1968). But when stop-and-frisk as a policy scales to hundreds of thousands of encounters per year in a single city and when the pressure from management is for volume and not their quality, few may be emulating the good police work of Officer McFadden in front of the jewellery store on his regular beat in downtown Cleveland, Ohio. Instead, a risk is that their apparent race, age, social class and gender may provide the principal flags by which officers identify hot people.

Third, the collateral damage of a crime prevention strategy generating large numbers of unwarranted stops of persons targeted for being who they are may include undermining the legitimacy of the police and perhaps that of the state. Legitimacy is one of the fundamental cornerstones of democracy. It underlies obedience to the law and to the directions of the authorities who protect it. It keeps them from needing an officer on every corner to secure order. If by their actions police undermine their own legitimacy—including by heedlessly sweeping through neighborhoods in a thin blue line—the broader political consequences of SQF ("stop, question, and perhaps frisk" as it has been labeled by a Chicago chief of police) could be significant.

But while there are skeptics, stop-and-frisk has vocal and active supporters and it is the strategy that many American police departments point to as evidence that they are trying to prevent crime. William Bratton, the Commissioner of the New York City Police at the time, put it this way:

> Stop-and-frisk is such a basic tool of policing. It's one of the most fundamental practices in American policing. If cops are not doing stop-and-frisk, they are not doing their jobs. It is a basic, fundamental tool of police work in the whole country. If you do away with stop-and-frisk, this city will go down the chute as fast as anything you can imagine.
>
> (Toobin 2013)

In New York as in Chicago and other places, euphemisms are occasionally employed to relabel stop-and-frisk. A New York City term is "investigative stops," and this will be used widely in this chapter. In Chicago, the chief of police—who served in New York City for 25 years—insisted on calling it "stop, question, and perhaps frisk," to signal that people could perhaps give a good enough account of themselves when they are approached. Since this research was conducted in Chicago, I will frequently label these stops "SQFs."

Stop-and-frisk as a policing strategy is certainly not confined to the United States. In the UK, searches are regulated and reported nationally. In 2008–2009, which is the last year that stops not leading to a search were recorded in the UK, police recorded more than 2.2 million stops and almost 1.1 million searches in a 12-month period (Shiner and Delsol 2015). Summarizing the results of a national survey of young people in France, Jobard et al. (2012) report that 28 percent of respondents recalled being stopped at least once in the course of the previous year. (As will be discussed below, the comparable stop rate for Chicago residents under age 35 was 40 percent.) Non-governmental survey studies of encounters are important in France as officially available data do not include information on the race of individuals (Zauberman and Lévy 2003). Some US cities release reports of their stopping practices, but surveys like that described here link people's stop-experiences to a broader range of process and outcome measures that may not reliably be recorded by the police, and probably will not be considered by them at all.

By 2013, SQF had become the primary crime prevention strategy in Chicago.[2] There, the most relentless stop-and-frisk pressure was not in the field; rather, it was internal, from police headquarters and directed at unit commanders, and from them down to line officers. The CompStat management system that was in place stressed hard numbers. The hardest number was the homicide count, which—unlike murder in other big American cities—was rising. The complementary number that seemed under the control of top management was the SQF count. The chief of police, who had arrived in the city from New York in late 2011, brought with him both CompStat (which he had been in charge of) and a firm belief in the redemptive power of stop-and-frisk. The weekly CompStat sessions, at which he grilled his unit commanders, sometimes became shouting sessions as he turned up the heat, exhorting them to produce ever-greater numbers of stops. As will be detailed below, 2014 featured an extremely large number of SQFs but closed with higher numbers of shootings and murders than the year before. The following year began as a virtual mirror of 2014, and by its conclusion shootings were up almost 30 percent over 2013, and the number of homicides rose from 2014 to 2015 by 13 percent. There was a sense of panic at police headquarters which was feeling the drumbeat of media criticism aimed at their inability to "do something" about this deadly trend. This chapter examines the consequences of Chicago's strategic response for the city's residents at this very moment, when SQFs reached their crescendo and then collapsed in the face of scandal and (perhaps) reform.

Measuring encounters with police

There are no national statistics on the frequency or outcomes of stop-and-frisk policing. Individual cities define these encounters in radically different ways. For example, New York City police complete a form for everyone they stop, and any further actions—including ticketing or arresting them, or seizing contraband—link to the stop record. In Chicago, on the other hand, police complete their local report only when there are *no* further consequences of the stop; if a stop-and-frisk is recorded, that is all that happened. Cities also use different forms of electronic and paper records. New York City's form includes many check-box responses to particular data needs, making it easy to analyze them statistically. In Chicago, by contrast, most of the form is a blank space into which officers key whatever text occurs to them to describe the event. As there are millions of these forms, analyzing them in any systematic way is virtually impossible. So while there are a few studies of individual cities, national trends are currently impossible to assemble using official records.

This examination of stop-and-frisk and its consequences is based on a survey of Chicago residents conducted during 2015. The sample to be questioned was selected to represent residents of seven race and class clusters that make up most of Chicago. The clusters were revealed by analyzing recent demographic and economic data for the city's 788 small census tracts. This identified geographic concentrations of poor and better-off African Americans, better-off and working-class Whites, long-settled and recently arrived Hispanics, and other recent immigrants, many of who are Asian. Representative samples of residential blocks located in each of these clusters were selected proportionate to their population size. Survey staff members next walked the sample areas, adding any residential addresses that did not appear on the United States Post Office's list for the block and removing incorrect or non-residential addresses. Then, sample addresses were randomly selected from the list for each block. Interviewers knocked on those doors and conducted personal interviews with a randomly selected resident age 16 and older. To encourage participation, potential respondents were offered a cash incentive of $40. The interviews could be conducted in either English or Spanish. This was significant for more than 30 percent of the Hispanics interviewed for this study were questioned in Spanish.

Up to ten contact attempts were made at each sample address, at varying times of day and days of the week, with the bulk of the attempts being made in the evening or on weekends. Follow-up validations were conducted for 10 percent of each interviewer's completed cases. The response rate for the survey was 28 percent, calculated according to American Association of Public Opinion Research standards. The factor that most affected the response rate was the frequency of sample addresses at which no contact could ever be made to determine if anyone eligible to participate lived there, or—in some cases—whether anyone was living there at all. Chicago's declining population and the high level of building abandonment characterizing many poor neighborhoods doubtless contributed to this. Another group that proved difficult to approach was affluent Chicagoans living in high-rise residential buildings. At addresses where someone could actually be contacted the cooperation rate was 52 percent.

A total of 1,450 residents were interviewed: 457 Whites, 436 African Americans, 437 Hispanics, and 121 persons of other races. Chicago's Hispanic community primarily has its origins in Mexico, and 44 percent of the Hispanics interviewed for this study were foreign born. Of all Hispanics, 26 percent reported they were not citizens. The terms Hispanic and "Latino" are used interchangeably in this report, as they are in daily life in the city. Respondents classified as "others" on race were 44 percent Asian in origin, primarily from the Philippines and Southeast Asia. Other blocs of respondents came from the Middle East and North Africa. Almost 40 percent of all "others" were foreign born, and in total 10 percent were not citizens.

Sampling weights were developed for the survey. They can be used to adjust the data for several factors. One component corrects for differences in the probability of selection for residents of multiple-adult households. Otherwise, individuals living in larger families would be less likely to be selected than adults living alone, who would always be chosen. In addition, respondents in each neighborhood cluster can be weighted to bring them into their correct demographic proportions across the seven study areas. In general, the descriptive statistics presented here are based on weighted data, but the multivariate analyzes that are reported are based on unweighted data. Weighting had little effect in the findings, in any event.

One purpose of the survey was to examine the frequency with which Chicagoans contact and are stopped by the police. Respondents were first presented with a number of questions about crime and disorder in their neighborhood, fear of crime, their participation in community organizations, and their responses to local problems. Next, they were asked about their neighbors and things they may have done to prevent crime. Further questions gathered their general impressions of the police on several dimensions, including how much they trusted them. Only then did the survey turn to their personal experiences with the police. Respondents were presented with multiple and redundant verbal cues to aid them in thinking about their involvement in police-initiated encounters. Respondents were first asked if they had *ever* been involved in a vehicle stop.

> Next I'm going to ask you about times that you may have been stopped or in contact with the Chicago police. Have you ever been in a car or on a motor-cycle that was stopped by the Chicago police, or have you never been in a car or motorcycle that was stopped by the Chicago police? You could have been the driver or passenger.

This was followed by a similar question about having ever being stopped "when you were out walking, or shopping, or just standing around?" There were also open-text questions about being stopped in other circumstances or for other reasons; responses to these were hand-coded. In response to the "have you ever…"-questions, 72 percent of those interviewed recalled being stopped by Chicago police.

Follow-up probes were next used to determine which if any of the encounters respondents recalled had occurred in the past 12 months. A 12-month recall period was used in order to estimate a yearly stop rate. In addition, respondents' ability to recall in detail what happened during these contacts could be greater if they were focusing only on relatively recent events. If respondents recalled being involved in more than one police-initiated encounter during the past year, they were asked which was the most recent of those events. This number was significant—almost 30 percent of those stopped in the past 12 months were stopped more than once during the period. In this circumstance, the most recent of multiple contacts provides a reasonable random selection from among them. Incident details were then gathered in follow-up questions about what happened during their only or most recent encounter, if it had occurred in the past year. The questioning sequence thus captured some data on respondents' experiences further in the past (in response to the "have you ever…"-questions) and the number of times they had been stopped during the year but details concerning what happened were gathered only for a specific incident that occurred within the past 12 months. The interviews were conducted continuously during 2015, so those taking place early in the year referred mostly to events that occurred during the latter part of 2014, while interviews conducted later mostly referred to 2015 events.

The frequency of SQFs

The analysis presented here examines the frequency and character of SQFs, sometimes in contrast to police enforcement stops, which generate citations and arrests. This distinction is based on respondents' descriptions of their experiences. If they reported being arrested or taken to a police station or if they received a traffic ticket, the encounter is classed as an enforcement stop. In Chicago, most enforcement encounters involved traffic stops; in 94 percent of enforcement encounters, respondents were either driving or they were a passenger in a car that was stopped. Only 6 percent reported being arrested or taken to a police station after being stopped while on foot. Across all enforcement stops, 97 percent of respondents received a ticket, 13 percent reported being arrested, and 19 percent said they were taken to a police station for further processing.

However, if at the conclusion of their encounter with the police they were not cited or formally sanctioned, and instead were free to walk away, the encounter is categorized as an SQF. The "frisked" component of the category is appropriate, for although no formal action was taken against them, the vast majority were questioned and asked for their identification. Many targets of SQF also reported being searched, threatened, handcuffed, and roughed up or even injured—particularly if they were African Americans, Hispanics or members of other minority groups. In contrast to enforcement stops, 46 percent of all SQFs involved respondents who were on foot rather than driving. A majority (56 percent) were stopped near their home, in contrast to 36 percent of enforcement stops.

Based on this, 29 percent of adult Chicagoans recalled being stopped by police in the past year. Among those who were stopped, 75 percent described what is classified here as an SQF investigatory stop, while 25 percent described being formally sanctioned following an enforcement stop. Methodological differences between surveys makes it difficult to compare this to other cities or other times. A survey I conducted in Chicago by telephone more than a decade earlier using otherwise very similar methods found a 20 percent stop rate (Skogan 2006). This was almost a third smaller than the comparable figure for 2014–2015 and clearly a large number.

As in many American cities, the frequency and social distribution of stop-and-frisk has been a subject of political contention in Chicago. At about the moment that this survey was completed, the Chicago police were engulfed in a tremendous scandal over charges (actually, over the fact) that they were concealing horrific acts of brutality in order to protect themselves and the political ambitions of the city's mayor. The resulting firestorm of criticism led to the creation of a special commission (the Police Accountability Task Force) to investigate the situation and recommend changes to the city's policies and practices. Based on administrative records, the Task Force's 200-page report observed that in the summer of 2014, the Chicago police stopped more than 250,000 people. As a rate per 10,000 residents, this was more than four times the comparable rate for New York City at the peak of its stop-and-frisk era (Police Accountability Task Force 2016: 36).

Another focus of attention among those concerned about police conduct was the distribution of those stops in the population. Of the 250,000 stops conducted that summer, 72 percent were of African Americans, 17 percent were of Hispanics, and 9 percent were of Whites (Police Accountability Task Force 2016: 10). The Task Force report included extensive documentation of other enormous racial disparities in the actions of Chicago police officers. These ranged from whom they shot (74 percent African Americans) to whom they downed with Tasers (76 percent African Americans). There was an extensive analysis of racial disparities in traffic stops (72 percent African American), arrests for loitering (82 percent African American) and investigatory stops (72 percent African American) (Police Accountability Task Force 2016: 35–47). About one-third or less of the city's population is African American, in contrast. Disparities targeting Black Chicagoans were so one-sided that one point I took away from the Task Force's charts was that there was little room left for extra attention to the city's Hispanic population. They also make up about one-third of the city's population but on many measures they did not hugely differ from Whites.

The survey was designed to capture many of the experiences that concerned the Task Force and others in the city. It was completed just as the scandal broke, so it and accompanying media coverage of police–community relations could not have affected the survey's findings. Unlike studies based on administrative forms, it does not "double count" individuals who are stopped more than once; as we shall see, this is quite common. It gathers reports of encounters directly from individual citizens, and these can be related to other analytic variables and to their assessments of how they were treated. Figure 11.1 examines the distribution of SQF ("investigative") and enforcement encounters described in the

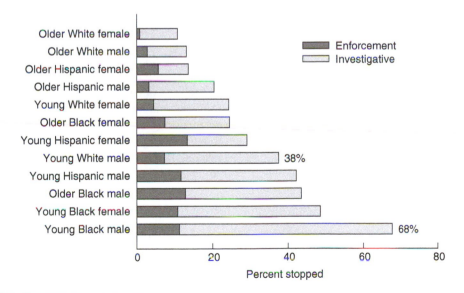

Figure 11.1 Stops by age, race, and sex.

survey. It categorizes Chicagoans by age ("young" is age 16–34), sex and race (persons of "other" races are excluded, as they were too few in number for this detailed analysis). It reports the percentage of respondents in each age-sex-race category who were stopped during the past year, dividing stops between enforcement and investigative encounters. A version of this figure appeared in the final report of the Police Accountability Task Force.

Several important points are illustrated in Figure 11.1. First, in Chicago *being stopped for investigative purposes is the predominant experience residents have with the police*. Every group represented in Figure 11.1 mainly reported being stopped for investigative purposes rather than being ticketed or arrested. The least-often stopped group (11 percent in the course of a year) was older White females, and they were six times more likely to be stopped for investigation rather than for an actionable offence. Among young Black males, 17 percent of those stopped were arrested or ticketed while 83 percent were involved in an SQF. Overall (the bars in Figure 11.1 do not represent equal numbers of people), 22 percent of Chicagoans reported being caught up in an investigative stop and 8 percent were formally sanctioned by ticketing or arrest, almost a 3–1 ratio. The wide net being cast by Chicago's SQF practices was one of its most surprising features.

A second feature of police–citizen encounters in Chicago is that they *vary widely in frequency*, and *among young people, men and African Americans being stopped is a common rather than an exceptional circumstance*. Statistically, age was the largest determinant of being stopped; note that being "young" describes six of the seven most-stopped groups in Figure 11.1. Overall, 31 percent of those interviewed who were under age 35 (the "Millennials" in this sample) were caught up in SQF, as were 23 percent of Chicagoans age 35–50. Race came next in terms of predicting the probability of being stopped for questioning. About 30 percent of African Americans were involved in SQF, in contrast to 16 percent of Whites and 20 percent of Hispanics. Gender was the third best predictor of being stopped. In total, 18 percent of females and 28 percent of males recalled being stopped for questioning. In addition, lower-income individuals and short-term residents of their neighborhood were more likely to be involved in SQF encounters (this is not depicted in Figure 11.1). There was also a tendency for foreign-born Chicagoans, and especially non-citizens within this group, to avoid being stopped by the police, either for enforcement or investigative reasons. This is consistent with their general tendency to be circumspect regarding potential encounters with law enforcement officials (Skogan 2009).

Finally, age, race, and sex conspire to create *a huge SQF rate among young African American men*. As Figure 11.1 illustrates, in the course of just one year, 56 percent of young Black males were subjects of SQFs, and 68 percent were stopped overall. They were five times more likely to be stopped for investigation than to be formally sanctioned. A survey I conducted in 2003 came to virtually the same finding—in that year, 71 percent of young African American men reported being stopped for any reason by the Chicago police. The major difference between the two surveys, which were conducted more than a decade apart, was an increasing stop rate for young African American women, from 39 percent in 2003 to 49 percent during 2015 (Skogan 2006: 295).

What happens during SQFs?

Most people stopped by Chicago police are not ticketed, arrested or taken to a police station. Instead, a very large majority of street stops are investigative SQFs. They involve ID checks, questioning, and searches of vehicles and persons. Chicagoans also report being on the receiving end of threats, handcuffing, and physical force even during investigative stops, although in the end there was no reason to hold them. Being on the receiving end of these intrusive police actions was much more common among African Americans, Hispanics and persons of other races.

A great deal transpired even during investigative stops; Figure 11.2 details some of the actions taken by the police during SQFs. As it documents, a majority of non-White Chicagoans faced an ID check; police demanded identification from about three-quarters of Blacks and Latinos who were stopped, and from more than 80 percent of those of other races. For Whites, the comparable figure was 56 percent. Searches were less common during SQF encounters but they were also disproportionate in their impact. About 25 percent of African Americans who were involved in a vehicle stop reported that their vehicle was searched. For Hispanics involved in traffic stops, that fraction was 20 percent, while for Whites it was 6 percent. An even larger percentage of all Blacks and Hispanics who were stopped—about 30 percent of each group—were personally searched, in contrast to 9 percent of Whites. Figure 11.2 summarizes both vehicle and personal searches in the course of SQFs in one number, which was

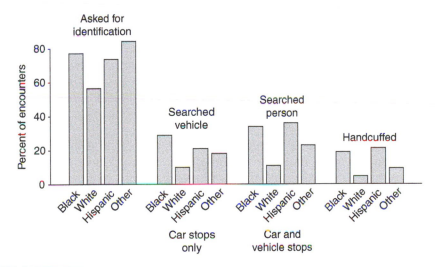

Figure 11.2 Police actions during investigative stops, by race.

in the mid–30s for both Blacks and Latinos. In addition to race, the demographic correlates of being searched included age: Chicagoans age 16–35 were most likely to be searched, as were lower-income and less educated people who were swept up in SQF encounters.

A perhaps surprising fraction of Blacks (19 percent) and Hispanics (21 percent) were handcuffed in the course of being questioned but then eventually released. Although the survey did not probe this point, handcuffing could have been precautionary by the police rather than in response to any violent action by the citizens involved, for in the end none were arrested. Figure 11.2 also reports a summary measure of the use of force in Chicago SQFs; use of force is examined in detail immediately below. In summary, about 35 percent of African Americans and 30 percent of Hispanics and persons of other races reported that they experienced use of force of some sort, including verbal threats, the display of weapons, and being physically accosted. Among Whites involved in SQFs, the comparable figure was 14 percent. In enforcement stops (which are not detailed here), all of these percentages were substantially higher. As for searches, Chicagoans age 16–35 were most likely to report that force was used and that they were handcuffed, as were lower-income and less educated respondents.

Respondents who had been stopped were questioned in some detail about any police use of force during the encounter. Their responses can be classified along a commonly used "force continuum" developed by policing scholar David Klinger (Klinger 1995). At the bottom of this continuum is *shouted commands*. Respondents caught up in SQF encounters were asked: "Did they shout or curse at you, or did they not shout or curse at you?" Overall, 23 percent reported being shouted at. Next on list comes *verbal threats of use of force*. Respondents were asked: "Did they verbally threaten to use force against you, or did they not verbally threaten to use force against you?"; in total, 13 percent were threatened in this way. The frequency of *weapon threats* was measured by responses to two questions: "Did they verbally threaten to use a weapon, or did they not verbally threaten to use a weapon?" and "[d]id they take out a weapon, such as a gun, a club, or a Taser, or did they not take out a weapon?" Officers were described as taking out a weapon in 10 percent of SQFs, and threatening to in another 6 percent. Finally, the use of *physical force* was indicated by positive responses to the question: "Were you pushed, grabbed, kicked or hit, or were you not pushed, grabbed, kicked or hit?" In total, 13 percent of those caught up in investigative stops were pushed or shoved.[3]

Figure 11.3 arranges these descriptions of use of force, from shouting at the bottom to the use of physical force at the top. Each respondent was placed in their highest position on the scale, based on their description of what happened at the scene. The overall height of each bar illustrates the proportion of each racial group that was subject to any kind of force, and those percentages are reported. Figure 11.3 illustrates the large racial disparities in the use of force reported by our respondents. At the top, the use of physical force was particularly disparate: 14 percent of African Americans and 20 percent of Hispanics who were stopped in an SQF reported being shoved or pushed around, in

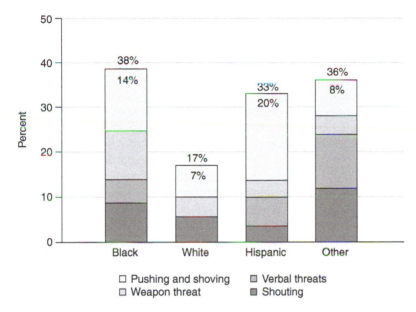

Figure 11.3 Use of force in investigative stops, by race (percent of all investigative stops).

contrast to 7 percent of Whites. (These percentages are also presented in Figure 11.3.) African Americans were almost three times as likely as Whites to be threatened by a weapon (11 percent versus 4 percent).

Overall, compared to Whites (17 percent), Blacks (at 38 percent), Hispanics (33 percent) and persons of other races (36 percent) were about twice as likely to have been subjected to some form of force before being released. It is important to note that very few respondents, 2 percent, reported being injured in any way during an investigative encounter, and that outcome is not presented in Figure 11.3.

Are police in Chicago just "rounding up the usual suspects"? In the popular film *Casablanca*, Captain Renaud of the local police substituted frantic activity for actual police work, ordering his officers to "round up the usual suspects" rather than actually investigate a murder. The political context of this study of SQF made such often-meaningless roundups a distinct possibility. At the department's CompStat management meetings, the chief of police roared at commanders who failed to produce ever-increasing numbers of stops. This translated into continuous pressure at the district level to make stops for the purpose of "laying hands on people" (conducting a search) and completing forms documenting contacts. Officers in many districts were exhorted at roll call to bring back stop reports. One officer reported being told to go to a park "... and get a couple of kid's names. I was compared to another officer who will fill out contact cards by the dozen daily." Another described his strategy: "We contact card the same piss bums and drunks week after week to keep the numbers up. I data warehouse checked one of our regular beggars and he has over 100 contacts this year." In some districts, officers reported that they were called in and questioned by their lieutenant if they returned from a tour of duty without any completed stop-and-frisk forms. Making stops was widely understood to be department policy but in the view of many close observers—including me—the actual implementation of the policy had become almost pathological.

In the survey, respondents describing vehicle and pedestrian stops that had occurred during the past 12 months were asked how frequently these kinds of incidents had happened to them in the past year. Blacks and Hispanics who were involved in SQFs proved to constitute the usual suspects. Black targets of SQFs reported experiencing 3.8 stops in the past year; for Hispanics, the stop average was 2.5. Whites reported being stopped an average of 1.7 times in the past year.[4] Respondents whose SQF was a foot stop rather than a vehicle stop reported experiencing almost twice as many recent encounters. Compared to enforcement stops, targets of SQF were more likely to be stopped multiple times. About 60 percent of those reporting enforcement encounters were stopped only once in the year, while about 60 percent of SQF subjects were stopped more than once.

The impact of SQF on trust in the police

The next question is, what is the impact of SQF encounters on resident's views of the police? Do they have any larger consequences for policing or for society? Here, I focus on *trust in the police*. In research, trust is viewed as one of the products of policing, caused to an important extent by the quality of service that police deliver to individuals and the reputation they develop in the community as a whole. It is also seen as a key component of legitimacy, one of the bedrock concepts of democratic theory. This section examines the impact of investigatory and enforcement stops on trust. Questions examining trust topics were asked early in the survey, before there was any discussion of recent experiences respondents may have had with the police. Trust questions were mixed among others examining aspects of police performance and the extent of police powers. This section describes in detail the distribution of trust in Chicago and the impact of encounters with the police upon it. A multivariate statistical analysis including a variety of correlates of being stopped is presented which further highlights the important role played by race in evaluating Chicago's SQF strategy.

Trust is evidenced when citizens believe that police try to do the right thing, acting on behalf of the best interests of the people they deal with. In this view, people may trust police if they seem to embody the norms and values of the community and when they think police are sincere and well-intentioned (Van Craen 2016). Trust is sometimes labeled "motive-based trust" because it is a belief regarding the intentions of the police, that "their heart is in the right place" and they mean well even if they do not always succeed. Trust generates confidence in the future behavior of the police and, when it is strong trust, can help sustain public support when there are occasional breeches and the police do not manage to live up to expectations, including their own. In procedural justice theory, it is procedurally fair treatment that generates trust in the police because citizens infer from how they are treated whether or not the police have good intentions. In Tyler's (2004) view, trust is one of the most crucial components of procedural justice theory as it underlies legitimacy—which is defined by an obligation to obey police and the law. The more people trust the police, the more likely they are to support them and act in accordance with their requests.

Why could involvement in SQFs undermine trust? This question returns to our discussion at the outset of the potential pitfalls of pursuing a crime prevention strategy that is based on extensive stop-and-frisk. Police casting a wide net, intervening in the lives of a broad spectrum of citizens in order to announce their presence to the community and send the signal that they are to be feared, could easily undermine any belief that police motives are to be trusted. Claims that SQF stops are being initiated in response to truly suspicious behavior, which is one basis of their legality, lose credibility. Instead, people may feel besieged, even in their own neighborhoods. They can feel that being stopped, and stopped repeatedly, is demeaning, and it certainly can send a signal that people like themselves are not respected. A high-volume SQF strategy like that adopted in Chicago may also not command careful management of the quality of stops. Procedural justice theory emphasizes the importance of officers letting citizens speak up, listening to what the public has to say, carefully explaining their actions, and being respectful and polite (Van Craen 2016). But, based on this survey, too often SQF in Chicago more resembles "confront and command" policing than procedurally just policing. This is particularly true among African Americans and other large minority groups, who are—as we have seen—more often harshly treated during these stops. Being stopped is also potentially dangerous—recall from Figure 11.3 that among all but White Chicagoans, more than 30 per cent reported being threatened or worse by the police during SQFs. Tyler and Huo's (2002) original formulation of motive-based trust involved the belief that police are doing their best for the people with whom they are dealing. SQFs do not send that message.

Enforcement stops could work differently. Note that they likely involved relatively clear wrongdoing. Those caught up in them had been speeding, driving while intoxicated or in a reckless manner, or were otherwise involved in actions that got them (mostly) ticketed, arrested, and/or taken in. Tyler and Fagan (2008) argued that under these circumstances, police enforcement actions may not undermine trust, as such stops typically have a clear legal basis. People may not be *happy* about being sanctioned, and it would not be surprising if being ticketed or arrested rebounded against the views of the police held by those on the receiving end. But—especially if police handle the incident in a professional manner— they do not have much cause for complaint, and they probably know that. In contrast, a pernicious feature of SQF is that doing nothing wrong may not inoculate people against being swept up.

In the survey, trust was measured by responses to six questions. They are presented in Table 11.1. The questions focus on perceptions of officers' character

Table 11.1 Measures of generalized trust in police

How often do police try to find the best solutions for people's problems in this neighborhood?

How likely is it that people's basic rights will be well protected by the Chicago police?

How likely is it that the leaders of the Chicago police will make decisions that are good for everyone in the city?

How sincere are police working in this neighborhood about trying to help people with their problems?

How honest are police working in this neighborhood?

How much of the time can the police be trusted to make decisions that are right for the people in this neighborhood?

(sincerity and honesty); their responsiveness to community concerns (finding "best solutions" while "trying to help with their problems"); their attention to the common good (making decisions that are "right for the people" and "good for everyone in the city"); and their commitment to lawful policing ("basic rights well protected"). Each question provided respondents with five responses to choose from. The response categories for each question varied appropriately, including positive categories such as "definitely will," "extremely likely," "always," and the like. Responses to the six questions were strongly correlated (an average of +0.59) and they formed one factor that explained 67 per cent of their total variance. Averaging the responses into one index created a trust-in-police scale with an alpha reliability of 0.90. On a five-point scale the average (and median) score was in the positive range (3.3). There was a visible (but not statistically large) grouping of low scores; as we shall see, these were linked to characteristics of our respondents and the experiences that they recently had.

Figure 11.4 illustrates the relationship between race, experience with the police, and trust in the police. It compares the views of respondents who were involved in enforcement stops and those who were the targets of SQF encounters with each other, and with Chicagoans who had not been stopped by the police during the same 12-month period. For Figure 11.4 (but not for the statistical analysis that follows), the measure of generalized trust in the police was categorized, breaking out respondents who averaged in the moderately-trusting range and those scoring in the high-trust range. Other respondents located themselves nearer the distrustful end of the scale, so the overall heights of the bars in Figure 11.4 illustrate the percentage of Chicagoans who held generally trusting views.

First, Figure 11.4 illustrates the *strikingly lower level of trust among Chicago's African Americans*. Overall only 44 percent of Black Chicagoans evidenced any trust in the police. This figure was much higher for Hispanics (68 percent) and for persons of other races it was 61 percent. More than 80 percent of Whites reported some level of trust in the police.

Second, compared to respondents who did not report a recent SQF, *those caught up in enforcement and investigative stops were less trusting of the police.*

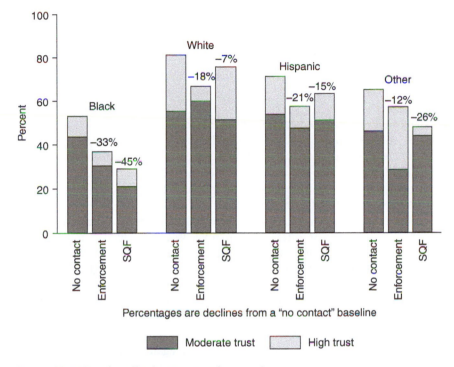

Figure 11.4 Trust in police by stop experience and race.

Figure 11.4 documents the percentage difference in support between baseline "no contact" respondents and those who recalled being stopped by the police. Across the board—and even among Whites—support was lower among those who were targets of enforcement stops and SQFs. The relative effects of SQFs and enforcement stops were mixed among African Americans, subjects of SQF reported lower levels of trust than even those caught up in enforcement stops, and the same was true of the diverse band of Asians, mix-race respondents and foreign-born people gathered in the "other races" category. Among Hispanics, differences in trust between the two targeted groups were small, and for Whites experiencing an SQF had little impact on trust in the police.

It is important to note that many of the "no-contact" respondents depicted in Figure 11.4 were doubtless aware of the character of policing in their community. With stop rates at the high levels described here, word was almost certainly getting around within poor and minority neighborhoods concerning what was happening to their relatives, friends, and neighbors. People draw lessons concerning policing from what they see and hear, and not just from their own direct experiences (Antrobus et al. 2015). This indirect experience would have a negative impact, probably a substantial one, on the views of the no-contact respondents described in Figure 11.4.

Figure 11.4 does not report on the statistical significance of any of the contrasts in levels of trust reported there. Rather, that is incorporated into a multivariate analysis of the impact of encounters with the police on trust that also includes determinants of attitudes toward the police in addition to race. This enables us to jointly compare the relative impact of each type of stop while accounting for differences in how often they occur and differing levels of trust between people of various backgrounds, most starkly among African Americans.

Table 11.2 reports two measures of the impact of all of those factors on trust. The "B" column of Table 11.2 reports standardized regression coefficients. They assess the relative impact of the listed variables on trust, and should be compared to one another down that column. The significance of each of the listed factors is reported as well, and except for gender all of the coefficients reported in the trust columns were reliably different from zero.

Table 11.2 suggests that SQFs in Chicago had about the same negative impact on trust in the police as differences in trust associated with being ticketed, arrested, or taken to a police station for further processing; those "B" coefficients were essentially identical in magnitude. Underplaying the potentially delegitimizing effects of an aggressive SQF crime prevention strategy would be a mistake. The consequences of those stops are as serious as ticketing and arresting people. Not surprisingly, race was the most important factor at play in Table 11.2. Net of other factors African Americans displayed much lower levels of trust than did Whites (who provide the baseline against which all of the race effects in the table are contrasted). They were followed by Hispanics, other racial groups and young people, all of whom were also significantly disenchanted with the police even controlling for their recent experiences with being

Table 11.2 Regression analysis of the impact of encounters

	Trust in the police		
	b	*B*	*sigf*
Constant	3.47		0.00
Investigative stop	−0.20	−0.09	0.00
Enforcement stop	−0.29	−0.10	0.00
Black	−0.58	−0.32	0.00
Hispanic	−0.12	−0.06	0.04
Other race	−0.20	−0.07	0.01
Age 15–35	−0.17	−0.10	0.00
Income	0.03	0.09	0.00
Male	0.02	0.01	0.68
	$R=0.38$ $R^2=0.15$		
	$N=1,450$		

Note
Column 'b' presents unstandardized regression coefficients; column 'B' presents standardized regression coefficients; the 'sigf' column presents significance values.

stopped. Note, however, that Hispanics and others stood out much less than African Americans in this regard. Social status, represented here by household income, also plays a notable role. Net of these other factors, better-off Chicagoans reported more trust in the police. There were no significant interactions between race and the stop measures, in their relationship with trust.

Conclusions

This chapter examined some of the consequences of stop-and-frisk as a crime prevention strategy in Chicago. It first documented that being targeted by stop-and-frisk was not an extraordinary occurrence but an extremely common event. The survey indicates that during that during a one-year period, almost 30 percent of the city's residents reported being stopped. Of those, 75 percent were stop-and-frisk encounters, so in total SQFs swept up 22 percent of the adult population. Further, stops were far more common among young people and racial minorities. Among young, male African Americans, 68 percent reported being stopped in a year, and most of those were stop-and-frisks. Blacks and Hispanics were also repeatedly targeted and stopped multiple times in the course of a year, especially while they were out walking.

Second, when compared to Whites, the city's African American, Hispanic, and other minorities were more likely to be caught up in abrasive encounters with the police. SQFs are not "quick and harmless" encounters. When they were stopped, the city's racial minorities were more likely to be searched, handcuffed and roughed up during investigative stops before they were let go. The force used was largely verbal, involving shouting and verbal threats—unless they were African Americans. In that case about half of the force that officers employed involved threatening them with a weapon or pushing them around.

Third, stops influence people's judgements concerning the trustworthiness of the police generally. Being targeted by an SQF had about the same negative impact as being stopped and ticketed or arrested. Trust is threatened when police stop people but do not turn up any reason to hold them. It is undermined by these kinds of demeaning and meaningless experiences. SGFs send the message that their targets are not respected. Casting a broad net that scoops up large numbers of persons to no avail thus undermines public confidence in the police. The effects of stop-and-frisk were greatest among (especially) African Americans, who reported the most frequent and most abrasive contacts with the police, and the smallest among Whites. Hispanics fell between the two on many measures, reporting lower stop rates, and the independent effect of being Hispanic on trust in the police was much smaller than that for African Americans.

None of these findings would be a great surprise in Chicago's Black and Brown communities. Just as the survey was completed, a police-brutality scandal led to investigations and a report on the extent of stop-and-frisk and other police operations that confirmed many of the conclusions detailed in this chapter. A *New York Times* poll of Chicago following the release of that report found that dissatisfaction with police conduct was broad as well as deep (Davey and

Russonello 2016). In the poll, only one-third of all city residents thought the police were doing a good job. Whites were more positive than Blacks or Hispanics but even a majority of them would not give the police high marks. Almost 60 percent of Chicagoans thought that officers were not punished harshly enough if they used excessive force. A majority of residents (including 52 percent of Whites) agreed that police are more likely to use deadly force against Black people and more than 40 percent of every group thought that African Americans and Latinos are treated unfairly by the city's criminal justice system either "always" or "most of the time" (Davey and Russonello 2016). As too often happens in policing, a policy rooted in criminological theory and perhaps cost-effective (in the largest sense of "costs") when employed judiciously, was scaled up beyond its capacity to be conducted responsibly, in a desperate attempt to stem a resurgent tide of violence in the city. The brutality scandal that then opened SQF to public inspection and debate may have thus magnified its impact on public opinion and the city's politics. Whether ensuing efforts at reform manage to stem SQFs or if they return to a prominent place in the bag of tactics that constitutes the city's crime policy, remains to be seen.

Limitations of this research

In assessing encounters with police, the primary alternative to surveys is examining forms filled out by officers, and limitations imposed by survey methods have to be evaluated in that light. The survey may have underrepresented the experiences of city residents who are difficult to find and interview. This is always a challenge in survey research, so in addition to making ten or more personal visits to locate difficult-to-find respondents we also weighted existing respondents so that the analytic sample matched Bureau of the Census estimates of the age, gender, and race composition of each of the seven study areas they were selected from. In this instance, gender proved less important than age and race but generally all three play a role in studies of police–community relations, so representing them proportionally is important. Of course, city residents who were arrested and remained incarcerated for about one month or longer would have been lost to our call-back process. This number was probably small; only 3 percent of respondents reported being arrested in the past 12 months, and most jail stays in Chicago are relatively short. However, no amount of weighting is likely to adequately represent the experiences of those with longer jail stays. Respondents may also have chosen not to tell us about their experiences. To counter that, this study invested significant resources in interviewer training and quality control, and the interviews were conducted privately, in respondent's homes.

Notes

1 This research was supported by a grant from the John D. and Catherine T. MacArthur Foundation. The survey described here was conducted by the Survey Research Laboratory at the University of Illinois, directed by Jennifer Parsons.

2 This and other descriptions of the inner working of the agency are based on my personal observations of CompStat and other meetings and interviews with participants in the process. The recorded crime statistics cited here are all based on my own analyses of agency data.
3 Responses to a final open-ended question asking about any "other" uses of force were coded into the main categories.
4 These means are based on a 5 percent trim of the data, a procedure that discounted very high-frequency estimates of the number of times they were stopped that were contributed by a few respondents, especially for SQF encounters.

Bibliography

Antrobus, E., Bradford, B., Murphy, K., and Sargeant, E. (2015). 'Community norms, procedural justice, and the public's perceptions of police legitimacy', *Journal of Contemporary Criminal Justice*, 31: 151–70.

Davey, M. and Russonello, G. (2016, May 6). 'In deeply divided Chicago, most agree: City is off course', *New York Times*, online. Available http://nyti.ms/1TsnqGE (accessed 29 December 2016).

Jobard, F., Lévy, R., Lamberth, J., and Névanen, S. (2012). 'Measuring appearance-based discrimination: an analysis of identity checks in Paris', *Population*, 67: 349–76.

Klinger, D. (1995). 'The microstructure of nonlethal force: baseline data from an observational study', *Criminal Justice Review*, 20: 169–86.

Police Accountability Task Force (2016). *Recommendations for Reform: Restoring Trust Between the Chicago Police and the Communities They Serve*, Chicago.

Shiner, M. and Delsol, R. (2015). 'The politics of the powers', in R. Delsol and M. Shiner (eds.), *Stop and Search: The Anatomy of a Police Power*, London: Palgrave-Macmillan, 31–56.

Skogan, W. (2006). *Police and Community in Chicago: A Tale of Three Cities*, New York: Oxford University Press.

Skogan, W. (2009). 'Policing immigrant communities in the United States', *Sociology of Crime, Law and Deviance*, 13: 189–203.

Terry v. *Ohio*, 392 U.S. 1 (1968).

Toobin, J. (2013, May 27). 'Rights and wrongs: a judge takes on stop-and-frisk', *The New Yorker*, online. Available www.newyorker.com/magazine/2013/05/27/rights-and-wrongs-2 (accessed 29 December 2016).

Tyler, T. (2004). 'Enhancing police legitimacy', *Annals of the American Academy of Political and Social Science*, 593: 84–99.

Tyler, T. and Fagan, J. (2008). 'Why do people cooperate with the police?', *Ohio State Journal of Criminal Law*, 6: 231–75.

Tyler, T. and Huo, Y. (2002). *Trust in the Law: Encouraging Public Cooperation with the Police and Courts*, New York: Russell-Sage Foundation.

Van Craen, M. (2016). 'Understanding police officers' trust and trustworthy behavior: a work relations framework', *European Journal of Criminology*, 13: 274–94.

Zauberman, R. and Lévy, R. (2003). 'Police, minorities and the French republican ideal', *Criminology*, 41: 1065–100.

12 Good cops, bad cops

Why do police officers treat citizens (dis)respectfully? Findings from Belgium

Maarten Van Craen, Stephan Parmentier, and Mina Rauschenbach

Introduction

A burgeoning number of recent studies have demonstrated the importance of procedurally fair policing. Procedural fairness has been shown to foster trust in the police, police legitimacy, and several other forms of cooperative and supportive behavior among members of the public (Jackson et al. 2012; Murphy et al. 2014; Sunshine and Tyler 2003; Tankebe 2008; Van Craen and Skogan 2015a). Yet, recurrent citizen complaints and continual media reports of abusive and discriminatory treatment indicate that fostering procedural justice in the ranks is a great and permanent challenge—even in the most democratic societies. Excessive police force remains a prime issue of concern, in addition to other types of disrespectful and authoritarian treatment. Despite substantial inroads made by police forces around the world, media reports of corruption and police violence, as well as pervasive public perceptions of unfair treatment, continue to damage the reputation of police and undermine their legitimacy, especially among minority groups (Tyler 2005; Van Craen 2013; Van Craen and Skogan 2015b; Warren 2010).

This observation raises an intriguing question: many policymakers, academics, and citizens want fair policing but how do we best achieve it? To answer this question, we need to gain more insight into the factors that shape police officers' behavior. What makes police officers behave in procedurally fair or unfair ways? In recent papers, Van Craen (2016, 2017) has argued that part of the answer lies in the way police supervisors deal with officers. He found that the extent to which officers' behavior toward citizens was guided by the principles of neutrality, respect, voice, and accountability depended on the extent to which supervisors' behavior toward officers was characterized by these same principles. This "fair policing from the inside out" approach comprises a range of mechanisms that may explain this link, yet until now they have been insufficiently examined (for a first—partial—evaluation, see: Van Craen and Skogan 2016). The study on which we report here is part of a comparative project that aims at evaluating the value and generalizability of this theoretical framework.

In this chapter we hone in on one particular dimension of procedural fairness: respect. Research suggests that respectful treatment is a key factor shaping public trust in the police and popular views about police legitimacy. Stoutland (2001: 250), for instance, concluded—on the basis of ethnographic research—that respect is a crucial determinant of citizens' attitudes toward the police: "Respect was such an important expectation for community members that it often seemed to be the largest factor in determining whether they granted credibility to the police department." Given the importance of respectful treatment, it is necessary then to address which factors lead police officers to engage in respectful or disrespectful behavior. Building on the "fair policing from the inside out" approach (Van Craen 2016a, 2016b), we argue that respectful treatment by police supervisors in turn fosters respectful policing toward citizens. Or, to put it another way, that the extent to which police officers' behavior toward citizens is guided by the principle of respect depends on the extent to which supervisors' behavior toward officers is characterized by this principle.

(Dis)respect is a multifaceted issue. Stoutland (2001) has observed that citizens often felt disrespected when the police were rude and discourteous; when the police were arrogant and belittled people; when they felt the police were prejudiced and treated them differently because of their race or socioeconomic status; when the police did not take them or their complaints seriously; when the police failed to respond (quickly) when they reported an incident; and when police harassed people or used excessive force.

We do not deal with the issue of excessive police force in this chapter. This subject has been addressed in a number of recent articles (see, for instance: Bradford and Quinton 2014; Haas et al. 2015; Tyler et al. 2007; Van Craen and Skogan 2017). In this chapter we focus instead on minor forms of disrespectful treatment, like using harsh language or assuming an intimidating attitude toward citizens. "Minor" here only refers to the fact that they have no physical consequences for citizens. Minor forms of disrespect, however, do strongly determine public perceptions of and support for the police (Stoutland 2001). The scientific literature on the police indicates that minor forms of disrespectful treatment occur predominately in police encounters with offenders, and they are often a *reaction* to disrespect by offenders toward the police (Easton et al. 2009; Van Maanen 1974, 1978). Yet, we think that the way in which police officers deal with citizens is also the result of a social learning process that takes place inside the police organization itself. Heavy-handed and verbally aggressive behavior by supervisors, for instance, may lead officers to believe that such types of conduct are appropriate ways to exercise authority, make people comply, and/ or solve problems. This may encourage them to engage in similar behavior. Moreover, these forms of procedurally unfair supervision may increase the likelihood that officers treat citizens disrespectfully by arousing negative emotions (such as frustration and anger). In the next sections we further explain these mechanisms and empirically test the hypotheses derived from them.

Supervisors' influence

Supervisor modeling

Applying key ideas of the "fair policing from the inside out" approach (Van Craen 2016a, 2016b) to the principle of respect, we examine two mechanisms that may link (dis)respectful supervision to (dis)respectful policing. The first is supervisor modeling. The supervisor modeling thesis draws on elements of social learning theory (Bandura 1971). This theory argues that most behavior people display is learned through the influence of models. That is, people learn how to behave by observing and imitating other people's behavior (a process called "modeling"). Observers are most likely to imitate models with high status, power, or competence, as these attributes lead them to believe that their model's behavior is appropriate to the situation and has been rewarded in the past. In the management and organizational psychology literature, this theory has been applied to employee–supervisor relationships to help understand organizational socialization (Weiss 1977). Specifically, it has been argued that employees learn how to behave in a work context by observing and imitating other people in the organization. The high status, power, and/or competence of supervisors increase the likelihood that employees will choose them as role models. Supervisors' behaviors signal to employees the expectations and intended norms of the organization. This information encourages those at the lower levels to emulate these apparently adaptive behaviors, especially when they believe that engaging in similar behavior will lead to organizationally mediated rewards.

Research in commercial organizations has shown that modeling is a relevant factor in understanding employees' behavior. Ruiz-Palomino and Martinez-Cañas (2011), for instance, have demonstrated that supervisor modeling can shape ethical behavior in the banking and insurance sectors. More specifically, they found that the perceived ethical behavior of supervisors can stimulate employees' intention to behave ethically. Through a process of supervisor modeling, ethical leadership increases the likelihood that employees will behave in an ethical way as well. Another illustrative example is Robertson and Barling's (2013) study on the role of social learning in shaping pro-environmental behaviors in organizations. They argued that when employees witness their leaders engage in pro-environmental behaviors, they learn how they can engage in such behaviors themselves, and that those behaviors are normatively expected, valued, and rewarded in their organization. These perceptions motivate employees to imitate their leaders and behave in similar ways. Empirical research has confirmed that leaders' workplace pro-environmental behaviors indeed stimulate employees' workplace pro-environmental behaviors.

In light of this, we hypothesize that police officers model respectful supervision in their dealings with citizens. When officers experience their supervisors treating them graciously and tactfully, they observe respect in action and experience the importance of this principle. This may encourage officers to be courteous and tactful themselves in their dealings with citizens. There is, further, also reason to assume that police officers imitate disrespectful supervision. Tests of social learning theory have revealed the power of negative behavior modeling as well. This issue has been studied considerably in the context of child-parent relationships. Muller et al. (1995), for instance, used a social learning approach to explain the intergenerational transmission of aggressive behavior. They hypothesized that an individual's tendency to manifest aggressive behavior is a consequence of the observational learning that takes place when receiving corporal punishment from parents. Empirical research among parents and their children (college students) confirmed this hypothesis. Greater levels of corporal punishment by one's own parents predicted greater levels of corporal punishment by new parents when dealing with their children. Similarly, children who received more corporal punishment from their parents were more likely to exhibit subsequent aggressive behaviors. Complementing these findings, a study by Mihalic and Elliott (1997) showed that girls who witnessed parental violence as a child— parental violence was measured as parents physically hurting each other—were more likely to be a violent adolescent—measured as hitting teachers, students, and/or parents—than those who did not witness parental violence. By extrapolation, modeling negative behavior implies that officers will also imitate supervisors' disrespectful behavior. Verbally aggressive behavior by supervisors, for instance, will lead officers to believe that such conduct is an appropriate way to exercise authority, make people comply, and/or solve problems. This will encourage them to engage in similar behavior.

Negative emotions

In addition to supervisor modeling, negative emotions may play a role in generating and explaining a link between procedurally unfair supervision and procedurally unfair policing. To theorize this mechanism, Van Craen (2016a, 2016b) combined elements of general strain theory (Agnew 1992) and frustration-aggression theory (Dollard et al. 1939). General strain theory states that strains generate negative emotions (such as frustration and anger). Agnew (1992: 50, 2001: 320) defined strains as "relationships in which others are not treating the individual as he or she would like to be treated." He classified the most common strains in three categories: events/conditions that involve goal blockage, the loss of positive stimuli, and the presentation of negative stimuli. Van Craen (2016a, 2016b) inferred from general strain theory that procedurally unfair supervision can involve different types of strain. For example, biased and disrespectful treatment implies the presentation of negative stimuli. Not allowing officers to give input is a case of goal blockage. And making decisions that affect officers—for instance, changing their tasks, watch, or beat—without giving them an explanation often results in a painful loss of positive stimuli. According to general strain theory, such strains cause negative emotions (such as frustration and anger).

Negative emotions are uncomfortable and thus create a pressure to reduce the degree of emotional tension. One way to do this is through aggression.

However, occupational constraints make it unlikely that aggravating supervisors will become the target of this aggression. Rather, it has been argued that when retaliation or punishment is feared from aggravating persons, aggression toward these persons will likely be controlled and redirected toward or displaced onto less powerful targets (Dollard et al. 1939; Marcus-Newhall et al. 2000; Miller 1941). In this particular case, aggression toward police supervisors would likely lead to disciplinary sanctions or even dismissal, so one might plausibly expect aggression to be displaced onto other targets, such as citizens. The probability that citizens will become targets of displaced aggression may be increased by the context in which police–citizens interaction occur. Psychological theorization and research suggest that interactions that take place in a negative setting are likely to trigger displaced aggression (Marcus-Newhall et al. 2000). Therefore, as many police–citizen contacts occur in a negative context, it is highly probable that citizens will be "chosen" as targets. We suggest that by arousing negative emotions among officers, disrespectful treatment by supervisors will increase the likelihood that officers are verbally or physically aggressive toward citizens.

Citizens' influence

When studying disrespectful policing we of course have to take into account the role of citizens—and, particularly, those who are offenders. Most obviously, it is often difficult to arrest offenders of serious crimes in a polite and courteous way. But also, we know from studies carried out in different eras and countries, that the way officers treat citizens depends on the degree to which citizens challenge their definition of the situation, their identity, and their authority (Easton et al. 2009; Loftus 2010; Van Maanen 1974, 1978). Disrespectful treatment toward offenders is often a reaction to what officers perceive as disrespectful behavior toward themselves by perpetrators of minor crimes, people who cause disorder, or perpetrators of traffic offenses. In these cases, negative emotions (such as frustration and anger) are likely to play a role as mediating factors. Disrespectful citizen behavior may cause frustration and anger in and of itself but it may also trigger a broader set of frustrations. Van Maanen (1978: 323) concluded on the basis of ethnographic research that disrespectful policing toward those who challenged officers' authority provided an expressive outlet for much of the frustration engendered by policing: "To the patrolman, one particular asshole symbolizes all those that remain 'out there' untouched, untaught, and unpunished." Disrespectful police actions, according to Van Maanen (1978: 323),

> release some of the pent-up energies stored up over a period in which small but cumulative indignities are suffered by the police at the hands of the community elites, the courts, the politicians, the uncaught crooks, the press, and numerous others. The asshole stands, then, as a ready ersatz for those whom the police will never—short of a miracle—be in a position to directly encounter and confront.

Finally, we consider it plausible that contact with offenders can also indirectly affect the treatment of law-abiding citizens by creating a knock-on effect. The emotional tension caused by encounters with offenders—both from the offenses themselves and from the disrespectful behavior toward officers—may not have completely subsided when officers later come into contact with law-abiding citizens. Consequently, a residual internal pressure to reduce emotional tension may encourage police officers to behave untactfully or unkindly toward law-abiding citizens.

Hypotheses and conceptual model

Based on these arguments, we hypothesize that disrespectful supervision is related to disrespectful policing both directly (modeling hypothesis), and indirectly, via negative affect. Likewise, we hypothesize that contact with offenders is both directly and indirectly (via negative affect) related to disrespectful policing. The hypothesized relationships are illustrated in Figure 12.1.

Context of the study

To test our hypotheses, we use data collected in Belgium (for more information on the data collection, see below). Policing in Belgium is guided by the

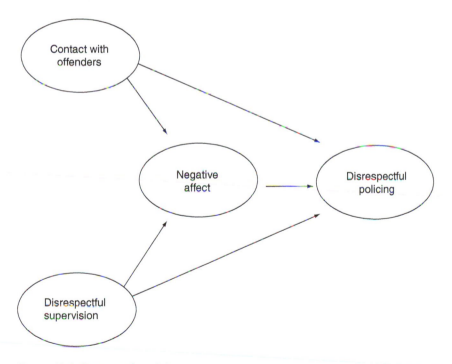

Figure 12.1 Conceptual model.

community policing model. Belgium introduced this model at the turn of the millennium, after it was confronted with the Dutroux case. In 1996, Marc Dutroux was arrested for the abduction of six girls. Two of them were found alive but help was too late for the four others. In response, nearly 300,000 people expressed dissatisfaction with the police and judiciary in an unusually large public demonstration known as the "White March." The Belgian government used this as an impetus for far-reaching police reform. In 1998, the governing parties, supported by most of the opposition parties, decided to merge the different existing police forces into what has been called "the integrated police, organized at two levels: the federal level and the local level." At the local level, 196 local police zones were created (since then, this number has been reduced to 189), each of which has their own police chief and considerable autonomy to address local problems. The role of the federal component is to complement that of the local police zones: the federal police has more specialized duties, is charged with supra-local tasks, and supports the local police zones wherever necessary. To further ensure unity in the integrated police force, a single status was introduced that applies to officers at both levels, and a new, quasi-identical uniform was implemented for officers of the federal and local police (only a few details differ). Additionally, a common logo was designed for both components of the integrated police force, and an identical training program was developed for all officers (Bruggeman et al. 2009).

Along with the new organizational structure, policymakers introduced a new community policing model. The implementation of this model has been gradual however. In 2003, authorities explicitly defined community policing in Belgium based on five pillars: external orientation, problem solving, partnership, accountability, and empowerment (Vande Sompel et al. 2003a, 2003b). This community-oriented approach has been complemented with information-led policing. The objective of this combined approach—which guides the role of both the federal and the local police—is to work toward "excellent policing" (Bruggeman et al. 2007). This implies, among other things, "establishing and maintaining a trust relationship between the population and the police" (Bruggeman et al. 2007: 19). Surveys of the general population show that, in the last ten years, trust in the police in Belgium is relatively high, compared to trust in other institutions (Van Craen and Ackaert 2006; European Social Survey (ESS) 2010; ESS 2014). Yet, in certain groups, such as ethnic minority groups, levels of trust in the police are well below the national average (Van Craen and Ackaert 2006; Vancluysen et al. 2009). In the past few years, both the media and academic researchers have reported widespread beliefs about police discrimination and disrespect toward ethnic minority groups. These factors negatively affect minorities' trust in law enforcement (Van Craen 2012, 2013; Van Craen and Skogan 2015b). Research has also revealed that certain ethnic minorities, especially male youths, are more frequently perceived by police as exhibiting disrespectful or challenging behavior (Easton et al. 2009).

Recently, in November 2016, Belgian police were criticized by Human Rights Watch, a nongovernmental watchdog organization, for treating Muslims disrespectfully and aggressively during operations following the Brussels terrorist attacks. Other cases that have attracted media attention were, among others, those in which disproportionate police force was used against mentally ill and aggressive juveniles, non-mentally ill youths (on the street and in pubs), and demonstrators. Minor forms of disrespectful treatment occur as well (Easton et al. 2009) but most of them go unnoticed by those who were not present at the scene.

Methods

Data

The data we use to test our hypotheses are derived from an officer survey conducted in the city of Ghent in 2015. Ghent is the second-largest city in the Dutch-speaking part of Belgium and has roughly 260,000 inhabitants. About 30 percent of them are not of Belgian descent. The "local police zone Ghent" consists of six police districts, each of which has one main police station (some have a few smaller police stations in addition). The Ghent Police Department consists of about 1,000 officers. The four main units—in terms of number of officers—are Neighborhood Policing, Interventions, Traffic Police, and the Local Criminal Investigation Force. The first two units have approximately 300 officers and the latter two approximately 100.

In total, 510 police officers of the Ghent Police Department were interviewed. The fieldwork ran from March to June 2015. All officers of the four largest units—Neighborhood Policing, Interventions, Traffic Police, and the Local Criminal Investigation Force—and of a few smaller units were invited to participate in the survey. The questionnaire was distributed at briefings/team meetings and the officers were asked to fill out the questionnaire immediately. Special efforts were made to prevent/limit social desirability effects. Supervisors were often present when officers answered the questionnaire but the research team ensured that they did not walk through the room when the questionnaires were completed. The researchers also guaranteed anonymity and confidentiality. Respondents' names were not asked and completed questionnaires were only handed to members of the research team. No one working for the Ghent Police Department was allowed to see the completed questionnaires, nor were they allowed access to the data file. To further assuage officers' potential worries of being identified, the number of questions about personal background information was limited and age was measured using 11 five-year categories. Social desirability may nonetheless still have influenced some answer distributions.

Data was gathered at 39 briefings/team meetings and 63 percent of the potential respondents (all officers of the selected units) filled out the questionnaire. In comparison with similar officer surveys in other countries, this is a relatively high response rate (see, for instance: Bradford et al. 2014; Skogan et al. 2015). Hardly anyone refused to fill out the questionnaire. Nonresponse was often due to non-attendance at briefings/team meetings (some officers had to work on the street, had a day off, or were ill) and certain units' limited team meetings.

About 70 percent of the respondents were male and 30 percent female. Most respondents held the lowest or second-lowest rank (86 percent in total) and only a small group of respondents held supervisory responsibilities. Large groups of respondents worked for the "Interventions" unit (42 percent) or the "Neighborhood Policing" unit (34 percent). About 11 percent worked for the Local Criminal Investigation Force and 8 percent for the Traffic Police. Compared to the broader police population, officers in the "Interventions" unit were slightly overrepresented and officers of the "Traffic Police" slightly underrepresented but the overall composition of the dataset closely resembled that of the population.

Measures

The core theoretical concepts—disrespectful supervision, contact with offenders, negative affect, and disrespectful policing—were all measured using multiple indicators (see Table 12.1). The items measuring (perceptions of) disrespectful supervision employed a six-point Likert-type response scale ranging from 1 (strongly agree) to 6 (strongly disagree). Answers to questions dealing with negative emotions and disrespectful behavior toward citizens could be indicated on

Table 12.1 Operationalizations and factor loadings (CFA)

Disrespectful supervision:	
• My supervisors sometimes use harsh words.	0.74
• My supervisors can sometimes be less than tactful in their communication with officers.	0.70
• The attitude and talk of my supervisors sometimes come across as intimidating.	0.88
Contact with offenders:	
• During work, how often do you come in contact with perpetrators of serious crimes?	0.58
• During work, how often do you come in contact with perpetrators of minor crimes?	0.84
• During work, how often do you come in contact with people who cause disorder?	0.85
• During work, how often do you come in contact with perpetrators of traffic offenses?	0.56
Negative affect:	
• Does it happen that you feel upset because of events that happened at work? (anger)	0.80
• Does it happen that events take place at work which make you angry? (anger)	0.90
• Does it happen that you feel you are being thwarted at work? (frustration)	0.65
• Does it happen in your job that you are unable to attain your own goals? (frustration)	0.51
Disrespectful policing:	
• I use harsh language toward citizens.	0.60
• I am not very tactful toward citizens.	0.65
• I assume an intimidating attitude toward citizens.	0.74

Notes
Model fit statistics: Chi-square=181.328; d.f.=72; $p < 0.001$; RMSEA=0.055; CFI=0.954.

a six-point Likert-type response scale ranging from 1 (never) to 6 (very often). The frequency with which respondents came into contact with different types of offenders was measured using a seven-point Likert-type response scale ranging from 1 (more than eight times a day) to 7 (less than once a week). The variables "disrespectful supervision" and "contact with offenders" were reversed coded to facilitate the interpretation of the results. We used confirmatory factor analysis (CFA) to simultaneously estimate and validate the key measures. Table 12.1 presents an overview of the operationalizations and factor loadings.

Findings

We employed structural equation modeling (SEM) to test the expected relationships. We developed a structural equation model specifying the hypothesized links between the four theoretical variables and the influence of two additional variables which have been commonly used in research on police officers' perceptions and behavior: age and gender (0 = female; 1 = male). Age was measured using 11 five-year categories to ensure anonymity. Figure 12.2 illustrates the results of the SEM analysis. In this figure only the significant effects are depicted.

The results indicate that there is an empirical link between perceptions of disrespectful treatment by supervisors and disrespectful officer behavior in dealings with the public: The latent variable "disrespectful supervision" is positively and significantly correlated with the latent variable "disrespectful policing." The results further suggest that perceived internal disrespect has an indirect impact on external disrespect through negative affect. The latent variable "disrespectful supervision" is positively correlated with the latent variable "negative affect," and negative affect is in turn positively associated with "disrespectful policing."

Encounters with offenders also shape disrespectful policing. The latent variable "contact with offenders" is positively correlated with the latent variable "disrespectful policing." The more often officers come into contact with offenders, the more frequently their behavior is characterized by external disrespect. Interactions with offenders also seem to have an indirect impact on external disrespect through negative affect. The latent variable "contact with offenders" is positively correlated with the latent variable "negative affect," and negative affect in turn is positively associated with "disrespectful policing."

Finally, we note that age and gender determines officers' behavior toward citizens. Age influences officer behavior directly through contact with offenders, and indirectly through negative affect. The age variable is negatively correlated with the latent variable "disrespectful policing": the older officers are, the less likely they are to treat citizens disrespectfully. Furthermore, age has a strong impact on the frequency with which officers come into contact with offenders: older officers are less likely to deal with offenders. And, as we have mentioned above, the less often officers come into contact with offenders, the less often their behavior is characterized by external disrespect. Age also has in indirect

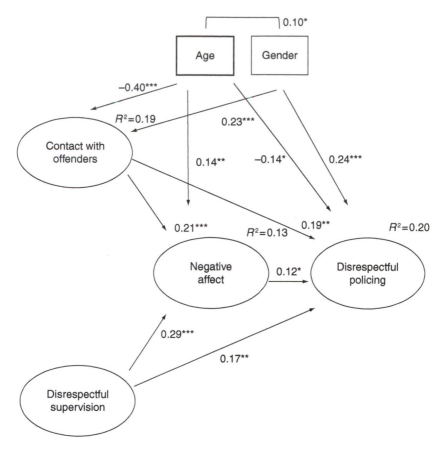

Figure 12.2 Factors explaining disrespectful policing.

Notes
Chi-square = 209.725; d.f. = 95; $p < 0.001$; RMSEA = 0.049; CFI = 0.955
$*p < 0.050; **p < 0.010; ***p < 0.001$.

impact through negative affect. The age variable is positively correlated with negative affect: the older officers are, the more often they feel angry and frustrated. Negative affect, in turn, is positively associated with "disrespectful policing."

Figure 12.2 indicates two ways in which gender shapes officers' behavior toward citizens. First, there is a direct link with external disrespect. Gender is positively correlated with the latent variable "disrespectful policing." This means that men are more likely to treat citizens disrespectfully than women. In addition to this direct link, there is also an indirect link between gender and disrespectful policing. Gender is positively correlated with the latent variable "contact with offenders." Men come into contact with offenders more frequently than women, leading them to behave more disrespectfully toward citizens.

We found no significant effects between age and gender on perceptions of disrespectful supervision. As far as the principle of respect is concerned, female and male officers report feeling treated by supervisors in the same way, as do younger officers and older officers.

Conclusion and discussion

Our findings and theoretical approaches complement a growing body of literature on the importance of procedural justice in police organizations. In this domain, researchers have shown particular interest in the relationship between procedurally fair police supervision and officers' (attitude toward) the use of force. Extant literature on this subject suggests that internal organizational procedural justice and the fair use of force by police officers are indirectly linked through officers' compliance with rules and orders. Research has also shown that fair supervision increases officers' compliance with their supervisors and the policies of the organization (Bradford et al. 2014; Tyler et al. 2007). Furthermore, scholars have argued that compliance is a factor in preventing the excessive police use of force (Haas et al. 2015; Tyler et al. 2007). Empirical tests which evaluate all aspects of this mechanism are scarce, yet there is still some evidence to support it. A recent study by Haas et al. (2015) in Buenos Aires—where police violence is a significant problem—has found that perceptions of internal procedural justice foster compliance with supervisors and policies, and consequently encourage police officers to accept the existing restrictions on the use of force.

Research has also suggested that the link between internal procedural justice and the endorsement of restrictions on the use of force may be mediated by officers' identification with their organization and their perceptions of self-legitimacy. Bradford and Quinton (2014) found that when police officers feel fairly treated by their organization, they identify more strongly with it and establish a firmer sense of their own legitimacy. These factors, in turn, enhance officers' commitment to the use of proportionate force. In analyzing the relationship between fair supervision and officers' use of force, Tankebe and Meško (2015) placed a similar emphasis on the mediating role of officers' self-legitimacy. Yet no recent attempts have been made to further theorize and clarify the role of officers' identification with their organization. Bradford and Quinton's study indicated that identification with the police organization and self-legitimacy are very strongly correlated but so far the question of whether the former shapes the latter or whether these mediators are two aspects of the same thing remains unanswered.

Besides this issue, there are several other gaps in the literature. First, compared to excessive use of force, minor forms of disrespectful citizen treatment have received much less attention. Second, most of the previously mentioned studies have focused on attitudes toward the use of force, not actual police behavior. This limitation is important, as officers' behavior may not (completely) reflect their attitudes. Overwhelming support for procedural fairness principles of "voice" and "accountability," for instance, does not mean these principles are frequently put into practice (Van Craen and Parmentier 2015). Explanations for this incongruence could be high workloads and the low status of these responsibilities in officers' hierarchy of priorities (for research on the latter aspect, see: Loftus 2010). Further, it seems likely that professionalism or the fear of being sanctioned can motivate officers to act in ways that do not correspond with their personal beliefs. Therefore, both officers' attitudes/views and behavior deserve more scholarly attention. Third, newly developed theoretical insights can be used to further disentangle the relationship between (aspects of) fair supervision and (aspects of) fair policing. In the study we reported here, we have taken steps toward filling in the latter three gaps. First, the research focus was not directed on the excessive use of force but on minor forms of disrespectful treatment, like using harsh language and assuming an intimidating attitude toward citizens. Second, we have moved beyond explaining officers' attitude toward (dis)respectful policing and instead measured their actual behavior. Third, we used key ideas from the "fair policing from the inside out" approach (Van Craen 2016a, 2016b) as a framework to advance empirical knowledge on (dis)respectful policing.

More specifically, we hypothesized that disrespectful policing partly flows from disrespectful supervision, and that disrespectful supervision shapes disrespectful policing both directly (modeling hypothesis) and indirectly, via negative affect. We expected that the way in which police officers deal with citizens would partly be the result of a social learning process that takes place inside the police organization. Heavy-handed and verbally aggressive behavior by supervisors, for instance, may lead officers to believe that such types of conduct are appropriate ways to exercise authority, make people comply, and/or solve problems. This may encourage them to engage in similar behavior. Moreover, we expected that these forms of procedurally unfair supervision would increase the likelihood that officers treat citizens disrespectfully by arousing negative emotions (such as frustration and anger). Disrespectful behavior toward citizens may be a way to reduce the degree of emotional tension that is caused by disrespectful supervision. Furthermore, we hypothesized that disrespectful policing partly flows from contact with offenders. Building on the existing literature on police–citizen interactions and broadening our reflections on the role of negative emotions, we expected that contact with offenders would shape disrespectful policing both directly and indirectly, via negative affect.

Our empirical findings seem to confirm all of these hypotheses. We found a positive correlation between the variables "contact with offenders" and "disrespectful policing," which suggests that contact with offenders directly influences the extent to which officers' behavior is characterized by the principle of respect. In addition, we found that "contact with offenders" correlates positively with "negative affect," and that negative affect in turn is positively associated with "disrespectful policing." This suggests that interactions with offenders can also have an indirect impact on external disrespect through negative affect.

Summarizing these findings, we conclude that more frequent interactions with offenders can lead officers to engage in disrespectful policing more often. We note that in certain cases, a heavy-handed approach may be required and can be part of the legitimate execution of police duties. Arresting offenders of serious crimes, for instance, is often difficult to carry out in a gentle or friendly way. However, disrespectful policing is also partly the result of contact with perpetrators of minor crimes, perpetrators of traffic offenses, and people who cause disorder. We emphasize that a SEM model in which "contact with offenders" is operationalized with only the latter three indicators yields similar results as those shown in Figure 12.2. This is in line with previous research, which indicates that disrespectful policing is a reaction to what officers perceive as disrespectful behavior by perpetrators of minor crimes, people who cause disorder, or perpetrators of traffic offenses. These people are perceived as disrespectful when they challenge officers' definition of the situation, their identity, or their authority (Easton et al. 2009; Loftus 2010; Van Maanen 1974, 1978). Our study suggests that disrespectful policing to some extent is a means to reduce the degree of emotional tension that is caused by the (perceived) disrespectful behavior of offenders. In addition to this, it seems also likely that contact with offenders can shape external disrespect by arousing negative emotions in reaction to the offenses themselves. The nature of our data did not enable us, however, to separate these two mechanisms and assess their relative explanatory power. This is a limitation that could be addressed in future research.

Another limitation is that we have no information on the types of people that are treated disrespectfully. Does contact with offenders lead *only* to the disrespectful treatment of the offenders with whom officers have interacted, or does it also affect the treatment of law-abiding citizens? On the basis of our data, we cannot give an empirically supported answer to this question, as our study only measured disrespectful behavior toward citizens in general. We do, however, consider it plausible that contact with offenders also affects the treatment of law-abiding citizens. The emotional tension that is caused by offender contact—in reaction to the offenses themselves and/or the disrespectful behavior of offenders—may not have completely subsided by the time officers come into contact with law-abiding citizens. Consequently, a residual internal pressure to reduce emotional tension may lead police officers to behave toward law-abiding citizens in a way that is not very tactful or kind. Future research could evaluate this hypothesis and contribute to advancing cumulative scientific knowledge by scrutinizing officers' behavior toward both offenders and law-abiding citizens. To address these limitations, it may be valuable to complement survey research with participant observation and mixed methods research.

The main focus in this chapter was on the relationship between disrespectful police supervision and disrespectful policing. The two claims we made regarding this relationship seem to be confirmed by our empirical results. We found a positive correlation between (perceived) disrespectful supervision and disrespectful policing, which suggests that supervisor modeling plays a role in shaping officers' behavior toward citizens. Officers' tendency to manifest disrespectful behavior on the street is, to some extent, a consequence of the observational learning that takes place when experiencing disrespectful supervision. In addition, we found that (perceived) disrespectful supervision positively correlates with negative affect, and that negative affect in turn is positively associated with disrespectful policing. This suggests that experiences of being treated disrespectfully by supervisors also indirectly shape external disrespect, through negative emotions. Disrespectful behavior toward citizens to some extent is a way to reduce the degree of emotional tension that is caused by disrespectful supervision.

One could remark that the impact of negative affect on disrespectful policing in our model is not very strong, and conclude from this that negative emotions only play a limited role in shaping officers' behavior toward citizens. We think, however, that the actual influence of negative affect on disrespectful policing is stronger than what we were able to measure. Two observations lead us to make this claim. First, it seems likely that our study—and survey research in general— underestimates the frequency with which police officers behave disrespectfully toward citizens. When survey questions deal with a sensitive topic, there is a risk that respondents answer in a socially desirable way. Therefore, we suppose that the actual frequency of disrespectful policing is somewhat higher than the one reported by officers here and that the coefficient in our model underestimates the strength of the correlation between negative affect and disrespectful policing. Second, we note that survey research is often based on well-reasoned reflections by respondents on their emotions and behavior, while the negative affect thesis explains impulsive actions and reactions. Given the nature of survey research, it is possible that it is too limited to demonstrate the full explanatory power of this mechanism. In psychology, many of the displaced aggression studies have used experimental designs (Marcus-Newhall et al. 2000). So, further reflection on how to more comprehensively test our hypotheses is needed, and it may turn out that studies using complementary methodologies will find a stronger influence of negative affect.

Another aspect that deserves more attention is the role of stress in shaping disrespectful treatment of citizens. Negative emotions and stress are highly correlated (Cannaerts 2016), and stress may mediate the relationship between disrespectful supervision and disrespectful policing (and the relationship between contact with offenders and disrespectful policing) as well (Van Craen 2016b). Following general strain theory, one can conceptualize internal procedural unfairness as a strain. However, building on the job strain model (Karasek and Theorell 1990) and Noblet et al.'s (2012) thinking about the relationship between organizational justice and work stress, one can theorize that perceptions of internal procedural unfairness *cause* strain. Strain/stress, in turn, may decrease officers' level of external procedural fairness as it leads people to react more impulsively and less deliberately (Keinan et al. 1987). All of this implies that strain/stress may be conceived as a factor mediating the relationship between disrespectful supervision and disrespectful policing, and as a factor associated with frustration and anger (Van Craen 2016b). In a similar way, stress/strain is also likely to link contact with offenders and disrespectful policing.

Summarizing our findings with regard to the subject of police supervision, we can conclude that disrespectful leadership inside the police organization often leads officers to engage in disrespectful behavior on the street. This conclusion has important implications for policy and strategies aimed at fostering procedural fairness in the police ranks. Police organizations that instruct police officers to treat citizens respectfully can and should help them meet this expectation by providing good examples and setting the right tone in their internal leadership practices.

Bibliography

Agnew, R. (1992). 'Foundation for a general strain theory of crime and delinquency', *Criminology*, 30: 47–87.

Agnew, R. (2001). 'Building on the foundation of general strain theory: specifying the types of strain most likely to lead to crime and delinquency', *Journal of Research in Crime and Delinquency*, 38: 319–61.

Bandura, A. (1971). *Social Learning Theory*, New York: General Learning Press.

Bradford, B. and Quinton, P. (2014). 'Self-legitimacy, police culture and support for democratic policing in an English constabulary', *British Journal of Criminology*, 54: 1023–46.

Bradford, B., Quinton, P., Myhill, A., and Porter, G. (2014). 'Why do 'the law' comply? Procedural justice, group identification and officer motivation in police organizations', *European Journal of Criminology*, 11: 110–32.

Bruggeman, W., Devroe, E., and Easton, M. (2009). *Evaluatie 10 jaar politiehervorming* [Ten years of reforms of the police: an evaluation], Brussels: Federal Police Council.

Bruggeman, W., Van Branteghem, J.-M., and Van Nuffel, D. (2007). *Toward an Excellent Police Function*, Brussels: Politeia.

Cannaerts, M. (2016). *Stress, frustratie en jobtevredenheid bij de politie* [Police officers' sense of stress, frustration, and job satisfaction], Leuven: KU Leuven.

Dollard, J., Doob, L., Miller, N., Mowrer, O., and Sears, R. (1939). *Frustration and Aggression*, New Haven, CT: Yale University Press.

Easton, M., Ponsaers, P., Demarée, C., Vandevoorde, N., Enhus, E., Elffers, H., Hutsebaut, F., and Moor, L. (2009). *Multiple Community Policing: Hoezo?* Ghent: Academia Press.

European Social Survey Round 5 Data (2010). NSD – Norwegian Centre for Research Data, Norway – Data Archive and distributor of ESS data for ESS ERIC.

European Social Survey Round 7 Data (2014). NSD – Norwegian Centre for Research Data, Norway – Data Archive and distributor of ESS data for ESS ERIC.

Haas, N., Van Craen, M., Skogan, W., and Fleitas, D. (2015). 'Explaining officer compliance: the importance of procedural justice and trust inside a police organization', *Criminology and Criminal Justice*, 15: 442–63.

Jackson, J., Bradford, B., Hough, M., Myhill, A., Quinton, P., and Tyler, T. (2012). 'Why do people comply with the law? Legitimacy and the influence of legal institutions', *British Journal of Criminology*, 52: 1051–71.

Karasek, R. and Theorell, T. (1990). *Healthy Work: Stress, Productivity, and the Reconstruction of Working Life*, New York: Harper Collins.

Keinan, G., Friedland, N., and Ben-Porath, Y. (1987). 'Decision making under stress: scanning of alternatives under physical threat', *Acta Psychologica*, 64: 219–28.

Loftus, B. (2010). 'Police occupational culture: classic themes, altered times', *Policing and Society*, 20: 1–20.

Marcus-Newhall, A., Pedersen, W., Carlson, M., and Miller, N. (2000). 'Displaced aggression is alive and well: a meta-analytic review', *Journal of Personality and Social Psychology*, 78: 670–89.

Mihalic, S. and Elliott, D. (1997). 'A social learning theory model of marital violence', *Journal of Family Violence*, 12: 21–47.

Miller, N. (1941). 'The frustration–aggression hypothesis', *Psychological Review*, 48: 337–42.

Muller, R., Hunter, J., and Stollak, G. (1995). 'The intergenerational transmission of corporal punishment: a comparison of social learning and temperament models', *Child Abuse and Neglect*, 19: 1323–35.

Murphy, K., Mazerolle, L., and Bennett, S. (2014). 'Promoting trust in police: findings from a randomised experimental field trial of procedural justice policing', *Policing and Society*, 24: 405–24.

Noblet, A., Maharee-Lawler, S., and Rodwell, J. (2012). 'Using job strain and organizational justice models to predict multiple forms of employee performance behaviours among Australian policing personnel', *The International Journal of Human Resource Management*, 23: 3009–26.

Robertson, J. and Barling, J. (2013). 'Greening organizations through leaders' influence on employees' pro-environmental behaviors', *Journal of Organizational Behavior*, 34: 176–94.

Ruiz-Palomino, P. and Martinez-Cañas, R. (2011). 'Supervisor role modeling, ethics-related organizational policies, and employee ethical intention: the moderating impact of moral ideology', *Journal of Business Ethics*, 102: 653–68.

Skogan, W., Van Craen, M., and Hennessy, C. (2015). 'Training police for procedural justice', *Journal of Experimental Criminology*, 11: 319–34.

Stoutland, S. (2001). 'The multiple dimensions of trust in resident/police relations in Boston', *Journal of Research in Crime and Delinquency*, 38: 226–56.

Sunshine, J. and Tyler, T. (2003). 'The role of procedural justice and legitimacy in shaping public support for policing', *Law and Society Review*, 37: 513–47.

Tankebe, J. (2008). 'Police effectiveness and police trustworthiness in Ghana: an empirical appraisal', *Criminology and Criminal Justice*, 8: 185–202.

Tankebe, J. and Meško, G. (2015). 'Police self-legitimacy, use of force, and pro-organizational behavior in Slovenia', in G. Meško and J. Tankebe (eds.), *Trust and Legitimacy in Criminal Justice. European Perspectives*, Cham: Springer International Publishing, 261–77.

Tyler, T. (2005). 'Policing in Black and White: ethnic group differences in trust and confidence in the police', *Police Quarterly*, 8: 322–42.

Tyler, T., Callahan, P., and Frost, J. (2007). 'Armed, and dangerous (?): motivating rule adherence among agents of social control', *Law and Society Review*, 41: 457–92.

Vancluysen, K., Van Craen, M., and Ackaert, J. (2009). *Gekleurde steden. Autochtonen en allochtonen over samenleven* [Coloured cities. Majority and minority group members on living together], Bruges: Vanden Broele.

Van Craen, M. (2012). 'Determinants of ethnic minority confidence in the police', *Journal of Ethnic and Migration Studies*, 38: 1029–47.

Van Craen, M. (2013). 'Explaining majority and minority trust in the police', *Justice Quarterly*, 30: 1042–67.

Van Craen, M. (2016a). 'Understanding police officers' trust and trustworthy behavior: a work relations framework', *European Journal of Criminology*, 13: 274–94.

Van Craen, M. (2016b). 'Fair policing from the inside out', in M. Deflem (ed.), *The Politics of Policing: Between Force and Legitimacy*, Book Series: Sociology of Crime, Law, and Deviance, Volume 21, Bingley, UK: Emerald, 3–19.

Van Craen, M. and Ackaert, J. (2006). *De Veiligheidsscan. Instrument voor een lokaal veiligheids- en leefbaarheidsbeleid* [The Safety Scan. Tool for a local safety and livability policy], Antwerpen: Maklu.

Van Craen, M. and Parmentier, S. (2015). *Survey politie Gent 2015: Beschrijvende resultaten* [Ghent officer survey 2015: Descriptive results], Leuven: KU Leuven.

Van Craen, M. and Skogan, W. (2015a). 'Trust in the Belgian police: the importance of responsiveness', *European Journal of Criminology*, 12: 129–50.

Van Craen, M. and Skogan, W (2015b). 'Differences and similarities in the explanation of ethnic minority groups' trust in the police', *European Journal of Criminology*, 12: 300–23.

Van Craen, M. and Skogan, W. (2016). 'Achieving fairness in policing: the link between internal and external procedural justice', *Police Quarterly*, online. Available http://journals.sagepub.com/doi/pdf/10.1177/1098611116657818 (accessed 20 January 2017).

Van Craen, M. and Skogan, W. (2017). 'Officer endorsement of use of force policy: the role of fair supervision', *Criminal Justice and Behavior*, 44: 843–61.

Vande Sompel, R., Ponsaers, P., Vandevenne, Y., and Van Branteghem, J. (2003a). *De pijlers van de gemeenschapsgerichte politiezorg in België* [The pillars of community (oriented) policing in Belgium], Brussels: Directie van de Relaties met de Lokale Politie.

Vande Sompel, R., Ponsaers, P., Vandevenne, Y., and Van Branteghem, J. (2003b). *Bronnen van community (oriented) policing en de toepassing ervan in België* [Origins of Community (oriented) Policing and Carrying It into Execution in Belgium], Brussels: Directie van de Relaties met de Lokale Politie.

Van Maanen, J. (1974). 'Working the street: a developmental view of police behavior', in H. Jacob (ed.), *The Potential for Reform of Criminal Justice*, Beverly Hills, CA: Sage, 83–130.

Van Maanen, J. (1978). 'The asshole', in P. Manning and J. Van Maanen (eds.), *Policing: A View from the Street*, Santa Monica, CA: Goodyear Publishing Company, 221–38.

Warren, P. (2010). 'The continuing significance of race: an analysis across two levels of policing', *Social Science Quarterly*, 91: 1025–42.

Weiss, H. (1977). 'Subordinate imitation of supervisor behavior: the role of modeling in organizational socialization', *Organizational Behavior and Human Performance*, 19: 89–105.

13 Trust in the Finnish police and crime reporting – findings in the context of Nordic countries

Juha Kääriäinen

Introduction

Public trust in the police has been the subject of a considerable body of research in recent years. Trust in the police is deemed vital for promoting cooperation between the police and citizens. The underlying assumption is that a secure society is created through cooperation between the authorities entrusted with security (such as the police) and citizens.

Cooperation between citizens and the police in safeguarding public order or preventing crime can be examined from a number of perspectives, only one of which is the reporting of offences to the police for criminal investigation. Common sense suggests that public trust in the police and the willingness of citizens to report offences or anti-social behaviour should go hand in hand. If victims or persons close to them believe that the police are helpful, honest, and efficient public servants, they will naturally turn to the police for help. The theoretical literature in the field also assumes that public trust in the police automatically increases citizens' willingness to report offences or anti-social behaviour to the police (e.g., Jackson *et al.* 2012; Tyler and Huo 2002).

However, the existence of a correlation between trust and willingness to report is controversial at best, according to the surprisingly limited available empirical evidence. The few studies that have been conducted (see below) do not seem to confirm the hypothesis that public trust in the police translates into increased readiness among citizens to report offences.

In this chapter, I explore why public trust in the police and the reporting of offences do not correlate as common sense and the theoretical literature would suggest. Of course, it is a long way from correlation to causation. But even if we restrict ourselves to discussing the correlation between different variables, we must still address the question of which mechanisms can explain them. When searching for mechanisms, it is useful to consider not only the individual micro-level but also the macro-level of societies. Why do societies differ considerably in the levels of public trust the police and in the levels of willingness to report crimes to the police?

For this chapter, I have reviewed a number of studies in the field. I have also analysed two sets of survey data collected in Finland: the fifth wave of the

European Social Survey and the Police Barometer – a biennial survey conducted by the National Police Board in Finland – for 2012 and 2014. Both datasets are based on personal interviews and are representative of the Finnish population aged 15 to 74.

Quality of police work and public impressions of the police

What precisely are we referring to when we discuss 'trust in the police'? In research in this field, it has become customary to adopt one of two perspectives on trust: the instrumental or the procedural perspective (Sunshine and Tyler 2003).

The instrumental perspective refers to how well the police perform. The idea is that if citizens think or know that the police get results, they will trust the police. In this model, trust is based on what citizens know about the efficacy (can it work?), effectiveness (does it work?) and efficiency (is it worth it?) of police work.

First, efficacy depends on whether the work done by the police has an impact, i.e. whether it improves citizens' security or quality of life – and whether efficacy can be proven under optimum conditions, e.g. in a randomised test. Can it be proven that active reporting of offences increases security in the community? Second, effectiveness is related to whether police work has the anticipated effect in everyday life, i.e. whether police work actually improves the security of citizens or even their sense of security. And if it does improve security, how does it do so, and whose security does it improve? Third, efficiency is a measure of whether the results attained are worth the trouble and money. Is it always worthwhile investing in police work? And even if police work has been shown to be effective, what is its efficiency ratio? If the work is effective but its costs outweigh its benefits, it is of little use.

If we were to consider the instrumental perspective on trust as the principal consideration in deciding whether to report an offence to the police, we would have to assume that ordinary citizens have actual and reliable information on the efficacy, effectiveness, and efficiency of police work. I find this an unrealistic assumption. Even researchers are unlikely to be in possession of such information. Naturally, citizens have various impressions of the effectiveness or efficacy of police work, but the question of how these impressions are formed is highly complex. Of course, this may involve personal encounters with the police, but public opinion is also shaped by newspapers, TV, films, literature, and our culture in general.

The procedural perspective on trust, in contrast, concerns how equally and fairly the police operate. For example, citizens have observed that the police favour ethnic and other majorities over minorities. This could include a variety of unethical practices such as excess use of force, corruption, and unprofessional behaviour. Such factors have been found to have a greater impact on public trust than instrumental factors. It would therefore seem that citizens do not expect the police to be efficient as much as they expect them to be fair and equal and to observe good professional conduct (Jackson *et al.* 2012; Tyler and Huo 2002).

Here, too, we can see that while impressions can be affected by negative personal experiences, there may also be other factors in play.

In addition to personal experience of dealing with the police, public impressions of the police are influenced by how the police are depicted in fiction – crime literature, TV series, and films. In most fiction, the police are shown in a positive light as heroes fighting for good against evil (Reiner 2008). A similar scenario underlies news reports on crime. On the other hand, the mass media do criticise police actions from time to time. Scandals have recently arisen concerning the use of excess violence by the police, particularly against members of ethnic minorities. Studies of the impact of such scandals indicate that in some cases they do indeed have a negative impact on the public image of the police, at least in the short term (Lasley 1994; Weitzer 2002), but in some cases that kind of impact has not been found (Kääriäinen *et al.* 2016; Thomassen *et al.* 2014).

To summarise, when we study public trust in the police, we are actually studying public impressions that may have other roots beyond personal experiences of what the police actually do and how they do it. Impressions are influenced by the mass media, but other factors, discussed below, are also involved. In any case, if as our baseline assumption we state that public trust is based above all on impressions, the lack of correlation between public trust in the police and the reporting of crime is hardly surprising. In northern Europe, for instance, although most of the population has a highly positive opinion of the police, a large percentage of offences remain unreported.

Willingness to report crime and public trust in the police

The debate in recent years has emphasised the importance of trust in the relationship between citizens and the police. Improved cooperation between the authorities and citizens is viewed as a positive outcome of such trust. Empirical surveys or questionnaires typically probe the willingness of respondents to cooperate with the authorities, e.g. their willingness to report any offences they observe to the police (Jackson *et al.* 2012).

A typical survey setup can be seen in the questionnaire for the European Social Survey Round 5 (2010). Table 13.1 illustrates data on Finland collected for this survey. It cross-tables the respondents' trust in the police with their hypothetical willingness to report the theft of a wallet they have witnessed.

The results reveal a weak correlation: Spearman's rho is 0.11 for the association between trust in the police and willingness to report a property crime to the police. This is consistent with earlier studies exploring citizens' experiences of police work and their attitudes to cooperation with the police (e.g. Jackson *et al.* 2012, Tyler and Huo 2002). It is surprising how weak the correlation is. On the one hand, we may claim that the question concerning willingness to report is at least partly equivalent to the trust indicator: attitudes towards or impressions of the police. In this light, it is surprising that the correlation is so weak. On the other hand, it is also surprising that the small minority of Finns who do not trust the police at all are nevertheless very keen to report the theft of a wallet: 82 per

Table 13.1 Trust in the police and willingness to report a property crime to the police in Finland (per cent)

Spearman rho = 0.11 (p < 0.001)		How likely to call police if you see a man get his wallet stolen?			Total
		Not very likely or not at all likely	Likely	Very likely	
Trust in the police	0–4	18	29	53	100 (N=79)
	5–6	6	42	52	100 (N=151)
	7–8	4	36	59	100 (N=783)
	9–10	4	28	68	100 (N=849)
Total		5	33	62	100 (N=1,862)

Source: ESS, round 5.

cent of those who trust the police the least would be prepared to report the offence. In my view, this indicates that willingness to report crime to the police does not necessarily demonstrate a willingness to cooperate with the authorities, but something else, perhaps a moral sense of duty – something that seems common to almost all Finns regardless of whether they trust the police or not.

Actual reporting of crime and public trust in the police

The fact that someone claims that they would be prepared in principle to report an offence to the police does not mean that they would actually do so. If that was the case, the police would be overwhelmed with reports of offences, at least in Finland. Surprisingly few studies address the connection between public trust and actual reporting of crime. Heike Goudriaan (2006) has conducted extensive research into reporting behaviour and its relationship to public trust in the police. Based on her examination of an extensive body of Dutch material, she concluded that neither at the individual level nor at the community level reporting behaviour correlates with trust in the police (Goudriaan 2006; Goudriaan *et al.* 2006). Instead, she noted that the greater the social cohesion and socio-economic wellbeing of a community, the more willing its members are to report offences (Goudriaan 2006).

Barbara Warner (2007) examined the extent to which neighbourhood characteristics in US cities are related to residents' likelihood of using two different forms of informal social control: direct informal social control (i.e. direct intervention) and indirect informal social control (i.e. mobilising formal authorities). Her findings indicate that the number of social ties a respondent has increases the likelihood of direct informal social control but not indirect informal social control. In contrast, social cohesion and trust between the community members decreases indirect informal social control but does not have a significant effect on direct informal social control. Faith in the police was not found to affect either formal or informal social control.

In their study on sources of informal social control in Chicago neighbour-hoods, Eric Silver and Lisa Miller (2004) found that neighbourhood attachment and satisfaction with police were significantly and positively associated with neighbourhood levels of informal social control. They argued that when resi-dents are satisfied with their neighbourhoods, they feel a greater sense of responsibility for maintaining local order and are therefore more willing to engage in informal social control. In addition, they found that when residents view the police as a viable and responsive local resource, they are more willing to intervene informally when young people misbehave.

Robert Davis and Nicole Henderson (2003) examined willingness to report crimes among residents of six ethnic communities in New York. They found that willingness to report crimes was not strongly linked to perceptions of police effectiveness or police misconduct. It was, however, linked to measures of com-munity empowerment. People who said that their ethnic community was likely to work together to solve local problems, and those who believed that their com-munity wielded political power, were more likely than those whose communities were politically weak to say that they would report crimes.

A recent German study by Nathalie Guzy and Helmut Hirtenlehner (2015) also examined the connection between trust and actual reporting behaviour and managed to identify a surprising correlation: The less the respondents trusted the police, the more likely they were to report an offence. The authors explained this finding by referring to a methodological problem concerning the sequence of events. Reporting behaviour was gauged by a question that asked about the past 12 months, while trust was gauged with reference to the time of the survey. Trust must therefore be considered a dependent rather than an independent factor in this study. Be that as it may, the findings of Guzy and Hirtenlehner are interest-ing and challenge us to examine the relationship between public trust and actual reporting behaviour more closely and thoroughly.

Crime reporting in the Finland

The following is a discussion of some observations from the Police Barometer, a survey conducted regularly in Finland. For this analysis, I combined the data from the 2012 and 2014 surveys (Ministry of Interior 2012, 2014).

The first point of interest is the reporting rates for certain types of offence (Table 13.2). We should note that actual reporting behaviour varies considerably, depend-ing on the type of offence concerned: The rate is highest for serious property offences and lowest for sexual offences. In property crime cases, the high willing-ness to report is likely connected to insurance claims: To get compensation from the insurance company, the offence must be reported to the police. It is also note-worthy that more than half of all violent crime remains unreported. This might be connected to the nature of the violence in Finland, about half of which is perpet-rated by unknown or semi-familiar individuals (Danielsson and Kääriäinen 2016).

The next point is the most important for our purposes: What is the correlation between public trust and actual reporting behaviour? It should be noted that my

Table 13.2 Reporting rates (per cent) for some types of offences in Finland

Did you report to the police when you last were a victim of...	... house break-in or an attempted house break-in?	80
	... car theft or an attempted car theft?	75
	... property theft?	65
	... damage to property?	52
	... other crime or inflicted harm?	47
	... an assault	45
	... an armed threat?	40
	... sexual harassment or violence?	26

Source: Police Barometer 2012 and 2014, cumulative data (Ministry of Interior Finland).

material encounters the same problem as the one of Guzy and Hirtenlehner (2015): The offence and reporting behaviour predated the question about trust. We must therefore be careful to refer to the relationship between these two factors as correlation, not a causal relationship.

Table 13.3 shows the association coefficients between trust and actual reporting behaviour by type of offence. We should note that a statistically significant correlation is only observed in the case of theft, and even there the coefficient is rather low ($V=0.11$). However, we should note that in some types of crime like house break-in or sexual harassments a low number of cases causes the statistical non-significance.

Although problems are always associated with the use of cross-sectional data, these findings indicate that actual reporting behaviour is influenced by many factors besides trust in the police.

It has been proposed that the reporting of an offence is preceded by a rational decision-making process weighing up the costs and benefits of reporting it (Felson *et al.* 2002; Gottfredson and Gottfredson 1987). Perceived benefits may include advantages such as the protection provided by the police: A victim is in distress and needs help, and the victim or someone else therefore calls the police. Another commonly perceived benefit would consist of bringing the perpetrator to justice in order to be punished by a court. In the case of property offences, the perceived benefit may be the recovery of property or receiving compensation based on an insurance claim. Perceived costs may include the various harmful impacts caused to the person reporting the offence, such as damaging their relationship with the perpetrator, being ostracised within their community, fear of revenge or the time and trouble required for participation in the eventual trial (Felson *et al.* 2002).

We know from actual reporting behaviour that only some reasons for not reporting an offence have anything to do with the police, and that only some of those reasons are related to impressions of or attitudes towards the police. Table 13.4 gives data for Finland, based on the Police Barometer surveys from 2012 and 2014, in particular on the behaviour of victims of assault. Some 13.5 per cent of respondents reported that they had been a victim of assault at some point in their lives. Just over half of these (54 per cent) had never filed a report of the offence. Table 13.4 includes a summary of the reasons given by respondents for non-reporting.

Table 13.3 Crime reporting and trust in the police: associations (Cramer's V) by some crime types

			How much do you trust the activities of the police?
Did you report to the police when you last were a victim of:	House break-in or an attempted house break-in?	Cramer's V Sig. (2-tailed) N	0.22 0.07 151
	Property theft?	Cramer's V Sig. (2-tailed) N	0.11 0.031 732
	Damage to property?	Cramer's V Sig. (2-tailed) N	0.05 0.731 493
	An assault?	Cramer's V Sig. (2-tailed) N	0.05 0.85 283
	Car theft or attempted car theft?	Cramer's V Sig. (2-tailed) N	0.17 0.06 263
	An armed threat?	Cramer's V Sig. (2-tailed) N	0.16 0.43 108
	Sexual harassment or violence?	Cramer's V Sig. (2-tailed) N	0.18 0.18 160
	Other crime or inflicted harm?	Cramer's V Sig. (2-tailed) N	0.12 0.33 242

Source: Police barometer 2012 and 2014, cumulative data (Ministry of Interior Finland).

The most common reason for not reporting an offence would seem to be regarding the incident as a private matter and not wishing to involve the authorities. This is less about a lack of trust than reluctance to resolve the matter in public. Domestic violence is a case in point: Victims are reluctant to report their partner or spouse to the police. This category probably also includes other cases in which the perpetrator and victim are either closely involved or at least acquainted with each other. We should also remember that violence (like crime in general) tends to cluster at the individual level: The same people tend to be involved in multiple offences, sometimes as perpetrators and sometimes as victims. When a conflict escalates into violence, this is often as the result of a process provoked and exacerbated by both parties. For instance, a typical Finnish homicide is the result of an altercation between two persons who are drunk

Table 13.4 Reasons for non-reporting of assaults in Finland. Multiresponse frequencies

		Responses		Per cent of cases
		N	Per cent	
Why not reported assault	Not serious enough a crime to report	12	14	16
	Thought the police would not be able to do anything	14	16	19
	Thought the police would not be interested/bothered	2	2	3
	Thought it was not a police matter	4	5	5
	Thought it was private/personal	20	23	27
	Reported to other authorities	7	8	9
	Fear/did not dare/fear of reprisal or violence by offenders*	4	5	5
	I was a child/young*	1	1	1
	The offender was a relative/ acquaintance/someone I know*	1	1	1
	Someone else reported it*	1	1	1
	The matter was resolved by talking/ negotiating*	2	2	3
	Did not report for some other reason*	6	7	8
	Can't say	13	15	18
Total		87	100	118

Source: Police Barometer 2012 (Ministry of Interior Finland).

Note
* Categorised open-ended question.

where it might be a matter of chance which one becomes the perpetrator and which the victim.

The second most common reason for not reporting an offence involves believing that the police could not do anything about it. This may involve a lack of trust in the ability of the police to investigate the case successfully and bring it to prosecution. However, in my view such a reason does not simply concern a lack of trust but also a realistic perception that the case would have been difficult or impossible to investigate successfully. If, for instance, the perpetrator is unknown and no property was lost, the victim may decide not to report the offence due to the perception that this would serve no useful purpose.

The third most common reason for not reporting an offence is believing that the offence was not sufficiently serious. In fact, this is one of the key factors governing the willingness to report an offence as detailed in the literature (e.g. Goudriaan *et al.* 2004). Unsurprisingly, serious property offences and violent offences are reported. But when is an offence sufficiently serious to warrant reporting it to the police? This is a question that victims of offences or anti-social behaviour clearly respond to in very different ways. It is a matter of tolerance: How great a social deviation we will tolerate, what kinds of deviation we will tolerate and by whom. The threshold for reporting an offence is probably lower if we wish to maintain social distance from the perpetrator. In a recently published article, Tim Reeskens (2013) notes that tolerance of social deviation is related to generalised trust: Deviations are tolerated most by those who trust their fellow citizens. Or to look at it another way: Deviations are tolerated least by those with little social capital.

The results reported in Table 13.4 indicate that most reasons for not reporting an offence have nothing to do with the police. In this light, it is hardly surprising that there is no correlation between public trust in the police and willingness to report an offence.

Comparative research is needed

Rule of law and the police

As detailed above, most studies at the individual level and at the local community level indicate that public trust in the police is unrelated to actual behaviour in reporting offences. What, then, is the association between these factors if we compare entire societies with one another?

Figure 13.1 shows a scatter plot of the relationship between public trust and reporting behaviour in certain European countries. The figures on reporting are derived from International Crime Victims Survey (ICVS) data collected over ten years ago, since no newer material is available (van Dijk et al. 2007). They describe the reporting of some property and violent offences in the one-year period preceding the study. The figures on trust are from European Social Survey (ESS) data collected around the same time.

Figure 13.1 shows independence between these factors, the country-level correlation being $r=-0.05$. In other words, both public trust in the police and reporting behaviour vary considerably from one European country to another – but totally independently. In addition, Finland and Iceland seem to be outliers in that figure, as compared to Denmark or Sweden, for example, crime reporting rates are much lower level.

In the absence of comprehensive datasets, it is difficult to explain these observations. The only comparable data available on reporting behaviour are from the ICVS, which is outdated and lacks certain relevant variables that may explain variations in reporting behaviour. My conclusions are therefore largely speculative.

First of all, we should ask why the level of trust in the police varies so much from country to country. Is it a question of the quality of police activity or a broader social phenomenon?

Perhaps one of the most promising substantial explanations seems to be related to the rule of law principles followed in society. According to the World

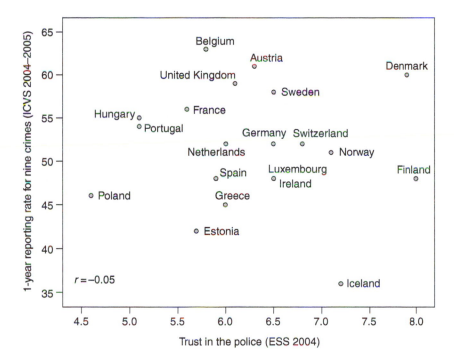

Figure 13.1 Trust in the police and crime reporting rates in 20 European countries in 2004–2005.

Sources: ESS 2004 and ICVS 2004–2005 (van Dijk *et al.* 2007).

Justice Project's (2016) definition, the rule of law is a system in which the following four universal principles are upheld (see also Barendrecht 2011):

1. The government and its officials and agents as well as individuals and private entities are accountable under the law.
2. The laws are clear, publicised, stable, and just; are applied evenly; and protect fundamental rights, including the security of persons and property and certain core human rights.
3. The process by which the laws are enacted, administered, and enforced is accessible, fair, and efficient.
4. Justice is delivered timely by competent, ethical, and independent representatives and neutrals who are of sufficient number, have adequate resources, and reflect the makeup of the communities they serve.

The rule of law index by the World Justice Project is relying on household and expert surveys to measure how the rule of law is experienced in practical, everyday situations by the general public and experts. The latest 2016 index has been collected in 113 countries.

Figure 13.2 illustrates the close correlation between the rule of law index and public trust in the police in some European countries in 2014. People trust the police in countries where they trust in the accountability, efficacy, and fairness of the public administration in general. In other words, the finding suggests that trust in the police is one expression of the fact that the entire system of government in society is (not) perceived as legitimate, transparent, and efficient.

Finland, like other Nordic countries, is doing well in the rule of law measurement. How is this reflected in the Finnish police organisations? At least four things can be mentioned.

First, the police activity is regulated in detail by laws and regulations. In Finland, police activity is regulated by the Police Act 872/2011 (Ministry of the Interior Finland 2011). The general sections of the Act 872/2011 (Ministry of the Interior Finland 2011) state, inter alia, that:

- police have to respect fundamental and human rights;
- police action shall be reasonable and proportionate with regard to the importance, danger and urgency of the duty;
- police shall not take action that infringes anyone's rights or causes anyone harm or inconvenience more than is necessary to carry out their duty;

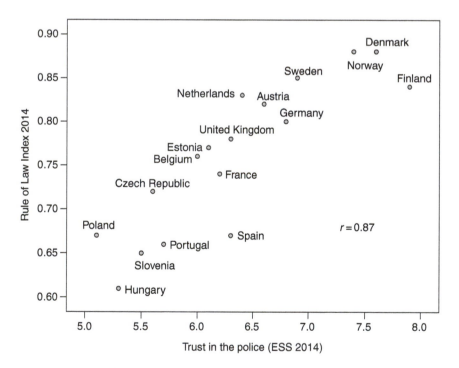

Figure 13.2 Rule of law and trust in the police in 17 European countries in 2014.

Sources: World Justice Project 2016 and ESS 2014. For Czech Republic and Estonia, Rule of Law Index is measured in 2015.

- police may exercise their powers only for the purposes provided by law;
- police shall act in an appropriate and objective manner and promote equal treatment and a conciliatory spirit. Police shall seek to maintain public order and security primarily through advice, requests, and orders.

In addition to these general principles, there are a number of detailed provisions in the Police Act on, for example, the general powers of the police, security checks undertaken in police premises, technical monitoring and rights to information, secret methods of gathering intelligence, gathering intelligence from telecommunications networks, extended surveillance, covert intelligence gathering, and technical surveillance.

Provisions on the criminal investigation of offences are laid down in the Criminal Investigation Act 805/2011 (Ministry of Justice Finland 2011a) and provisions on the coercive measures used in the criminal investigation of offences are laid down in the Coercive Measures Act 806/2011 (Ministry of Justice Finland 2011b).

Second, in Finland, like in other Nordic countries, the national police organisation is highly centralised. It means that there is, in principle, a uniform police force in the country. The National Police Board, operating under the Ministry of the Interior, is in charge of the performance management of local and national police units. Local police consists of 11 police departments. The local police departments are in charge of core policing operations like the maintenance of public order and safety, crime prevention, and the promotion of traffic safety. The national police units are the National Bureau of Investigation and Police University College. The National Bureau of Investigation specialises in the prevention of serious and organised crime. The Police University College is responsible for police training, and for research and development in the police field (Police of Finland 2016).

Third, police training in Finland is based on the Act on the Police University College (amendments up to 1164/2013 included in Coercive Measures Act, Ministry Justice Finland 2011b). The law requires, for example, that police training must be based on freedom of scientific research and education, and the quality of the education must be evaluated regularly by the independent organisation. The three-year course 'Bachelor of Policing' leads to a bachelor's degree in police work.[1] The bachelor's degree qualifies a person to the positions of police officer, such as a Senior Constable. A Master of Policing degree at the Police University College focuses on management skills and supervisory tasks. The degree qualifies holders to commanding positions, such as Chief Inspector and Superintendent.

Fourth, according to the principles of rule of law, activities of the authorities must be controlled. There are two supreme overseers of legality in Finland: the Chancellor of Justice, who reports to the Government and to Parliament, and the Parliamentary Ombudsman. Their tasks and powers are largely the same. Both oversee the legality of the actions of authorities and officials. If someone thinks that a police officer or another police administration official has committed misconduct while in office or neglected to perform their official duties, that person can put the matter forward for investigation by filing an administrative complaint. It is submitted to a senior police authority or directly to the highest judicial authority: the Parliamentary Ombudsman or the Chancellor of Justice (Parliamentary Ombudsman 2016).

Social capital, welfare state, and the police

In a study conducted using Finnish data (Kääriäinen and Sirén 2011), we found what seemed to be an interesting link between reporting behaviour and social capital at the individual level, specifically what might be called generalised trust. It seemed that those who were most active in reporting offences had little trust in either the police or their fellow citizens. Reporting behaviour would thus seem to correlate negatively with social capital: A person who has relatives, friends, neighbours, colleagues, and other networks to provide informal security may only turn to the authorities when in serious danger. Similarly, those who do not have a community or network to provide them with security and who are without response options may be more likely to go to the police.

Comparative studies of social capital have shown that the highest levels of generalised trust, trust in institutions, and other social capital may be found in countries with the smallest income differentials, the best social security, a well-functioning democracy, and reliable public administration (Kääriäinen and Lehtonen 2006; Van Oorschot and Arts 2005). As one aspect of institutional trust, public trust in the police is highest in such countries.

Figure 13.3 illustrates the close correlation between generalised trust and public trust in the police. It seems very clear that people trust the police in countries where people also trust one another. If we have social capital, this means that we can rely on the support of and assistance from the community and the unofficial social controls that the community can provide.

The theoretical literature explains public trust in the police by the actions of the police: how efficient, fair or helpful the police are perceived to be. This is an important and understandable assumption. But beyond that, especially if we wish to understand why public trust in the police varies so greatly from one society to another, we must need to identify complementary factors related to the differences between societies. There is, to my knowledge, not any reliable evidence suggesting that public trust in the police is higher in northern Europe than elsewhere in the world specifically because our police officers are more efficient or fairer than others. We need much more detailed comparative research on police–citizen relations in different societies to understand better the quality of police work and its relation to citizens' experiences. Study designs based on conventional survey methods alone are not adequate because those citizens who have the most experience of police usually respond less frequently to these surveys, with the possible exception of school surveys targeting the adolescent age group. More qualitative and multi-method research is needed on the police–citizen relations in real situations and in different social environments.

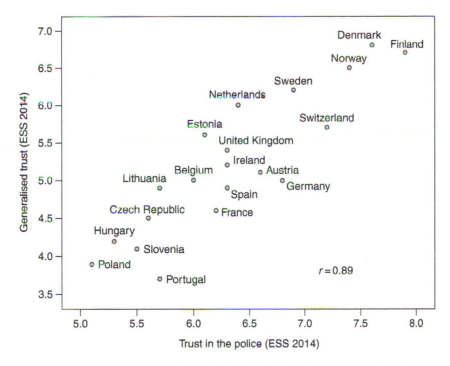

Figure 13.3 Generalised trust and trust in the police in 20 European countries in 2014.
Source: ESS 2014.

It is possible that part of the explanation lies in the role of the police in society, i.e. what citizens, experts, and politicians expect the police to do with regard to solving problems in society at large. The social status and significance of unofficial social control is closely related to this issue.

Reporting an offence to the police often translates into a breach of trust between individuals. If I report my neighbour to the police due to a disturbance, I can be sure that my neighbour will not say hello to me for a long time. Based on my knowledge of Finnish society and culture, I can confidently state that although we have great trust in the police, the threshold for reporting disturbances and offences to the police is also high. This is partly due to our relatively homogeneous socio-economic population structure, our well-functioning social networks, and our high level of generalised trust. As Reeskens (2013) notes, trust increases tolerance of social deviations, which is no doubt reflected in reporting behaviour.

Above, we have found that trust in the police is highest in the Nordic countries. These societies have been characterised by a strong welfare state as guarantor of the social security and rights of the population. Welfare states attempt to control social risks by equalising income differentials and by providing high-quality public services to the population. Active welfare policy also appears to have been fruitful: The Nordic countries tend to thrive quite well in various quality of life measurements (Eurostat 2015). The welfare model also seems to be supported by the population: In the Nordic countries, people rate the quality of governance to be at a good level and are willing to finance it through taxation (Svallfors 2013).

On the other hand, the Nordic welfare societies have been characterised as reacting to crime as a social problem rather than a matter of strict order and security. This can be seen clearly in prisoner rates. Although the crime rate in the Nordic countries in itself is not significantly different from other European countries, the number of prisoners per capita in the Nordic countries is significantly lower than the rest of Europe. This has been the result of conscious penal policy, which seeks to overcome tough sanctions and to intensify the social rehabilitation of the criminals (Lappi-Seppälä 2012). The policy seems to have the support of the people: The trust of the population towards the legal system is quite high in the Nordic countries (Jackson *et al.* 2014). The same applies to the number of police officers per capita: In the Nordic countries, there are fewer police officers per capita than anywhere else in Europe (Lappi-Seppälä 2012). So it seems that the police are trusted the most in countries where the number of police is minimal.

Hence, it can be argued that citizens' trust in the police appears to be closely linked to the general equality and fairness of society; those with the least trust in the police usually come from the lower strata of society where experiences of discrimination are more common. For example, Frank *et al.* (2005: 215) note that satisfaction with the police is lowest in the lowest-income category in the United States. In a similar vein, it has been found that unemployed and those suffering the greatest economic hardship in Europe trust the police less (Kääriäinen 2007). It seems that fair distribution of welfare in society increases citizens' trust in the police and other institutions of society. It has also been found that trust in the police is strongly connected to citizens' overall satisfaction with the functioning of their country's political system and economy (Thomassen and Kääriäinen 2016). In addition, it seems that political orientation and values matters, too. In his analysis of the effects of political ideology and ethnic identity on assessments of police fairness in France, Roché (forthcoming) found that political conservatism and punitive attitudes emerged as strong positive predictors of the phenomena.

Moreover, many studies have indicated that satisfaction with the police is lower among ethnic minorities than among the native population. Most of these studies are based on observations from the United States (e.g. Carter and Radelet 2002: 226–9; Frank *et al.* 2005; Weitzer and Tuch 2005). In Europe, the European Union Minorities and Discrimination Survey by the European Union Agency for Fundamental Rights indicated that there is much room for improvement in European police forces: Minorities' trust in the police is at a lower level than that of the general population (e.g. Van Craen 2013). In Finland, it has been found that the Somali community's trust in the Finnish police is lower than among the rest of population (Kääriäinen and Niemi 2014).

As late as the early 1990s, Finland was very ethnically homogenous. Since then, immigration has increased rapidly: In the past few years, the annual volume of immigration has been around 10,000–15,000 people. The largest groups of migrants are those who have Russian, Estonian, Somali, English or Arabic as their mother tongue. Despite the relatively rapid change, the proportion of people living in Finland and speaking a mother tongue other than Finnish, Swedish or Saami (the official languages of Finland) was no more than 6.2 per cent (Official Statistics of Finland 2016). In the future, the number of migrants is very likely to grow, and we will see how it is reflected in the development of trust in the police.

In conclusion, we need to study both the reasons for trusting the police and its consequences in a broader social context than previously. We need comparative research that takes account not only of the interaction between the police and citizens, but also the many factors stemming from the economy and culture of various societies that may affect citizens' expectations of the police. Ultimately, the question is what role the police play in addressing problems in any given society.

Note

1 The curriculum of the bachelor's degree and other information on the Finnish police training can be found online (Police of Finland 2017).

Bibliography

Barendrecht, M. (2011). 'Rule of law, measuring and accountability: problems to be solved bottom up', *Hague Journal on the Rule of Law*, 3: 281–304.

Carter, D. and Radelet, L. (2002). *The Police and the Community*, Upper Saddle River, NJ: Prentice Hall.

Danielsson, P. and Kääriäinen, J. (2016). *Suomalaiset väkivallan ja omaisuusrikosten kohteena 2015 – Kansallisen rikosuhritutkimuksen tuloksia [Finns as a victim of violence and property crimes—results of the national crime victim survey]*, University of Helsinki, Institute of Criminology and Legal Policy.

Davis, R. and Henderson, N. (2003). 'Willingness to report crimes: the role of ethnic group membership and community efficacy', *Crime and Delinquency*, 49: 564–80.

European Social Survey Round 2 Data (2004). NSD – Norwegian Centre for Research Data, Norway – Data Archive and distributor of ESS data for ESS ERIC.

European Social Survey Round 5 Data (2010). NSD – Norwegian Centre for Research Data, Norway – Data Archive and distributor of ESS data for ESS ERIC.

European Social Survey Round 7 Data (2014). NSD – Norwegian Centre for Research Data, Norway – Data Archive and distributor of ESS data for ESS ERIC.

Eurostat (2015). *Quality of Life. Facts and Views*, Luxembourg: Publications Office of the European Union.

Felson, R., Messner, S., Hoskin, A., and Deane, G. (2002). 'Reasons for reporting and not reporting domestic violence to the police', *Criminology*, 40: 617–48.

Frank, J., Smith, B., and Novak, K. (2005). 'Exploring the basis of citizens' attitudes toward the police', *Police Quarterly*, 8: 206–28.

Gottfredson, M. and Gottfredson, D. (1987). *Decision Making in Criminal Justice: Toward the Rational Exercise of Discretion.* New York: Springer.

Goudriaan, H. (2006). 'Reporting crime: effects of social context on the decision of victims to notify the police', published Ph.D. thesis, Leiden University, online. Available https://openaccess.leidenuniv.nl/bitstream/handle/1887/4410/Thesis.pdf (accessed 19 December 2016).

Goudriaan, H., Lynch, J., and Nieuwbeerta, P. (2004). 'Reporting to the police in western nations: a theoretical analysis of the effects of social context', *Justice Quarterly,* 21: 933–69.

Goudriaan, H., Wittebrood, K., and Nieuwbeerta, P. (2006). 'Neighbourhood characteristics and reporting crime effects of social cohesion, confidence in police effectiveness and socio-economic disadvantage', *British Journal of Criminology,* 46: 719–42.

Guzy, N. and Hirtenlehner, H. (2015). 'Trust in the German police: determinants and consequences for reporting behavior', in G. Meško and J. Tankebe (eds.), *Trust and Legitimacy in Criminal Justice,* Cham: Springer, 203–29.

Jackson, J., Bradford, B., Stanko, B., and Hohl, K. (2012). *Just Authority?: Trust in the Police in England and Wales.* Abingdon: Routledge.

Jackson, J., Kuha, J., Hough, M., Bradford, B., Hohl, K., and Gerber, M. (2014, 1 September). 'Trust and legitimacy across Europe: a FIDUCIA report on comparative public attitudes towards legal authority', *SSRN,* online. Available https://ssrn.com/abstract=2272975 (accessed 8 February 2017).

Kääriäinen, J. (2007). 'Trust in the police in 16 European countries. A multilevel analysis', *European Journal of Criminology,* 4: 409–35.

Kääriäinen, J., Isotalus, P., and Thomassen, G. (2016). 'Does public criticism erode trust in the police? The case of Jari Aarnio in the Finnish news media and its effects on the public's attitudes towards the police', *Journal of Scandinavian Studies in Criminology and Crime Prevention,* 17: 70–85.

Kääriäinen, J. and Lehtonen, H. (2006). 'The variety of social capital in welfare state regimes – a comparative study of 21 countries', *European Societies,* 8: 27–57.

Kääriäinen, J. and Niemi, J. (2014). 'Distrust of the Police in a Nordic welfare state: victimization, discrimination, and trust in the police by Russian and Somali minorities in Helsinki', *Journal of Ethnicity in Criminal Justice,* 12: 4–24.

Kääriäinen, J. and Sirén, R. (2011). 'Trust in the police, generalized trust and reporting crime', *European Journal of Criminology,* 8: 65–81.

Lappi-Seppälä, T. (2012). 'Penal policies in the Nordic Countries 1960–2010', *Journal of Scandinavian Studies in Criminology and Crime Prevention,* 13: 85–111.

Lasley, J. (1994). 'The impact of the Rodney King incident on citizen attitudes toward police', *Policing and Society: An International Journal,* 3: 245–55.

Ministry of the Interior Finland (2011). *Police Act 872/2011,* online. Available www.finlex.fi/en/laki/kaannokset/2011/20110872 (accessed 19 December 2016).

Ministry of the Interior Finland (2012). *Police Barometer 2012,* online. Available https://services.fsd.uta.fi/catalogue/FSD2838?study_language=en (accessed 8 February 2017).

Ministry of the Interior Finland (2014). *Police Barometer 2014,* online. Available https://services.fsd.uta.fi/catalogue/FSD3000?lang=en&study_language=en (accessed 8 February 2017).

Ministry of Justice Finland (2011a). *Criminal Investigation Act 805/2011,* online. Available www.finlex.fi/fi/laki/kaannokset/2011/en20110805.pdf (accessed 19 December 2016).

Ministry of Justice Finland (2011b). *Coercive Measures Act 806/2011,* online. Available www.finlex.fi/fi/laki/kaannokset/2011/en20110806.pdf (accessed 19 December 2016).

Official Statistics of Finland (2016). *Migration,* Helsinki: Statistics Finland, online. Available www.stat.fi/til/muutl/index_en.html (accessed 2 December 2016).

Parliamentary Ombudsman (2016, March 29): *The Parliamentary Ombudsman of Finland,* online. Available www.oikeusasiamies.fi/Resource.phx/eoa/english/ombudsman/index.htx (accessed 19 December 2016).

Police of Finland (2016). *About the police,* online. Available www.poliisi.fi/about_the_police (accessed 19 December 2016).

Police of Finland (2017). *Bachelor studies,* online. Available www.poliisiammattikor keakoulu.fi/en/bachelor_studies (accessed 7 February 2017).

Reeskens, T. (2013). 'But who are those "most people" that can be trusted? Evaluating the radius of trust across 29 European societies', *Social Indicators Research,* 114: 703–22.

Reiner, R. (2008). 'Policing and the media', in T. Newburn (ed.), *Handbook of Policing,* Abingdon: Routledge, 313–36.

Roché, S. (forthcoming). 'The "silver bullet" to policing: a mirage? An analysis of the effects of political ideology and ethnic identity on assessments of police fairness', *International Journal of Police Strategies and Management.*

Silver, E. and Miller, L. (2004). 'Sources of informal social control in Chicago neighbor-hoods', *Criminology,* 42: 551–84.

Sunshine, J. and Tyler, T. (2003). 'The role of procedural justice and legitimacy in shaping public support for policing', *Law and society review,* 37: 513–48.

Svallfors, S. (2013). 'Government quality, egalitarianism, and attitudes to taxes and social spending: a European comparison', *European Political Science Review,* 5: 363–80.

Thomassen, G. and Kääriäinen, J. (2016). 'System satisfaction, contact satisfaction, and trust in the police: a study of Norway', *European Journal of Policing Studies,* 3: 437–48.

Thomassen, G., Strype, J., and Egge, M. (2014). 'Trust no matter what? Citizens' percep-tion of the police one year after the terror attacks in Norway', *Policing,* 8: 79–87.

Tyler, T. and Huo, Y. (2002). *Trust in the Law: Encouraging Public Cooperation with the Police and Courts,* New York: Russell Sage Foundation.

Van Craen, M. (2013). 'Explaining majority and minority trust in the police', *Justice Quarterly,* 30: 1042–67.

Van Dijk, J., van Kesteren, J., and Smit, P. (2007). *Criminal Victimisation in Inter-national Perspective,* Den Haag: Boom Juridische Uitgevers.

Van Oorschot, W. and Arts, W. (2005). 'The social capital of European welfare states: the crowding out hypothesis revisited', *Journal of European social policy,* 15: 5–26.

Warner, B. (2007). 'Directly intervene or call the authorities? A study of forms of neigh-borhood social control within a social disorganization framework', *Criminology,* 45: 99–129.

Weitzer, R. (2002). 'Incidents of police misconduct and public opinion', *Journal of Crim-inal Justice,* 30: 397–408.

Weitzer, R. and Tuch, S. (2005). 'Determinants of public satisfaction with the police', *Police Quarterly,* 8: 279–97.

World Justice Project (2016). *What is the Rule of Law?* Online. Available http://world justiceproject.org/what-rule-law (accessed 19 December 2016).

Index

Page numbers in *italics* denote tables, those in **bold** denote figures.

Taylor & Francis eBooks

Helping you to choose the right eBooks for your Library

Add Routledge titles to your library's digital collection today. Taylor and Francis ebooks contains over 50,000 titles in the Humanities, Social Sciences, Behavioural Sciences, Built Environment and Law.

Choose from a range of subject packages or create your own!

Benefits for you

>> Free MARC records
>> COUNTER-compliant usage statistics
>> Flexible purchase and pricing options
>> All titles DRM-free.

Benefits for your user

>> Off-site, anytime access via Athens or referring URL
>> Print or copy pages or chapters
>> Full content search
>> Bookmark, highlight and annotate text
>> Access to thousands of pages of quality research at the click of a button.

REQUEST YOUR **FREE** INSTITUTIONAL TRIAL TODAY

Free Trials Available
We offer free trials to qualifying academic, corporate and government customers.

eCollections – Choose from over 30 subject eCollections, including:

Archaeology	Language Learning
Architecture	Law
Asian Studies	Literature
Business & Management	Media & Communication
Classical Studies	Middle East Studies
Construction	Music
Creative & Media Arts	Philosophy
Criminology & Criminal Justice	Planning
Economics	Politics
Education	Psychology & Mental Health
Energy	Religion
Engineering	Security
English Language & Linguistics	Social Work
Environment & Sustainability	Sociology
Geography	Sport
Health Studies	Theatre & Performance
History	Tourism, Hospitality & Events

For more information, pricing enquiries or to order a free trial, please contact your local sales team: www.tandfebooks.com/page/sales

Routledge
Taylor & Francis Group

The home of Routledge books

www.tandfebooks.com

Lightning Source UK Ltd.
Milton Keynes UK
UKHW020744091120
372966UK00010B/252